BROWNSVILLE

ALTER F. LANDESMAN

BROWNSVILLE

The Birth, Development and Passing of a Jewish Community in New York

Second Edition
with a foreword by
Dr. Louis Finkelstein

BLOCH PUBLISHING COMPANY, New York

To the memory of my sisters

SARAH AND GOLDIE

Foreword to Second Edition

By Dr. Louis Finkelstein

WHEN in my childhood and early youth, I lived in Brownsville, it was frequently called in Rabbinic circles "the
Jerusalem of America," as Vilna used to be called "the
Jerusalem of Lithuania." In my father's synagogue, there would
be service after service from early dawn until about nine A.M.,
each well attended, by people of different age groups—young,
middle-aged, and old. There were study groups in the afternoon
both in Talmud, and, for the less well prepared, in Mishna. There
were several people who spent virtually the whole day in the
synagogue, studying, with interruptions for prayer. When the
President of the congregation to which my father ministered was
inaugurated, on *Shemini Azeret* (having been elected during the
preceding week), he and my father would march through the
main street, Pitkin Avenue, at the head of a procession, which included almost the whole Congregation. When for some reason,
the Scrolls of the Torah had to be taken from one building to

another, they were also carried in a procession, followed by hundreds of people, walking down the streets, regardless of traffic. And my father's congregation was only one of many. There was for example a Hasidic congregation which I often visited, because their library contained commentaries on the Talmud rarely to be found elsewhere. There, too, people studied all day.

Most of the members of my father's congregation, it seemed to me, then, and it seems to me, now, observed the Sabbath, and meticulously adhered to the other commandments and rituals. Litigations between people were brought to my father to settle in accordance with Jewish law.

Immersed in these surroundings, I was quite unprepared to discover, as I grew older, that there was also another Jewish Brownsville. That Brownsville consisted of skeptics, agnostics, intellectuals, who violated the Sabbath and disregarded Jewish law generally. That Brownsville had apparently grown up during my boyhood days, unnoticed by those of us who were busy in the synagogue.

Both Brownsvilles produced a veritable *Who's Who* of people, who in later years became distinguished. Some became eminent in letters; others in industry; still others in the professions, in science, and in academic life. From time to time, I now come across people in their seventies who recall how in their childhood they sang in the choir which accompanied Cantor Kaminsky in my father's synagogue. Others tell how, as they grew up in Brownsville, they rebelled against the establishment. Some years ago, one of our great Universities appointed two University Professors (the first to hold that title and status there), one a scientist, who had won the Nobel Prize in physics, the other a historian and critic of art. Astonishingly, both were born and reared in Brownsville.

The rise and decline of Jewish Brownsville occurred, as my colleague, Professor Simon Greenberg—himself raised there—once reminded me, in a single human lifetime. When my father arrived there in 1902, the neighborhood was still finding itself. When he died in 1947, it had completely changed.

Rabbi Alter Landesman, the author of this volume, has performed a great service to future historians, American Judaism, and to the community generally, in recording the story of the curious phenomenon of the development of the two subcultures which grew up side by side in Brownsville, and their interrelation. He was in a unique position to draw up this record. For, since 1922, when he was graduated from the Jewish Theological Seminary of America, he was the Director of the Hebrew Educational Society in Brownsville. In this position, he came into close contact with the youth of the community. A shrewd observer, with a remarkable insight into human character, and a loving eye for human eccentricities and foibles, he has traced the evolution of the community with the eye of a social scientist.

He writes of people whom he knew well, as well as, inevitably, of some of whom he could know only by report. He does justice to the various sociological streams flowing through Brownsville, and compresses all this information into a single readable, delightful work.

His book will inevitably hold an important place among the histories of local Jewish communities, scattered over the United States, each of which could be the subject of a saga.

To tell the whole history of any community is virtually impossible. To "Namierize" Brownsville, showing how much each person there contributed to its peculiar American-Jewish civilization, and how it contributed to their culture, and to indicate why one person went one way, and another turned in another direction, would require many volumes, and be beyond the goal which Dr. Landesman set himself. It might also be beyond the scope of the reader who wishes to know what Brownsville was like. This work is addressed to such readers. Dr. Landesman is to be earnestly congratulated on this fine book, for which all students of contemporary Jewish life must indeed be grateful.

It is good to know that the book is now to be published in a second edition. I hope that although this community no longer exists physically, the values which it fostered will survive in the descendants of its descendants.

Preface

THIS volume is an attempt to present a full account of the beginnings, the growth and development, and the passing of the Jewish communities of Brownsville and East New York—well known neighborhoods of Brooklyn, New York.

I gratefully acknowledge my indebtedness to published materials, which I list in the Bibliography and Notes—books, studies, reports, biographies, memoirs, magazine articles, novels, newspaper accounts, and other printed matter containing historic data about the community.

I am grateful to the many individuals, institutions, and libraries who provided records, gave interviews, assembled data, and read portions of the manuscript. Special mention is due Samuel Hollander, Morris Zeldin, Dr. Lloyd Gartner, Dr. Israel Levinthal, Dr. Joseph Kaminetsky, Seymour Janovsky, Dr. Sophia Robison, Dr. David Farber, the Honorable Michael Kern, and also to Harry Handler, Joseph Koplowitz, and Jacob Wax of blessed memory. My thanks are due to Allan Sugarman for drawing the map and designing the jacket, and to Mrs. Rhoda Barnum and her assistants for typing the manuscript.

My special thanks are expressed to Dr. Alan Steinbach for editing the manuscript, and for his many valuable suggestions and improvements with regard to its style and content.

Mr. Charles Bloch, Mr. Soloman Kerstein, and Miss Elizabeth Abell of the Bloch Publishing Company were most helpful in seeing the book through publication, and my deep appreciation is expressed to them for their interest and encouragement.

At a time when Brownsville is undergoing a complete physical, social, and ethnic transformation, and its Jewish community has practically disappeared, this book is humbly offered, as a tribute to the community's pioneers, and as an historic record of a vital Jewish center that has made a distinctive contribution to the life of our great metropolis.

ALTER F. LANDESMAN

Brooklyn, New York
October 1968

Contents

Introduction

> *"Albert," she said timidly, "Albert"*
> *"Hm?"*
> "Gehen vir voinen du? *In New York?"*
> "Nein, Bronzeville. Ich hub dir schoin geschrieben."
> *"She nodded uncertainly, sighed . . ."*
> *Screws threshing, backing water, the Peter Stuyvesant*
> *neared her dock, drifting slowly and with canceled mo-*
> *mentum as if reluctant. . . .*
>
> Henry Roth, Call it Sleep [1]

BROWNSVILLE witnessed the development of one of the largest communities of East European Jewish immigrants during the last decade of the nineteenth century and the first two decades of the twentieth. Of the nearly two million Jews who migrated to the United States during that period from Russia, Poland, Austria, Hungary, and Rumania, the overwhelming majority settled in New York City.[2] Most of the newcomers established themselves in the lower East Side, and when it became overcrowded, many took up residence elsewhere. The construction of the Williamsburg Bridge at the beginning of the century, and the improvement of transit facilities, came in time to relieve the lower East Side. As a result, Brownsville became for large numbers their new home in the Golden Land (*Die Goldene Medina*), and for some three-quarters of a century, perhaps more than any other section of New York, it represented a center where the folksy, intimate mass life of the East European Jewish immigrant found full expression.

The rapid rise of Brownsville into one of the most populous and thriving neighborhoods—a city within a city—captured the interest of many. "It is doubtful if there is another like section of the earth's surface that developed so quickly as Brownsville," reads one newspaper account.[3] The genesis of this community was not due to the discovery in the soil of rich raw materials such as gold, silver, copper, or oil, which made other towns mushroom over night. Tailors were the original pioneers; sewing machines, flat irons, scissors, needles, and thimbles—these were the foundation materials upon which this vibrant community was built.

The growth of Brownsville illustrates the great urbanization of American society in the present century. Like the early villages of the Town of New Lots, East New York, and Brownsville, the United States was predominantly rural-born. The pioneer, the cultivator, the independent craftsman, the frontiersman—these were the precursors of the nation's hardy spirit and vigorous character.

Rural and agrarian society, however, was constrained to retreat before the inexorable, expanding urban industrialism. This urban upheaval has exercised a crucial and significant impact upon American history, effecting reforms in government, law, economics, religion, social attitudes, and human relations.

Urbanization goes hand in hand with technological progress, and during the period of the mass migration from Eastern Europe, technological advance was assuming major proportions in America. Industry needed all the manpower it could marshal. The Jewish immigrants were absorbed into the garment industry, which witnessed unprecedented business activity at the time. The rapid growth of cities brought with it changes in style and in the production of clothing. The apparel trades had become one of New York's major industries long before the East European Jews arrived, but these trades grew in importance in succeeding years.

A number of reasons impelled the Jewish newcomers to select employment in the garment industry. First, many of them were tailors before they arrived in America. Secondly, the economic position of the Jewish worker in the clothing trades was not at the bottom of the industrial complex. While the earnings were poor, other workers in New York and elsewhere were earning less. In fact, over the years the New York clothing industry offered a wage scale higher than any other clothing center, and in 1900 it compared favorably with other trades. Thus, for a large number of Jewish immigrants the clothing industry became a "vast economic frontier," and the sweatshop served as a training school where they learned not only the values of organized labor and of the union, but also how to become contractors or manufacturers on their own.[4]

The first Jewish settlers in Brownsville belonged to the proletariat. One of the most industrialized groups in the city, seventy per cent of them were engaged in 1892 in the needle industries. They were young people, strong, earnest, and adventurous, eager to pursue the life-quest in the village that offered more room, more air, and more opportunity for the families they had begun to rear.

Of the large influx of immigrants from Eastern Europe, many settled first in the East Side or Williamsburg, and later moved to Brownsville. This produced a building boom. Neither the reversals of 1893 nor the depressions that were to follow could impede further growth. A new Brownsville sprang up. Where formerly there were empty waste spaces, blocks of wood and brick were constructed. Brownsville developed from a small village into a large metropolitan urban district whose impact on the development of New York City was appreciable. Equally impressive was its role in the adjustment of these immigrants to the New World. It swelled into a busy, bustling center of Jewish life whose fortunes were followed not only by New Yorkers but also by immigrants throughout the country, who referred to it as the "Jerusalem of America."

Brownsville in later years was "no garden spot to the eye." Many immigrants, in order to escape the East Side slums, moved to this remote section of Brooklyn where they could enjoy a more inviting environment. And yet, although much land was available, the builders and speculators erected row on row of unattractive, dreary, railroad flats. In later years a residential section, with spacious and comfortable two- or three-family homes, was constructed. As for the older section, it began in time to decay and fester, and resembled more and more the Manhattan slums that had been abandoned. Truly, one can say that the suburbs of yesterday became the slums of today.

What else could one have expected? No town-planning went into the development of Brownsville. There was no outside support such as is available today. Most of the original private builders were confronted with numerous hardships and impediments. Periodic depressions were usually followed by bank failures, with subsequent difficulty in obtaining credit or disposing of property in hand.

So Brownsville grew—some of it fair to behold, most of it dull and unalluring. It was not a quiet or tranquil place. A number of observers have commented on the strident features—the noises, the smells of this teeming and bristling district. "I heard the constant din of sirens, police whistles, fire engines. A huge six-block square of junkshops, tinsmithies, stables, garages and miscellaneous small enterprises surrounded [the] main arteries. How it all rang and clattered and buzzed and smelled! There wasn't a quiet square yard in the whole district." [5]

The main thoroughfare was Pitkin Avenue. It ran for a mile through the heart of Brownsville, and became for a time one of the most important shopping centers in Brooklyn. Hundreds of stores of every description lined its sidewalks, displaying in well-dressed show windows every imaginable commodity, serving as a combination of Broadway, Fifth Avenue, and Wall Street. On weekends and holidays Pitkin Avenue resembled Times Square. It was packed and vibrant, full of movement, excitement, and color. Thousands of shoppers, strollers, and loungers moved along the avenue, pausing to shop, listening to the arguments of speakers on the street corners, or just enjoying a promenade or rubbing shoulders with crowds of people. Not far away, and in striking contrast was Belmont Avenue, with its market and its pungent blocks of pushcarts. The pushcart markets on Prospect Place and

Blake Avenue were also familiar sights. Next to Belmont Avenue ran Rockaway Avenue with its areas of furniture stores, remaining to this day a famous furniture mart. Sutter Avenue, extending through Brownsville and East New York, one of the main shopping districts of East New York, was another main artery of the section, as were Pennsylvania, Stone, Fulton, and Atlantic Avenues.

The Jews streaming into Brownsville formed a self-contained community, a little island within the village. Unlike the newcomers in other communities, they did not displace the earlier residents; they moved into new houses constructed for them on previously unoccupied land. While they formed the largest enclave, they were not the only immigrant group that moved into the town. Other immigrant ethnic groups, comparatively smaller in number, moved into the section at the same time. Russians, Poles, and Italians settled next to the Jews.

The newcomers who sweated in the Brownsville shops faced a two-fold problem of adjustment—adapting themselves to the new American environment, and adapting themselves to a new Jewish environment. Those who had come from the townlets (*shtetlach*) of Eastern Europe found themselves in a westernized, industrial urban society with a set of mores totally different from those they had grown up with. Although they were poor in material goods, the Jews brought with them a rich spiritual tradition. They came from compact Jewish settlements, and they yearned to preserve the customs and mode of life for which they had been persecuted and discriminated against in the old country.

Unlike the East Side—which became the concern of the social reformers—and the older settlers, the "Uptown German" Jews, who sought to help the newcomers in their Americanization, Brownsville was left largely to itself. Not only was the general community complaisant and indifferent about the Brownsville Jews, but even the older German-Jewish community did not come in direct contact with them. The Hebrew Educational Society, established in Brownsville by the Baron de Hirsch Fund and the older German Jewish settlers of Brooklyn, did not come into existence until a decade after Jewish settlement in Brownsville.

Nor were settlement houses established here as in the East Side, where they wielded an important influence. While the freedom to organize and develop its own life in its own way may have spared Brownsville the friction which characterized the East Side's struggle between the "Uptown and Downtown Jews," as well as the zealous efforts of various social workers to accelerate the Americanization pace, Brownsville was left to its own devices totally unprepared and without assistance.

In general, the period was one of change and social unrest among people everywhere. However promising the future, current conditions were hard and challenging and baffling. Americans were confronted with a variety of conflicting social problems.[6] On the one hand, the rapidly growing towns and cities were being populated by a multitude of immigrants and by masses of wage earners, most of them at the bottom of the social ladder, struggling to better their economic and social position. On the other hand, America experienced the phenomenal development of an industrial economy brought about by technological change, which gave rise to vast corporate bureaucracies and to the concentration of wealth and power in the hands of a few men.

During this era of great changes, even thoughtful and eminent Americans began to feel insecure about the permanence of the structure the American people had raised. There were disparate reactions. Some Americans, following the example set by Henry Adams and Henry James, fled to Europe. Others, like Edward Bellamy and Henry George, turned from the present to embrace the future through their Utopias. Henry George, in his *Progress and Poverty*, complained about the materialist appetites, the lust for wealth, "Get money—honestly if you can—but at any rate get money! This is the lesson that society is daily and hourly dinning into the ears of its members." He was frightened by the manner in which the large cities were developing. "Whence shall come the new barbarians?" he asked. "Go through the squalid quarters of great cities and you may see, even now, their gathering hordes."

The East Side and Brownsville were aroused by the various social reform movements. They were seething with social protest.

Radicals, social reformers, and all kinds of champions were trying to make the masses cognizant of the deplorable social and economic conditions under which they lived. On every possible platform these men emphasized and debated their concepts of the good society, of social justice, and of their religion of humanitarianism and brotherhood. In all this convulsing ferment, Brownsville was only a tributary of the main stream of social idealism and protest which flowed from the East Side. But because Brownsville was a compact and unique Jewish enclave, not as directly affected by the various international cross currents felt in the East Side, it had its own contribution to make. The various social reform movements were perhaps closer here to the Jewish masses.

Great social changes do not transpire without struggle. Indeed, they are usually accompanied by turbulence and violence. The labor struggles in the first decades of this century claimed their martyrs and victims. Many of the improvements and social reforms we now enjoy and take for granted, emerged only through the agitations and exertions of "prophetic shock minorities who had the zeal and energy to prevail over an apathetic or disinterested majority," to use a quotation from Jacque Maritain. Brownsville contributed its share of idealists and social reformers.

All kinds of movements found their followers in Brownsville. If Brownsville was "no garden spot to the eye, it was a lush garden for the mind" states Sol Hurok, the impressario who, for a time, was manager of the Brownsville Labor Lyceum. "Brownsville was a steaming microcosm of culture in the heart of Brooklyn, alive with intellectual striving and artistic hungers. In meeting rooms above the crowded stores, the air shook with furiously happy arguments. There was never any lack of audiences for speakers, for concerts. . . . In those days music was not big business—but music thrived in Brownsville." [7]

Various educational forums dotted the neighborhood, where proponents of all causes found adherents. Dr. Nathan Krass, later Rabbi of Temple Emanuel in New York City, crowded the auditorium of the Hebrew Educational Society to its rafters at his Sunday afternoon forums, and Mr. Nathan Seidman for many years packed the auditorium of P.S. 84 with his lecturers.

There was "such a love of learning, such a respect for ideals and idealists, as I have encountered nowhere else," writes Samuel Tanenbaum, another son of Brownsville. "The library was something more than a place where one went for books. Here one met men and women who had little formal schooling, who worked in factories and were socialists, anarchists, Zionists, Macfaddenites, chiropractors, atheists, food faddists, sun worshippers, Buddhists; men and women who wanted so much from life—to be great writers, to be great humanitarian leaders, to be innovators of world-shaking importance." [8]

Margaret Sanger decided to open the first birth control clinic in Brownsville in 1916 because it had a large population of working class Jews, always tolerant of new ideas, willing to listen and to accept advice whenever the health of mother or children was involved—"Here there would be at least no breaking of windows, no hurling of insults into our teeth."

Jews first settled in East New York about 1850. They were German-Jewish immigrants who followed their earlier German compatriots who had immigrated to the village in the 1840's. What stands out in the life of these early German Jewish settlers is their complete integration into the life of the German-American community of East New York in whose midst they lived. They not only participated in the activities of the various German societies, but also were the organizers and leaders in some of them. They found it natural and evidently pleasurable to spend their lives in the German-American cultural milieu.

The character of this Jewish group differed from the great wave of East European Jewish immigrants who settled in the town in subsequent years. They were not so readily absorbed into the mainstream of life. Their large number, and the compactness and folk character of their immigrant colony, enabled them not only to maintain the old world religious cultural values, but also to create new ethnic institutions and to introduce modifications of traditional forms.

Of primary importance was the creation of a Jewish labor movement. It transformed the Jewish immigrant workers into a social force that left its mark on the life of the Jewish community as well as on the country's entire labor movement. If the contractors who moved to Brownsville anticipated being spared the struggle of the unionization movement, or being relieved from some of the anti-sweat shop rules, they were soon disabused. Here a union movement was developed which fought hard and incessantly to improve working conditions and which played a decisive role in the promotion of progressive social legislation. A strong socialist movement also evolved, and from 1917 to 1919 the socialists controlled the political situation.

The pioneers who created the Jewish labor movement in this country were primarily socialists. They belonged to the intelligentsia, were cosmopolitan in spirit, and under the influence of the Russian Revolutionary movement, many of them employed the Russian language as their vernacular. Their objective was not to create a *Jewish* labor movement, separate and apart from the non-Jewish workers; rather they strove to integrate the Jewish proletariat in the American unions and in the American Socialist Party. "However," as Dr. Bezalel Sherman points out, "in the very process of initially injecting a socialist spirit into their unions, they created a gulf between the Jewish labor movement and the general labor movement in the country" that was far removed from a class approach to social problems.[9] Hence the Jewish unions formed an entity of their own, modeling themselves not on their American counterparts, but rather on European socialism.

While the founders of the Jewish unions were indifferent to Jewish culture, they soon discovered they would need to use the Yiddish language if they wanted to organize the Yiddish speaking Jewish workers. Thus, parallel with the rise of the Jewish labor movement, and indeed largely as its consequence, there developed a broad secular culture that found expression in a Yiddish literature, press, theatre, and educational system.

The Jewish labor movement remained aloof from the Jewish community until the First World War. A change took place after the War, when some of the leading socialists, including the Brownsville socialists like Shiplacoff and others, became active leaders in the Labor Zionist rescue efforts on behalf of the Jewish people. Significantly, at the time the Jewish workers became active in Jewish projects, the Jewish Labor Movement had ceased to exist as an independent entity; it had become an integral part of the American Labor movement.

Although the labor leaders were anti-religious, and the first trade unions were founded as secular socialist organizations, vast numbers of the Jewish immigrant workers remained Orthodox in religion and were determined to maintain their cultural identity. The first synagogues in Brownsville were organized in the sweatshops, and the membership of the numerous synagogues that were soon established was made up of these workers. In fact, the arrival of the East European Jews stimulated a revival of Orthodox Judaism in this country.

Important as was the role played by the labor movement, it by no means constituted the totality of Jewish life. Spiritual factors burgeoned as well. Brownsville accepted its share in the challenge to assure the continuity of Jewish life. It participated in all movements and activities dedicated to the survival of Jews and Judaism in the United States. Here lived and worked some of the pioneers of the spirit who displayed a passionate devotion to Jewish learning and education, to the revival of the Hebrew language, to the growth of Zionism as a bastion in religious and secular circles, to the synagogue, and to the idealism inherent in the Jewish heritage. Brownsville contributed a number of leaders to the Conservative movement in Judaism, which advocated a gradual and moderate accommodation of Judaism to modern life, and which was gaining strength at this time. Brownsville participated in the effort of the New York *Kehillah* to organize the Jewish community in the first decades of the century, in the organization of the American Jewish Congress, in the various war relief projects for their stricken brethren abroad, and in other comparable enterprises. Not always feeling at home in the agencies and services established by its older fellow German-Jews, Brownsville created its own institutions and formed its own communal bodies, which enriched the life of the entire community. Hospitals, homes for the aged, orphanages, day nurseries, *Gemillut Hasadim* societies, communal Talmud Torahs and Yeshivas, were built here, as well as numerous other philanthropic, social, and fraternal organizations which are functioning to this day.

Nothing came easily in this immigrant community; everything had to be started from modest and tenuous beginnings. The residents had to struggle diligently and perseveringly to procure essential public benefits—schools, playgrounds, paved streets, health improvements, transit facilities, and the like. Many civic groups, among them the Brownsville Board of Trade, the Pitkin Avenue Merchants Association, and the Brownsville Neighborhood Health and Welfare Council, labored long and indefatigably to obtain whatever forward steps were achieved. Few of the social welfare measures which every modern American takes for granted were in vogue. But the Brownsville immigrant community was not easily discouraged, having experienced hardship before they arrived here. In 1900, 40.5 per cent of all immigrants arriving in this country possessed less than $30 on landing, and only 5.6 per cent had more.[10] Low as was their standard of living here, however, it exceeded their European scale. There was no one to lean upon, no one to blame; they had to create their own resources; they had to blast their building materials out of their own quarry of hope and resourcefulness. Their faith in a better future was invincible. It must be conceded that Jews were different in some respects from their fellow immigrants. Most of them were artisans, and in many instances of urban origin, but more important, they avouched great faith in education, both as an end in itself and as a means to carve a better future. Jewish parents, anxious to spare their children the hard lot they had known, made many sacrifices to keep their children in school.

For many of the first generation, Brownsville was a completely Jewish world; it came closest to the life of the European *Shtetl* most of them had known. The language in the home was Yiddish, the newspapers that came into the home were Yiddish, and the store signs were in Yiddish. The synagogues were always assured a *Minyan* (quorum). Small wonder that many resided in Brownsville for decades without learning to speak English. They gave little thought to leaving their residence for other sections.

Even for the American-born generation there were Jewish links which could not easily be eradicated. Some of the streets bore the names of Jewish personalities—Herzl Street, Strauss Street, among others. On almost every block there was at least one synagogue, and on some two or three, to which neighbors came thrice daily for religious services. The newsstands displayed the Yiddish dailies and weeklies next to the English newspapers. The public parades on special occasions—Jewish Flag Day and Flower Day—and the street-corner meetings on Jewish issues served as constant reminders of Jewish life.

On the Jewish holidays the public schools were practically unattended. Whether religiously observant or not, no children attended school on these days. The restaurants and bakeries served Jewish dishes. One could tell the approach of the Sabbath by the aroma of Sabbath dishes being prepared by the Jewish housewives. As Friday night approached, the pushcarts left the streets and some of the stores began to close. The hustle and bustle preceding Passover and the High Holy days announced their arrival long in advance. What youngster would go without a new suit on Passover, or attend synagogue without a new hat on Rosh Hashonoh? On Kol Nidre night Pitkin's stores were all dark. The Avenue became the leading promenade, the Fifth Avenue for the entire community. It was a sight to behold!

But despite the insulating effects of the immigrant community and institutions, Jewish life could not remain unchanged; the old-world Jewish culture could not be imported here. The European *Shtetl* had a history and a tradition, a self-imposed discipline, and a respect for rabbinic authority. Here each group was left to its own, free to follow its ways. Intellectuals began to arrive here who had lived and studied in the larger European centers. They were exposed to the secular forces which were beginning to influence large numbers, and some were responsible for the strong socialist, anti-religious and anti-Zionist trend which was introduced in the community. Many were determined to break loose from the *shtetl* way of life, which appeared to them too circumscribed and authoritarian. They were seeking new adventures in the large city and in the new land.

The immigrant community was not always successful in bridging the gap between the old country and the new, and therefore personal and social tragedies ensued. The life of the American-born generation of Jewish youth was particularly affected. A number of Jewish writers have in recent years attempted to depict the impact which life in the Jewish quarter imposed on their emotional, spiritual, cultural, and psychic life. In many cases the cleavage between the generations was fraught with heart-rending consequences. Wholly without roots in the Jewish past, many of the second generation were, if not hostile, indifferent to their parents' way of life.

"This explosive tension made it possible," wrote Professor Morris R. Cohen, "for the same family to produce saints and sinners, philosophers and gunmen." William Poster, who himself was raised in Brownsville summed it up: "What wrenching occurred as out from under the tremendous corpus of the centuries—old Jewish development lying motionless as a whale cast up on a strand of the great continent—crept the children, breathing a bewildering mixture of the heavy, humanity-laden air of the Old World and the thin atmosphere of the New! . . . Relations between children and parents reached an extreme of imbalance, not only among the Jews, but also in all of America that was going, at different rates, through a prolonged crisis of transplantation in which scarcely anyone has had more than an inkling of what is to be preserved or destroyed, what will grow and what decay. . . ." [11]

The Jewish district sought simultaneously to retain its cultural identity and to accommodate itself to American conditions of life. It participated energetically in political activity, and adapted itself to new forms of recreation and social life. However, Brownsville acquired not only the assets which have made urban America appealing, but also, alas, some of its glaring faults. All large cities have been plagued by gangsterism at frequent intervals. "The lawlessness of American Society," suggests Mrs. Constance M. Green in her *Rise of Urban America*, "which later generations would trace to the frontier, had its roots perhaps equally deep in the fierce competitiveness of the American city."

In the early 1940's Brownsville shocked the nation by the District Attorney's exposure of an incredible crime syndicate called the "Combination." Later it came to be known as "Murder, Inc."—a cutthroat racket operating for a number of years across the entire country, committing killings to order. The inquiry revealed the national scope of the Combination's connections, but the crime revelations fell mainly upon Brownsville. This was a shockingly new phenomenon in Jewish life. The Jewish gangster was without precedent, a product not of Jewish but of American urban life. Naturally, the handful of malefactors brought grief and disgrace not only to their parents, but also to the community. But this sad interlude in Brownsville's history has been counterbalanced by the larger number of wise, constructive sons who brought glory to the community. Many who lived here became world famous by their worthy contributions to the welfare of mankind.

Despite its early characterization as a village where one walked "knee-deep in mud" and where "nanny goats roamed," urban Brownsville was an attractive American-Jewish Center. There were warmth, color and tradition. It was not an impersonal place with stretches of apartment houses where one scarcely knows his neighbor. People were interested in each other. True, some parts were marked by squalor, poverty, and sordidness. There were the agonies of feeding and safeguarding the family, and the pain of adjustment to a new land; but there were also rich and middle class families, business men, professionals, educators, and spiritual leaders, among others. It was a community teeming with life, with idealism and aspirations, and rich in movements and "isms."

In her stimulating study, *The Death and Life of Great American Cities,* Mrs. Jane Jacobs analyzes some of the factors and processes that go into the seemingly mysterious and perverse behavior of cities, what makes for their decay, and what gives life and spirit to them.[12] Brownsville's continuous existential span as one of the largest concentrations of Jewish settlement for seventy-five years in Metropolitan New York is in itself a noteworthy phenomenon. This may be attributed to various factors. The ethnic cohesiveness; the many local improvements and transit facilities extracted from the City authorities; the convenient shopping areas; the comparatively low rentals; the construction of new homes and new sections for those who changed their incomes or their tastes; the neighborhood's leadership; the many religious, educational and social institutions—all these contributed to the stability of the section. Until the 1940's there was always a new wave of immigrants, and therefore a less affluent group to take over the homes abandoned by the older settlers. The most recent groups to move here, only a few years ago, were some Israelis and Cuban Jews.

As the neighborhood experienced dilapidation and decay, many interested groups became concerned, unwilling to see their old community expire. They sought to ameliorate the situation by encouraging builders to repair and to renew. When these efforts failed, they prevailed upon the public authorities to demolish the old section and construct on it a new low income housing project. The heart of Brownsville, accordingly, the old and original Brownsville settlement, saw the bulldozer, which symbolizes the transformation of many urban sections caught in the maelstrom of change and dispersion. A large blighted area with its old tenements was erased, and on its site were erected a number of public housing projects. The bulldozer has not yet completed its task. Several more areas are scheduled to feel its giant strokes, to make room for additional public housing projects.

None of this, however, helped to revive or update Brownsville. Not only the landscape, but also the district itself, has changed radically. From an almost solidly Jewish community it has become a solidly non-Jewish area into which Negroes and Puerto Ricans have moved. The large concentration of public housing projects planned primarily for low-income families has created an economically, socially, and racially segregated neighborhood with all the economic and social ills associated with such communities—overcrowded schools, shabby housing, poor health, juvenile and adolescent delinquency, and a disoriented family life.

The Brownsville Jewish Community is no more, but its story merits telling even if the feverish pulsations of its former heart can not be adequately recaptured. It was not an homogeneous community but quite differentiated, an urban section abounding in contrasts of light and shadow. To some, Brownsville meant home; to others, it was a suburb of the Lower East Side where "nanny goats" roamed. Some saw Brownsville as the "Jerusalem of America," others as an area where radical labor-union people lived. To some it came to mean the spawning place of "Murder, Inc.," to many it was the locale of Gerald Greene's "last angry man," which Paul Muni brought to the screen, the locale which boasts many commanding figures, famous personalities, scientists, doctors, lawyers, politicians, writers, teachers, and philanthropists. This ambivalent attitude has prompted both favorable and unfavorable portrayals. Former residents to this day, even after having moved to other sections, look with nostalgia and a sense of loyalty and pride to their old neighborhood. Others who could never endure or accept it hesitate to admit they spent their youth in the community.

Whatever may be one's feelings towards the Brownsville community, it forms a valuable chapter in the history of the East European Jewish immigrants during the past three-quarters of a century. It is with further aspects of this story that the following pages are concerned.

The First Jews in East
New York

I

New Lots and the Villages of East New York and Brownsville

PRIOR to 1886, Brownsville and East New York formed part of the town of New Lots, which lay within the present eastern section of Brooklyn, extending from Ralph Avenue to the Queens County Line, and from Fulton Street and the Cemetery Hills to Canarsie and Jamaica Bay. Within these boundaries there developed over the years the widely known sections of Brownsville, East New York, New Lots, Highland Park, Arlington, and Cypress Hills, each with its traditions, history, and unique characteristics.

New Lots was one of the earliest American settlements. Its history goes back almost three hundred years to about 1670, when the Dutch acquired land in this region. It was the scene of important military operations during the Revolutionary War. Sir Edmond Andros, second English Governor, granted a separate patent, or charter, for New Lots on March 21, 1677, with the new lands laid out in individual plots or plantations. Some of the settlers had emigrated from the Netherlands, settling in New Amsterdam or elsewhere before removing to Flatbush (*Flackbos*) or Midwout, one of the Dutch towns founded around the middle of the seventeenth century and now part of the Borough of Brooklyn.

New Lots remained a subordinate village of the town of Flatbush until 1852, when it established its local independence. It continued as an independent town until it was annexed to Brooklyn in 1886 as the Twenty-sixth Ward. During the period of its independence, three other villages developed within the town of New Lots—East New York, Brownsville, and Cypress Hills.

The village of East New York owes its name and existence to John R. Pitkin, a native of Connecticut and a far sighted businessman, who came to the village in 1835. He was so impressed with the lands lying between the hills on the north and Jamaica Bay on the south that he conceived the idea of founding a new city to rival New York and giving it the name of East New York.

The last and most dramatic of the four villages that constituted the town of New Lots was founded during the Civil War. On January 25, 1861, another New Englander, a native of Vermont named Charles S. Brown, bought a parcel of land at a public auction. Later, he acquired additional land, and for more than a decade he actively engaged in the development of the village which came to be called by his name—Brown's Village, or Brownsville. When Brooklyn merged with New York in 1898, the entire district became part of New York City.[1]

The First Jews in East New York

There were no Jews among the Dutch pioneers who settled New Lots in the seventeenth century. The Jews arrived about 1850, when a large group of Germans settled in the East New York section. A study of the early records reveals, however, that from the very beginning Jewish itinerant traders or merchants came in contact with residents of the town of Flatbush, of which New Lots was a part. Soon after Flatbush was formally settled (1652), a small group of Sephardic Jews, Dutch-Brazilian refugees, arrived in New Amsterdam in September 1654. Although the refugees did not receive a friendly welcome, and were subjected to economic disabilities, they managed after a struggle to establish a foothold in this new land.

One of the most colorful and influential personalities among the first Jewish arrivals in 1654 was Asser Levy.[2] A champion of civil and religious liberty among the early settlers, he took the lead in demanding and obtaining civic rights for himself and his fellow Jews. He was licensed as a butcher, dealt in real estate and various commodities, owned a tavern, and was a fur trader. He arrived as a penniless immigrant, but when he died in 1681 he left a considerable estate. According to some historians, his family settled in Long Island after his death.

Asser Levy's wide range of business dealings brought him in touch with a large number of individuals in different parts of New York and adjoining territory. The early records of the Town of Flatbush contain a number of references to his dealings with Dutch residents of Flatbush. Through legal records available to us we can identify Asser Levy and the town's folk in Flatbush. These records deal with lawsuits brought before the authorities, most of the time by Levy, as plaintiff. This would indicate his involvement in many activities, since only a small portion of business transactions lead to litigation.

Among the defendants were a number of individuals who became owners of lots, or "plantations" in the New Lots of Flatbush. A separate patent for the New Lots of Flatbush was granted by Governor Andros on March 21, 1677. Later, on April 2, 1680, the land was subdivided among the original owners of plantations in Flatbush into forty-seven lots.

In four records which concern Asser Levy, we find two cases involving a Minne Johannes, who appears to have resided in New Lots in 1675. His name appears in the New Lots charter granted by Governor Andros in 1677, and when the tract was subdivided, he was allotted three of the forty-seven lots.[3] In one of these cases in 1676, Asser Levy, plaintiff, complained through his attorney that Minne Johanness owed him 400 guilders seawant value. The case had been referred previously to a jury, which brought in a verdict in the plaintiff's favor. The court approved the verdict and issued a judgement accordingly.[4] On June 19, 1677, Asser Levy appeared again as plaintiff against Minne Johanness, claiming 370 guilders seawant or merchantable wheat equivalent in value, and 50 guilders to cover court expenses. The defendant, through his attorney, George Cooke, agreed to the full sum.[5]

Several earlier cases in which Asser Levy was involved with Flatbush residents indicate that Asser Levy bartered goods and products and traded in a variety of articles. On February 10, 1668, he appeared as a plaintiff against Antoni Jansz,[6] who owed him for the following articles purchased on November 22, 1667:

One load of flax weighing 176½ pounds at 10 striver per pound—florins 138-5.
one axle—fl. 24
nine pounds grease at 25 striver per pound. fl.-11-5
twenty-five pounds of grease at 25 strivers per pound—florins 315.
one comb, and thread—fl. 5-16
 Total florins—210-9

In several other cases in which Asser Levy appeared as plaintiff against Flatbush residents, the constable and overseers judged in favor of Asser Levy and ordered the plaintiffs to pay their debts.[7]

One of the well-known families in Flatbush and New Lots was the Strycker family, whose ancestor Jan Strycker settled in the town in 1654. Some members of the family went to live in New Lots at the time the land was divided. We find that on August 15, 1683 one of the Stryckers, Pieter, who resided in Flatbush, bought from "Abraham Franckfoort, a Jew residing in N.Jorck," a Negro male man for the sum of 1025 guilders.[8]

The Flatbush Town Records contain later references to Jews who were associated with the Spanish Portugese Congregation, Shearith Israel; to a Moses Levy in 1723, to a Naphtali Hart Myers in 1747, and others. Interesting as these names are historically, they only indicate that Jews came to this region and had commercial dealings with the residents of the town. This is borne out by other references, which indicate that Jewish traders and peddlers had visited the region before it contained a Jewish settlement.

The Bookman and Midas Families

The first Jewish family to settle in New Lots was the Bookman family, whose members, together with the Midas family, which was related to it, were among the earliest and best known citizens in East New York. These families continued to reside in the town for more than a century, from about 1850 until 1962.

Our earliest reference to the family is found in the 1855 State Census of the Town of New Lots,[9] which lists M. Bookman and members of his family. Mr. Bookman was at that time fifty years of age, a naturalized citizen, a native of Germany, a merchant by trade, and had resided in the town for five years. His wife Fanny was fifty-two years of age, and his daughter Barbara was eighteen. Their frame dwelling was valued at $1,400.

Adolph Bookman, aged twenty-two, clothier, is listed in the 1855 State Census of the neighboring town of Flatlands. Although we have carefully studied the census information of that period, we cannot state whether there were other Jews among the 444 families that dwelt in New Lots at that time. The difficulty arises from the fact that no statistics were kept on a religious basis, and the names of the Jews were similar to those of their German neighbors.

In the early 1850's Max and Adolph Bookman established the firm of M. A. Bookman, which became one of the leading dry goods and clothing establishments in New Lots. It was located on the southwest corner of Jamaica and Georgia Avenues. It did an immense business and attracted customers not only from New Lots but also from the surrounding towns. Max Bookman was a tailor by trade, and his wife, Fanny, a weaver. The last reference to them is found in the State Census of 1875, in which Max Bookman is listed as the father, seventy years of age, and Fanny as the mother, seventy-four years of age.

Adolph Bookman was, for thirty-eight years until his retirement, a leading merchant in East New York. Born in Augsburg, Germany, on August 17, 1832, he arrived in this country as a young man, established a country store in the fisherman's village of Canarsie, and later removed to East New York. In 1855 he married Babette (Barbara) Hecht, and both lived to celebrate their golden wedding anniversary on August 10, 1905.

Adolph Bookman and his family took leading roles in the affairs of the town. Adolph was one of the charter members of the Union Hook and Ladder Company, of the Volunteer Fire Department of the Old Town of New Lots, and was among the first trustees of the East New York Savings Bank. He was one of the founders and a president of the first synagogue of the town, and one of the oldest members of the Hillel Lodge of Order B'nai B'rith.

Adolph Bookman died on November 17, 1909, in his seventy-seventh year, at his residence in 1829 East New York Avenue. He was survived by his widow, a daughter Jennie (Mrs. Judah P. Friedman), four sons—Morris, Ralph, Joseph, and Simon—ten grandchildren, and two great grandchildren.

Babette Bookman, widow of Adolph died four years after the death of her husband, on April 24, 1913, at the Bookman residence, in her seventy-eighth year. She was noted for her charities and for her gracious and engaging personality. She was long prominent in the Knights and Ladies of Honor and in the Order of Eastern Star, in which she had proposed over two hundred members.

The Bookmans carried advertisements of their store in the various local papers. A few of these advertisements are not only of interest for the history of the family, but also reflect the conditions of the time. The Bookmans sold not only ready-made clothing, but also made clothing to order. Our earliest advertisement comes from the *Kings County Advertiser*, dated May 6, 1857.

M. & A. Bookman, Dealers in Foreign and Domestic Dry Goods would respectfully call the attention of the inhabitants

of East New York and vicinity to their large and well assorted
stock—Lawn Marinos, Alpaca Muslin de Lains, mourning
goods etc., Shawls, A large assortment of Ready made Cloth-
ing—Vests, Overcoats, Frock Coats, also pantaloons, boys
caps, straw hats, Ladies and Misses gloves. All kinds of cloth-
ing will be made to order, warranted to Fit.

By strict attention to business they hope to merit the
patronage of the public. Vermont Avenue near Railroad
Depot & on Jamaica Plank Road opposite Stage Office. East
New York, L.I.

A similar advertisement was carried in *The East New York*
Journal, Sept. 9, 1858, and in *The Sentinel,* July 6, 1872, the
advertisement reads in part:

THE LEADING HOUSE
OF EAST NEW YORK

M. & A. BOOKMAN
(Established 1852)
Dealers in Foreign and Domestic Dry Goods. A well assorted
stock of cloth and cassemeres, and all kinds of clothing will
be made to order. We buy for cash and sell as low as any
other House.
M. & A. Bookman—corner of Jamaica Plank Road and
Georgia Ave.

The location became known as Bookman's Corner, and on April
11, 1887, the Brooklyn Council renamed Livingston Place
"Bookman Place."

Morris Bookman, eldest son of Adolph, followed in his father's
footsteps and established the House of Morris Bookman in 1876.
He became a first class practical tailor, personally superintending
all the operations of his staff of competent workers, which
consisted of some twenty employees in 1886.[10] At that time, this
enterprising merchant-tailor and clothier had two stores in East
New York—one at the corner of Fulton and Jamaica between
Georgia and Alabama Avenues, and a second one at Atlantic
Avenue between Sheffield and Pennsylvania Avenues. Morris

Bookman was regarded as one of the most esteemed of the East New York eminent merchants.

Adolph Bookman's only daughter, Jennie, married Judah P. Friedman, who was engaged in the same business as her father. In *The East New York Weekly Sentinel* of Saturday, April 10, 1880, the following advertisement appeared:

1880 SPRING AND SUMMER STOCK 1880
NOW READY
GRAND DISPLAY!!!!
FRIEDMAN & BOOKMAN
LEADING CLOTHIERS
OF LONG ISLAND.
FULTON AVENUE & JAMAICA PLANK ROAD
BETWEEN ALABAMA AND GEORGIA.

All of Adolph Bookman's sons became prominent citizens in East New York. Morris, Ralph, and Simon were members of the New Lots Exempt Firemen's Association. For a time Ralph carried on the same kind of business in partnership with Henry N. Bach. The old homestead at 1829 East New York Avenue was occupied by Joseph and Simon for a time. In a house nearby, at 1809 East New York Avenue, lived the oldest son, Morris. The last of the Bookmans to reside there, Morris Bookman, died in the spring of 1962 at the age of seventy-seven.

The Midas family was also well known in East New York. Mrs. Regina (Rachel) Midas, who died in 1936 in her ninety-fifth year, was the oldest resident of New Lots at the time. Born in Buttenheim, Bavaria, on June 24, 1842, she immigrated to the United States in 1859, and lived with her sister, Mrs. Babette Bookman. On August 5, 1860, she married Bernard Midas. She was associated with a number of organizations, and was particularly active in the organization of Temple Sinai and of the Hebrew Benevolent Society of East New York, of which she was treasurer for twenty-one years. Mrs. Midas, known throughout the community as Aunt Molly and as the old matriarch of East New York, was blind at the end of her life. On the fiftieth anniversary of the annexation of New Lots to Brooklyn on October 4, 1931, celebrated with a parade in East New York, Mrs. Midas rode in the automobile with Judge Edward Richards, spoke through the microphone, and shook hands with scores of well wishers.[11]

Her husband Bernard was one of the outstanding leaders of the community. He, too, came from Bavaria, and in 1860 he established his wine and liquor store in East New York on Vermont Avenue and Jamaica Plank Road. He was twice elected to the important position of Commissioner of Charities of Brooklyn, serving from 1875 to 1881. He was also treasurer of the Union Free School, District 2, and was instrumental in the purchase of Jamaica Plank Road (now Jamaica Avenue) from a private corporation. He was a member of the New Lots Exempt Firemen's Association, and was affiliated with a variety of fraternal and social organizations. Together with his wife and a niece, Rosa, who married Mr. A. Dennon, he lived at 135 Jamaica Avenue. Mr. Midas died in 1904, and Mrs. Midas in 1936. Mrs. Rosa S. Dennon died in 1956 in her eighty-ninth year.

Philip Midas, a brother of Bernard Midas, was born in Bavaria in 1845. He served in the Army during the American Civil War, enlisting in 1863 for a period of three years as a private in the 34th New York Volunteer Regiment. He was promoted, after some twelve months of service, to Orderly Sergeant. In 1865 he was still listed as a representation recruit, and remained in the same regiment as Orderly Sergeant.

Soon after the end of the Civil War, the Louis M. Hamilton Post No. 82 of G.A.R. was organized, and met every second and fourth month at Christian Cook's on Jamaica Plank Road near Sheffield Avenue. Philip Midas became the senior vice-commander of the post.

On February 10, 1878, the German Press Association of New Lots began to publish a German language weekly newspaper— *The East New York Laterne*. C. W .C. Dreher became its editor, and later its sole proprietor. It became a successful and influential enterprise until February 10, 1883. In the Spring of that year Philip Midas became publisher, editor, and sole proprietor. He was the first Vice-Grand of the Rainbow Lodge 409, U.O.S.B., which was installed on July 23, 1874 at Bernet's Hotel. He was also a charter member of Von Mensch Lodge 765 F. and A.M., an offshoot of the Tyrian Lodge, comprised of some of the most prominent German citizens of the town, which met twice a week at the Masonic Hall at the corner of Atlantic and Butler Avenues.[12]

Other Jewish families settled in East New York in the 1860's, 70's and 80's. In the 1865 State Census we find the family of Joseph Kaufman, aged thirty-one, who was a merchant in New Lots. He and his wife Sarah were natives of Germany. There was also Coleman Cohen, a salesman, first listed in the 1892 census. He was a native of Prussia, and his wife was named Eliza. His children are listed as Richard, twenty-five years old (1867), Harry M., twenty-one, Hattie G., eighteen, and Lottie. During the Civil War, Coleman Cohen enlisted in the Thirteenth Regiment, in which he attained the rank of Captain. He saw action in most of the major engagements, and was wounded in the Battle of Bull Run. He died on April 4, 1933.

A well-known physician in the East New York section was Dr. Adolphus G. Meyersburg, graduated from New York University Medical School in 1875. He was one of the first medical examiners of the Prudential Insurance Company, and he died at his home, 157 Bradford Street on August 19, 1922,[13] in his seventy-fourth year.

What stands out in the life of these early German Jewish immigrants is their complete integration into the life of the German-American community of East New York. They not only participated eagerly in the programs and activities of the various German societies, but also were the organizers and leaders of some of them.

In 1881 the residents of New Lots organized the Glenmore Rod and Gun Club of Long Island, which became a member of the Long Island Sportsmen's Association. Its purpose was to improve its members in the arts of wing-shooting, the handling of guns, and the enforcement of the game and fish laws of New York. The club was headed by Bernard Midas as president. The first Ladies Bowling Club in Greater New York was formed in Hallem's Hall in East New York. It was called "The Lady Lexington Bowling Club," and among its members were Pauline Sachs and the wives of Adolph Bookman, Barney Midas, and J. P. Friedman.[14]

Paucity in numbers at that time prevented the Jews in East New York from forming a colony within a colony. They had much in common with their German neighbors, however, that was conducive to good neighborly relations. They conversed with one another in German, read the German newspapers, and generally remained deeply devoted to the German culture and civilization. The German community of East New York sought to preserve the life and habits they had brought from abroad through the establishment of social, fraternal, and cultural groups. They had their reading, dramatic, choral, and gymnastic societies. These German Jews no doubt moved into East New York because first they preferred to spend their life in the German-American cultural milieu, and secondly, because they felt they could best carry on their business enterprises and special crafts among their countrymen.

The Jewish settlers came mostly from Bavaria, and were prompted to emigrate from Germany in search of personal freedom and economic opportunities. There was, however, an additional motivation prompting the Jewish emigrant—the need for freedom from religious restrictions and disabilities. "Bavaria, with its Pharaoh-like registration laws, and its restriction of trade, stood first in the row of intolerant states, and made marriage and the right of residence almost impossible for Jews; naturally it furnished the first emigrants, just as it has since supplied the largest number," wrote I. J. Benjamin in his *Three Years in America* (1859-1862).[15]

Among the early Jewish settlers of East New York were also Russian and Polish Jews. In the State Censuses of 1865 and 1870 we find the family of Max, or Mark Blumberg, a tailor by trade. He was a native of Russia, while his wife, Hannah, or Harriet, was a native of Bavaria. They must have settled in New York in the late 1840's, for according to the 1865 State Census, all of their eight children were natives of New York.

Another early resident, Bernard Price, was a native of Poland, while his wife, Hannah, was from Hesse-Darmstadt. Mr. Price had a fancy store in New Lots for many years, and was well known in the Jewish community.

Morris Hamburger, a saloonkeeper, aged forty-five, is listed in the 1870 census as a native of Poland, his wife Anne as a native of England. His eldest daughter Julia, aged eighteen years, also born in England, was a teacher in 1873 in the local school which belonged to School District 2. For a long time she was the first and only Jewish school teacher in the town.

The Jewish population in East New York grew in the following years. When the 1892 State Census was taken, there were about a hundred families, comprising some five hundred individuals in the East New York Section of the Twenty-sixth Ward. A number of them had lived in the United States for many years—since the early 1850's, 60's, 70's, and 80's. This is indicated by the fact that most of the children are listed as natives of the United States. While many were natives of Germany, there was now a considerable number of Jews who had emigrated from Russia, Poland, England, and Austria (Galicia).

A majority of the early settlers of East New York were merchants, shopkeepers, or skilled artisans, with their stores along Atlantic and Jamaica Avenues. They resided on Herkimer Street, Wyona, Arlington, Alabama, Georgia, Elton, Schenck, Pennsylvania, and elsewhere. A number of them were tailors; some were cigar-makers, peddlers, shoemakers, and other craftsmen. They included Israel Lipsky and his wife Sarah, both natives of Germany who had six children, all born in the United States. Mr. Lipsky had two department stores, one at Atlantic and Pennsylvania Avenues, the other at Atlantic Avenue and Hendrix Street.

Charles Dattlebaum, aged thirty-nine, and his wife Fannie, both natives of Germany, were storekeepers. One of the sons is the well known physician, Dr. M. J. Dattlebaum who has practiced in Brooklyn for many years, and was president of the Kings County Medical Society.

William Isaacs, a native of Germany, with his wife Esther, and their five sons and three daughters (all of them born in England, where the Isaacs lived before coming to this country)ˉ, were well known glaziers in East New York. Lazarus Sachs and Abraham Levy were also glaziers.

The Sam Nedis Department Store on Atlantic Avenue was a well-known shopping center. Mr. Nedis, its owner, was a native of Austria who lived here with his wife Annie and their children. Goodman Department Store on Atlantic Avenue was another well known shopping place. Samuel Furmansky, Louis Krieger, Samuel Schreiber, a native of Germany, and his American-born wife Carrie, were merchants. David I. Lubin owned a fancy store. Abram Abrams, a native of Russia, aged forty-two, and his wife Bertha, a native of Germany, were store-keepers. Abraham Brash aged sixty, and his wife Rosalie were natives of Germany, and Jacob, aged twenty-two, were storekeepers.

An important role in the political life of Kings County was played by Judge Israel Frederick Fischer.[16] Born in Manhattan on August 17, 1858, he attended public high school, studied law in the office of Henry S. Bennett, and was admitted to the bar in 1879. In 1887 his family moved to East New York. He was elected chairman of the Republican committee of Kings County in 1889, and served until 1891. Between 1888 and 1890 he served as a member of the Executive Committee of the Republican State Committee. In 1894, and again in 1896, he was elected to Congress to represent the Fourth Congressional District of Kings County. In May 1899, President William McKinley appointed Fischer a member of the U.S. Board of General Appraisers, which consisted of nine members. In 1926 Congress reorganized this Board into the United States Custom Court, and in 1927 Mr. Fischer was appointed chief justice by President Coolidge and later reappointed by President Hoover. He retired in 1933, after thirty years of service. The Fischers lived in East New York at 83 Arlington Ave., but in 1938, toward the end of Judge Fischer's life, they lived in New York City. Judge Fischer participated actively in the affairs of Union Temple and of the Brooklyn Federation of Jewish Charities.

Another well-known family in this section was the Morris and Rosalie (Lehman) Katsky family, natives of Germany. Their son

Alexander was born on June 5, 1873, and after a career in professional baseball between 1890-1900 as catcher for the famous Baltimore Orioles, he became active in Jewish philanthropic and religious organizations, serving as grand-master of Order B'rith Abraham.[17] His sister Addie married Isaac Sargent, a prominent lawyer who represented the Brownsville District in the State Assembly in 1908-1909, was a member of the State Constitutional Convention in 1915, and president of the Hebrew Educational Society. They resided for many years on Herkimer Street.

THE MURDER OF SARAH ALEXANDER AND THE CONVICTION OF PESACH N. RUBENSTEIN

All of New York was aroused and shocked by a sensational murder case in 1875 in the town of New Lots.[18] On December 14, 1875, a farmer of Jamaica Plank Road in East New York informed the police that one of his laborers had found a woman's body in his field. Proceeding to the designated place, the police found the woman's body with her throat slashed.

Careful investigation by the Brooklyn police authorities soon established the identity of the murdered woman as Sarah Alexander, a Polish Jewess, nineteen years old, who resided at Essex Street in the lower East Side of Manhattan. Circumstantial evidence pointed to her cousin, Pesach Nathan (Nissim) Rubenstein, as the murderer. Sarah Alexander had arrived eighteen months earlier in this country, and during the first ten months she lived as a housemaid with her cousin, a Mr. Rubinstein, at Bayard Street in Manhattan. She became very intimate with her employer's son, whom she attended day and night during a long and severe illness. After leaving the house of her cousin, she was employed in a tailoring house on Division Street, and on Sunday afternoon, December 12, she visited her cousin.

The District Attorney of Kings County, Winchester Britton, and police detectives soon established enough evidence to arrest Pesach N. Rubinstein. He stoutly maintained his innocence. He was about twenty-eight years of age, a peddler who kept a small jewelry store at Bayard Street, and had a wife in Poland who was expected to arrive in a few days. A number of persons of East New York, who had ridden on Sunday evening in the car from Broadway to East New York, identified the woman as having ridden with them, and also gave a full description of her male companion. According to their testimony, both got out at the termination of the road in front of the Howard House at about six-fifteen in the afternoon and went off in the direction of the Jamaica Plank Road. Rubenstein's family engaged eminent counsel to defend their son. Every effort was made to save his life.

There was strong circumstantial evidence against the accused. A post-mortem examination revealed that the woman was pregnant at the time of her death. This explained the motive. The accused had been sexually intimate with her and knew she would soon become a mother. Fearing to have the fact come to the knowledge of his wife, who was expected to arrive by every steamer, he determined to kill the girl.

A resident of East New York called at Police Headquarters and identified Pesach Rubinstein as the man he had seen on the Roosevelt ferry boat with the woman. The police measured the impression of the man's and woman's feet where they scaled the fence into the lot, and found that Rubinstein's boots corresponded exactly with the larger impress. The boots were still covered with the peculiar soil of East New York. The knife, which was found in the corn stalk about seven feet from the body, was identified, and its purchase traced to an obscure little shop.

Moreover, the defendant had told six or seven persons, including P. J. Alexander, that he had dreamed that Sarah had been killed ten miles from New York. This was regarded as crucial evidence of knowledge of the murder before it was discovered. In his memoirs, Abraham Cahan suggests that Pesach, as a religious Jew, was fearful lest Sarah might not receive a Jewish burial, and so was led to tell of his dream.

On December 22, 1875, the coroner's inquest was concluded, and the jury rendered their verdict: "We find that Sarah Alexander came to her death by violence at the hands of Pesach N.

Rubinstein, on or about the twelfth day of December 1875, in the Town of New Lots, and that the death of the child was consequent in the death of the murder."

After a long trial, Pesach Rubinstein was found guilty. Desperate efforts were made to save him. On March 17, 1876, a stay of execution was granted by Judge Brady. This seemed to be reasonably justified since nothing but circumstantial evidence had been adduced against him, and the testimony to prove an alibi was left unimpeached. But before his case came up for a hearing in the Supreme Court, Pesach Rubinstein died in his cell on May 9, 1876. It was not certain whether he committed suicide or succumbed to physical exhaustion and terror.

All the newspapers gave much space to this appalling murder case. It was the first crime of such violence charged to a Jew, and it cast a sad cloud on the Jewish community, especially on the Russian Jewish community, who were recent immigrants. Some of the base elements in the community used the convicted murderer's name as an insulting epithet by calling after Jews, "Rubinstein, Rubinstein!" The murder also gave rise to a popular street song, "My Name Is Pesach Rubinstein."

The case left its lamentable aftermath in New Lots, where one of the sections came to be known as "Blood Hollow." As Alfred Osterland explains it: "It so happened that during the time they were searching for the murderer of Sarah Alexander in good old East New York, and the section was alive with reporters assigned to the case, Atlantic Avenue in the Essex, Eldert Section—was being graded and paved, and one of the laborers was injured. Some one removed the laborer's bloody jumper and threw it down the new embankment into the hollow (Misener's Pond). One of the reporters wrote up a story next day entitled 'Bloody Shirt Found in Hollow,' trying to connect it with the Rubenstein-Alexander murder case. Thus the section came to be known as 'Blood Hollow.' "

This section later became notorious as the habitat of the Blood Hollow Gang, which engaged in battles with the *Bohne-Viertels* and other gangs.

Founding of Congregation Bikur Cholim *(Temple Sinai)*

It was not until 1885 that a synagogue was established in New Lots.[19] Several previous attempts were made to conduct religious services on a regular basis, but they were unsuccessful. Religious services were held at Schiellin's Hall, at the corner of Atlantic and Vermont Streets, as early as 1880. While there were probably fewer than fifty Jewish families in the section prior to 1880, the organization of a synagogue seems to have been a belated effort.

This may be attributed to several factors. Practically all of the early settlers were shop-keepers along Jamaica Plank Road or Atlantic Avenue, and were occupied on the Sabbath and holidays. Moreover, as has been already noted, some of the early settlers became so involved in the German culture and social activities on the one hand, and in the general activities on the other, that there was little time, and perhaps inadequate interest and motivation, to pursue their Jewish interests more intensively.

In 1885, while visiting a house of mourning, a group of men prominent in the business and communal life of East New York suggested at this *Minyan* that a congregation be formed in order to meet the religious needs of the community. When a sum of five hundred dollars had been accumulated, they purchased, in 1886, the frame structure at 101 Wyona Street, formerly owned by Trinity Episcopal Church. The congregation was incorporated on January 19, 1886, as Congregation *Bikur Cholim* by the following individuals: H. Copperman, President; Isaac Stamper, Vice-President; Ralph Bookman, Secretary; Louis Krieger, Treasurer; A. Wiesenbach, Financial Secretary, and the following Trustees: Jacob Basch, Judah P. Friedman.

As the name indicates—"Visiting the Sick"—the synagogue was to serve not only as a place of worship, but also as a benevolent institution. The founders and early members included the families of Adolph and Babette Bookman, Bernard and Regina Midas, Aaron and Rosa S. Dennon, Mr. and Mrs. Samuel Gumpel,

Theodore Eisner, Henry Kraushar, Samuel J. Schreiber, Coleman Cohen, and others. Among the rabbis who served the congregation were A. Cantor, between 1892 and 1895; Julius F. Loeb, between 1896-1898. In 1897 the number of members listed for the congregation is fifty; in 1899, seventy-nine. The total amount of money raised in 1899 was eighteen hundred dollars. The value of the synagogue property was placed at eight thousand dollars on which there was an indebtedness of two thousand dollars.

The American Jewish Year Book for 5661 (1900-1901) records the congregation as having fifty members and twenty-two seatholders. Services were conducted on Fridays and Saturdays under the spiritual guidance of Ignatz Diamond. The officers were: President, Adolph Bookman; Vice-President, B. Sacks; Treasurer, I. Schreiber; Secretary, Ralph Bookman; Trustees: Hyman Cooperman, I. Gregen and H. Sacks. It conducted a religious school which had at the time ninety-five pupils and six teachers. The congregation owned a cemetery at Bayside, Long Island.

On May 12, 1899, the Ladies Hebrew Benevolent Society of the Twenty-sixth Ward was founded. It met at 97-101 Bradford Street on the second Tuesday of the month. Its officers were: President, Mrs. Pauline M. Sachs; Vice-President, Mrs. G. Nathan; Treasurer, Mrs. B. Midas; Secretary, Mrs. M. Gold; Trustees: Mesdames A. Dennon, R. Traube, R. Brenner, J. Frankel, G. Meyersburg, and the officers. One of the objectives of the society was to maintain a Sunday-School in the ward. When the Temple Sisterhood was organized it took over the activities of the Sunday School.

On April 11, 1920, ground was broken for a new structure for the Congregation on Arlington Avenue, at the corner of Bradford Street. On June 27, 1920, the cornerstone was set, and on November 27, 1921, the new building was dedicated, one of the finest in East New York at the time, at a cost in excess of one hundred thousand dollars. Sometime thereafter, two adjoining lots on Arlington Avenue were also acquired, on which a modern center was erected in 1955. In this Arlington district's Jewish Center the Religious School, the Men's Club, the Young Folk's

League, the Parent-Teacher's Association, and various other groups meet. It was during this period that the congregation, originally chartered as Congregation *Bikur Cholim,* and popularly known as the "Old Wyona Street Synagogue," became known as "Temple Sinai."

Among the rabbis who have ministered to the congregation are Dr. Maxwell L. Sacks, (1920-1929), Rabbi Morris Rose, and Rabbi Ralph Silverstein, the present spiritual leader. Among the officers and members who have been active in the congregation are Adolph Weisfeld, Julius Josephson, Jacob H. Cohen, Philip I. Carthage, Dr. Milton Schreiber, Henry Kraushar, Dr. Martin Maliner, Henry Friedman, Henry N. Cooper, Samuel Starfield, William Gold, Israel Lazarowitz, Theodore Eisner, Dr. Abraham Eisen, Sidney Gaffen, Martin Lichtenstein, and A. Frederick Meyerson.

The German-Jewish group, here as elsewhere, remained for a long time steadfast in the habits it had acquired in Germany. Invoking the pattern of life of the general German-American community, they spoke the German language, read the German-American press, and belonged to the many German-American organizations which flourished in the community. The German-Jewish immigrant evidently found it natural and pleasurable to spend his life in the German-American cultural milieu. But his German heritage was primarily a cultural one. He perceived quite clearly that his future was closely bound up with the general American community and with those other elements of the population whose social and political status predominated. His children spoke English in the home, attended the district public schools, and sought to become an integral part of the general community. In their businesses, too, which consisted mostly of general stores, the German-Jewish group sought to cater to all the population of the town, including the Dutch pioneers, the English, the Scotch-Irish, and the others.

In many respects the character of this German-Jewish group differed from the great wave of East European Jewish immigrants who settled in the town in subsequent years.[20] The new group affected the growth of every section of the town, and the area became one of the most populous Jewish neighborhoods in Greater New York. The growth in population was particularly due to the large influx of Jews in the late eighties in the adjoining village of Brownsville, with which the next chapter concerns itself.

Jews Move to Brownsville

II

WHEN JEWS first acquired property in Brownsville in 1886, the village had a population of about four thousand living in some five hundred small cottages, mostly one-and-a-half-story frame structures. One could see farmers plowing their fields, cows and sheep pasturing in the meadows, and cherry and apple trees blossoming in the orchards or by the roadside. One could be lost in the bushes and woods on what became later the busiest thoroughfares, Hopkinson and Pitkin Avenues; one could go fishing in the neighboring ponds known as Silver Lake and Shady Lake.

Only a few farms were still held by the original Dutch families of pioneer days. The Vanderveers still owned their farms with their orchards west of Bristol Street to Howard Avenue, along Pitkin Avenue (Eastern Parkway). The old Williamson, Hotso Van Sinderen, and Lott lands had changed hands, and were cut up either into lots or smaller farms.

Practically the whole settlement was to the west of Rockaway Avenue. To the east, except for a few houses, it was all farm land

and swamps. In addition to the Thatford and Culver farms, there were the Lewis milk farm located around Belmont (Bay Avenue) and Rockaway, and extending to East New York Avenue; and the Wilson farm between Sackman and Christopher Avenues. Mr. Lewis was an enterprising farmer who sold hay and feed, and he owned the Lewis Hotel, on the corner of Osborn and East New York Avenues. There were various other kinds of stores where one could buy life's necessities.

Besides the various trades and crafts, some of the residents worked for neighboring farmers, and others for the "boss"-tailors in New York, bringing home the bundles of cut garments and returning them when finished. These boss-tailors advertised in the local papers such as *The Record* and *The Sentinel*, offering work. The pay was scant; one received fifteen cents for completing a pair of knee pants. Three people, working a day, could complete a dozen pairs.

Despite the rural character of the village—no paved streets, no sewers, no gas lights—the Twenty-Sixth Ward of Brooklyn, of which Brownsville was part, had much to recommend it to the real estate investor. The town enjoyed perfect railroad transit via both steam and elevated railroads. In time, improvements such as sewers and water could be expected, as well as other conveniences.

The farmers of Brownsville soon realized that it would be more profitable for them to cut their farms into lots and build on them. Gilbert S. Thatford, who next to Charles S. Brown was responsible for the promotion of the village of Brownsville in its early years, was one of the first to envisage the possibilities of a vast development. He had issued a map of his lands, prepared by surveyor Martin Johnson in December 1877. Together with others, he asked a number of men with connections in the East Side to serve as brokers and to induce their friends to buy lots.

In 1886, Mr. Thatford succeeded in interesting Aaron Kaplan, an East-Side real estate agent, to purchase lots in Brownsville. A record in the Kings County Register's office dated July 17, 1886, refers to a conveyance of property by Mr. Gilbert S. Thatford and his wife, Eliza, both residing in the town of New Lots; to Mr.

Samuel Phillips, and to Aaron Kaplan, both of New York City.[1] The latter bought from Mr. Thatford, for the sum of $1,000, lots indicated on the Thatford Map as Lots Numbers 401 to 407 inclusive. On July 6, 1887, Mr. Kaplan bought thirteen additional lots—Numbers 363 to 375 inclusive on Thatford Map—for the sum of $2,400, subject to two mortgages amounting to $2,100.[2] All the land was located on the corners of Riverdale (Rapalje Avenue), and Osborn Street (Ocean Avenue), and Riverdale and Thatford Avenues.

Every community likes to know the name of its first settler. While we know that a number of Jews came to live in Brownsville during 1887, the early chroniclers differ as to who was the first Jewish settler.[3] It appears that Jacob Cohen and his family settled about the same time as Isaac Krupitsky. The latter, however, came alone, and was followed later by his family, which arrived from Europe the following summer. It would appear therefore, that the Jacob Cohen family was the first family to make its residence here, but that Isaac Krupitsky had preceded them as an individual resident.

In an interview in 1928 with Sidney Blatt, for *The Brooklyn Guide,* Jacob Cohen, then an old man residing at 27 Grafton Street, stated about his early settlement: "Brownsville was all farms, all farms, I say. And there was only one Jew who lived here before me. His name was Isaac Krupitsky. I don't know whether he lives now, but he was influential in helping me make my home here."

In view of this definitive statement by Mr. Cohen, this writer is prepared to honor both of these pioneers—Jacob Cohen and Isaac Krupitsky.

Isaac Krupitsky came here as a young man. He is listed in the 1892 State Census as a tailor, thirty-five years of age. With him are listed his wife Sarah and their children, Jacob and Celia. His son, the late Dr. Jacob Krupp, became a well-known physician in Brooklyn. On May 31, 1887, Isaac Krupitsky and Benjamin Marshak bought from Gilbert S. Thatford some property including six lots (Numbers 394-399 on Thatford Map) for two thousand dollars, of which three hundred dollars was paid in cash.

Benjamin and Rebecca Marshak sold their share to Mr. Krupitsky on April 9, 1888.[4] He started his factory in his home with six machines, on which he put to work the tailors he brought with him from the East Side.

Jacob Cohen was a small boss-tailor in New York, where he arrived about 1880. For reasons of his wife's health he decided to move to the "country." He bought a house on the corner of Blake and Sackman Street, moved into the village, and was for many years a manufacturer of boys knee-pants on East New York Avenue and Bristol Street. The first *Minyan* (public worship) was held in his home. He owned his own *Sepher Torah* (Scroll of the Law), which his mother had brought with her from Poland when she followed him to America.

Elias Kaplan, a clothing contractor, gave impetus to the growth of the village of Brownsville into a hustling and bustling community when he decided to transfer his large shop with its workmen from the East Side to Brownsville. That move not only started the ball of industry rolling to the village, but prompted the influx of a considerable Jewish population. Aaron Kaplan, the real estate agent alluded to earlier, and Gilbert Thatford were largely instrumental in persuading Elias Kaplan to bring his shop to Brownsville. Realizing the advantages of having a large shop in the village, they offered assistance that finally induced Elias Kaplan to make the move. A deal was arranged whereby four lots were sold on May 26, 1887, to Mr. Kaplan for $1,600; $325 in cash.[5] Thatford agreed to build him a two-family house at 175 Osborn Street, a cottage with a big porch, and between the two, a two-storey shop, all for a sum slightly more than $5,000; $1,000 down, and the balance in small monthly payments. It was also arranged that Thatford would build a number of two-family houses for the shop's married workers at a cost of $1,100 each; $100 down, and the balance in monthly payments of $10.

When the buildings were completed, Elias Kaplan moved to Brownsville with a large group of workmen. He brought a large supply of kerosene lamps to light up his shop, where the working hours started early and continued until the late hours of the night.

Along with Mr. Kaplan came Herman Moskowitz who designed clothes—a skill commanding prestige and a good salary in the clothing industry. Mr. Moskowitz took a house at 184 Watkins Street. The unfortunate death from diphtheria of two of his children in his home on congested Houston Street induced him to leave New York and move to the country, but the advent of Elias Kaplan and his associates had initiated a movement which brought other Jews to Brownsville.

Elias Kaplan had been born in the small town of Rittewa, Russia, in 1847. His father, a cutter of women's coats, had taught him the trade, and in time he became an expert in the design of new styles. In 1882, at the age of 35, he and his family immigrated to America, landing in the East Side of New York. For three months after his arrival he worked as an operator with a boss-tailor in New York. Finding himself handicapped by the unwillingness of tailors to work under a "green" boss, he proceeded to revolutionize the industry by eliminating tailors and using only machine operators in the manufacture of women's coats. For many years he was the first and only boss to employ needy Poles, Russians, and Slovenians whom he found jobless, penniless, and untrained. These men he converted into capable operators, pressers, fitters, and bushelmen. It was not long before Kaplan ranked among the most important boss-tailors, "the Prince of the business." This title fitted him in those days. To quote Jacob Wax, the chronicler of early Brownsville, "He (Kaplan) had a commanding figure, tall and erect, a handsome, round face framed in a black beard, thick eyebrows, and a proud bearing." [6]

Kaplan played a leading role in the establishment of a variety of institutions that were necessary for the new community. Residing in Brownsville at 43 Bristol Street, he died at the age of eighty-six; his wife at the age of ninety-five. In addition to their three children born in Russia, Mr. and Mrs. Kaplan raised four children in the United States—Louis, Israel, Sadie, and Charlie. Louis Kaplan, who became a doctor, was born on June 8, 1882, at 112 Ludlow Street and attended the local public schools of Brownsville, Erasmus Hall High School, and graduated in 1904 from Long Island University Medical School. He has continued to practice medicine in Brooklyn, and still lives on Eastern Parkway.

Among the Jews who bought property in Brownsville and built homes for either themselves or others during their first years of settlement from 1886 to 1887 were, according to the deeds of sale recorded in the Kings County Register's Office: Samuel Phillips and Aaron Kaplan (July 17, 1886), Hyman Kaplan (Feb. 4, 1887), Elias and Anna Kaplan (May 26, 1887), Isaac Krupitsky (May 31, 1887), Isaac Gross, (July 28, 1887), Samuel Samuelson (July 18, 1887), Harris Max (Aug. 12, 1887), David Kline (Aug. 12, 1887), Isaac N. Axelrod (Aug. 16, 1887), Samuel Levy (Sept. 6, 1887), Morris and Anne Mintz (Sept. 8, 1887), Israel Moskowitz (Sept. 6, 1887), Isaac and Meyer Hoffman (Oct. 8, 1887), and Isaac Glaser (Aug. 16 and Oct. 4, 1887).[7]

The growth of the Jewish population during the first few years was on the whole very gradual. The Jewish section, which centered east of Rockaway Avenue on Thatford, Osborn, Watkins, Liberty, Glenmore, Belmont, and Riverdale Avenues, was a small, deserted corner surrounded by a large Christian community. While some of the Jews moved to Brownsville for a variety of reasons, the majority were not yet ready to give up the teeming life of the East Side, with its many associations and its rich cultural and social life, to withdraw to an undeveloped village which took hours to reach from New York, and where one had to wear rubber boots and trudge through mud and slime to obtain the necessities of life.

As the builders accelerated and intensified their real-estate efforts, and as local improvements were introduced, the population began to grow faster. Besides Aaron Kaplan, others tried to interest their Manhattan friends in buying real estate in Brownsville. Gilbert S. Thatford, Andrew Culver, and Mr. Lewis were among those who were ready to sell their land, and there were builders ready to build houses on it. One of the first builders was John Powers, father of James Powers, now President of the New York Board of Elections. John Powers built seven houses on Thatford Avenue. Business houses were constructed for $2,500 with $500 in cash; residences for $1,000 with $200 in cash. Herbert Smith, a lawyer from Court Street, bought Lewis's farm and cut it into lots, and Arthur Hurst, a well-known lawyer and his son, helped in the development by loaning money on mortgages.

The New York State Census of 1892 provides interesting data concerning the Jews who had been settled in Brownsville for the first four or five years. The religious affiliation is omitted in this census as in other census records, but it is comparatively easy to distinguish the Jewish from the other names listed in the area. The distinctive names which the East European immigrant familes bore, and the other data concerning them which are included in the census, furnish good clues for judging whether or not the family is Jewish.

In 1890, Ward 26, which embraced the villages of New Lots, East New York, Cypress Hills, and Brownsville had a total population of 29,505 (14,957 males, 14,548 females). Most of them (20,325, or 72 per cent) were either foreigners or children of foreign parents. A small, group, 784 in all, were natives of Russia and Poland. Of these, 459 were 15-years-old and over, and 109 were natives of Hungary. By 1892 the total population of the ward increased to 38,591. On the basis of their names and other data included in the census records, we counted about 4,000, or slightly more than 10 per cent, to have been Jewish.

Aside from several hundred Jews who resided in East New York and in other parts of Ward 26, most of the Jews, approximately 3,600 lived in the 1st, 2nd, and 3rd election districts in Brownsville. They constituted about half of the total population in these three districts. The largest cluster of Jews, 2,671, lived in the 2nd district, whose total population was 3,352. It embraced Thatford, Osborn, Watkins, Riverdale, Livonia, Glenmore, and Rockaway near Sutter, Blake, Belmont, Watkins, and surrounding streets. Another community of Jews, some 800, resided in the 3rd election district, which centered around Sackman, Christopher, Blake, and Stone Avenues near Pitkin Avenue. It contained a total population of 2,359, of whom 648 were aliens. A small group of Jews—117 in all—resided in the 1st election district; its population was 1,326 and it centered around Rockaway Avenue, East New York Avenue, and Chester Street.

Most of the Jews who came to Brownsville were born in Russia. They comprised a large contingent of Jews from Lithuania and White Russia, who came in the 1880's because of poverty and governmental restrictions, and Ukranian Jews who fled the periodic pogroms there. The second largest group came from Galicia, a province of Austria, where deteriorating economic conditions due to government policy prompted many to come to America. As is indicated in the following table, the number of Jews from the other countries was not very great.

Jewish Population in 1892 and
Countries of Origin

Russia	1,695	70 per cent
Austria	369	15 per cent
(Galicia)		
Poland	186	7.7 per cent
Hungary	55	2 per cent
Roumania	47	
England	34	
Germany	29	
Total	2,415	

Occupationally, the Jews of Brownsville were mainly concentrated in the garment industry in 1892. Some 70 per cent of all gainfully employed—659 out of a total number of 943—were engaged in tailoring of some sort, while 96, or 10 per cent, were artisans, mostly in the building trades (36 carpenters, 18 painters, 2 plumbers, 2 tinsmiths); 27, or 3 per cent were shopworkers, including 8 bakers, 7 cigar-makers, 5 machinists, 4 printers. A large group—124, or 13 per cent—were tradesmen. In this group were included 30 grocers, 14 butchers, 25 peddlers, 10 dairymen, and 16 liquor dealers. There was a wide variety of other crafts and small trades in which the Jews engaged. There were the teachers, the musicians, the druggist, the builders, the farmer and the like. All were to be found among the early Jewish settlers of Brownsville, some represented by only a few individuals.

The first Jews to move to Brownsville were young people,

strong and adventurous. They were prepared to challenge the rigors of life in the village, which provided more room and air for the young families they had begun to raise. This is indicated by the age distribution of the Jews who lived in the Brownsville district in 1892.

Age	Number	Per cent
Under 5	782	.218
5–9	560	.156
10–14	324	.09 plus
15–19	338	.094 plus
20–30	897	.249
31–40	437	.122
41–50	169	.046
51–64	76	.021
65 and over	11	.003
Total	3,594	.999 plus

Almost 93 per cent of the total Jewish group were under forty years of age. Only 256 individuals, or 7 per cent, were over forty. Most of the residents were young parents, for the largest group in this table is represented by infants under 5 years of age, and by young children between 5 and 9 years of age.

They came here as families. There were some unmarried persons who boarded with others, but their number was inconsequential.

The family character of the East-European Jewish immigrants differed from groups such as the Irish and the Italians, who came originally to save enough money to return home and establish themselves on a sounder economic basis. The Jews came not only to improve their economic lot, but also to seek the place of refuge America offered them. And they intended to remain here. Some, who could not adjust themselves to the new country, returned to their former homes, but in some cases, made a second attempt to return here. The overwhelming majority had neither the desire nor the ability to leave for they had burned all their bridges behind them.

Among 3,280 individuals, we identified 657 Jewish families in the 1892 State Census in Brownsville. The table below indicates the size of the families at the time.

No. of Families	No. of Children	Total No. of Children
45	0	0
106	1	106
144	2	288
134	3	402
90	4	360
68	5	340
36	6	216
19	7	133
10	8	80
1	9	9
3	10	30
1	11	11
Total 657		1,975

The average number of children per family was 3. The size of some of the families probably increased later, since the young parents had only recently started raising families. This is probably true of most of the 45 families who are listed as having no children.

The family size—5 persons to the family—varies little from the 4.70 persons to the family for the entire Ward 26 in the 1890 Federal Census, which listed 6,277 families, totaling 29,505 persons in all. There were some large families. Some 20 per cent had more than 5 children, and a few as many as 7, 8, 9, 10, even 11 children. These created the impression that families in those days were inordinately large.

In many respects, the character of the Brownsville population differed little from that of the Lower East Side from which they had recently moved.[8] A census of Jews in New York City, undertaken in August 1890, by the Baron deHirsch Fund, showed 111,690 Jews stemming from 28,801 families in the 7th, 10th, and 13th Wards. Of these, 60,257 (54 per cent,) were children—23,405

(21 per cent,) under 6 years of age; 21,285 (19 per cent) from 6-14, and 15,567 (14 per cent) over 14. The size of this total age group was about the same in Brownsville, 55.8 per cent. The size of the group under 14 was about the same as in the Lower East Side, but the group over 14 was smaller in Brownsville. This was due to the fact that the East Side settlement, being older, had more children of adolescent age—14 per cent in the East Side against 9.4 per cent in Brownsville. Occupationally, 70 per cent of the Brownsville Jews as against 60 per cent in Manhattan were engaged in the needle trades. Brownsville's small settlement specialized in the tailoring trade.

The health of the newcomers compared favorably with that of the native population. Dr. John Shaw Billings's report on vital statistics in New York and Brooklyn (1894) [9] states that during a 6-year period the death rate in the Twenty-Sixth Ward was below the city average, but above the average for foreign children under 5 years of age. For those 15 years of age and upwards, judged by the mother's ethnic origin, it was 4.64 per 1,000 persons for Russians and Poles; 10.42 for Americans; 17 for the Germans; and 20.04 for the Irish. Malaria fever and whooping cough caused more than the average percentage of deaths—26.18 per 100,000 in the city, and 30.51 in Ward 26. Tuberculosis caused 303.24 deaths per 100,000 in the city, and 230.61 for Ward 26.

The Jewish population continued to grow apace. Between 1890 and 1900 the total population of Ward 26 more than doubled— from 29,505 to 66,086—and the Jewish population increased from less than 3,000 to more than 15,000. The large flow of immigrants from Eastern Europe and of former East Side residents into Brownsville brought about a building boom. Speculators bought land and allowed people to build houses for only a small down payment. The talk of the town centered around houses, lots, bonuses, and mortages.

Mrs. S. Axelrod's restaurant on Thatford Avenue between Pitkin and Belmont Avenue became the center of the real estate market. Tailors left their machines to dabble in real estate. A New York *landsmanschaft,* the Minsker Society, purchased land from Mr. Vanderveer, near "Pigtown." Prices continued to rise and to attract builders. Among those who entered the real estate business on a large scale were Louis Ratner and his brother Charles; Max Harris (Max the Builder); Simon Rose, Aaron Kaplan, Pincus Grodzinsky (the father of the well known Dr. Abraham J. Rongy) ; Hyman Meyerson, Barnett Levine, Solomon and Joseph Morris, Isaac Levingson, among others. Mortgages were given by Louis Hearst of Nassau Street, Schenck and Lanig of Nassau Street, and Herbert S. Smith and Kafna of Court Street. Then came one of the severest periodic depressions, the crash of 1893, which halted progress for a time.

The tailoring industry experienced a grave crisis, and home owners were unable to make payments on their mortgages. Foreclosures followed. Rent collectors were appointed. Land prices fell. Brownsville went back to tailoring, and normalcy returned very slowly. Poverty was generally very great. Brownsville was not yet the *Goldene Medina* (Land of Gold) .

Neither the setback of 1893 nor subsequent depressions, however, could long deter Brownsville's growth. Thousands of people who were moving into the community had to be housed. The building of the Williamsburg Bridge at the turn of the century brought the East Side of Manhattan closer to Brooklyn, and the construction of the Delancey Street approach to the bridge resulted in the displacement of 10,000 persons who had to find new homes. Some moved across to Williamsburg, and thence spread to other sections, including Brownsville.

The mass wave of East European Jewish immigrants into New York City was primarily responsible for the phenomenal growth of Brownsville and adjoining neighborhoods during the first two decades of the present century. Between 1880 and the outbreak of World War I some two million Jews—over one-third of the Jewish population in Eastern Europe—left their native lands. Most of them—some ninety per cent—migrated to the United States, the majority settling in New York City.

The reasons which impelled such vast numbers to leave Russia, Poland, Galicia and Roumania have been told in great detail in a number of studies.[10] Some of the reasons were common to all emigrants forced to uproot themselves. The mass flight of the

Jews, however, mirrors a dimension evoked by the unique repressions, persecutions, and strictures to which the Jewish group alone was cruelly subjected. In consequence of this unprecedented flow of immigrants and of former East Side residents, a new Brownsville arose. Where formerly there were empty spaces, there now stood blocks of brick and stone buildings. But before we turn to that phase of our story, let us pause for a while to examine some phases of the life of the early Jewish settlers in Brownsville.

Life in the Early Jewish Settlement of Brownsville

III

DURING THE early settlement, Brownsville was a small town. There was none of that colorful, and pulsating Jewish life for which it was later to be noted; life proceeded at a leisuely pace. Some of the early settlers tended to struggle against acclimatization to their new surroundings. They tried to duplicate the life of the *Shtetl* (townlet) of Eastern Europe from which they came. To the outsider, who occasionally looked in, Brownsville appeared to be a replica of an East European *Shtetl*. In reality, it was as different from the *Shtetl* of Lithuania and Poland as the American setting was from the European. In describing "Brooklyn's Ghetto" in *The New York Sun* in December 1899, the writer states: "One in whom curiosity has been aroused or stimulated by Zangwill's *Children of the Ghetto* need not journey to London or Jerusalem in quest of a community in which ancient social customs are observed, and religious rites and traditions handed down from century to century are still venerated. For in Brooklyn there is a Ghetto, large in population, inflexible in its orthodoxy, and notable in the hardships it is obliged to endure."

When the Jewish immigrants formed their little island within the village of Brownsville, they did not displace the earlier residents from their homes, as they did in some of the older sections of the city, where the new arrivals took over the old tenements held by the older settlers. The immigrants of Brownsville moved into new houses, which were built for them on large stretches of land. Unfortunately, much of the building was done in haste and without adequate planning. Rows of frame houses, frame factories in back yards, frame privies, and small, frame tenements were quickly and cheaply constructed. The result was a duplication of the experience of other congested areas—so much so that Jacob Riis in the late nineties stigmatized Brownsville as a "nasty little slum." [1] In describing "Brooklyn's Ghetto" in December 1899, the writer states that "most of the houses are without sewers or decent drains. Families are so huddled together in the sweat-shop tenements that even the ordinary precautions of cleanliness are next to impossible. The goat, cat, or dog, is as much a member of the family as the baby, and makes itself generally at home with him in the living room. The streets are nothing but mudholes—and where the streets are not miry with filth, they are deep in dust. There is only one bath, or common wash house, in Brownsville, and on Fridays, Saturdays, and Sundays it is invariably crowded to the doors."

A Family Moves to Brownsville

Charles Reznikoff, a native son of Brownsville and well known as author and poet, has given us in his published writings an intimate glimpse of life of the early immigrants, and explains why members of his family, like so many others at the end of the century, came to live in Brownsville. [2]

Sarah Yetta's family sought to dissuade her from venturing on a journey to America. "Who goes there but bankrupts, embezzlers, and those who have wrecked their lives here?"

Despite the objections, Sarah Yetta, after a number of weeks required to cross the Russian border, and after a trip of three weeks across the Atlantic in an old ship, finally reached the East Side.

One day Sarah and Nathan Reznikoff decided to visit Sarah's cousin in Brownsville. After traveling about four hours they found him. He was a tailor, out of work and very poor. He took them for a walk to show them what Brownsville was like. "Our houses are small and built of wood, but our rooms are comfort. able," he told them. "We have no paved streets, but we see the sun and moon from the moment they rise until they set. When it rains the streets are muddy, and when it isn't raining, dusty; but we do not smell the garbage in the barrels that stand on the side. walks. Many have shops there, and their work is brought from New York in express wagons that charge only ten cents a bundle."

When the days became hot, and the windows had to be closed because the elevated trains that ran on Allen Street used soft coal, and the smoke of the engines blew into the windows, the Reznikoffs decided to move to Brownsville. They rented a store and three rooms on Thatford Avenue for nine dollars a month. By August, Sarah and Nathan had saved a hundred dollars—enough to furnish the three rooms and to get married. The wedding took place in their neighbor's parlor. "There were some radicals among the guests who were opposed to religious ceremonies. They remained downstairs in the store." Later, when seated at the tables, the eldest guest scolded Sarah Yetta and Nathan, saying they were foolish to be married by a rabbi. Nathan said, "It would be foolish for your children to be married as we were, but you know how our parents would feel if we were married otherwise. It is better for us to be foolish than to hurt them. Most of those there said that I was right, and those who thought otherwise said no more."

Brownsville's Sweatshops

Most of the gainfully employed residents of Brownsville were engaged in some form of tailoring. Work was hard, but they were glad to have work. The New York manufacturers and wholesale merchants, and the contractors who received work from them, established "outside shops" in Brownsville because they believed they would be able to produce their goods at a lower cost. The contractor in his small workshop relied on an extensive division of labor, or the "sectional system." Many hands performed different tasks. The unskilled immigrant help, regardless of their vocational background, could learn in a short time to perform one of the many operations into which the completion of the garment was divided. Some operations required greater skill and commanded higher pay. The designers and cutters usually worked for the manufacturer; the machinists, operators, pressers, finishers, fitters, fellers, basters, and buttonhole-makers worked for the contractors.

To get as much work out of the employee as possible, the task system was introduced. As described in a U.S. Census report, the work was done in the following manner: "Each team consists of three men—an operator, a baster, and a finisher. Outside the team there is, as a rule, a presser, a girl for sewing on buttons and making buttonholes, and a bushelman or fitter. Each member of the team has his particular part of the coat to make, and in a short time gains such an efficiency in his work that the team is able to turn out an increasing number of coats."

In evaluating this system, the U.S. Industrial Commission had this to say in one of its reports: "By this queer cooperative production in the form of team work, combined with the personal interest of piece work, the Hebrew tailors in New York have devised what is perhaps the most ingenious and effective engine of over-work known to modern industry." [3]

The contemporary newspaper account describes the situation as it prevailed in some of the shops in Brownsville under this system: [4] "Here most of the men and women, the youths and maidens as well, are under the thrall of taskmasters, under the domination of modern taskmasters—the sweatshop contractors.

"The people who live in it (Brownsville) are, by sheer force of circumstances, out of employment for four months of the year. Their mission in life is to make cheap clothing for the metropolis. In winter they work like slaves day and night, but the majority do not have enough to last them through the enforced idleness of summer. The time of famine is upon them now."

Some of the sweatshop conditions were very bad in those early days. Dr. Black, in a report to the Health Department, had this to say of one of his visits to a sweatshop: "In one shop, at 11 o'clock in the evening, was found a man working at a sewing machine, his wife in bed, asleep, and three children taking basting threads out of garments. The room was in the basement, and in a filthy condition. . . .

In describing another sweatshop he stated, "This is a 3-story, frame, double workshop, 65 feet by 42 feet by 10 feet, having 14 windows. There are 2 sinks on each floor, with 1 2-inch iron trap for both, and a 3-inch pipe wasted through the roof. The faucets are leaking on the 1st and 2nd floors, depriving the 3rd floor sinks of water. There is a hand-hole-covered 2-inch trap under the 3rd floor sink. The ceiling is wainscotted. Three hoppers are in the yard, 1 stopped up. The floor in the closets is disgustingly filthy; 133 people have but 2 closets for use. The yard is full of rubbish and ashes."

In the light of this gloomy picture, one asks why so many Jewish immigrants took to the needle trade. There were a number of overriding reasons. For many who landed here, it was their original trade, in which they had worked in Europe or trained themselves before leaving for the States. Due to the sectional system, those with no vocational preparation (and these were in the majority) could learn in a short time to perform one of the many operations into which the manufacture of a garment was divided.

Most of the new arrivals came with very little capital; many were almost penniless and could not remain long without work; they had to take the first jobs offered them. Many were met in Castle Garden by relatives or contractors who were employed in these trades and could recommend jobs for them. Above all, it was the only significant industry in the hands of the Jews, and they could understand the language of their fellow workers. Many of the newcomers were unwilling to leave New York. Hard manual labor, such as work in steel mills or on railroad construction, was alien to their experience and background. Another reason was that the contracting system and residence in New York permitted the observance of religious traditions by those desiring to do so. These immigrants were young, robust, and hopeful, resolved to establish their homes and to seek their fortunes. Ready and willing to do any work that could be procured, their ambition was to gain experience and save sufficient money to enable them to become bosses.

The new immigrant had no direct contact with the rich manufacturer, but only with the contractor, who usually came from the same country, even the same town. Since the contractor worked as hard, and put in the same long hours as did the employees, there was not the same class conflict between them as there was between the non-Jewish immigrant who worked for the railroad magnate or in the coal mine. Consequently, the Jewish labor movement which later developed derived from the unique immigrant community's economy.[5]

The *"Landsmanshaft"* spirit which prevailed frequently in the shop, the homesickness, the new relationships and new meanings which the new immigrants had to work out for themselves, often under harsh circumstances, are portrayed by the great Yiddish writer, Shalom Asch, in his penetrating classic, *Uncle Moses.*

The needle trades were by no means the only industry in which Jews were engaged. Some were employed in tobacco, construction, and other industries. Many were storekeepers or little shopkeepers. All worked hard and long. The life of the small storekeeper who lived in the rear of his store and worked with the other members of his family was not easier or more profitable than that of the other workers. So long as there was work, the people were happy. A dollar earned in those days went a long way—for new furniture, for a phonograph, even for the luxury of a gold watch or some other coveted object. It was in times of depression, when unemployment became rampant and credit unavailable, that acute suffering prevailed.

The Depression of 1893

Wretched times struck the community during the depression of 1893.[6] The distressing conditions in parts of Brownsville are graphically described in *The Brooklyn Eagle* of Sunday, December 24, 1893.

"If," said Dr. Israel Kaufman of Stone and Sutter Avenues to a reporter, "If something is not done, and that quickly, to alleviate the sufferings of the people of Brownsville, we shall have a widespread famine on our hands. I have travelled considerably and have never witnessed such suffering from cold and hunger. The distress is simply appalling."

Dr. M. A. Cohn who lived on the same avenue, near Blake Avenue, was equally emphatic in his statement of the situation. "Brownsville is suffering from hunger. Many are on the verge of actual starvation."

Mr. Frank Rosenberg, Commissioner of Deeds, whose office is on Stone Avenue near Blake, said, "The distress is really shocking. See the children picking clinkers and cinders from yonder dirt heap! Those cinders have been sifted three times before, and probably children who are still poorer than they will sift them again. Yes, the people help one another, but the rich are now becoming poor and can hardly get along themselves. Our local resources are exhausted. We have no organized committee but (we) are doing the best (we) can. It is bad now, the situation is fearful, but is hourly growing worse."

America was a *Goldene Medina,* but with modifications. Like the other periodic upheavals this depression passed, and Brownsville went back to a normal, even an accelerated pace of progress.

The Belmont Avenue Market

A very lively place in the growing community was the market place on Belmont Avenue, between Thatford and Stone Avenues. It comprised a number of small shops and stands ranged along the sidewalks on each side of the asphalt thoroughfare. It was a particularly active place on Thursday and Friday mornings, when street vendors took possession of the sidewalks, and throngs of people congregated to shop for the Sabbath. Within the confines of these few blocks every conceivable kind of merchandise, from collar button to fresh fish, was offered. The fowl was bought alive and killed by the *Schochet* (slaughterer according to ritual law). The vendor would test the eggs by holding them up to a light. All varieties of vegetables, barrels of salted herring, and huge baskets filled with loaves of rye bread were abundant. It was quite patent that the market was a necessity, but how to maintain it has remained an unsolved problem to this day. It was suggested as early as 1896 that the city build a market and rent stalls. The same subject is still being discussed.

Many complaints were lodged at the health office against the sanitary condition of the neighborhood. In August, 1896, Commissioner Emery ordered an investigation. The sanitary inspectors, Dr. S. G. Clarke and Arthur H. Bogart, reported that since the market street lying between Thatford and Watkins Street was ungraded and unpaved, it was unfit for a market. They recommended that it be transferred to a street that was paved, graded, and sewered. Dr. R. M. Wyckoff suggested to the City Works Commissioner that the street be asphalted, but it was made clear that no monies were available. Besides, only the paved streets in Brownsville were cleaned under the street-cleaning contract. The situation was continually a bone of contention. According to a report by Dr. Robert A. Black, Assistant Sanitary Superintendent of the Health Department, a systematic program of disinfecting was carried on for an entire year, and on November 29, 1899, Thatford, Dumont, Osborn, Blake, and Sutter Avenues were thoroughly disinfected as part of the great effort to maintain them in a sanitary condition.

Relations With Their Neighbors

With their experiences of the European Pale of Settlement behind them, and with pogroms still vivid in their minds, the new settlers had no heart for seeking homes among strangers. They developed a self-contained enclave far removed from the life of the people around them. Most of them, having lived in the small, relatively isolated and circumscribed *Shtetel* in Europe, tried to transplant here some of the institutions and the life pattern they knew in their native Lithuanian or Russian townlets. New Lots consisted of a patchwork of districts or streets inhabited by the various ethnic and social groups. The Old Dutch settlers continued to reside along New Lots Road, the Germans in their *Bohnen Viertel*. It became proverbial in the early days of German immigration that where the Germans come in, the "Yankees go out." The English, Scotch, and Irish had their districts, and now the East European Jews were establishing their section in Brownsville.

The experience of the newcomers in their relations with their neighbors was not different here than elsewhere. In East New York, where a tiny group of German Jews, mostly merchants, settled, there was not much of an obstacle to their social acceptance by the majority group. In taste, language, and culture these Jews were very much like their fellow German countrymen.

It was different with the new wave of East European immigrants who settled in Brownsville. They retained their peculiar way of life, their own jargon, foreign dress, curious foods, and their own unique customs, habits, and religious observances. All these appeared strange and alien to the older residents, and the familiar refrain, "Everything was so nice here, until those others came," began to be heard here. In the consolidation number of *The Brooklyn Eagle,* in January, 1898, one reads: "The village was at one time a very desirable place for residence for people of moderate means, but since the annexation, it has very much deteriorated by the settling of a low class of Hebrews who have disfigured many of the dwellings by converting them into small business places."

During the first few years, when the settlement was very small, the anti-Jewish feeling was not strong. According to the testimony of Jacob Cohen, one of the first settlers, it was "when many more Jewish families came into the community that the Christian elements resented it. The newcomers assumed the role of proprietorship by taking possession of the land, and the result, at times, was battles, and even bloodshed." [7]

By and large, the attitude towards the newcomers was no different from that in the Lower East Side, or in Williamsburg. On Cherry and other streets in the Lower East Side, clashes between Jewish and Irish boys were common. No cause was required for hostilities to start. It was enough that a Jewish boy appeared on the street for gangs to set upon him. In Williamsburg, matters became so serious that a Jewish Protective Association had to be organized in 1891 to spur city officials to suppress rowdyism against the Jews.

Brownsville, too, was plagued for a time by rowdy elements. But the new community solved the problem in its own way, determined that bullies would not be allowed to hinder the development of the community. The young population was strong and courageous, ready to fight off any one who entered its enclave or tried to interfere with it. A number of Brownsville residents organized themselves in the 1890's into a Hebrew Protective League. When the streets became safe, and the organization was no longer needed, the members joined the order Brith Abraham and called their lodge the Hebrew Protective Lodge 228. One of the founders and leaders was Samuel Feuer, who became one of the first walking delegates of the Cloakmakers Union in Brownsville.

The Brooklyn Eagle published in the 1890's news items dealing with the "Sensations of Brownsville." On July 16, 1892, writing up one of these sensational items, it had this to say of the Brownsville Hebrews: "Since their advent to this portion of the town not a day has passed without a fight of some kind. In fact, many an unfortunate Christian who has had occasion to pass through the streets of Brownsville at night has been roughly handled."

The afternoon of the Jewish New Year's Day—*Rosh Hashonah* —when observant Jews were accustomed to go to the river to recite the *Tashlich* prayers, was an opportune time for some of the hoodlums to stage an attack. On Rockaway and New Lots Avenues, where later stood the car barns, there were a stream and a lake for boating. Adjoining it, where now stands the Beth El Hospital, were woods. Some two years after the first Jews settled in Brownsville, they decided to go to that stream to recite the *Tashlich* prayers. No sooner did they near the stream than they were set upon with stones by a group of Canarsie hoodlums. Fortunately, the Jews were accompanied by a dog, who saved the day for them.[8]

On *Tisha B'Ab*—Fast of the Ninth Day of Ab—the pious Jews closed their shops, and having as yet no cemetery to visit, went fishing in the small lakes that existed at the time at Prospect Place and Saint Marks Avenue. Aware of the Crow Hill Gang that customarily hung out in that neighborhood around Bergen Street, the Jews were accompanied by some of their Polish workmen and a number of others who knew how to use their fists. Marty Rosenbloom, who later became an important political figure, was among them. They had hardly reached their destination when they were pummeled with bricks and stones, and with faces bloodied, they returned home.

It took time before these hostile situations stabilized themselves. There were many other misunderstandings and prejudices to which the early settlers were subjected. Integration in the general community and adjustments to the new world came about slowly, and not always easily.

Relations with the Police and Other Authorities

The first police station was in a store on Pitkin Avenue and Osborn Street, with Captain Thomas Prentiss in charge. Velsor was Captain in 1899.

The Brownsville residents were a law-abiding, temperate, and moral group. At the Kings County Penitentiary in Brooklyn, there were comparatively few Jewish males, and it was a rarity to find a Jewish girl or woman on the rolls. The matron of the police station in Brownsville stated that in her twelve years experience she could not recall a single instance of a Jewish woman having been arrested for drunkenness. Captain Velsor, in 1899, likewise reported that there was very little intemperance among the Brownsvillites, and that an arrest for immorality was an almost unknown occurrence in Brownsville.

Most of the complaints at the police station were for petty thefts, or misunderstanding about some bit of personal property. There were frequent quarrels. To Captain Velsor, the Hebrews of Brownsville appeared "rather a jealous lot, who quarreled a great deal among themselves. But woe to the outsider who attempts to intervene, and act as a mediator. He will regret that he was ever born." [9]

Brownsville Police Court

To avoid misunderstanding and unfavorable comment, the Jews of Brownsville developed among themselves a system of arbitration. This evoked even greater misunderstanding and criticism on the part of the general community, as the following incidents will illustrate.

The Jewish immigrants from Poland and Russia brought their old ways of living with them. In Russia and Poland, government officials had been worst enemies and detractors of the Jews and were therefore avoided or "paid off." Besides, in the well organized Jewish communities of Eastern Europe, it was a well recognized principle to keep litigations between Jewish parties before Jewish tribunals. These tribunals could serve only as voluntary courts of conciliation or arbitration.

It seems that in Brownsville, in 1895, a number of lay people, not the rabbis or the communal leaders, also decided to open several courts to settle disputes among the Jewish residents. They felt that their own people serving as arbitrators could understand their immigrant brethren better than judicial officers, to whom they would appear alien and peculiar. Coincidentally, during this period a struggle was being waged to unionize the Brownsville shops. Coercion was often used, and the labor leaders were reluctant to go to the police courts to air these cases.

The activities of the Brownsville Court excited unwholesome publicity. *The Brooklyn Daily Eagle* devoted much space to it, calling it "a mock court" and a "bogus court." In its issue of May 17, 1895, we find that Judge Harriman, magistrate of the Gates Avenue Court, was surprised to learn that there was another court in his area of jurisdiction, and that police officers Keys and Webb were conducting an investigation of it. According to the story, about ten days previously a resident who had a shop on Osborn Street had secured a warrant for the arrest of a resident on the charge of stealing clothing valued at one hundred dollars. The defendant stepped forward when called, but the plaintiff did not appear.

"What is the excuse?"

"Why the whole case was settled. It was tried before the court on Tuesday, and I was acquitted because you had no right to issue a warrant."

Lawyer Francis McCaffrey, who had been retained by the plaintiff, stated that he had tried in vain to bring his client to court. There is a court in Brownsville, he explained, which arrogates to itself the right to settle all disputes among Hebrews. "The court, of course, is not legally constituted and has no powers, but its decisions are generally binding. When my client took out this warrant he was ordered to withdraw it, and when he declined, a boycott was declared against his shop; all his employees left him, and his neighbors avoided him. Unable to endure being thus ignored, my client consented to go to their court. I remonstrated with him, but he was adamant in his refusal to come here."

"This is a most remarkable state of affairs," the judge stated. "I will adjourn the examination for a week and will bring your client here, or else will send him to the penitentiary."

On May 24, 1895, *The Eagle* reported that Gates Avenue Court was filled with people from Brownsville. Judge Harriman learned that during the previous three weeks, twenty-six cases in which Brownsville Hebrews were interested had been dismissed for want of prosecution. In most of these cases neither plaintiff nor defendant had appeared in court.

All the parties concerned were summoned to Court by Court Officer Keys, who rounded them up in Brownsville, arousing excitement wherever he went. On meeting one of them, Officer Keys gave him the choice of either reporting at the "Horse Market" on Saratoga Avenue at 7 o'clock that morning, or suffering dire penalties. All appeared, accompanied by friends.

Justice Harriman had the whole group of more than twenty arraigned before him, and demanded to know why the authority of his court was so contemptuously disregarded. In response, each individual exhibited a copy of a mutual agreement in which he had agreed to drop charges.

"Why did you do this?" the magistrate demanded. He called

upon one of the defendants, who explained that Barney Wolff, better known as the Mayor of Brownsville, had sent for him and demanded that he withdraw a charge of petty larceny which he had made against an individual. Both parties went to Wolff's office, where Wolff listened to both sides, ordered them to sign an agreement not to press the matter any further, and then assessed each of them one dollar for his services.

"Who is this Wolff?" inquired the magistrate.

The answer was that he was a notary public, and had jurisdiction over all cases between Brownsville Jews.

The Judge also learned that because Wolff's business had become too heavy, a second court had been recently established in Brownsville by a Herman Schwartz, who purported to be a law student and rendered judgements for one dollar per case.

Unable to try all the cases on that day, the Judge arrested two of the group, one a walking delegate of the union, and one of the amateur judges who furnished bail. A warrant was also taken out for the other "judge," and the Brownsville Courts were adjourned for a while.

On May 25, 1895, *The Brooklyn Daily Eagle* carried an editorial on the Brownsville Court, commending Judge Harriman for taking energetic measures to suppress the several Hebrew courts in Brownsville. "Too much cannot be said of maintaining the purity and integrity of the police justices courts. They deal with the poorest, most ignorant, and most helpless classes, and because of this fact there is the greatest reason why they should be conducted along lines of strictest honesty and impartiality. People should be concerned with the police courts, and should insist that they be placed in the hands of a better set of men than those who now preside over the greater number of them."

Judge Harriman continued to give his attention to the affairs of the "illegal" Brownsville police court. On May 27, he issued warrants for the arrests of two men on charge of conspiracy, and they were locked up in the Seventeenth Substation. The plaintiff charged that they had engineered a strike in his place, and a boycott that followed had practically ruined his business.

On June 14th of the same year, we find that Officers Keys and

Tracy of the Gates Avenue Police Court rounded up another group of Brownsville defendants, among whom were some of the community's best-known residents, who had had their cases settled in the Brownsville Court. The judge lectured them severely and announced he would try all cases. The defendants were paroled after promising to be on hand.

The community was not altogether without social dregs, thieves, and swindlers. If they did not reside in Brownsville, they found their way there from the East Side or elsewhere.

An interesting report of a robbery is contained in *The Eagle* of August 21, 1896. Rabbi Sobusky, a *Shohet* in Brownsville, killed chickens in his back yard. His son Isaac opened a small stationery store. By strict economy, the *Shohet* saved three hundred dollars to return to the Old Country before he died. On the evening of August 20, while taking care of his son's little store, a dark-complexioned man of about thirty-eight entered the store, purchased a box of writing paper, and asked if he could sit down and write a letter. As might be expected, he was invited to make himself at home. He proved a good conversationalist and asked the Rabbi about his contemplated trip abroad. The Rabbi replied that he was all ready, and drawing his roll of money from his pocket, proudly displayed it. He had hardly gotten the money in his hands when the stranger dashed a handful of pepper in his eyes and ran out of the store. Rabbi Sobusky shouted for help, but the stranger had fled.

Israel Raeder owned a three-story, brick, clothing factory on Watkins Street near Glenmore, where he manufactured coats for New York dealers and employed a large number of workers. Because the locality was still a lonely and unsettled place in October 1894, a watchman was employed. About 7:30 o'clock on Thursday night, October 4, 1894, while the watchman went out to eat, an express wagon drew up in front of the factory door. The factory door was opened, and a large sack of clothing was taken and put in the wagon. When the thief made a second trip, Sargeant Brady, on watch at the time, spied him and gave chase with a loaded gun. The fugitive surrendered and gave his name as C. F. Two bags and other samples valued at $2,500 were recovered. The police stated that the prisoner was a member of the famous Essex Street gang in New York.

The First Public Schools

The children of Brownsville attended the public schools, conversed in English, among themselves, and sought to become familiar with American life. Originally there was only one school in Brownsville—Public School 66, on Blake and Thatford Avenues. When Public School 73 was built in 1899 at Rockaway Avenue and McDougal Street, some of the children attended it. It was a long walk from Brownsville. In 1890 four classrooms, with 224 seats, were added to Public School 66 to accommodate the growing population. More space was made available by the construction of Public School 84 on Glenmore and Stone Avenues. It was first occupied in September 1892 and was enlarged by several additions in 1894, in 1901, and in later periods. Public School 109 on Dumont, Powell, and Sackman Streets was the next school to open for Brownsville students in December 1895.

According to a contemporary account of life in Brownsville,[9] the teachers in the three public schools found the Hebrew children, particularly in the primary grades, brighter and more eager to learn than the children of the other schools. This did not always hold true in the higher grades, where the education of a child ceased to be compulsory by law. On the contrary, the teachers found that parents were constantly trying to take their children out of the grammar grades before they should, in order to push them to work and assist in maintaining themselves. The school authorities had to be constantly on the alert to contravene this practice which prevailed among families where only one or two of the children, at best, could be allowed the luxury of a higher education. The others not only had to support themselves, but also had to help those who were continuing their education.

The Hebrew Educational Society did not start its activities in Brownsville until the end of the century. Prior to that time there was no public library or organized activity of any kind that could occupy the youngsters. Like all other neighborhood boys, they took to playing baseball. Professor Morris R. Cohen wrote: [10] "As there was no public library in Brownsville my intellectual food was restricted to *Die Arbeiter Zeitung* and the few paper books in my brother Sam's collection. But the lack of reading matter was fully balanced by the opportunity to play with the Jewish boys of the neighborhood far more than I had done in New York, or even in Minsk. It was in Brownsville that I was introduced to the various forms of boys' baseball.

"In those days the Brooklyn Baseball Club of the National League played in Eastern Parkway, not far from Rockaway Avenue, where we lived. I went almost every afternoon to watch part of the game through the various cracks in the fence. Once my brother Sam took me to a neighboring house from which the field was visible. At one time, when there was a tied game between Brooklyn and New York, and the gateman had left his post after the eighth inning, several of us actually went in, and I was thrilled to see my hero, Jouett Meekin, pitch and hold the Brooklyn team down. I also saw the new sensational first baseman, Jack Doyle, play for New York. I regarded myself as a New Yorker, and rooted for my home team so that the boys called me 'Giant.' "

The Eastern Park Ball Grounds in which the Brooklyn team played from 1891 to 1898 was located on four blocks. They were bounded on the north by Eastern Parkway (Pitkin Avenue), on the east by Vesta Avenue (Van Sindern Avenue), on the south by Sutter Avenue, and on the west by Powell Street. The size of these grounds was 460 feet on the north and south streets, and 860 feet on the east and west streets. Transportation was by way of the Liberty Avenue car line, from which one had to walk two blocks south, or by the Fulton Street elevated, from which one had to walk a block farther.

The Eastern Park ball field was originally prepared in 1890 by the Players League. At the end of the 1890 season, when the League collapsed, the ball field was taken over by the Brooklyns, who had played since 1883 in Washington Park. Here the team was known as the "Bridegrooms," because in 1890 some nine or ten members of the club decided to be married about the same time. The price of admission to the bleachers was twenty-five cents. Many of the Brownsville children had a grand time peeping through the cracks of the ball park fence, or else, by paying ten or fifteen cents, watching the games from homes on Powell Street.

It was a hardship for most of the fans to reach Eastern Park, and the attendance fell off during the period the team played there. Accordingly, in 1898, it moved back to the heart of Brooklyn, to the second Washington Park, which was bounded by Third and Fourth Avenues and First and Third Streets. There they played until the end of the 1912 season, when they moved to Ebbets Field in 1913.[11]

Besides the National League team, there were a number of local teams in Brownsville. According to an account by Simon Cohen, the most prominent Jewish baseball team was known as "Nine Spots." It played weekends with teams called "Stars," "Victories," and "Thirty-three" on the baseball field at Pitkin Avenue and Watkins Street behind P.S.84. The most popular semi-pro team was the Alerts, who played on Rockaway Avenue in the rear of the car barns. The price in the bleachers was ten cents, and a scorecard was given free. Those who could not pay the ten cents watched the game from behind the ropes. The manager solicited contributions from fans, who would drop a few pennies in a cigar box. The attendance was about three thousand. Ace Batch, third baseman, later played in the Brooklyn National League.

Like so many other Brownsville youths, Simon Cohen was also a baseball fan, and was catcher on a team that played in the vacant lot on Stone and Sutter Avenues. The youngsters had no money to buy a catcher's mask, and one Friday Simon Cohen was struck in the eye by a ball, and sported a black eye for a while. This would have been inconsequential were it not that on the following day, Saturday morning, he became *Bar Mitzvah* and was called to the *Torah* in the Synagogue. The black eye was naturally embarrassing to Simon's parents.

The First Hebrew School

Poor or rich, the Brownsville parents provided their children with some Jewish education. Each family contributed five to ten cents a week for the support of the Talmud Torah—the Hebrew School. Some well-to-do families had the Hebrew instructors come to their homes, but the other children attended the religious classes either before or after the regular school sessions. The instruction seldom went beyond the reading of the prayer book, translating a few portions of the Bible, writing Yiddish, and preparation for *Bar Mitzvah*. The instruction was conducted in Yiddish.

A Talmud Torah was established soon after the settlement of the Jews in Brownsville. The Hebrew Free School of Brownsville, popularly known later as the "Stone Avenue Talmud Torah," originated in 1892. Among its founders and early supporters were H. Simon, Dr. I. Kaufman, H. Meyersohn, D. Rosenberg, Elias Kaplan, I. Cohen, Solomon Reuben, Simon Rose, Rabbi M. C. Rabinowitz, A. Volitsky, A. Belanofsky, S. Grally, Aaron Kaplan, Nathan Kovinsky, and I. Levingson. Until 1902 it met in a house on Thatford and Belmont Avenues. In that year it moved to a frame building at 386 Stone Avenue.

In the grand parade arranged to welcome Rabbi Judah Wistinetsky in 1894, the leaders and children of the Talmud Torah took an active part.[12] M. Moss, president of the school, rode on horseback, accompanied by policemen and followed by the principal of the school, Israel Lifshitz, and a hundred and sixty Talmud Torah children with their teachers. All the pupils of the Talmud Torah were boys. One of Rabbi Wistinetsky's first activities was to establish a school for girls. A society was organized to support this school, with Mr. Rosenfeld as chairman. The membership dues were five cents a week, and the tuition fees ranged from ten to twenty cents. The girls school grew rapidly, counting seventy students during the first year. Among the Hebrew teachers and Rabbis listed for Brownsville in the 1892 Census were Jacob Aaronson, William Brownstein, Hyman Eisenburgh, Nathan Getzhoff, Pincus Gudelowitz, Michael Kaplowitz, and Rubin Plotsky.

Zedakah and Gemilut Hasadism

The early East-European immigrants seldom, if ever, sank to pauperism. They were a hard-working class, ready to labor even under the harshest conditions to eke out a living. Unlike the situation on the East Side, the older German-Jewish community in Brooklyn did not come to assist Brownsville until the beginning of the century, when the Baron de Hirsch Fund initiated the Hebrew Educational Society more than a decade after Jews settled here. The earliest Jewish leadership in Brooklyn was the establishment in 1878 of the Brooklyn Hebrew Orphan Asylum, which serviced the entire Jewish Community. It was first located on McDonough Street. In 1892 the old building was sold, and a large building was constructed on the edge of Brownsville at Ralph and Howard, Dean and Pacific Streets. There were periods of acute distress, but during these times there were mutual efforts to help one another. "Search in the records of the unfortunates that appeal for aid to the public charity organizations," reads a contemporary account, "and you find no mention of Brownsville. In their charities, as in everything else, these Hebrew people are a law unto themselves." [13]

The immigrant Jews brought with them Judaism's concepts of *Zedakah* and *Gemiluth Hasadim*—the human obligation to help the less fortunate. Charity was personal and genuine. Neighborly relations were close. Because the residents of a given block lived in close proximity and were therefore familiar with each family's circumstances, there was a readiness to help those in need, even to the point of self-sacrifice.

It is impossible to measure the amount of charity dispensed by those early immigrants either individually or through some organization. Practically every family had relatives abroad whom they assisted financially, or helped bring to this country by providing them with steamship tickets. Charity was also administered to help some "green" *Landsman*—townsman—get a start in the new country. The old world custom of *gehen kleiben*—house to house collections—was a common method that remained in vogue over the years. Appeals in the Synagogue, charity boxes—*Pushkes*—in the homes, were other means used to acquire funds for local needs and for institutions in Europe and in the Holy Land. In time, numerous societies were set up to render assistance in cash, in kind, or in personal service.

During the 1893 depression, the distress in Brownsville as elsewhere was appalling.[14] There was no organized committee, but active men like David Berger, the contractor, George Young, a lawyer and a hustler for charity, Mark Cohen, a cloakmaker on Thatford Avenue, Moritz Bloner, and others, went from house to house collecting food, coal, clothing, or money for the distressed to alleviate the suffering.

Physicians and other professionals conversant with the gravity of the crisis also helped as much as they could. Professor Morris R. Cohen relates how his mother became seriously ill giving birth to a baby daughter, who died during labor. "Her labor pains began earlier than was expected. I remember her cries of agony. She sent me for a doctor, but it was some time before I found a doctor to attend her. He was an old gentleman with a fine understanding of actual conditions. He attended mother for hours, and quietly accepted the one dollar which was all that we had left in the house after paying for the necessary drugs at the apothecary's. The doctor (I am sorry that I never thought of asking for his name) continued to come every day until my mother was out of immediate danger, and I think that my father managed to get together a few more dollars in order to pay him. . . ." [15]

As needs increased, societies were organized to meet them. To illustrate: a girl collapsed at work one afternoon in one of the shops and died. She had no relatives or friends to arrange for the burial. A few residents started immediately a *Hesed Shel Emeth Society*—Free Burial Society—and collected money for the funeral. They purchased a plot from the Oheb Shalom Congregation, which already owned land at the Washington Cemetery in Parkville. The Society was incorporated in 1895 and has continued to serve to the present time.

In the *Yiddishe Gazetten* of May 1894, there is an item in the Brownsville column under the title "Brownsville Pinkos," stating that one of the residents called the Board of Health to arrange for the burial of his child. The reason for this strange act was not known; either the resident did not believe in a Jewish burial, or he did not have the three dollars charged by the Society for the burial.

To provide clothes and shoes for the poor, a *Malbish Arumim*—Clothing the Naked—Society was organized in 1894. The need for a dispensary where the poor residents of Brownsville could secure free medical help became apparent very early. The three physicians who practiced here in the early years charged one dollar for a visit to the house, but that was sometimes beyond the reach of the families who were plagued by recurrent strikes and seasonal unemployment. At the suggestion of Rabbi Judah Wistinetsky, a Society for the Aid for the Indigent Sick was organized in 1895, with J. Koplowitz as its first secretary. A small store was rented at Thatford and Pitkin Avenues for its use. The Society paid for the services of the doctor. To supply coal, pay rents, and render other assistance, the Brownsville Relief Hebrew Charity was established a little later. Thus sprang up various aid societies which in subsequent years became important institutions.

Religious Life in Brownsville

As already stated, the first Jews who settled in Brownsville brought with them the traditions they saw practiced in their European homes. Orthodoxy, the Rabbinical tradition, was the dominant culture in the Russian Jewish Pale. Reform Judaism, as practiced by the older German-Jewish residents in the community, had no appeal for them. Even those who were affected by the *Haskalah* and other secular movements in Jewish life in the latter part of the nineteenth century were not attracted by the religious Reform movement. Those who departed from Orthodoxy—and there were many among the immigrants in this country—moved in the direction not of religious reforms but of a complete indifference to religion. Some became part of the core of radicals, even atheists, who later developed a Yiddish radical and secularist movement in this country.

Soon after the Jews settled in Brownsville they organized a *Minyan* for public worship.[16] By 1889 there were two separate *Minyanim,* one in the big factory of Elias Kaplan, which on Saturdays was transformed into a Synagogue. The other prayed in the back yard house of Jacob Cohen's house. A few days before the

Jewish New Year 5650 (1889), while Mr. Kaplan was busy preparing his shop for Holy Day religious service, he was visited by a committee of Jewish residents of the Atlantic Avenue and Fulton Street section to rent thirty seats for the High Holiday Services, stipulating that he should engage a good Cantor. This was the first official contact between some of the older Jewish residents of East New York, many of whom were German Jews who had settled considerably earlier, and the new Jewish settlement in Brownsville. Max, the builder, had accepted the position of Cantor for which he received an honorarium of fifteen dollars. A surplus of one hundred dollars was realized that year.

With this sum in the treasury, the meeting of both congregations was called by Elias Kaplan and Herman Moskowitz, at which time it was proposed that both *Minyanim* unite to build a Synagogue. The plan met with the approval of most of those present, and eighteen men pledged one dollar each towards the cause. At the suggestion of Mr. Moskowitz, the Synagogue was named *Oheb Shalom*—Loving Peace. Despite its peace-inspiring name, the congregation split for a time, but amity was soon restored.

In 1889, soon after the congregation was organized with Mr. Kaplan as president, two lots were purchased on Thatford Avenue from a Mrs. Mary Kramer for $400. Mr. Moskowitz the agent, received a commission of $50, which he turned over to the Synagogue. To get additional funds, another meeting was called at which 14 permanent seats were sold, ranging in price from $35 to $100 each, 10 per cent in cash, and the balance in payments.

When plans were made for the construction of the building, the estimates indicated that it would cost at least $5,500. As the committee was about to let the contract to one of the local builders, a Mr. Louis Ratner appeared. He came originally from Rakov, a town in the province of Minsk, and had built houses in New Haven, Connecticut, where he first settled. He agreed to construct the Synagogue for the same amount of $5,500, but he also promised to construct a beautiful Ark without extra cost. The Ark stands to this day.

To raise the large sum required for the construction of the

building, the community turned to Arthur Hurst, son of a lawyer who was the principal mortgager of Brownsville real estate and the owner of many vacant lots. When Arthur Hurst complained that the real estate business was bad, it was suggested that in order to encourage Jews to move into the community and buy houses, he should influence his father to help them get a mortgage to build the synagogue. It might initiate a general boom.

The older Hurst was even more enthusiastic than his son, and agreed to take a first mortgage for $5,500. The building was completed the following Passover. Hyman Moskowitz was elected president, and Elias Kaplan vice-president. Solomon Levine was the first *Shamash* (Sexton), *Baal Kore, Mohel* and *Shochet,* and Joseph Lack, the first Rabbi. Among the original members were Simon Schnapir, Solomon Morris, G. and A. Goldstein, George Young, Al Pasternack, Zigmund Rosenfeld, Max the builder, Louis Ratner, Simon Rose, Mendel Stark, Jacob Cohen, and Messers. Friedman, Goot, Gotther, London, Padansky, Wasserman, among others.

In time the building became too small for the growing congregation, and in 1902 the building was sold to the *Hebra Nahalath Israel* and removed to Chester Street between Pitkin and Sutter Avenues. A new Synagogue was constructed on Thatford Avenue near Belmont Avenue, and it continued to play a leading role in the congregational life of the community.

In 1894 the congregation engaged Rabbi Judah Hakohen Wistinetsky, a well-known Rabbi and scholar from Suwalki, Lithuania, as its spiritual leader. He came highly recommended. Prior to coming to America he edited and annotated the illustrious ethical work *Sefer Hasidim,—Book of the Pious*—by Judah ben Samuel he-Hasid of Regensburg, who died in February, 1217. Upon his arrival in New York, Rabbi Wistinetsky served for nine months as superintendent of the *Hahnosath Orhim*—Immigrant Aid Society—of which Kasriel Sarasohn, publisher of the *Yiddishe Gazetten,* was president. The community, feeling that a change for the rabbi was desirable, arranged that he become the rabbi of the new settlement in Brownsville, amid pomp and ceremony.

A detailed and graphic description of the ceremony was given in the *Yiddishe Gazetten* of May 18, 1894. There was a torchlight procession with a mounted policeman at its head, the Rabbi in the middle, and David M. Berger at the end. The Rabbi was met by a parade of music and carriages. Two carriages contained directors of the New York *Hahnosath Orhim,* and more than thirty carriages held Brownsville residents. The carriage of M. Moskowitz, the president, was followed by Mr. Moss, president of the Talmud Torah, on horseback, and by 160 children of the Hebrew School, marching with their teachers. The principal, Israel Lifshitz, and the teachers, with two of their pupils, carried a banner bearing the Hebrew words *Baruch ato B'voeho*—Blessed be thou in thy coming. When Mr. Moskowitz stepped out of the carriage, he handed the Rabbi a bouquet of flowers on which was inscribed, *Hebra Oheb Shalom, Shalom Aleihem.* The Synagogue was filled to capacity. Following the speakers, Rabbi Wistenetzky addressed his new community. He was then taken to his new home on Watkins Street near Belmont Avenue, which was especially fitted up for him. For a time he captured the heart of the entire settlement.

The lot of the Rabbi was not always an enviable one in some of the small towns in Eastern Europe, but there was a discipline and a tradition which was lacking in the new American communities. Consequently, the lot of these pioneer Rabbis was often difficult. Some of them, unable to adjust to the new conditions, were impelled to return to their native country. Rabbi Wistenetzky found himself in this category. He could not adapt to the American conditions and he ultimately returned to Suwalki.

As usual, the *Kosher* meat question was a source of friction, a bone of contention. In *The Brooklyn Eagle* of July 10, 1894, and in the *Yiddishe Gazetten,* it was reported that there had been one or two rough fracases in the streets, the Rabbi of the settlement had been mobbed, and the police had been called.

"According to the most reliable sources of information," reports the *Eagle,* "it all came about this way." It was a matter of common knowledge that the Rabbi's salary was guaranteed by Messrs. G. & D. Isaacs, wholesale butchers on Hudson Avenue, who were to be under the Rabbi's supervision. In return, the Rabbi promised to issue certificates to such Brownsville butchers as purchased from Isaacs. This had the effect of compelling every retail dealer to buy from Isaacs only. Serious trouble ensued. Some of the butchers rebelled. One Friday morning, a delegation of the trade visited an establishment next door to Isaacs, and ordered a quantity of beef. A member of the Isaacs firm at once offered two of the leading Brownsville butchers all the meat they could handle provided they undersold all other butchers. These two consented, and broadcast circulars stating they were prepared to sell meat at ridiculously low prices. This enraged the other butchers, and the rivals indulged in a rough and tumble fight on Pitkin Avenue on a Sunday afternoon.

On Monday morning the worst befell. Rabbi Wistinetzky set out in his buggy to visit the butcher shops, carrying his certificates and informed the butchers he could not be responsible for the *Kashrut* unless the meat was purchased from Isaacs. He had visited only a few when the news of his errand became public property. Fifteen or twenty butchers, together with their large families and several dozen sympathizers, surrounded the Rabbi's buggy, "overturned the vehicle, pulled the occupant from the wreck and mauled him unmercifully." He was cut and bruised before a large group of sympathizers headed by Louis Parmer came to his rescue. The two mobs were in a mood for bloodshed, but five policemen and a sergeant from Liberty Avenue station drove them off and carried the Rabbi back to the safety of his premises.

All Brownsville was agog. In the evening there was a large mass meeting in Parmer's Casino on Pitkin Avenue. There were many fiery speeches and great indignation that rendered the situation potentially explosive. After some turbulent discussion a committee was appointed to devise some method of punishing the rioters. Some warrants were issued from Gates Avenue Police court.

The meat and poultry problem continued to trouble Brownsville. On November 21, 1894, *The Eagle* reported that Harris Hillman and David Blumberg had applied to Health Commissioner Emery for a permit to operate a new abattoir, one of four in Brooklyn, erected at the corner of Christopher and Dumont Avenues. The commissioner, ready to grant the permit, was asked by a deputation from the Oheb Shalom Synagogue that it be granted the permit. He was even more puzzled when the Talmud Torah Society asked for the permit. "What is the meaning of all this competition?" asked the commissioner.

It was explained that the fees accrued from the killing of poultry would aggregate a few thousand dollars, and therefore a share of the profits was desirable. The Synagogue was willing to have Hillman and Blumberg operate for an annual contribution of $100. Hillman and Blumberg agreed, but only for 5 years. The Talmud Torah Society demanded 8 per cent of the profit, claiming that it alone was organized for charitable purposes. The commissioner suggested that they go home and try to arbitrate the matter.

Acting on the advice, the Society held a meeting at the home of Rabbi Wistenetsky, who acted as referee. It was decided that Oheb Shalom Synagogue receive $125 annually for 6 years, and that the Talmud Torah be treated generously at the annual distributions. When Commissioner Emery learned that an agreement had been reached, he granted a permit.

The competition among the *Shohetim*—slaughterers of animals according to ritual law—and also among the *Mohelim*—circumcisers according to Jewish law—sometimes resulted in unpleasant incidents, occasionally even in altercations which were brought to the attention of the police authorities.

All this was the price of freedom and free enterprise. The absence of a hierarchy and of discipline outside the congregation encouraged different synagogues and societies to conduct themselves capriciously in whatever ways the members willed.

After Rabbi Wistenetsky returned to his native town in Lithuania, Rabbi Simon J. Finkelstein accepted the position at Oheb Shalom in 1902, and ministered to the community until his death, April 16, 1947. The Hebra Torah, the Beth Hamidrash Ha-Gadol, Congregation Etz Chaim Machzikei Ha-Rav, Hebra Tehillim Keter Israel, and a number of other synagogues were organized in the early years.

The Jews were elated with their synagogues, but the religious women raised a cry for a *Mikvah*—Ritualarium. Poor transit made a trip to New York difficult and burdensome. Mr. Louis Ratner answered the need by building a bath house with a *Mikvah* on Belmont near Rockaway Avenue. Later, he installed a Russian Bath, which is functioning to this day.

The Zionist movement, concerned with the establishment of a Jewish homeland in Palestine, commanded a strong following in Brownsville. The *Hovevei Zion* of Brownsville according to a listing of some 300 associations of the *Hovevei Zion*—Lovers of Zion—in the United States in *Siphruth Zion* of 1898, was organized on December 28 of that year. It comprised a group with a membership of 50. Another group consisting of youth who called themselves *Naarei Zion V'Naarot Zion* is also listed.

Home and Social Life

Brownsville was by no means a homogeneous community even in the early days. It was quite differentiated, and time was required before the various groups felt at home with one another. There were the large number of Lithuanian and Russian Jews, a substantial number of Galician Jews, and smaller groups of Polish, Roumanian, Hungarian, and others. While they had much in common, there were differences in cultural background and outlook which had to be reconciled. In time they began to cut across lines of local origin, intermarried, and joined the same organizations and activities.

The majority of the population, having emigrated from the smaller and relatively isolated Eastern-European towns, were still under their cultural and religious impact. Some were illiterate, and others were limited in outlook and education. On the other hand, others were beginning to arrive who had lived, studied, and worked in the larger cities, and who had been exposed to the secular forces prevalent in Europe at the time. They were the intellectuals, social reformers, socialists and anarchists. The local police, headed by Captain Velsor in 1899, stated: "There are said to be some anarchists here who have an international reputation, but they hold their meetings in the most unobtrusive way, and if they even plot any mischief the police are not able to find it out." [17]

There was not much free time for diversion, but the people

were far from being solemn folk. There were many occasions when
they could indulge in play and fun. Brownsville generally enjoyed
holidays, and always managed to find time for special observances.
When the first rabbi was brought over from the East Side to the
Oheb Shalom Synagogue, there was a holiday with a parade,
horseback riding, music, and banners. The same Jews, except the
boss-tailors, enthusiastically paraded with their red flags on the
first of May, which was another holiday. When they routed a gang
of rowdies or missionaries bent on disturbing the peace of the
community, the victory was celebrated with a parade. When the
first dispensary was opened, there was a holiday in Brownsville,
and the celebration lasted until dawn. The introduction of gas
lamps in the Brownsville streets was feted with gladness. For years
the Purim Masquerade Ball conducted by the Stone Avenue
Talmud Torah was a local event, and no one dared to compete
with it by arranging an affair on that day. For months mothers and
daughters prepared the masquerade costumes for the mass event in
which orthodox Jews, socialists, and anarchists, and all others
participated. It was a gala communal holiday!

On Friday evenings and Saturday afternoons, the residents put
on their fine clothes and went on parade on Eastern Parkway
(Pitkin Avenue), pausing for ice cream. The gaiety was concluded with the Saturday night dance. For the observant Jew,
there was a genuine Jewish life on the Sabbath. Everybody ate the
Jewish Sabbath dish, the *Cholent*. After the meal the older folks
enjoyed the customary siesta, while the youngsters played in the
streets. Family events were occasions of social gatherings and
festivities. The *Brith*—circumcision ceremony—the *Bar Mitzvah*,
and the marriage ceremony were joyous occasions in which the
family, friends, and neighbors joined.

The most popular institution was the theatre. The first Jewish
actors in Brownsville were the parents of Sam Leawenwirt, buff
comedian, who played in English in London, and then in New
York. Mr. and Mrs. Sam Kestin worked during their early career
in the shop by day, and played theatre in the evening. Sanger's
Hall on Pitkin and Watkins Street was the locale for all actors and
stars who came from New York to entertain Brownsville
audiences.

Sanger's and other halls were used for concerts, lectures, debates, and entertainment. Those were the days when people waxed excited over the relative merits of a poet, editor, actor, or cantor. There was no dearth of crowds, excitement, parades, mass meetings, picnics, and other forms of diversion to fill the free moments.

The children, who usually spoke English not only in school, but even at home and among themselves, had their own diversions —ball-playing, parties, meetings, movies. There were the Oriole and the Surprise motion picture theatres on Pitkin Avenue. Two people were admitted for five cents. Those who had only two cents would stand outside and wait to match their pennies with those who had three cents. Live English shows were to be seen in the Liberty Theatre on Liberty Avenue, near Watkins, which was built by Lowe. Some of the early favorites presented there included *Chinatown Trunk Mystery,* and *Bertha, the Sewing Machine Girl.*

Many old men who were boys in those days, recall with delight those "good old days." Ben Holiber in the "Old Timers Column" of *The Brooklyn Eagle* on June 30, 1949, expressed the nostalgic feelings and fond memories of many who grew up in Brownsville in those early years:

> *"I was born in Brownsville, Brooklyn*
> *over fifty years ago*
> *When we had plenty of mud, sometimes*
> *eight feet of snow;*
> *Where the old lamplighter made*
> *his daily round.*
> *Only a few peaceful families*
> *were there to be found.*
>
> *Some of the pioneers I shall mention*
> *by name*
> *Who through the long years reached*
> *their fortune and fame.*
> *They were the Strongins, the Langsams,*
> *the Starks and the Rumphs,*

The Heatters, the Goldbergs, the
  Raphaels (Rayfiels) and the Strumphs.
There were many others back in those
  days—
For instance, the Grallas, the Goldsteins,
  and the Fiers.
They too lived in a lamp—lighted
  little old shack
In the Town of Brownsville, Brooklyn
  (more than) fifty years back.

The Cow Barn and milk farm
  once owned by Cohen
Stood at the corner of Pitkin
  and Stone
Along side stood the Hebrew School,
  the best we had.
The rabbi no doubt was
  Jack Holtzman's dad.

I remember the old firehouse of
  long ago,
The horse drawn engine plowing
  through the snow;
The little old police station
  off Osborn Street,
With just a handful of policemen
  patrolling the beat.

I remember the rugged roads,
  tall trees now gone,
Surrounded the houses where many
  a genius was born.
And the old red school house
  on Watkins Street—
We'd walk for miles—there
  we would meet.

In those days we were only
   barefooted boys—
No fancy clothes, no
   expensive toys.

Our parents toiled both
   night and day
To bring happiness some
   future day.

The time has come; we outlived
   those years,
We enjoyed much happiness,
   we shed many tears.
Although years passed on,
   friend drifted apart,
Always remember Brownsville, Brooklyn,
   Whence you got your start."

Brownsville's Growth to the Largest Jewish Community in New York

IV

BROWNSVILLE enjoyed a phenomenal growth during the early decades of the twentieth century. From a small suburban village it developed into the largest and most densely populated section in the Borough of Brooklyn. The improved transportation facilities rendered it possible for thousands living in overcrowded conditions in the lower East Side and Williamsburg to seek new homes miles away from their jobs in Manhattan and elsewhere. The opening to traffic of the Williamsburg Bridge on December 19, 1903, and of the Manhattan Bridge on December 31, 1909; the expansion of the West Side Subway through Brownsville and East New York; the extension of the B.M.T. Subway; the opening of surface lines such as the Douglas Street line, later known as the St. John's Place line, connecting Brownsville with the Brooklyn Bridge; the surface cars running through Rockaway Avenue to Canarsie, making transportation to Manhattan easier; the extension of the Fulton Street elevator—all were great factors in accelerating the development of the neighborhood. Many who had looked on those moving to Brownsville as on the pioneers who went with covered wagons in search of the West, now moved into what was only a few years before a suburban section.

Real estate values jumped. Hundreds of buildings were erected to provide housing for the newcomers. Between 1907 and 1909 the entire section west of Rockaway Avenue was cluttered up with diggers and excavators. Whole streets were cut through and piled with building materials and sewer pipes. In 1909 Dr. Coyne, president of the Brownsville Tax Payers Association, stated that lots originally costing $50 or more, had been sold within the previous two years at an average price of $3,000. Near Stone Avenue, lots were valued and assessed at from $12,000 to $15,000 each, "and none of them was in the market, even at this figure." A report of the building operations during that year, published in the *New York Herald* on January 17, 1909, indicated that they were quite extensive. On the north side of Pitkin Avenue, between Chester and Rockaway Avenues, three-story buildings with stores were built by Samuel Palley, at a cost that included the price of the lots, for $7,500 to $8,000 cash. Stores rented for about $75 a month, and flats with 5 rooms and bath for $30 a month. Rows of flats and stores on Pitkin and Amboy streets were built by Abraham Kaplan, stores renting for between $40 and $50, and suites for about $3 a room. The same applied to other parts of Brownsville and East New York. Solid blocks of apartment houses rose on Saratoga, Howard, Blake, and other streets.

In 1901 New York City adopted a building code regulating the construction and maintenance of buildings containing three or more dwelling units. Its aim was to make the new buildings safer against fire hazards, to permit more light and air, and to provide separate sanitary facilities. Many buildings constructed after the enactment of the code satisfied only the minimum requirements, while some were speculative and jerry-built. Brownsville did, however, witness the construction also of a large number of substantial brick buildings.

Builders of Brownsville and East New York

While Brownsville was a proletarian district inhabited by a vast population of workmen (mostly tailors), it also had its builders, businessmen, bankers, real estate operators, professional men, and others who played a leading role in building up Brownsville and adjoining sections.[1] Many of these men started out as poor immigrants, sweatshop workers or peddlers, and became important leaders in the building and business world. They are as much a part of Brownsville's story as is the story of the sweatshop. When they expanded their activities into other parts of the city, many of them moved to the Eastern Parkway and other sections of the Borough. There were those who made significant contributions to the religious and philanthropic projects in the community.

Most of these builders, immigrants from Eastern Europe, underwent arduous struggles in the early days. The periodic depressions and the bank failures which followed them, the difficulty in obtaining credit and disposing of property on hand at such times, tested the character and business acumen of the best of them.

One of the earliest and best known realtors and bankers was Samuel Palley, a vice-president of the Public National Bank of New York, who was in charge of the Brownsville branch of the bank on Pitkin and Watkins Street for many years until he was transferred to its main office on Delancey Street.

Among the early builders was Isaac Levingson, who came to this country in 1889 at the age of seventeen. He started as a presser in an East Side sweatshop, and when he accumulated a little money he came to Brownsville to enter the realty field. He began his operations first in Brownsville, and later expanded them throughout Brooklyn and Long Island.

Jacob Goell was another pioneer builder in Brownsville, East New York, Eastern Parkway, and other sections of the borough. Born in Poswel, Kovna, on July 15, 1871, he came to the United States in 1890. He first engaged in carpentry, and eventually in building. Among his numerous buildings were the large row of

apartment houses and stores on Sutter Avenue between Amboy
and Herzl Streets.

Charles Goell, six years younger than Jacob, received a good
Jewish education in European Yeshivahs before he was brought
here in 1891. After several years as foreman for a number of
structures, he set out for himself, first as a builder in the East New
York section of Brooklyn, and later in the Eastern Parkway and
Flatbush sections, building hundreds of buildings of various
types.

Morris Weinberg came to Brownsville in 1895 from Russia
where he was born on January 15, 1878. He engaged in the
wholesale newspaper business between 1895 and 1901. Organizer
and treasurer of the Metropolitan News Company between 1901
and 1906, he went into the building business at that time,
constructing several hundred apartment houses and family
dwellings in Brownsville, East New York, and subsequently in
Eastern Parkway. He purchased the huge Van Siclen Estate in East
New York, and is best known today as the President and Publisher
of the Jewish daily, *The Day-Jewish Journal.*

For many years Harry Strongin had his real estate offices at 1662
Pitkin Avenue. He was born in Manhattan on August 12, 1889,
and at the age of twelve came to Brownsville. He built many
apartment houses in Flatbush and elsewhere, but is particularly
known for his contributions to the development of Pitkin Avenue
as an important thoroughfare, and for his plans in the construction of the East New York Terminal on Junius Street.

Among the many other builders who had a share in building
Brownsville and East New York were, to mention a few of them,
David Isacowitz and his sons, Bernard and Murray, Samuel
Sassulsky, Abraham Kaplan, Israel and Louis Halperin, Max
Alpert, Moses and Samuel Bernstein, Max Feldman, Samuel
Coffey, Jacob Siris, and the Meislin brothers.

Development of Business Centers

Along with the building of homes, came the development of a
number of business centers. "To write the story of Brownsville

without mentioning Pitkin Avenue," according to Samuel L. Peckerman, one of Brownsville's old-timers and active workers, "would be like telling the story of the landing of the Pilgrims and omitting Plymouth Rock."

This thoroughfare, which runs for a mile or so through the heart of Brownsville, was for a time next to Fulton Street, one of the most important shopping centers in Brooklyn. It was Brownsville's chief support and one of the main reasons for its existence. Hundreds of stores of every description lined its sidewalks, displaying every commodity in well-dressed show windows. Pitkin Avenue, from Stone Avenue to Ralph Avenue— some 14 blocks—in 1942 counted 372 stores doing an annual business of some $90,000,000, and employing some 1,000 people. There were 8 banks, 43 men's clothing stores, 26 ladies' ready-made-to-wear shops, 44 shoe stores, as well as haberdasheries, furriers, jewelry stores, hat stores, house furnishings, restaurants, cafeterias, liquor stores, and the Loew's Pitkin Theatre with 3,600 seats constructed at a cost of over $3,000,000. People came to shop here, especially on week-ends, from all parts of Brooklyn and other parts of the city.

Some time elapsed before Pitkin Avenue became a leading shopping mart. The first Jewish settlers in Brownsville patronized the East Side shopping avenues such as Division Street, Grand Street, Hester Street, or Avenue A. Gradually the Brownsville pioneers opened little shops in their homes. Soon millinery, clothing, shoe, and a variety of other stores began to appear. As the population grew, the small, wooden houses were razed, and in their place arose the beautiful shops which have made Pitkin Avenue famous. Differing in some respects from the shopping avenues of the East Side, it attracted customers not only from Brownsville, but also from all parts of Brooklyn, Staten Island, and Long Island. Its shops were open all week until late in the evenings, and contained specialty or more individualized articles than were available in the department stores, and they were one-priced stores, guaranteeing their wares. Belmont Avenue, Stone Avenue, and Sutter Avenue also became important retail centers, and Rockaway Avenue became famous as a furniture mart.

A number of industries were established here—the manufacture of men's, women's, and children's clothing, embroidery works, iron works, and other industries such as the Rubel Coal and Ice Company, Shapiro and Aronson Chandeliers—giving employment to a specialized class of workers.

To conform to Jewish ritual practices, many food stores were established. Hundreds of meat, dairy, and grocery stores dotted the neighborhood. Osborn Street became the wholesale fruit and vegetable mart. One of the first settlers to establish a milk farm in Brownsville was Shlomo Greenberg (1861-1933). After coming to this country in the 80's from Zabludowa, Russia, he settled in Brownsville, bought a few small farms, and established a milk farm, which became well known in Brownsville. Jewish Brownsville may be said to have been raised on Greenberg's milk. When he grew older he transferred the business to his family, who conducted it as the Linden Farm Milk Company and the Hegeman Farm Milk Company.

The Holland Family also has resided in Brownsville from the beginning and engaged in the milk business. Mrs. Sarah Holland has continued to this day to take an active interest in the life of the community.

Banks and Bankers

Brownsville was serviced at different times by a number of banks—The Public National Bank, The State Bank, The Twenty-Sixth Ward Bank, The Union, The Homestead, The East New York Savings Bank, The Morris Bank, The Provident Loan Society, The Municipal Bank, The Bank of the United States, The Modern Industrial Bank, The Food Dealers, Manufacturers Trust Company, The Bank of North America, to mention a few.

Before the days of Federal Bank Insurance and the merger of many of New York banks into giant financial institutions, the local bank and the local banker, who usually lived in the neighborhood, exercised a significant role in the life of the community. Samuel Palley of The Public National Bank, and Julius Josephson and

Samuel Barnett of The Municipal Bank were among the local bankers in this category.

A man to whose guidance and assistance many builders and businessmen of Brownsville owed much was William B. Roth. Mr. Roth was born in Eepeyes, Hungary, on October 1, 1864, and as a youth studied in the Yeshivahs. At the age of nineteen he immigrated to America, landing in New York on November 20, 1883. He became associated in July 1890, with The State Bank located at Grand and Suffolk Street, and during his thirteen years with that institution he came in contact with Brownsville residents who traveled to Manhattan to deposit their savings in the bank. Mr. Roth visited the new and growing community a number of times.

In July 1903 he succeeded in persuading The State Bank and its president, Armand Cohen, to embark on the hazardous undertaking of establishing a branch office in Brownsville, then estimated to have a population of fifteen thousand, with himself as manager. The first office was located at the corner of Glenmore and Stone Avenues, where for a year and a half Mr. Roth served as banker and guide to many of the Brownsville pioneers. He tried to guide and teach his first business clients, mostly in the tailoring and contracting businesses, sound business methods that might prevent failures. This was not an easy undertaking in the pioneering community, and Mr. Roth sometimes appeared hard, obstinate, and overbearing.

Mr. Roth and his aides helped local merchants and builders recover from serious financial crises in 1907, 1914, 1920, and 1921, which threatened insolvency to many caught unawares by the business depressions. The Jenkins Trust Company at the corner of Pitkin and Rockaway Avenue failed in 1907, with disastrous results to depositors. Mr. Roth aided the community to recoup its losses. In the same year The Union Bank, located at East New York and Atlantic Avenues, closed its doors, and again Mr. Roth helped to liquidate the assets for the benefit of the crash victims. When Max Kobre's bank failed in 1914, Mr. Roth and George W. McLoughlin, later president of The Brooklyn Trust Company, helped to save large sums of money for Brownsville investors. In

1920 Mr. Roth was made vice-president of The State Bank. When the bank merged with The Manufacturers Trust Company, he resigned to become president of The Food Industrial Bank. He was associated with practically every religious and educational agency in the community, and is particularly known as the founder and president for many years of Temple Petach Tikvah.[2]

Trade Associations and Neighborhood Councils

In Brownsville there were always one or more organizations whose purpose it was to keep the residents alert to their community's needs, to help develop local neighborhood spirit and civic pride, and to coordinate the community's welfare. A main objection of the early residents of New Lots to annexation to Brooklyn, and later to New York City, was fear of increased taxes. This was demonstrated by the increase in taxes on two lots and a house at 197-9 Bristol Street, which was torn down to make room for Public School 263. In 1869 the taxes on the property was $2.84. In 1891, when Brownsville was part of the City of Brooklyn, taxes increased to $31.82. In 1933, when it was part of Greater New York, taxes rose to $170. It is noteworthy that during this continuing increase the property took on no noticeable physical change.[3]

Many people complained about the over-assessment of real estate, and the expensive insurance rates. To deal with the problem, the Brownsville Tax Payers Association was formed with Dr. N. J. Coyne as the moving spirit. In 1909 it had as many as four hundred members.

A significant force in the early history of the community was the Brownsville Board of Trade, organized about 1905 by George Tonkonogy, William Sugarman, Sol S. Schwartz, Samuel Telsey, Alexander Drescher, and others. The most prominent businessmen and leaders of the neighborhood were associated with it. As a result of its campaign for improvements, new schools were built, streets asphalted, proper lighting obtained for the streets, and transportation facilities improved. The first president of the

Brownsville Board of Trade was George Tonkonogy. He was succeeded in turn by William Sugarman, Alfred A. Sclickerman, and Simon H. Kugel. In 1912 Simon H. Kugel was president, Moses Bernstein and Morris Weinberg, vice-presidents, Alexander S. Drescher, secretary, Herman Lefkowitz, treasurer, and Max N. Koven, financial secretary.[4]

When the Board disbanded, the Pitkin Avenue Merchants Association took over some of its functions. While the Association was primarily concerned with improving business on Pitkin Avenue and guarding its prestige as one of the main shopping areas in the city, it also participated in the general welfare and improvement of the community. Its membership of some 250 businessmen included the most prominent citizens of the community. Among those who served as presidents of the Association were Abraham Stark (now Brooklyn Borough President), Joseph Feinberg, Abraham Gratenstein, Samuel Zweig, Irving Glick, J. Launsbach, Philip Klewansky, Samuel Stofsky, and B. Port.[5] Mr. Harry Singer served for many years as its field secretary.

There were other business associations in Brownsville—the Belmont Avenue Merchants Association, of which David Gumberg was president for many years and Sam Weiss, vice-president, the Sutter Avenue Merchants Association, and the Rockaway Avenue Merchants Association.

Betsy Head Playground

The Board of Trade took an active interest in obtaining the Betsy Head Playground, whose erection in Brownsville demonstrates the great public spirit displayed by the community. A Mrs. Betsy Head of Islip, Long Island, had bequeathed a considerable sum of money for the establishment of a recreation center where it would do the most good. By 1913, some four years following her death, the Betsy Head Fund, which was held by the city, amounted to $187,746. Each of the five boroughs had been trying to obtain the funds for a playground in its own section. After protracted consideration, the Public Recreation Commission, which had the matter in charge, decided in favor of Brownsville and left to its influential citizens the selection of the site.

Brownsville won the coveted prize because of its tremendous public spirit. It was the only district whose people offered to bear a portion of the cost. At a mass meeting held on November 14, 1912, in the Stone Avenue Talmud Torah, it was decided that the cost of purchasing the site be borne by the Brownsville citizens by assessment on the property adjoining the playground in an amount not to exceed ten dollars a lot. As might be expected, not all concurred. There was objection to the levy on the part of some of the property owners. The opponents of a local assessment insisted that the city should pay for the land, and they arranged their own mass meeting. To counteract this anti-playground move and to make propaganda for the cause, a mass meeting was held at the Hebrew Educational Society, under the auspices of the Playground Advisory Committee. It was addressed by General W. Wingate, former Alderman Alex S. Drescher, Dr. Charles S. Bernheimer of the Hebrew Educational Society, Dr. Michael A. Cohn, and Simon Kugel.

In addition to mass meetings, fifteen thousand signatures were obtained from residents of the neighborhood, urging the Board of Estimate to establish the proposed playground. A committee of three hundred people was then appointed under the leadership of Simon H. Kugel, Dr. Charles S. Bernheimer, Jacob Wax, Editor of the Brownsville Post, Alexander Drescher, and others for the purpose of impressing on the Board of Estimates the need for such a playground. A committee of three taxpayers, named by the Brownsville Board of Trade, was appointed to pick a committee of ten, to be known as the Brownsville Playground Advisory Committee, to represent the district and to recommend to the Commission a site for the playground. This Committee consisted of George Tonkonogy, Dr. Charles S. Bernheimer, Jacob Goell, William Roth, Dr. Michael Cohn, Rabbi S. Finkelstein, Dr. Saul Badanes, Simon Kugel, and Alexander S. Drescher. Several sites were suggested, but for a time the committee could not agree. However, when the Recreation Commission notified the members that if they did not agree at once Brownsville would lose the playground, personal desires were submerged, and a unanimous report was rendered.

The committee recommended the acquisition of four blocks

bounded by Blake, Hopkinson and Dumont Avenues, and Bristol Street, as a playground for mothers and children, and the three blocks bounded by Livonia, Hopkinson, and Dumont avenues and Douglas Street (Strauss) as an athletic field for baseball and football. The total area encompassed 10.41 acres.

The entire Betsy Head Fund was used to convert the property into one of the finest playgrounds in the country, at a cost estimated to be about $500,000. At the ground breaking ceremony which took place on October 14, 1914, Commissioner McAvery congratulated the district upon having secured the playground. "The victory was an earned one, hard fought for."

The playground was dedicated in 1915. In 1916 Mrs. Issac R. Rice presented, in memory of her husband, the memorial gate and fountain in the main entrance known as the Isaac L. Rice Memorial. The central figure of the fountain is a javelin thrower in action, by the sculptor Louis St. Laune.

The Brownsville Neighborhood Health and Welfare Council

Various committees, assemblies of civic minded residents, and communal organizations were organized from time to time in Brownsville, East New York, and New Lots, but few lasted over a considerable period of time. To have any important effect on a community, an organization needs time and continuity of leadership. This was achieved in a large measure by the Brownsville Neighborhood Health and Welfare Council. For a quarter of a century it was the voice of Brownsville calling for more active participation by the citizens of the community in public affairs.

Through the efforts of Dr. Alter F. Landesman, executive director of the Hebrew Educational Society, the Brownsville Neighborhood Council was initiated on May 14, 1938. It was brought to function on November 14, 1938, by representatives of some twenty civic associations in Brownsville and a number of individuals who headed social and business organizations affecting community welfare. In 1954 it merged with the Brownsville Health Council to form the Brownsville Neighborhood Health and Welfare Council. It continued to meet in the Hebrew Educational Society throughout its existence, being the oldest council in the city with a volunteer staff. It was strongest in the forties and early fifties, but lost some of its effectiveness with the change of neighborhood and leadership.

The first effort of the council was to effect a recognition by the community and the responsible civic authorities of the imperative needs of a low-rent housing project in Brownsville. The Housing Committee, under the leadership of its chairman, Milton Goell, arranged housing exhibits, lectures, discussions, and mass meetings, and contacted various housing authorities and public officials on behalf of a better housing program for our community. In 1940 Goell's study, entitled "Brownsville Must Have Public Housing," was published under the auspices of the Brooklyn Committee for Better Housing and the Brownsville Neighborhood Council, with a foreword by Rev. John Howard Melish, chairman, Brooklyn Committee for Better Housing, and an Introduction by Alter F. Landesman, president of the Neighborhood Council. As a result of its efforts and those of other progressive groups and individuals, a housing project was obtained for Brownsville. In 1942 the Council began a campaign for a health center in Brownsville. The Council's case for a new health center building was prepared by Milton Goell in a brochure entitled "For Better Health in Brownsville." These efforts helped to obtain the Brownsville Health Center on Bristol Street.

In 1944 Mr. Goell prepared a third brochure, "The Post-War Plan for Brownsville," in which he set forth the needs and proposed improvements in Brownsville. Nurseries, an enclosed market, a new post office, improved transit facilities, new parks, new playgrounds, new and rehabilitated housing, a recreation center, a social service center—these are among the projects dealt with in this study. His plan was presented at a public meeting held at the Hebrew Educational Society on February 8, 1945. The Honorable Louis H. Pink, who had written the foreword to this brochure, gave the introductory address, and Rabbi Landesman, honorary president of the Council, spoke about the function of the Neighborhood Council. Mrs. Sadie Doroshkin was chairman. In

1951, jointly with the East New York Dispensary, the Council published the fourth brochure by Mr. Goell entitled, "East New York Must Have Public Housing."

In addition to these activities, the Brownsville Neighborhood Health and Welfare Council was involved in a host of other problems. It succeeded in obtaining neighborhood improvements, and in calling attention to the need for many others. It employed various media to reach the ears of the residents of the community and of the civic authorities—Town Hall meetings, conferences, exhibitions, seminars and lectures, parades, newspaper articles, and the like. It spent much time and energy to improve sanitation, and to campaign against rat infestation. It espoused the building of an enclosed market on Belmont Avenue and the removal of the open pushcarts, but without success. It sponsored good-will dinners, sent speakers to Albany and to budget hearings of the Board of Estimates in support of the construction of new schools and school budget needs. It made surveys to determine the need for child-care centers, helped finance a part-time staff in the Brownsville Project Recreation Center, and campaigned for the reconstruction of Betsy Head Park. It participated in numerous projects in cooperation with the Brooklyn Council for Social Planning, the Brownsville Mental Health Clinic, the School Council, and various city agencies such as the City Youth Board, the Board of Education, and the Park Department, among others.

During the quarter-century of its existence, the Neighborhood Council was headed by the following presidents: Dr. Alter F. Landesman, who served as the first president and then as an honorary president; Milton Goell, Reuben Bennett, and Irving Tabb. They were assisted by a group of civic-minded citizens.[6]

In 1948 a series of mental health lectures—"Forums for Better Living"—was held at the Thomas Jefferson High School. Out of this program arose a permanent service in 1949, the East Brooklyn Mental Health Clinic, which was in part operated and supported by the citizens of Brownsville in cooperation with the Brownsville Neighborhood Health and Welfare Council. Louis Askwyth and Dr. Wolfson headed the group, and Anne R. Brodsky was honorary secretary. The Clinic was housed in the present District

Health Center building at 259 Bristol Street, which was opened on
June 14, 1949.

*Vital Statistics and Social Data—The Growth of the General
and Jewish Population*

The population of Brownsville increased rapidly between 1900
and 1925, when it reached its peak.[7] After 1930 it began to
decline. The downward movement was slight during the depression years. There was a much sharper decrease during the war and
postwar period. As incomes rose and newer homes were constructed in more spacious and more pleasant neighborhoods in
Brooklyn, many residents moved out. At first they moved to the
adjoining sections—East New York, New Lots, Eastern Parkway
and Crown Heights. Later they gravitated to East Flatbush,
Flatbush, and to other neighborhoods, and in recent years to
Canarsie, Mill Basin, and the suburbs in Long Island and
Westchester.[8]

Due to the disparate conceptions of Brownsville's geographical
limits, it is difficult to establish reliable comparative statistical
data. The figures must always be checked against the boundaries of
the area they include. Brownsville had come to mean more often a
state of mind than a specific geographic area. There is no real
natural dividing line between Brownsville, Eastern Parkway, and
East Flatbush. So far as the Jewish population is concerned,
Brownsville, East New York, and New Lots are substantially
alike.

For the period prior to 1910, the state and federal census figures
for Ward 26 denote the total population for the area formerly
known as the town of New Lots (which included the New Lots,
Cypress Hills, East New York and Brownsville sections). The total
population of the ward was 29,505 in 1890, 66,086 in 1900, and
177,605 in 1910. The Jewish population increased during these
years from 4,000 in 1892 to about 50,000 in 1905.

Other statistical units for the period after 1910, when the ward
was divided, must be employed. After 1930 the Department of
Health of the City of New York divided the city into a number of
health centers, each based on a population of some 300,000. As

defined by the New York Health Department, the Brownsville
Health District comprises, besides Brownsville proper, East New
York and Canarsie. The boundaries it designates for Brownsville
are Van Sinderen Avenue, East; East 91st Street, Clarkson and
Remsen Avenue, West; East New York Avenue, North; Hegeman,
Linden Boulevard and Avenue A, South.

Dr. Alexander Dushkin, in his study of the Jewish population of
New York City, based on his computation of Jewish children
absent from public elementary school on Yom Kippur, 1914,
estimated the Jewish population of the Brownsville District to be
102,000, and of the East New York-New Lots District 108,000
Jews. His boundaries for Brownsville approximate those adopted
by the Brownsville Health District.

In 1916 Brownsville and East New York (New Lots) constituted one of the largest Jewish sections in the entire city, exceeded
in population only by the Lower East Side. The population of
Brownsville proper, which numbered 146,813, was only a few
thousand less than Harlem's 149,091, which ranked next to the
East Side's 353,493. Besides, there were 78,677 Jews in the New
Lots-East New York area, making a total of 225,490 Jews for the
entire area, second only to the number of Jews in the Lower East
Side. In 1925 the Jewish population in Brownsville and New Lots
increased to 285,521—169,906 in Brownsville, and 115,615 in East
New York (New Lots). This increase made it the largest
concentration of Jewish population in the city, exceeding the East
Side's 264,178, Tremont's 121,129, Harlem's 114,869, and Williamsburgh's 104,905.

During the decade between 1916 and 1925 Brooklyn sup-
planted Manhattan as the center of Jewish population, containing
45.6 per cent of the total New York Jewish population. It
numbered 568,000 Jews in 1916, and 800,000—an increase of
40.07 per cent—in 1925. Brownsville was the most populous
Jewish section in Brooklyn both in 1916 and in 1925. Williamsburgh was second in size in 1916, but in 1925 New Lots
superseded it. In 1916 Brownsville, New Lots, and Williamsburgh
had more than 61 per cent of Brooklyn's Jewish population, but in
1925 the proportion of Jews decreased to 48.7 per cent.

Dr. Max Halpert, in his study of Brownsville—which includes

not only Brownsville proper, but also portions of East New York and New Lots—estimates, on the basis of sample studies of individuals and families according to the State Census figures of 1905 and 1925, that the Jewish population of Brownsville numbered 49,280 Jews in 1905, or 80 per cent of a total population of 61,687, and 250,340 in 1925, or 82 per cent of a total population of 304,330.

Two population studies have been made in the past two decades by the Federation of Jewish Philanthropies of New York, one in 1944, and the other in 1959. In the 1944 study, Brownsville and East New York, which were combined for statistical purposes and designated as "Section M," had a Jewish population of 203,000, or 60 per cent of a total population of 337,015. The section was subdivided into five Jewish districts, or clusters.

Jewish Population

1. Highland Park (District 36)	72,000
2, 3. East New York (Districts 37, 38)	70,000
4. Upper Brownsville (District 40)	66,000
5. Lower Brownsville (District 39)	64,000

(Contiguous with Jewish concentration in north-east corner of East Flatbush.)

In the 1959 study made for the Federation of Jewish Philanthropies by C. Morris Horowitz and Lawrence J. Kaplan, East Flatbush and Brownsville had a population of 125,734 in 1950, and 95,652 in 1958. East New York-Jamaica Bay had 73,829 in 1950, and 89,557 in 1938.

Proportion of Jews to Total Population

In view of the fact that the Jews of Brownsville, like those in other densely Jewish populated neighborhoods of New York, tended to concentrate in certain blocks and form distinctive Jewish population clusters, most of the reports about Brownsville read as if the population of the area were almost entirely Jewish.

The various statistical studies indicate that the proportion of

Jews to the total population differed from census tract to census tract. Jews were more concentrated in certain blocks than in others. A detailed study by Dr. Walter Laidlow of the religious composition of the New York population for the year 1920 according to census tracts and districts, indicates that in the area he denominates as "K8," and which approximates our boundaries for Brownsville proper, there were 81,404 Jews, or about 75 per cent out of the total of 109,880. About 11 per cent—12,262, were Roman Catholics; 10 per cent—11,498, were Protestants, and about 4 per cent—4,716, were Greek Orthodox. Jews were more concentrated in the area between Sutter and Livonia, Saratoga, and Van Sinderan avenues (Census Tracts 878,910, 912,914) where they constituted 80 per cent of the population—21,778 Jews, 2,490 Roman Catholics, 1,912 Protestants, and 1,271 Greek Catholics.

In the East New York-New Lots District (K10-K10b) according to Dr. Laidlow's study, there were 77,148 Jews, constituting about 51 per cent of a total population for the entire district of 154,918. In this section lived 40,559 Protestants, 33,065 Roman Catholics, and 4,209 Greek Orthodox Catholics. Here, too, there were clusters of Jewish settlement where Jews constituted a larger percentage of the total population. In the blocks between Van Sinderan and New Jersey avenues, Belmont and Dumont avenues (Census Tracts 1,134 and 1,156) lived 14,188 Jews, or some 80 per cent of a population of some 17,679.[8]

According to the Federal Census of 1930, many countries were represented as birthplaces of the residents of the district. The predominant number, 221,857, or 74.5 per cent of the foreign white stock (most of whom were Jews) came from Eastern Europe, Russia, Poland, Austria, Hungary, and Roumania. Ten per cent—29,928—came from Italy. The 7,478 Negroes constituted 2.5 per cent of the total population of 298,122.

Age Distribution

All the studies of the age distribution of the Jewish population indicate that the Jewish population was definitely younger than the total population of New York. The Jews who first moved into Brownsville were young people. In 1892 almost 93 per cent of the Jewish group were under 40 years of age, and 37.4 per cent were infants and children under 10 years of age. Dr. Max Halpert, in his sample study of 12,517 Jews in Brownsville in the 1925 State Census, found 81.2 per cent to be under 44 years of age as compared to 83.15 per cent found for that age group in 1925 by the Jewish Communal Survey for all of New York's Jewish population. He found as many as 50 per cent under 20 years of age, as compared to 40.69 per cent for that age group in the Jewish Communal Survey, and 38.77 per cent estimated for the entire United States white population in 1923.

Sex Ratios

While Jewish immigration to the United States between 1899 and 1910 was essentially a family movement, the number of males nevertheless exceeded the number of females. Of the 1,074,442 Jews who emigrated during these years, 607,882, or 56.6 per cent were males, and 466,620, or 43.4 per cent were females. In time the situation normalized, and the ratio was about equal. Dr. Julius B. Maller, in his study of 407,223 people in 15 Health Areas predominately Jewish in 1930, found 203,964 males, 203,259 females—50.09 and 49.91 per cent as against 50.11 and 49.89 per cent for the entire city. He found slightly more females in Brooklyn. Dr. Max Halpert's sample study of 1925 of 12,517 Jewish individuals, reported 6,434 males, and 6,083 females (51.4 per cent and 48.6 per cent), although he found some variations within the various age groups.

Size of Families

The average size of the family in 1892 was 5 persons, slightly larger than the 4.70 per cent persons in the average family for the entire Ward 26 in 1890. Dr. Max Halpert's study of 12,570 Jews in the 1925 State Census also indicated that the most common family consisted of 5 persons; there were 554 such families out of a total of 2,106 families with 6,982 children. He found a considerable number of families with a larger number of children—114 with 6 children, 51 with 7 children, and 17 with 8 children. Twenty-one families had 9, 3 had 10, and 2 had 12 children. Horowitz and Kaplan, in their 1959 study found an average of 3 to 4 person families. The Brooklyn average was 3.71 in 1940, and 3.36 in 1950.

Birth Rate

The study of the Bureau of Jewish Research found that the Jewish birth rate in 1925 was lower in Brooklyn than for the general population—18 per thousand for the Jewish population as compared with 22.62 per thousand for the general population of Brooklyn. Dr. Julius B. Maller, in his study in 1930 of 15 Health Areas of which 10 were in Brooklyn, also found the birth rate somewhat lower in the Jewish areas—16.9 in the Jewish as against 17.5 in the others. The birth rate for all of Brownsville, including both the Jewish and nonJewish population for 1930, was 18.7 per thousand as against a borough rate of 19.3.

The Health Status of the Jews

Despite the hard conditions under which the Jews in Brownsville had to live in the first decades of this century, they were a healthy lot—certainly as healthy as any other group.

In 1929 the Brownsville Health District in Brooklyn had the lowest mortality rates of the entire City of New York—7.6 per 1,000 population.[9] In 1930 its lower death rate of 7.4 per 1,000 was only matched by the Williamsbridge-Westchester District in the Bronx. This was a little less than the finding of the Jewish death rate for all of New York by the Jewish Communal Survey of 1925. According to its study, the Jewish death rate in 1925 was 7.91 per 1,000 of population as compared with New York City's rate of 11.7 per 1,000. It explained this lower rate partly on the basis of the youth of New York Jews.

Dr. Julius B. Maller in his study of 15 Health Areas, predominately Jewish, found the Jewish areas to be safer places to live. The ratio of homicide was only one half as high as for the city (0.3 versus 0.6 per 10,000); accidents occurred one half as frequently (3.5 versus 7.0 per 10,000), and suicide was slightly less (1.7 to 2 per 10,000 in the city).

Occupational and Industrial Classification—Economic Status

Since Brownsville was only a section of a large community, it is difficult to make any comparisons with other communities, or to determine the economic status. Dr. Julius Maller, in his study of Jewish neighborhoods in New York City in 1930, found that in economic status, as revealed by home values and rental, the Jewish areas were identical with the rest of New York.

What stands out in the various studies that have been made concerning the economic status of the section is the fact that Brownsville continued to be populated through the years by a predominantly wage-earning class. It should not be thought of as a place of abject proverty. It had its wealthy and middle classes, but most of those who continued to reside there belonged to the lower economic group.

In a sample study made by Dr. Halpert of the occupations of 459 families living in Brownsville in 1905, he found that a large number, 57 per cent (a lesser proportion than the 70 per cent we found in 1892) worked in the needle trades. The others were to be found scattered in small numbers among the various skilled and unskilled trades, professions, shops, and businesses.

Those of the second generation who continued to reside in Brownsville in 1905 continued substantially to work in the same occupations as their parents, particularly in the skilled crafts. They were also to be found as the first generation in the needle trades. There was some upward mobility among them, some of them entering clerical and sales positions, while some of them were beginning to find employment in new occupations such as plumbing, glazing, driving, jewelry making, printing, and other crafts.

In the subsequent years, Brownsville continued to be the home of a large Jewish working class. Aside from the needle trades, many engaged in the building and construction industry as carpenters, bricklayers, plasterers, roofers, and glaziers. The electric trades, plumbing, printing, clock- and watch-making, and the jewelry business also attracted considerable numbers. The native-born tended to veer away from their parents' occupations. They were hardly to be found in the tailoring and garment-making trades; these were left mostly to the foreign-born. The native-born, however, were found in large numbers in the needle trades and other industries working as salesmen, clerks, book-keepers, shipping clerks, mail clerks, messengers, and drivers. The native-born also entered the newer crafts, particularly the mechanical crafts, as they opened up. In a sample study of 3,660 individuals in Brownsville based on the 1925 State Census, Halpert found 59 per cent in the crafts and operators category, 21.2 per cent in clerical and sales, 17.1 per cent in professional and managerial, and 2.7 per cent in the private household and laborers category.

There was a large number of small businesses. Although working longer hours, and perhaps earning not much more than the wage worker or salaried employee, it represented to many an economic advance and an improvement over the sweatshop conditions into which many of the older immigrants had been initiated. As numbers of the population succeeded in moving upward economically, or entered the professional fields and found positions elsewhere, they moved out of Brownsville. New waves of arriving immigrants became workers or small shopkeepers at first, like the Jewish immigrants before them, and many of them settled in the low-rent area of Brownsville, replacing those who had moved out of the working class and were seeking newer homes in other sections.

Radical and Social Reform Movements

V

At the turn of the century, when Brownsville began to teem with thousands of newly-arrived immigrants from Russia, Poland, and other East-European countries, a number of Jewish intellectuals came to live in Brownsville. It was a period of social unrest among people everywhere. Various groups and movements were founded purposing to achieve social reforms through a reorganization of the economic, political, and religious institutions. There was also unrest among women, who felt they had been dislodged from a definite niche in the social fabric of modern civilization. This gave rise to a feminist movement, which advocated woman suffrage, the right to birth control, and other reforms.

Some of the intellectuals, Socialists, and Anarchists who settled in Brownsville joined the radical and social reform movements. They began to awaken the masses to the deplorable social and economic conditions under which they lived, and sought to inculcate them with ideas of how to improve the social order. On every available platform, on street corners, and in the lecture hall, these champions discussed and debated their concepts of the good society of social justice, of humanitarianism, and brotherhood.

A strong Socialist movement was fostered in Brownsville, and from 1917 to 1919 the Socialists controlled the political situation. Radical groups sprang up from time to time which differed widely in ideology and program for action. In the public mind, however, their adherents were all lumped together and referred to as Anarchists or "Reds," and Brownsville became known for a time as the "Red District."

August Claessens, well known Socialist leader, had this to say after traveling throughout the land: "Brownsville had the liveliest crowd. Here was built that labor and Socialist beehive— the Brownsville Labor Lyceum. Here was planted the cooperative bakery. . . . Here, the now-noted impressario, Sol Hurok, got his start. For a couple of years Harry Kritzer managed a very successful forum in the Academy of Music, and thousands of persons flocked to listen to prominent debates and lectures. During the 1917 campaign, hundreds of street meetings were held. Pitkin Avenue, Brownsville's Great White Way, was especially the thoroughfare to a new America for the thousands and thousands of young men and women attending these great Socialist meetings." [1]

Brownsville was only a tributary of the main stream of social idealism whose source was to be found in the Lower East Side, where a cosmopolitan group of social thinkers flourished. On the East Side, large numbers of American and English social reformers converged, conscious of a new epoch. Among them were the German Marxists, who formed the backbone of the Socialist Party, Russian revolutionaries, political refugees from various lands, victims of injustice here and abroad, Jewish intellectuals who had fled Russia, non-conformists, visionaries, and prophets harboring dreams of all kinds of Utopias.[2]

The East Side was also the arena for the vast group of Jewish intellectuals who for two generations exerted a profound influence on the masses of Jewish immigrants. They not only wrote and lectured, but were also frequently seen and heard in other immigrant settlements like Brownsville. These intellectuals in-

cluded Abraham Cahan, Dr. Chaim Zhitlowsky, Dr. Isaac A.
Hourwich, Dr. C. Spivack, Morris Hillquit, Paul Kaplan, Dr. B.
Morrison, Emma Goldman, Ephraim and Meyer London, Ben-
jamin Feigenbaum, Michael Zametkin, Leon Kobrin, Morris
Rosenfeld, Dr. H. Zolotrow, Dr. Max Girsdansky, and Alexander
Harkavy.

Jewish radicalism was derivative. As Professor Maurice G.
Hindus has pointed out, it had its origin not in Jewish but in non-
Jewish associations. It drew its inspiration from German, Russian,
French, and other foreign sources. The leaders of these movements
were mostly non-Jews.[3] "The fact that Marx and LaSalle were
Jews does not invalidate this statement. They were Jews only by
birth. Intellectually, they lived in a world that was not only alien
to Jewish thought, but which Jews at that time regarded as hostile
to Judaism. Marx and LaSalle were steeped in Western, that is,
modern Gentile culture. Had they followed the traditions of their
ancestors and devoted themselves to the study of Jewish lore and
Jewish learning, they might have become famous Rabbis but not
social philosophers, economists, leaders of the proletariat."

Once the Jewish intellectual was wooed into radical thought, he
plunged into the revolutionary movements with an unquenchable
enthusiasm. "It must be owned," said Professor Hindus, "that the
heritages he (the Jew) brought with him from the Jewish world
facilitated his process of acclimatization and his rise to a position of
prominence and leadership."

A number of reasons may be invoked to explain this phenomenon. First, many of the Hebraic beliefs, traditions, and ideals
harmonized with the purposes and methods of the radicals. Both
exalted the oppressed and championed the underdog; both
scorned the wrong-doer and espoused human dignity; both
preached social justice, kindness, and mercy. Secondly, as the son
of an oppressed people that suffered persecution, injustices,
discriminations, the Jew was more susceptible to movements
which promised to establish a cooperative commonwealth with
equality for all. Finally, being of an intellectual bent of mind,
with a long tradition of a love for knowledge and mental
stimulation, the Jew found the radical groups, with their debates

and discussions, and their quests for innovation, particularly intriguing.

The radicals and Socialists stirred a counter effort on the part of many leaders and humanitarians to present what they regarded as a more positive and balanced view. Institutions and movements were initiated for the purpose of bridging the widening gap between the classes in American cities. One recalls the great teachers—Edward King, Thomas Davidson, Myra Kelly; the Ethical Culturists—Felix Adler, Stanton Coit, Dr. David Muzzey; the settlement houses and their leaders, Lillian Wald, Mary Simkhovitch, Charles Stover, Dr. David Blaustein, Isaac Spectorsky; journalists like John Swinton, Hutchins Hapgood, Jacob Riis. They postulated the hypothesis that the East Side and Brownsville were *sui generis* and not quite typical of America; it was, rather, what the stream of newcomers from the Old World had helped to make them. Many joined the ranks of evolutionary Socialists. The socialism of this group, according to Professor Morris R. Cohen, was a "protest against economic conditions which denied to so many of us, and to our less fortunate brothers and sisters access to the riches of the spirit. . . . And so our socialist activity, though often cast in Marx's materialistic terms, was directed primarily to the conquest and democratization of the things of the spirit." [4]

There was, however, a considerable group who, fed by the negative, critical, and pessimistic literature of the middle-nineteenth-century, were persuaded that social and economic improvement could be achieved only by the introduction of a new social order. The devastating results of this rebellion against all political, social, and religious systems, and its negative effect on the development of Jewish life in this country are felt to this day.

"The world that we faced on the East Side at the turn of the century presented a series of heartbreaking dilemmas," wrote Professor Morris Raphael Cohen, ". . . and having been immersed in the literature of science, we called upon the old religion to justify itself on the basis of modern science and culture. But the old generation was not in a position to say how this could be done.

. . . Because no distinction was drawn between ritual and religious conviction and feelings, the very word 'religion' came to be discredited by many liberal people who, whatever might be said about their errors, at least attempted to think for themselves."

The development of religious sentiment was stunted among the young, and cynicism or pessimism came often to displace the natural idealism of youth.

"However we resolved this dilemma," continues Professor Cohen, "and whatever concessions we made to the old ritual, the loss of the religious faiths which had sustained our parents through so many generations of suffering left a void in our lives which we tried with every fiber of our beings to fill in one way or another. All our organizations and circles were attempts to fill this void. None of these attempts amounted to very much in the long run until the advent among us of a wandering Scottish philosopher who had been the spiritual inspiration, in England . . . [of] the Fabian Society, as well as one of the founders of the Aristotelian Society, and who was destined to give many of us on the East Side the same kind of inspiration. . . ." [5]

To Morris R. Cohen and to hundreds of others it was the Scottish philosopher, Professor Thomas Davidson, who brought meaning and inspiration. To hundreds of sweatshop workers, uprooted from their old environment and rich Jewish life, it was the socialist message as it was presented to them that filled the void. They embraced it with the same piety they and their parents formerly had felt in the performance of their devotional practices.

A group of intellectuals, falling under the spell of this East-Side radical movement, undertook to spread their doctrines in Brownsville. These intellectuals consisted at first of a number of professional people—Dr. Michael Cohn, a physician; Dr. N. J. Coyne, a dentist; Dr. Rosenson, a physician from Russia, and Dr. I. Lack, a student of dentistry.

Dr. Simon Frucht, who became a well known heart specialist and has practiced medicine in Brownsville for many years, moved to Brownsville. In his early youth he had lived on the East Side and belonged, with Professor M. R. Cohen and others, to the Marx

Circle, which was later discontinued. When Dr. Frucht came to Brownsville he organized with others a branch of the Thomas Davidson Society, which met in the Hebrew Educational Society Building on Pitkin and Watkin Streets. Albert Halpern and the barbers Bernard and Swenton were also very active. Every week quarters were collected in the community to help pay for lecturers. The first speakers brought there were Abraham A. Cahan, B. Feigenbaum, and M. Zametkin.

In the late 80's and early 90's, Anarchism, with its negation of all laws of social progress, had a peculiar fascination that attracted many adherents. These outstripped the Socialists in numbers and influence.[6] Many of the Socialists who became prominent at a later period began as Anarchists. Anarchism is diametrically opposed to Socialism, advocating in its purest form the complete emancipation of the individual from society. Socialism, on the other hand, implies the supremacy of the collective, social body over the individual. The Anarchist denies the gradual evolutionary course of societal development. A few individuals ready to sacrifice themselves for the welfare of the oppressed population can bring about the social revolution. All great revolutions and all public benefits have been forced upon mankind by the dedicated minority. Political actions are impotent. The Anarchist believes in the weapons of the "propaganda of the word," and "propaganda of the *deed.*"

Pierre Joseph Proudhon was the first thinker to formulate this ideology, later modified and popularized by Michael Bakounin. In the 90's its chief proponents were Prince Kropotkin of Russia and Johann Most, a native of Germany, who more than any other leader influenced the American anarchist movement. This movement enjoyed considerable strength in Chicago and Philadelphia. After the Haymarket tragedy had exploded the folly of men "who consider dynamite bombs as the best means of agitation," the prestige of the anarchist movement declined, and the Socialist Labor Party which had fought it gained the ascendency. Well-known leaders of the anarchist movement, like Emma Goldman and Alexander Berkman, vigorously spread its doctrines.

Leon Kobrin, the Yiddish writer and dramatist, describes in his autobiography the profound influence of the anarchist and radical movements on the young immigrants.[7] Particularly aggressive in their campaign against religion, the Anarchists mocked it with their Yom Kippur balls and their "Red Pesachs," when they circulated leaflets parodying the solemn holiday prayers with revolutionary slogans. It is hard to imagine how much antagonism and heartache this aroused among vast masses of the Jewish Community.

In September, 1890 the New York Anarchists arranged a Yom Kippur Ball at the Lyceum in Brooklyn. Tickets of admission read: "Grand Yom Zom Kippur Ball with theatre arranged with the consent of all new Rabbis of liberty Kol Nydre Night and Day in the Year 5611, after the invention of the Jewish idols, and 1890, after the birth of the false Messiah, in the Brooklyn Labor Lyceum, 61-67 Myrtle Street, Brooklyn. The Kol Nidre will be offered by Johann Most. Music, dancing, buffet, Marseillaise, and other hymns against Satan." The cellar of the Lyceum was stocked with beer, bread, bologna, ham, cheese, and fruit for the lunch counter.

Prominent Jews of Brooklyn were outraged, and attempted to stop the affair. When the courts refused to intervene, they petitioned Mayor Chapin to forbid the meeting on the grounds that it would lead to disturbance and riots. The Mayor acquiesced and ordered the police to prevent the meeting and disperse the people without opening the hall. For his action Mayor Chapin was severely criticized. *The New York Sun* carried the following editorial on September 25, 1890: "The Constitution of the United States guarantees the freedom of speech and the right of the people peacefully to assemble. The Constitution of the State of New York guarantees that right. Until the right of free speech has been abused, no crime has been committed. No matter how unpleasant or violent or vile is the programme announced for a public meeting—the time for the police to interfere is when the law is broken, not before.

"The suppression of the meeting of the infidel and anarchist Jews of Brooklyn by the police of that city, under verbal orders from Mayor Chapin, after the courts refused to prevent the meeting by injunction was an extraordinary proceeding.

"To close the doors of their hall, and the mouths of their

speakers before any law had been broken was a colossal blunder, no matter how good the intentions of the authorities responsible for the order of the police." [8]

Many advocates of Anarchism fought for its philosophy which negated "the cursed trinity—religion, state, and capitalism." The anarchist papers, such as the *"Freie Arbeiter Stimme,"* and Johann Most's *"Freiehit,"* were read devoutly. The radicals displayed in their homes the pictures of their heroes—Kropotkin, Marx, and others. Some named their children after their favorites, such as Bakounin or Engel, and others even renamed themselves after their favorite hero or philosopher, such as Herbert Spencer.

Dr. Michael Cohn

One of the most prominent radicals of Brownsville was Dr. Michael Cohn, a popular physician and a leader in the Anarchist movement.[9] Dr. Cohn was a dynamic supporter, lecturer, writer and fiery agitator on behalf of the anarchist movement for a half century. Born in a typical religious home in December, 1867, in the town of Makov, in the province of Lomze, he received the religious education common at that time. His father was a carpenter who later went into the forestry business. At the age of twenty-one, Dr. Cohn escaped from Russia which also meant to him an escape from military service, from strict parental control, from a strict religious life, and other restraints. In America he fell into a radical circle, and in order to support himself, he became a tailor, working in one of the shops by day and studying by night. He studied medicine in the College of Physicians and Surgeons of Baltimore, Maryland, and was graduated in 1893.

An Anarchist by conviction, and gifted with fluency of speech, he devoted his free time to lecturing and addressing gatherings. This brought him into conflict with Orthodox Jews in Baltimore. On September 10, 1890, prior to the Succoth holiday, he debated with Orthodox representatives in Baltimore on the subject, "Are religion and socialism compatible?"

The four Orthodox speakers presented their case without any interruption. When Michael Cohn arose, the audience became disorderly. Someone screamed "Fire!" and the meeting dissolved.

Cohn got into difficulties with the police in Baltimore, and for almost two days was confined in jail. With his fiery temperament and fluency of pen, he wrote a dozen letters entitled "Letters from Prison to the London *Arbeiter Friend*." Frumkin, a naïve youth at that time, comments in his memoirs on the profound impression these epistles made on him. Reading Cohn's attacks on the capitalist order and his tirades against the evils of the social order, it never occurred to him, he states, to ask, "What does it all have to do with the Baltimore prison where he was confined only a matter of hours?"

In time, Frumkin came to understand that the prison was only a foil for the impulsive and impetuous anarchist to write a series of propaganda articles.

Cohn married a girl who was even a greater idealist than himself—Anne Netter, whose father had a grocery store at 16 Suffolk Street. Netter's home behind the little grocery store became, according to Emma Goldman, "the oasis for the radical element, an intellectual center," and many assembled there "to make evenings real intellectual feasts." From her early childhood, Anne became part of the group, and captivated the hearts of those who frequented her father's home. Edelstadt, the editor of the *Freie Arbeiter Stimme,* spoke of her as the "little good Netter."

The Cohns moved to Brownsville and established a home and office on Stone Avenue, where he soon became a successful and popular doctor. Dr. Michael Cohn was a man of contrasts, unlike the stereotype of an anarchist. There was the practical man who not only engaged in the practice of his profession, but also participated in the Brownsville real estate boom. He was reputed to have been the first to own an automobile in Brownsville. He was more than a doctrinaire anarchist. He responded warmly to all appeals of social and philanthropic organizations. He was interested in promoting public improvements, and as a member of the first Board of Directors of the Hebrew Educational Society, he served for a time as chairman of the House Committee. He took an interest in the Home for the Aged, in various hospitals, and other social and eleemosynary endeavors.

There was also the unswerving idealist in him. His whole being focused on the Anarchist doctrines. At the meetings of his group, or when visiting the cafes in the East Side, he became a different person—the idealist, the agitator, the propagandist.

He spent much time, effort, and money, to sustain the *Freie Arbeiter Stimme*. On his trips abroad he took a lively interest in the international anarchist movement. In 1900 he sent reports from Europe about the Congress that was being planned in Paris. In 1926 he became treasurer of the Rudolph Rocker Committee that was interested in publishing Rocker's works. Rudolph Rocker was a German labor leader who was very influential in radical circles at the beginning of the century. At the Kropotkin Memorial Meeting held in the Manhattan Opera House, he was one of the principal speakers. He continued to lecture on anarchism throughout his life.

In 1927 Dr. Cohn became absorbed in the movement to save Sacco and Vanzetti. He published a pamphlet in English on the case, and spent several weeks in Boston participating in demonstrations and protest meetings.

In 1931 he was elected secretary of the Anarchist Federation, and worked very hard carrying on a large correspondence, calling meetings, and laboring to keep the periodical alive. He disregarded criticism that he was a "capitalist far removed from the labor movement," and was often accused of not contributing sufficiently to the cause in accordance with his means. He published books and articles in English and Yiddish. He wrote articles in Yiddish on current problems for the *Freie Arbeiter Stimme,* the *Zukunft,* and *The Forward.* There was always the aura of the agitator and the propagandist about him in whatever he did.

After he retired, he went to live in Loyola, San Diego, California. On July 10, 1939, at the age of seventy-one he suddenly died of a heart attack. According to Frumkin's Memoirs, on which our account is largely based, Cohn reflected in his personality more than any other Jewish anarchist the development of the anarchist movement in the United States.

Emma Goldman, the famous anarchist, a native of Kovna,

Russia, who came to New York in 1889 at the age of twenty, frequently came to Brownsville to deliver lectures. Michael and Anne Cohn were her "dear comrades," who "were in the lead with large sums of money" on behalf of the cause. For a time Emma Goldman and her friend, Ed Claus, even lived in Brownsville. They opened an ice-cream store not far from the race track, but after three months, gave up the losing business and returned to New York.[10]

When speakers like Abraham Cahan, B. Feigenbaum, and other radicals came to speak in Brownsville, many were horrified at their radical ideas. Parents were distressed when they discovered their children in possession of the *trefa* books or periodicals. They sought to combat this "pernicious evil" in every possible way, including the use of force. At times it was quite dangerous for a Socialist speaker to come to Brownsville. When Feigenbaum, an antireligionist spoke, he was bombarded with cans, old shoes, and corn cobs. Abraham Cahan relates that after a long and tedious trip to Brownsville from New York to address a meeting, he was greeted by a mob of rowdies who would not let him hold the meeting. They whistled and continued to shout "Hurrah! Hurrah!" Such experiences did not, however, deter the radical groups from persisting in their activities.

A group of American-bred Socialists soon began to flourish in Brownsville.[11] The sons of two families who moved to Brownsville at the turn of the century became leaders in the movement. One of the families was that of Abraham Wolff, who moved from New York with his young son, Barnet. Mr. Abraham Wolff, at first a workingman and later a grocery-store-keeper, was a pious Jew who conducted a *Minyan* in his own home. On the family's way to America, Barnet was born in Paris, France, and was less than a year old when he was brought to New York. He was brought up in Brownsville, and received a general and Jewish education. He became active in the Socialist and labor movements, first spreading the Socialist doctrine in Brownsville, and then holding very important posts in the Jewish labor movement. In 1917-1918 he served as alderman of the City of New York, representing Brownsville. Most of his activities were, however, associated with the Workingmen's Circle, on whose National Executive Committee he served as vice-president in 1924-1925, and as treasurer in 1930. For almost ten years he was manager of the Sanitarium for Consumptives in Liberty, New York. He distinguished himself as a speaker and as an organizer, and was a delegate at many Socialist and Workingmen Circle conventions. "Barney," as he was affectionately known, died on August 15, 1944, at the age of sixty-five, leaving behind him a fine family of three sons and a daughter who have done well in the educational and professional fields.

Abraham Shiplacoff

The Shiplacoff family, whose son Abraham became a distinguished leader of the socialist and labor movements in this country, moved to Brownsville from Woodbine, New Jersey, the Jewish agricultural settlement.[12] Abraham Shiplacoff was born December 13, 1877, in Chernigov, Russia, and at the age of twelve came with his parents to the United States. He began to work in a tailoring shop, participating in the organization of the union and assisting in strikes. He worked by day and attended school by night. In 1905 he was graduated as a teacher from the State Normal and Training School for Teachers of New York. As a socialist, he did not find it easy to get a position as a teacher, and for several years he went from one job to another. In 1913 the editor of *The Forward,* who knew Shiplacoff for his articles written under the pseudonym of *Der Bronzviller Melamed*— "The Brownsville Teacher," offered him the position of labor editor.

Drafted for various positions in the labor movement, Shiplacoff was respected by friend and foe alike for his idealism, self-sacrifice, and amiable character, and he became one of the most popular labor and Socialist orators in the country. Active in the political efforts of the Socialist Party, he was elected to the New York State Assembly as the "lone Socialist," in 1915, receiving more than seven thousand votes. Men and women and children paraded through the streets on that auspicious night. He was reelected with one colleague the following year, and later with nine others, and remained assemblyman until 1918. In that year he was drafted to be a candidate for congressman, but failed the election. In 1919 he was elected a New York City alderman, serving for two years.

According to Algernon Lee, Shiplacoff was one of the strongest opponents of Communism in American labor ranks, and as a member of the national executive committee of the Socialist Party, he voted to expel the Communist members. He was active in the agitation against the execution of Sacco and Vanzetti, and was a leading fighter against Nazism. He was among the few Socialists raised in this country who came close to the Yiddish masses, and among the first founders of a separate Yiddish Socialist branch of the Socialist Party, and at its beginning was its secretary. Out of it later grew the Jewish Socialist Federation—later the Jewish Socialist *Verband.*

In his relations to Zionism and Judaism, Shiplacoff followed the classic pattern of the Socialists of his time. He was violently opposed to it all. Toward the end of his life, however, he underwent a great change. His Jewish consciousness revealed itself, and he returned to his spiritual heritage. He became a devotee of Israel and of its labor movement. He served as chairman of the National Labor Committee for Israel, and made several trips to Palestine and Europe on behalf of the Jewish Labor Committee.

After a lingering illness he died on February 7, 1934, at the age of 56. At his funeral in the Forward Hall he was mourned by his wife, a daughter, two sons whose names were William Morris and Frederick Engel, and a host of friends among whom was Joseph Sprinzak, delegate of the Palestine Histadruth. His memory is perpetuated in a public playground in Brownsville. He rests in the Mt. Carmel Cemetery of the Workmen's Circle, surrounded by the graves of his co-workers.

Brownsville was represented at conventions of Jewish socialist sections of New York and vicinity which took place from the end of the century on. At the convention on July 5, 1891, New York, Philadelphia, Hartford, Boston, Newark and Brownsville were represented, as well as labor organizations. It was decided to issue the *Zukunft,* with Philip Krantz as editor, and to send Abraham Cahan as an American Jewish Labor delegate to the Congress of the Second International, which was to be held in Brussels. At that Congress Cahan proposed a resolution voicing the opposition of International Socialism to anti-Semitism. Some of the Jewish leaders among the European socialist parties, embarrassed by the resolution, privately urged Cahan to withdraw the proposal. When he persisted, a compromise resolution was adopted condemning both anti-Semitism and philo-Semitism.

Brownsville participated in the Party Days held in Philadelphia on April 17, 1892, in Newark on December 30, 1893, and in New York in 1895, as well as in other cities. In the 1893 Party Day Brownsville was represented by the Yiddish Section and Socialist Campaign Club. It was decided at this convention to delete from the agenda the subject, "Our Position on Religion," since it belonged to the decision by the entire international movement.[13]

The William Morris Educational Club

In their youth, Barnet Wolff and Abraham Shiplacoff became disseminators of the Socialist gospel in Brownsville. At first they carried on their propaganda in English among the young students. First there was the Irving Literary Society. Then Shiplacoff, while still a student at the Jamaica (Long Island) Teachers Training School, organized the William Morris Educational Club, named after the English Socialist poet who led the Socialist League in England. Through the League and its organ, *Commonweal*, the League spread education toward revolution.[14] Most of the Brownsville intellectuals belonged to this society.

In 1903 the William Morris Club became a branch of the Socialist Party, and was installed by William Konig, a German anarchist whose father was a Socialist Democrat in Germany.

The Brownsville Labor Lyceum

When the Russian immigration was bringing to America Bundists, Socialists, and other radicals who began to organize their unions and groups, Shiplacoff and Wolff decided to conduct their meetings in Yiddish, and admitted the revolutionary newcomers.

For its headquarters the labor movement took over the building called the New Palm Gardens and transformed it into a Labor Lyceum, one of the first of its kind in the East. The new venture needed a director, and Mr. Sol Hurok accepted the position. "One morning," writes Mr. Hurok, "I was routed out of bed to find fire engines banked three-deep against the building. When the firemen left there was only a shell."

Money was raised for a new building, which was constructed subsequently on Sackman Street. A four-story building, quite large for the community, was built mainly from the proceeds of collections and donations.

The Lyceum became the center of a variety of activities and served as the headquarters for all local unions and the Workingmen's Circle branches. It was indeed the seat of the Socialist movement. During the election campaigns it rallied speakers, flooded the district with political literature, arranged monster mass meetings, and was the center of Socialist propaganda. During strikes, which were quite numerous, the Labor Lyceum was the main assembly hall for the strikers. Money was raised for the relief of strikers. As there was no reserve in the treasury, when the Amalgamated Clothing Workers had their big strike, contributions for the soup kitchen were collected through a house-to-house canvas.

At no time was the Lyceum an idle place. It bulged with educational, musical, and social activities. Under the direction of the indefatigable Sol Hurok, the famous impresario who for a time was manager of the Brownsville Labor Lyceum and also managed some of the successful campaigns of the Socialist Party, more music programs were introduced by the Labor Lyceum than by any other institution. Sunday evenings were usually set aside for the "big" concerts with top-flight artists who attracted large audiences. These musicales were probably the starting point of Hurok's career.

Every day had its activity in the Labor Lyceum. There were socials and dances. Friday evenings were devoted to meetings and debates; Saturday was ball night; Sunday morning and afternoon were given over to lectures. Socialists, anarchists, and proponents of various causes would air their views in the debates and lectures in the halls of the Labor Lyceum. On Friday nights Emma Goldman, Dr. Michael Cohn—the Brownsville Anarchist—and other intriguing leaders expounded their theories of free love, the essential goodness of man, the abolition of police and jails, and the like. In those days the lecture forums were popular enough to attract large audiences to hear erudite dicussions on sophisticated subjects such as "The History of Philosophy," "From Greek to Modern Times," "Kropotkin, Spencer, and Marx," "Dickens, Zola, Flaubert, as Interpreted from the Viewpoint of the Class Struggle," and others. In those early days antedating radio and television, the forensic duel of wits, public debates, forums, and discussions became a popular form of public amusement which attracted audiences by the thousands.

To meet the growing demand, a group of popular and skilled platform speakers were developed. The Socialists boasted a number of masters in this art. Among the most gifted of these was Charles Solomon of Brownsville. A frequent subject of debate was "Socialism versus Capitalism." Professor Edwin R. Seligman of Columbia University, usually speaking on behalf of Capitalism, participated in numerous forums, repeating over and over again his side of the argument, ostensibly enjoying his role as a target for heckling by the vast audiences of young radicals.

In 1919 the Sunday afternoon forums included such speakers as Albert A. Knott, an editor of *The Nation,* who spoke on "Evolution of Rebels," Algernon Lee, Louis P. Lochner, Alexander Fichandler, Elizabeth P. Flynn. At every lecture there was also a program of vocal and instrumental music. Classes in English, History, Socialism, and international labor questions were opened in the Lyceum by the Rand School. Shiplacoff was in charge of the English class, Norman Thomas of the history class, David P. Behrenberg of the class in Socialism, and Lochner of the International Labor Movement.

A Socialist Sunday School was also maintained in the Lyceum to inculcate in the young the Socialist cardinal principle of class consciousness. The Labor Lyceum was also the scene for the celebration of holidays and special events—Labor Day, May Day, the Fourth of July, the anniversaries of the French Revolution, the Paris Commune, the Haymarket victims, the Hazelton and Colorado miners, to mention a few.

There was no room for religion or Zionism in this hotbed of radicalism. The old Zionists of Brownsville recall how they were heartened when Mr. Poliakoff, the leader of its Socialist Band, included a Hebrew melody as part of a program in one of his concerts.

The Americanization of the immigrant, the catastrophies which befell the Jewish people, all tended in time to mellow and modify the extreme position held by the Socialists. The relations between Jew and Jew, and between Jew and non-Jew, became more tolerant. There was also a change in population and in the character of the labor movement. The Labor Lyceum, no longer needed, was converted into a factory. Later it was torn down to make more room for a public park and playground, which were established by the City of New York in 1938 and named after Abraham Shiplacoff.

Margaret Sanger Opens in Brownsville the First Birth Control Clinic in America

VI

THE OPENING of the first birth control clinic in America on October 16, 1916, at 46 Amboy Street, Brownsville, was "an event of social significance," according to Margaret Sanger, founder of the movement. The avalanche of nation-wide publicity in the daily press, which followed the spectacular raid on the clinic after its first week of operation, put Brownsville once again in the limelight.

The circumstances surrounding the choice of Brownsville for her first experiment are described in great detail by Mrs. Sanger in her autobiography and in her other writings.[1] Early in 1912, Margaret Sanger tells us, she came to a sudden realization that her work as a nurse and her activities in social service were entirely palliative, and consequently futile to relieve the misery she saw all about her. To awaken the womanhood of America became her mission. She traveled to Europe in 1914 and found that birth control information had been more widely disseminated among the mass of the people in Holland than in any other country. Profoundly inspired by what she saw in Holland, she envisioned the establishment of a "chain" of clinics in every center of America, and the engagement of research specialists to bring the subject to modern scientific standards.

To create favorable public opinion for such clinics, she felt it necessary to establish a model. The selection of a place for the first of such clinics was of major importance. She considered all the difficulties—the indifference of women's organizations, the resentment of social agencies, and the opposition of the medical profession. Then there were the laws of New York State, which prohibited the dissemination of such information except through physicians, and then only for the care or prevention of disease.

While pondering on a location, five women from the Brownsville section of Brooklyn crowded into Margaret Sanger's room "seeking the secret" of birth control. Each had four or more children who had been left with neighbors. One of the women had recently recovered from an abortion which had nearly proved fatal. They told Mrs. Sanger of their suffering, the high cost of food, the meager income of their husbands (when they worked at all), and the constant worry and fear of another baby hanging over them. They felt that a clinic in their neighborhood would be a blessing.

Mrs. Sanger decided there and then to open her clinic in Brownsville. She and Fania Mindell of Chicago plodded through the streets the next day. They not only failed to receive encouragement from the social agencies in the neighborhood, but also were asked to keep out of the district. "We do not want any trouble," the agencies told them.

"I preferred a Jewish landlord," states Mrs. Sanger, one of eleven children of Michael Higgins, a stonecutter in Corning, New York. Mr. Rabinowitz, a Brownsville landlord, was the answer. He was willing to let her have Number 46 Amboy Street at fifty dollars a month. Mrs. Sanger knew that Brownsville had a large population of working-class Jews who were interested in health measures, always tolerant of new ideas, willing to listen and accept advice involving the health of mother or children. She felt that "here there would be at least no breaking of windows, no hurling of insults into our teeth; but I was scarcely prepared for the popular support, the sympathy and friendly help given us in that neighborhood from that day to this.

"The Brownsville section of Brooklyn in 1916 was a hive of futile industry—dingy, squalid—peopled with hard-working men and women, the home of poverty which was steadily growing worse in the tide of increasing responsibilities. Early every morning weary-eyed men poured from the tenement houses that crouched together as if for warmth, bound for ten or twelve hours of work. At the same time, their women rose to set in motion that ceaseless round of cooking, cleaning, and serving that barely kept the young generation alive. A fatalistic, stolid, and tragic army of New Yorkers dwelt here, most of them devout Jews or Italians, all of them energetic and ambitious, but trapped by nature's despotism. It was not a section unique in New York City; Manhattan Island was and still is dotted with such dismal villages."

To publicize the opening of the clinic, five thousand handbills in English, Yiddish, and Italian were printed, and for several days Mrs. Sanger and her friends distributed them from house to house.

On the morning of October 16, 1916, Margaret, her sister Ethel, and her friend Fania opened "the doors of the first birth control clinic in America, the first anywhere in the world except the Netherlands." Would the women come? Margaret, her sister, and Fania hardly had time to ready themselves for the official reception when Fania called, "Do come outside and look."

Halfway to the corner at least 150 women were standing in line. Margaret and her companions took from 7 to 10 in a group, explaining to them simply what contraception was, and suggesting that abortion was wrong. At 7 o'clock in the evening women were still coming. One hundred and forty passed through the doors the first day, and the others were told to come the following day. These were not people only from Brownsville. They came from Massachusetts, Pennsylvania, New Jersey and the far ends of Long Island—"Jews, Christians, Protestants and Roman Catholics."

The clinic continued without interference for 9 days, and then was raided by the vice squad. The 464 case histories were confiscated. The street was packed when the patrol wagon came rattling to the door. Masses of people spilled out to the pavement, milling around excitedly. The police made Mr. Rabinowitz, the landlord, sign eviction papers, on the grounds that Mrs. Sanger was "maintaining a public nuisance." In the Netherlands such a clinic was cited as a public benefaction.

As a result of the raid, the clinic was closed, and four separate cases were assigned for trial. Jonah J. Goldstein, then a young lawyer, offered his legal services and represented them in Court. The sensational aspects of the trials made good copy for papers. Mrs. Sanger's sister Ethel was sentenced to thirty days in the workhouse on Blackwell's Island on East River.

After Ethel had gone 103 hours without eating, Commissioner Lewis ordered her to be forcibly fed. At Mrs. Sanger's trial on January 29, 1917, at the Court of Special Sessions before Judge Freschi, 30 Brownsville mothers had been subpoenaed by the prosecution, but about 50 appeared. Margaret Sanger received a 30-days sentence. At a mass meeting at Carnegie Hall, organized for that evening by a Committee of 100, with Helen Todd as chairman, the mothers of Brownsville were given places of honor on the platform.

The fiftieth anniversary of the founding of the first Birth Control Clinic was the occasion of many observances in 1966. Few, not even Margaret Sanger herself, could have envisaged how worldwide the movement would become.

The Workers, Their Trade Unions and the Jewish Labor Movement

VII

THE LARGE proletariat that settled in Brownsville played a significant role in the development of the Jewish Labor Movement comprising the trade unions, the Socialist Party groups, the Workmen's Circle, and the Yiddish Socialist Press. Most important was the development of the Jewish trade union movement which took years of education, persistent effort, and bitter struggle to achieve. The story of these unions and their role in the general labor movement has been told by a number of labor historians.[1] We shall limit our account to those aspects which affected the Brownsville Jewish workers.

By the time Jews settled in Brownsville, some progress had already been made in the unionization of the various industries in which Jews were employed, but the unions were as yet weak and unstable. The United Hebrew Trades—*Vereinigte Yiddishe Gewerkschaften*—organized on October 9, 1888, had grown by 1890 to twenty-two unions with almost six thousand members.

If the contractors or boss-tailors who moved into Brownsville thought they would find it easier to conduct their shops here than in Manhattan, they soon were disabused. The vast number of workers engaged in the needle trades concentrated in Brownsville rendered it easier for labor leaders to organize them and to compel loyalty to unionism. This was not always achieved peacefully. Force was invoked by both sides.

Brownsville labor was among the first to organize. In 1892 the jacket-makers of Brownsville established a union, a local of the Knights of Labor. Alter Caspar, who later became a lawyer, was its secretary, and Jacob Wax its walking delegate. The Knights was an American Union, founded by Uriah Stephens, a garment worker. As early as 1885 a group of Jewish garment workers sought and gained admission to the Knights, one of the strong American unions of the time, and offering most promise to the harassed worker. The Brownsville union leaders soon began to demand full recognition, closed shops, and a twelve-hour day— seven A.M. to seven P.M. The bosses refused, and the first strike in the industry began in September, 1896. Work was left half-finished in the shops to force a settlement, but the bosses—all former operators and pressers—banded together and moved from shop to shop finishing the work.

Twenty pickets attacked one of the bosses, who was getting the best of the fracas when Jake (Jacob) Wax appeared. Jake later described his encounter thus: "On seeing A. with his knees on two of our men, I grabbed a rocking chair from a nearby secondhand store and brought it down on his head, opening it up like a fountain. Thirty stitches had to be taken on A's head." Wax was arrested and released on bail. While out, he came face to face with his opponent. "Seeing me, he became enraged and handed me a wallop on the nose. I fell down, and like a prudent man, fainted. A friendly doctor bandaged me up heavily before I went for A's arrest." [2]

The Cloakmakers Strike

In the famous Cloakmakers strike of 1894, Brownsville furnished the most loyal strikers. Mr. Abraham Rosenberg, in his memoirs, describes the behavior of Brownsville as follows: [3] "The only ones that had no scabs among them were the Brownsville cloakmakers. All their shops were closed, and the whole village lay under siege. No one could leave the town unless he had a pass from the Strike Committee. All who wanted to go to New York, had to go to the elevated stations, and pickets were placed there to guard the stations day and night. A few Brownsville residents who did work as scabs in New York were packed into sacks during the night and taken away in a butcher's express. A few scabs dared to come to Brownsville during the strike to visit their families. They were escorted by a funeral procession, never to be forgotten. They were brought in a patrol wagon, guarded by a half dozen policemen on horseback who rode in front of and behind them. All men, women, and children of Brownsville followed them with black candles crying *Zedakah Tazil Me-Movit*—'Righteousness saves from death.' And when the scabs reached their homes alive, they did not dare to step out during the entire weekend. Policemen guarded their homes day and night. When the time came for the scabs to return to New York on Monday morning, the same funeral procession followed. A few scabs wanted to move to New York during the period of the strike, but there was no expressman who would move them."

While Brownsville was a strong fortress, the New York strikers were too demoralized, and the strike of 1894 failed. Joseph Barondess, that colorful personality of the labor movement, "King of the Cloakmakers," resigned from the leadership of the union after this strike. He suffered hunger and dire need. He lived in penury for a time in Brownsville, and there were times, according to Mr. Rosenberg's memoirs, when he was too impoverished to pay the five dollars monthly rent. Were it not for his friends, he would have been evicted after that long and weary twenty-week strike.

Joseph Barondess arrived in the United States in 1888 and worked in various trades before becoming a labor leader in the 1890's. He was jailed and denounced as an anarchist.

One of the sad experiences in his life was the "Jamaica Episode." A former union man named Greenberg opened a shop in the woods near Jamaica, Queens, to avoid the unions. Although his shop was well protected by barbed wire and dogs, some of the members of a special picketing committee reached the shop and removed the scabs. During the scuffle, the stove used by the pressers was overturned, and the foot of the contractor's little girl was burned. The pickets left the shop, taking the trolley car to East New York.

The contractor immediately telephoned the East New York Police Station that his factory was attacked by a band of ruffians, and asked that the group be arrested. When the committee stepped off the trolley car in East New York, the police stood ready for them. Most of them managed to get away with the other passengers. Because his coat was torn in places and spattered with mud, only one member of the union, Rheingold, was suspected by the police and arrested.

The manufacturers and the police seized upon the incident. One paper came out with a scare headline that the cloakmakers union had poured vitriol on the foot of the child. Detectives went to the union headquarters and arrested twelve members of the executive committee, although none of them had ever been in Jamaica. The same evening Mr. Barondess was taken into custody and was confronted by a union member who testified he had witnessed Barondess distribute bottles of vitriol to members of the committee, and had even tested it on a piece of cloth.

Barondess was held under $20,000 bail, and the others under $10,000 bail. The union was able to raise only enough money to release Barondess. The other prisoners languished in the Jamaica prison until the trial 10 weeks later. After a trial which cost the union $45,000, a huge sum at that time, the defendants were released with the exception of Rheingold, who was sentenced for 5 years and 9 months.

The union collected tens of thousands of signatures on petitions to Governor Sulzer, and six months later Rheingold was set free.[4]

After Barondess retired from the labor leadership, he entered the insurance business, but remained ever ready to serve the labor cause. A popular orator, he became a prominent Zionist leader, and was for a time a member of the Board of Education of New

York City. In those days a section of the city was assigned to each member of the Board for his supervision. Brownsville came under the supervision of Barondess.

Another union organized early was the Children's Garment Makers Union, local Assembly 1110, Assembly District 40, Knights of Labor, with H. Bendfeldt as treasurer, and G. Horowitz as secretary. Meyer Silverman was the walking delegate, and a powerful one. Reference has already been made to the court case in which he was involved on June 3, 1895, because he told one of the bosses who had preferred charges against one of his employees that unless he withdrew the charges, all his men would be called out.

The next day the workmen struck and the boss sent for the delegate to make terms. All adjourned to the office of a lawyer, where the boss-tailor was told that the men would be allowed to return to work on his paying twenty-six dollars, giving a bond of two hundred dollars, and pledging not to make trouble in the future. The twenty-six dollars, it was explained, would be expended as follows: one dollar for the lawyer, five dollars to cover the claim by the defendant, and twenty dollars in damages to the employee—one dollar an hour for the time he was in jail before a bondsman was secured. The bond which the complainant was obliged to sign was in reality a union contract. He agreed to give his men a ten-hour work day, pay them union wages, employ only union men, permit the walking delegate to enter the place at his pleasure, and settle all disputes with his employees as the union may direct. The complainant absented himself from the court as he had promised.[5]

During this period practically every trade and industry was being organized. Some of the unions had their origin in Brownsville, and some of the local unions met here.

In September, 1892, 9 bakers in Brooklyn organized themselves into a union, which ceased to exist the following year. A year later several baker-bosses suggested that their workers organize a sick benefit society, and on *Rosh Hashana*—New Year—several Brooklyn bakers came to Brownsville to discuss the matter. During the deliberations it was suggested that instead of a society to protect the bakers during illness, it would be more advisable to organize a union which would afford protection at all times. This plan found favor, and a union was organized.

On October 8, 1894, 35 bakers applied for a charter to the International Bakers Association, and Local 163 was installed. Two weeks later the local presented a series of demands to their bosses, which were granted. For 14 years the Brownsville bakers belonged to the Brooklyn Local 163. On April 24, 1909, when the number of Jewish bakeries had increased in Brownsville, 125 workers organized themselves as Local 87, which grew to 400 members in 1915.[6] In a comparatively short time the union doubled its membership and was able to assist other locals.

The International Barbers Union has existed in the United States since 1887, and the barbers of the East Side organized themselves in 1894. In 1911 a local of the Barbers Union was organized in Brownsville with Barnett Jacobs as manager. Now Local 657 of Brownsville undertook to organize all barbers of Greater New York in 5 locals of the International Barbers Union of America. D. Menkin of the Brownsville Local was helpful in the success of the effort. In 1917 Local 657 had 155 members, with Louis Lubinsky as its president.[7]

A large group in Brownsville was engaged in making wrappers, kimonos, housedresses, and bathrobes. Conditions in the industry were bad—long work hours and low pay. In 1901 a union of these workers in New York was organized by the United Hebrew Trades, but it was very weak. Local 41, organized by the Brownsville workers, was much stronger. It called a number of shop strikes and managed to gain a shorter week with higher pay.

In 1910 the United Hebrew Trades again organized the New York wrapper- and kimono-workers, and amalgamated them with the Brownsville Local into the Wrapper, Kimono, House Dress, and Bathrobe Makers Union, Local 41 (ILGWU), which carried out a series of strikes. In January, 1913, a general strike was declared in which some 2,000 workers of New York, Brooklyn, and Brownsville participated. A settlement was reached in February which won for the workers a 50-hour week and a 10 per cent wage increase. In 1917 the union had 1,200 members, and 2 of its chief officers were residents of Brownsville—Miss Sarah Spanier, president, and Israel M. Chatcuff, secretary.[8]

The first wet-wash laundry in New York was opened in Brownsville in 1912. The owners sent out drivers with horse and wagons to collect the bags. No matter how many pounds were pressed into the bag, it was all washed for 50¢. If one did not have enough laundry to fill a bag, a neighbor's laundry was often included. This prompted the drivers to organize a union.

One cold evening in the winter of 1922, when some one hundred laundry drivers were assembled in the Brownsville Labor Lyceum to organize their union, armed gangsters entered the hall shouting, "Get out of this hall!" When the workers were driven outside, they were attacked by a large group with revolvers and blackjacks.

The fight lasted some fifteen to twenty minutes, without a policeman in sight. The next day Mr. Shiplacoff, who was the Lyceum manager at that time, called a conference of all officials of the tailors, cloakmakers, bakers, carpenters, and of other unions at the Labor Lyceum, and it was decided to organize a Laundry Drivers Union in Brownsville. The owners of the laundries met later with Mr. Shiplacoff and agreed to compensate the injured laundry drivers. On June 14, 1923, the Laundry Drivers Union became a local of the International Teamsters and Chauffeurs Union, Local Number 810, and drew the drivers of all neighborhoods of Greater New York into the Union.

Many locals, some with large memberships, met in the neighborhood.[9] The Cloak and Shirt Makers Union, Local 11, of the International Ladies Garment Workers Union (organized in 1908) had a membership of 2,500 in 1917. It met on Sackman Street, with J. Rosenzveig as president and H. Batsky, as secretary. The United Brotherhood of Tailors, Local 213 (organized in 1895), with a membership of 1,000, met at 105 Thatford Avenue. H. Saperstein was president and Sam Levy, secretary. Local 214 of the Amalgamated Clothing Workers of America (organized in 1915) met in 1917 at 99 Thatford Avenue, with a membership of 250. I. Galushkin was president and J. Angelman, secretary. Local

159 of Knee-Pants Makers (organized 1894), with a membership of 300 in 1917, also met here under the presidency of M. Sprung.

Many Jews entering other industries were interested in becoming identified with their unions. As building activity proliferated in new Jewish neighborhoods, Jewish workers sought to enter the building trades, but found the unions closed to them. The workers in these unions feared that the admittance of Jews might lower the standards. Through excessive initiation fees, as much as $100, and by requiring applicants to pass a difficult examination, the unions were able to limit the membership. Thus barred from the building trade unions, Jews formed their own unions with the aid of the United Hebrew Trades. They organized under the names of Alteration Painters Union, Alteration Carpenters Union, Alteration Mason and Bricklayers Union, Alteration Plumbers Union, and Alteration Electrical Workers Union.

Several years transpired before these unions were admitted as locals of the international unions. In 1904 the Jewish Painters Union Local 1011 was the first to receive a charter from the Brotherhood of Painters. Jewish workers in other trades passed through similar vicissitudes before achieving recognition.[10]

While each local union had its own unique configuration, the Brownsville workers shared in common experiences which affected organized labor as a whole. The economic depressions of 1893, 1907, and the 1930's, the World Wars, the unremitting conflict between capital and labor, the arduous organizing campaigns and the violence eventuating from strikes, the lock-outs and injunctions, the ideological differences which evoked quarrels and party splits, the personality clashes among the labor leaders, the New Deal legislation, the founding of the American Labor Party and the Liberal Party—all these phenomena which made up the story of the labor movement during the past three quarters of a century were national in scope, transcending all local issues. The labor sector of Brownsville shared in the national economic changes, and at the same time contributed to the general development of the Jewish labor movement.

In 1897 and 1898 Brownsville and the entire Jewish labor movement became involved in the bitter struggle between the Socialist Labor Party (S.L.P.) which was backed by Dr. Daniel DeLeon and his party press, the *Abandblatt,* and the Social Democracy of America (S.D.A.) founded on June 18, 1897, under the direction of Eugene Debs, which received the backing of *The Forward* and its editor, Abe Cahan. The S.D.A. attracted numerous adherents among Jewish labor in New York. Locals were established in Brownsville and in other parts of the city.

The struggle between the S.L.P. and S.D.A. was reflected in the dissension within the unions. The United Hebrew Trades feuded with the Federated Hebrew Trades of Greater New York, organized September 22, 1897. The two federations accused each other of harboring groups of scabs. In 1899, after a two year conflict, the two federations merged under the name of the United Hebrew Trades. The S.D.P. and S.L.P. united in 1900. In Brownsville, the revolutionaries of the S.L.P. did not wait until the official merger, but began joint meetings with the S.D.P. In 1901 both parties united, assuming the present name of The Socialist Party.[11]

Several attempts were made to organize the garment workers into an over-all national union. In August 1896 the United Brotherhood of Cloakmakers Union was formed, and by 1897 it had a membership of ten thousand with seven "walking delegates." Dues were originally 5¢ a week; the entrance fee was $1 in 1897, and $5 in 1899. The union assisted in organizing the Federated Hebrew Trades of Greater New York. As a result of unsuccessful strikes and injunctions, the organization became weak. Another effort to effect a stronger national organization resulted in the formation of the present International Ladies Garment Workers Union.

Brownsville was one of the few locals represented in the organizing convention of the International Ladies Garment Workers Union. In answer to a call to all cloakmakers, ladies tailors, and skirtmakers in the United States and Canada to convene in New York on June 3, 1900, to organize a national body, 12 delegates met in the Labor Lyceum in New York. They represented some 2,000 members of the cloakmakers unions in New York, Philadelphia, Newark, Baltimore, and Brownsville. Quoting from the minutes of that first meeting; "At 2 P.M. the convention reconvened. A credential was presented from Brownsville Cloakmakers for delegate Ginsburg, who was duly admitted."

At this convention it was resolved to organize the International Ladies Garment Workers Union, and to affiliate with the American Federation of Labor. Herman Grossman was elected president. The organization grew in numbers, and in 1901 was able to pay its secretary a salary of $15 a week. The economic depression of 1907 particularly affected the women's clothing industry. The income of the International from all its locals for the year of 1907 was $3,446. The phenomenal growth of later years and its present strength hardly bear a resemblance to its humble beginnings.[12]

Industrial unionism was another issue in organized labor.[13] When the Industrial Workers of the World (I.W.W.) was organized, it appealed especially to the Young Russian Jewish Revolutionary émigrés. In August, 1905, they organized the makers of wire frames for women's hats in New York as the first Jewish industrial union.

The first mass meeting of the union was held in Brownsville at the end of August, 1905, with addresses by Charles Sherman, president, Dr. DeLeon, and others. The I.W.W. also organized some ten to fifteen unions with a membership of several thousand, and aroused the apathetic workers by their elaborate May Day Parades, and their interest in various causes. Other labor groups did not always approve the methods of these *Industrialnikes,* as they were called, but they were generally regarded as an asset to labor.

Some thirty years later, with the rise of the C.I.O., industrial unionism became again a live issue. When the question was raised at the American Federation of Labor Convention in 1935, both Sidney Hillman, leader of American Clothing Workers, and David Dubinsky, of the International Ladies Garment Workers Union, were among its most vigorous advocates. In 1938, when it became clear that John L. Lewis intended to make C.I.O. a permanent body, Sidney Hillman and his union remained with the industrial group, while David Dubinsky returned to the A.F.L.

The cooperative movement struck roots at the beginning of the century among the Jewish working class and inspired interested individuals to hold a convention in the Rand School on December 20, 1909.[14] Dr. Nachman Syrkin, the Labor Zionist, was among the leaders of the movement. In 1910 the Cooperative League bought a hat factory from the Union Hatters Corporation and opened a number of cooperative outlet stores. One of these stores was on Pitkin Avenue. However, the cooperative proved unprofitable and was sold in 1911, and the league was dissolved in 1914.

The movement was continued by the Industrial and Agricultural Cooperative Association, which grew out of the Universal Cooperative Association, founded by J. Sekader in 1912. The association succeeded in organizing a number of cooperative businesses in New York. As for Brownsville, the only cooperative undertaking that existed there through the years was a cooperative bakery.

During the first decade of the century the Jewish labor movement began to exhibit a maturity and responsibility that became a source of strength in subsequent years. In 1900 only a small fraction of the 200,000 Jewish tailors were organized on a permanent basis. Many kept aloof because of the continuous quarrels among the Socialist groupings and parties, and the crisis over the party press. Nor did the frequent strikes help matters.

On July 22, 1901, some 25,000 tailors of New York, Brownsville, and Newark declared a general strike, demanding a 59 hour week and the elimination of the contracting system. In a resolution printed in *The Forward* on May 15, 1901, they voiced their grievances; "Finally, whereas the conditions are such at the present time that we can no longer exist because the contractor is only a tool of the manufacturer to exploit the worker, we have at the present time come to the conclusion that it would be ridiculous on our part to start a fight against the sweater. We, the delegates, of The United Tailors, of all the local unions among the garment workers of New York, Brooklyn, Brownsville, and

Newark resolve that when the appropriate time will come, we will refuse to work for the contractors, and we want it known by the manufacturers of the tailoring trade that it is up to them to establish shops under their control and responsibility."

The general strike of 1901 lasted several weeks and was only partially successful. In July 1902 the workers struck again for the same demands, but the outcome was regarded as a failure. The general strike of 1904 for a "closed shop" was regarded only as a partial victory. The tailors were becoming discouraged because the periodic strikes were of little avail. The 1907 depression did not help matters.

The workers and leaders painfully came to realize that periodic strikes were a questionable instrument to bring success. These struggles required much planning and preparation. A special conference of tailors unions in New York, Brooklyn, Newark, and Brownsville was held to discuss and analyze the consequences of too frequent strikes.

The "Uprising of the Twenty Thousand" shirt-waist makers, which was initiated at a meeting in Cooper Union in November, 1909, terminated for a time the demoralization that engulfed the Jewish trade unions. The enthusiastic response to the call for a general strike by the young women workers in this relatively new branch of the needle trades, and the favorable reaction by various communal groups, brought victory to the strikes within two months. They won a fifty-two hour week, four paid holidays, and improved conditions.[15]

The "Great Revolt" of the cloakmakers followed a few months later.[16] The preparation for the strike was made under the supervision of the General Executive of the International and Cloakmakers Joint Board, which consisted of seven locals. The two locals from Brownsville that were added did not at the time belong to the Joint Board, but were only represented on the Strike Committee. Some sixty-thousand workers in the cloak and suit trade were involved in this struggle, which lasted for some ten weeks. The workers suffered hardship, even starvation, but they held on.

Mass meetings, parades, demonstrations, injunctions, police

interference—all were part of this acrimonious struggle. An aroused public opinion hastened the efforts at settlement. Prominent Jews came forth to assist—Louis D. Brandeis and Louis Marshall, famous lawyers; Benjamin Schlesinger of *The Forward;* Julius Henry Cohen, counsel for the employers, and Meyer London for the workers—all worked hard to bring about an end to the strike. It initiated a period of collective bargaining in the industry. On September 1, the Protocol of Peace was finally drawn up, and many of the evils of the shops were abolished. Wages were raised and Price Committees established; hours were reduced to fifty per week; ten legal holidays a year were granted. Grievances and controversies were left to the final judgment of a "chief clerk" representing the public. An Impartial Chairman was chosen and paid by both sides. Selected for his neutrality as well as for his familiarity with industrial problems, he assumed a new importance.

During this period, the men's clothing workers, affiliated with the United Garment Workers (U.G.W.), were also undergoing a struggle.[17] The new leaders, who included Sidney Hillman and Joseph Schlossberg, clashed with the old-guard U.G.W. leadership, and at the end of 1914 the insurgents formed themselves into the Amalgamated Clothing Workers of America, with Sidney Hillman as president. The United Hebrew Trades recognized the union, but Samuel Gompers, president of the American Federation of Labor, attacked it as a dual union and refused it official recognition. Abraham Shiplacoff, an organizer of the Amalgamated Clothing Workers and at that time secretary of the United Hebrew Trades, went to the 1915 Convention of the American Federation of Labor in San Francisco, where he gave his answer to the criticism of Samuel Gompers.

World War I, an open-shop offensive following the war and the brief post-war depression, affected organized labor. The Jewish trade unions were particularly affected by the attempts of the Communists during the 1920's and 1930's to capture the unions. The Communists almost succeeded in seizing control of the needle trades unions, but were defeated after a long, vehement struggle.

The internecine war in the I.L.G.W.U. was responsible for the violent Communist-led strike of 1926, which lasted six months and cost over three million dollars. The leftist officials were finally ejected, and Morris Sigman and his group gained control of the industry.

The conflict with the Communists was just as fierce among the furriers. The Communists also attempted to infiltrate the Amalgamated Cothing Workers, but the struggle there was not so severe, and Sidney Hillman and Joseph Schlossberg, the union's leaders, were able to cope with the opposition.

Prior to the late 1930's the labor movement was plagued by undesirable elements, even by racketeer infestation. Violent strike-breaking was an accepted mode of industrial relations, and both manufacturers and unions resorted to it. Some of the strong-arm men came from the Jewish neighborhoods of the East Side, East New York, Brownsville, and elsewhere. The racketeers were ultimately driven out, and for many years now the clothing industry has been a paragon of good labor-management relations.

The depression in the 1930's brought a resurgence of sweatshop conditions; longer hours, piece work, and a general deterioration of shop conditions. A number of organizations in Brownsville came under the influence of leftist groups. In May, 1933, a baker's strike in Brownsville by twenty-seven bakeries aroused great excitement. At a mass conference held in the Labor Lyceum on Sunday afternoon, May 14, in which forty-eight organizations represented by eighty-three delegates participated, a resolution wholeheartedly endorsing the strike was unanimously adopted. It said in part: "While wages are being cut, hours increased and relief cuts imposed upon employed workers, the bosses, under the lead of the capitalist administration, are boosting prices on products of everyday necessities for the workers."

The Roosevelt era with its New Deal measures, stimulated a renascence in the life of the Jewish unions. Not only the trade unionists, but also nearly all Brownsville residents became staunch Roosevelt supporters.

In 1935, when the N.R.A. codes were declared unconstitutional by the Supreme Court in the poultry market case brought by the

Schechter brothers of Brownsville, the International Ladies Garment Workers Union, the Amalgamated Clothing Workers Association, and the Hatworkers Union continued, through voluntary employer-union bodies, to maintain the standards, membership, and many of the activities made possible while the N.R.A. codes existed.

With the elimination of the racketeers and the Communist influences in the unions, and with the introduction of liberal measures during the Roosevelt era, the trade unions were able to focus their attention on other interests. As the trade unions grew in numbers and in influence, and gained better working conditions through the years, "the revolutionary temperament chilled, and opposition to capitalism diminished," in the words of Joseph Schlossberg.

The unions did not repudiate socialism, they drifted away from it. They continued, however, to pioneer in improving the general security and lot of the workingman. They concerned themselves with the problems of unemployment, workers' education, recreation, health work, public education, responsibility for the efficient conduct of the industry, and scientific investigation and research in the formulation of policies and programs. Above all, they cultivated a more lively interest in Jewish communal affairs, dispelling, at least partially, their original intransigence and doctrinaire opposition to Jewish affairs. They formed the Jewish Labor Committee to assist the victims of the Nazi terror; they helped organize a boycott of German goods, engaged in rescue work, and took an interest in the establishment of the State of Israel.

With the decline of the Brownsville Jewish community, the activities of the Jewish trade unions also declined. The Labor Lyceum on Sackman Street was closed. The one time Jewish trade unions with a predominant Jewish membership underwent a striking metamorphosis, although some of the unions maintained Jewish leadership.

Ben B. Seligman, writing about Jewish Labor in the United States, deplored the decline of the typical Jewish trade unions. He wrote: "Here was a movement, in origin a remarkably viable blend of European and native elements, that gave to American civilization a unique union organization—an enlightened national industrial union superimposed upon a variety of craft locals. As a by-product it created a union philosophy that paid attention to the educational and welfare needs of its members, as well as to hard-headed 'business.' And it sought, in varying degrees of effectiveness, to infuse its economic program with political meaning." [18]

The Workmen's Circle

Founding fraternal orders, of which the first and largest was the *Arbeiter Ring*—Workmen's Circle—constituted another significant project of the Jewish Labor Movement.[19] It was launched on April 4, 1892, by a group of radicals in the East Side, to meet a need for mutual aid, social contacts, educational activities for members, and the establishment of cooperative enterprises. On September 5, 1900, after the formation of several branches of the Workmen's Circle, it was decided to organize a fraternal order, and after weathering difficulties and struggles the order was finally chartered in 1905 by the State of New York. The East Side organization became Branch Number 1, the group in Harlem, Branch Number 2. In June, 1899, a Brooklyn Branch was installed with twenty-nine members.

The Brownsville Branch of the Workmen's Circle, designated Number 11, was established after the first convention in New York on March 29-31, 1901. Its founding caused considerable controversy in the radical community. A workmen's sick-benefit and aid society—*Der Arbeiter Kranken Unterstizung Ferein fun Brownsville* had been established in Brownsville, and when the Workmen's Circle was reorganized on April 4, 1900, the society was invited to become a branch of the *Arbeiter Ring*.

The society decided to hold the invitation in abeyance until after the convention in order to convince itself of the progressive character of the Workmen's Circle. In the interim, however, ten members of the society organized a new group under the name of the International Aid Society, and decided to affiliate immediately as a branch of the Circle. The officers of the older society, fearing competition from the new group and the possibility of forfeiting the right to become a branch, resolved not to wait until the convention, and applied for admission to the Executive Board of the Workmen's Circle. The Executive Board deemed it unwise to show preference to either of the two groups. Instead, the Board called a mass meeting in Brownsville and informed the community that anyone might join the new branch of the Workmen's Circle being formed in Brownsville. The sick-benefit and aid society protested this action at the convention, whereupon the Assembly voted to instruct the new Executive Board to study the matter further.

After the convention, another mass meeting was called. It was a tumultuous meeting, necessitating the appearance of the police. The Brownsville Workers Society contended that the meeting was called contrary to the decision of the convention. There were accusations and counter-accusations, which were published in the press. The Brownsville Society wrote an open letter of two columns in *The Forward,* and the Executive Board retaliated with three-and-a-half columns in two issues of *The Forward.* Despite the protests, twenty members registered in the new branch, and in May, 1901, they were installed as Branch 11 of Brownsville.

The Workmen's Circle concerned itself particularly with matters of health, and became known as the "Red Cross" of Jewish Labor. In 1910 it opened its Sanitarium for Consumptives in Liberty, New York, which continued to serve until 1955. It cared for 132 patients during its first year of existence. For a number of years, Barnett Wolff of Brownsville was its director. Among the benefits the Circle afforded its members in the early years were sick payments of six dollars a week for a period of twelve weeks a year, four hundred dollars insurance on the death of the husband, two hundred dollars on the death of the wife, funeral expenses, and cemetery privileges. At a time when the social welfare measures of today were undreamed of, such benefactions were of inestimable value to the poor workingman.

The early leadership of the Workmen's Circle lay largely in the hands of Jewish radicals who espoused the revolutionary class struggle ideology. Cosmopolitan and assimilationist in spirit, these leaders were opposed to any distinctive nationalist particularism.

In order to prepare the growing generation for the socialist legacy, a number of Socialist Sunday Schools were created.[20] These followed the pattern established in European socialist centers. The two-hour, weekly session, conducted in English, purposed to acquaint the children with the socialist doctrines and the labor movement.

The first Sunday School was opened in Harlem on November 10, 1906, and in the following year schools were opened in the East Side and in Williamsburg. Workmen's Circle Branches Number 11 and Number 139 of Brownsville and East New York opened a Sunday School in East New York in 1908, and another in 1910 on Alabama Avenue. By 1910-1911, there were ten such schools in greater New York with a registration of one thousand five hundred, but in 1914 the registration had dwindled. The wave of nationalism which swept the world permeated also the ranks of the Jewish socialists. A "young" group of bundists and labor Zionists pressed for the establishment of Yiddish Schools. The National Workers Alliance, which had united with the *Poale Zion,* were already conducting Yiddish day-schools. One had been established in New York by the *Poale Zion* as early as 1910.

At a number of annual conventions of the *Arbeiter Ring,* the subject of Yiddish schools was discussed. Dr. Chaim Zhitlowsky was among the leaders who supported this issue, but it did not receive a favorable vote.

The principle of establishing week-day schools was adopted at the 16th annual convention of the Workingmen's Circle held at the Brownsville Labor Lyceum May 2-8, 1916. The 104 delegates representing branches in 34 areas assembled at a critical period in the life of our people to decide on a number of grave internal issues. On May 3 the Cloakmakers Union of New York was locked out by the manufacturers. The dispute over the appointment of Zivyon (Dr. B. Hoffman) as secretary of the Order led to his resignation. Since the United States was about to enter World War I, a resolution was adopted opposing militarism and urging an immediate and just peace. The Order also passed a resolution calling for contributions on behalf of the Peoples Relief Committee to assist our stricken brethren across the sea.

At this convention a resolution was adopted by a vote of fifty-five in favor, forty-three against, two absent, and two abstaining, exhorting the branches of the Circle to join the Socialist Yiddish schools where they already existed, and to help establish them where they had not yet been formed.

The Education Commitee of the Order based its recommendation on the following statement of principles: "Our children receive their education only in the public schools where they do not receive any special Jewish knowledge. They grow up strangers to the Jewish community. Hardly any of them speak Yiddish. Many do not even understand it, with the result that they do not understand the masses, cannot communicate with them, and are alien to their customs and ideals. They look down upon them as a people of an inferior culture, occasionally even with contempt. Not infrequently this attitude is carried over by the children to their own parents. It is a sad fact that Jewish children are often ashamed of their parents who do not speak English fluently. Unacquainted with the Jewish literature, without any conception of the rich Jewish cultural treasures, the children grow up alien and often hostile to the Jewish people and all that is Jewish. By failing to give our children a Jewish education, we lose them gradually to ourselves and to our masses.

"Only a comparatively small number of children do receive a certain kind of Jewish education, but this type of education cannot satisfy us. They usually get their education in the *Talmud Torahs* and *Hedarim,* or in the so-called 'national radical schools,' but the *Talmud Torahs* and *Hedarim* inculcate only religion, and often a fanaticism from which we want to free our children. In the national radical schools the education is ultra-national, and mostly openly Zionistic.

"We want our children to get neither a religious nor a Zionist education, but a free Jewish education.

"We want first of all, that our children be able to speak correctly, to read, and to write Yiddish—the language of the Jewish masses. We want them to become familiar with the various facets of Jewish life—with the immediate American-Jewish life as well as with the life of Jews in other lands—in order that they may understand, and together with others, experience the joys of the

Jewish masses, as well as share in their sorrows. We want our children to be familiar with the rich Jewish cultural treasures— with Jewish literature, old and new, in order that they may be able to continue to create its culture. We want our children to be familiar with the history of the Jews in different lands, including America, and including the present time."

A very spirited debate followed the introduction of the resolution. Sol Hurok, a representative of Brownsville, opposed it on the grounds that the adoption of the resolution would indirectly endorse the radical nationalist schools maintained by the National Workers Alliance. N. Feinerman and others spoke in favor of the resolution, which was adopted. However, since no budget was voted, the resolution was not solidly implemented until after the Pittsburgh convention. A two-cents quarterly assessment for the support of such schools was put into effect on January 1, 1919. The assessment was increased to thirty-six cents a year per member in 1921, to sixty cents in 1925, and to eighty cents in 1927.

The first two Yiddish schools were opened in November, 1919 in Harlem, with Jacob Levine as teacher, and in Williamsburg with A. L. Goldman as instructor. The Brownsville school saw the light of day in April, 1919.

These *Arbeiter Ring* schools became busy centers of activities. They not only conducted the classes for children, but also printed a monthly, opened teacher training classes, introduced a wide variety of extra-curricular activities such as children's clubs, parents organizations, the publication of text books and reading material.

In the early years, these schools evoked considerable hostility. A report from the Board of the Brownsville school describes the opposition they had to contend with: "In the beginning our school encountered opposition from two sides. The Orthodox, convinced that Workmen's Circle schools undermined the foundation of Judaism, tried to have it closed. They took the cards announcing the school out of store windows, and threatened a butcher who displayed such a card to declare his meat *trefa* if he would not remove it. Opposition also came from some of the

Circle members themselves, who thought that the school was no different from a *Talmud Torah,* making religious Jews out of the children. They prevailed upon certain Brownsville branches not to send delegates to the school board. However, lately both sides have given up the fight."

The young guard, which found support in *The Day,* the new Jewish daily, continued its struggle to establish an educational department that would serve the adult membership as well. They were opposed by the old guard, who found their support in *The Forward,* which was still internationalist. An educational department with a sizeable budget was finally established, a number of books were published, and other activities introduced. It progressed until 1926, when a serious split between the leftist and rightist wings in the Workmen's Circle interrupted the progress. The leftists took over the control of most of the schools in the city, the high school, and Camp *Kinderland.* In time the situation normalized.

Over the years, the Order continued to grow and to broaden its scope of activities. In consequence of the many changes in Jewish life in America and in the Jewish labor movement, the Order also underwent an evolution. It is now more firmly anchored in the Jewish historical heritage.

Nahum Chanin, who retired after a number of years as general secretary of the Workmen's Circle, presented an incisive analysis of the ideological changes during the period. One of "our mistakes probably was that during the early years of our Order we took little interest in Jewish life. We were certain that Socialism will answer all Jewish questions. In this respect, we perhaps erred. But these were not only our mistakes. Jewish life in America changed so much and so rapidly. What we regard today as the mistakes of yesterday were not considered mistakes, and were right for the yesteryear, because the past was so different from the present. There was a time when we did not want to have anything to do with the Jewish bourgeoisie. Life has taught us however, that we are part of the greater Jewish people. All suffering and joy, all problems and achievements of Jewish life, are also ours. We now sit together around the same table; we work together for the common interests of the Jewish people. We strive as much as is possible, to find the best solutions for the Jewish problems here in America, and for all other Jewish settlements throughout the world."

Thus the Order continues. In the words of its official song, composed by Dr. Gingold:

> *"A friendship chain we forge,*
> *A chain of countless rings,*
> *To link a mighty band*
> *Of rings in every land."*

Yiddish Cultural Activities

VIII

The Yiddish and English Press

THE EAST EUROPEAN immigrant not only created a distinctive Jewish labor movement but also, in doing so, developed an extensive Yiddish culture, a Yiddish press, a Yiddish literature, a Yiddish theatre, Yiddish schools, and a secular Jewish nationalism. This was a great achievement, and Bezalel Sherman, in his interesting study of the Jew within American Society, has analyzed for us how the trade unions, which for all other workers were second to the school as an assimilatory factor, became for the Jewish workers the important instrument of ethnic cultural advance in the Yiddish language.[1] The fact is all the more striking when we realize that the founders of Jewish unions had little ideological interest in Jewish cultural activity, most of whom tended toward assimilation and looked down upon Yiddish as a patois. "However, in the very process of initially injecting a socialist spirit into their unions, they created a gulf between the Jewish labor movement and the general labor movement in the country," which was far removed from a class approach to social problems. This made for an ethnic separation. Moreover, since Yiddish was the spoken and mother tongue of most of the East European Jewish immigrants, of both workers and employers, certainly as far as most of those in the needle trades were concerned, it did not take long for the leaders to realize that if they wanted to reach these immigrants and to educate them, they would have to use the Yiddish language.

In all of this the Yiddish press played a dominant role.[2] In those days it was largely a party press to spread and fight for its ideology. To achieve its objectives it would generally select an editor with a combative temperament. Such militant journalists, as Abraham Cahan, Louis Miller, and S. Yanofsky exerted influence on the creation of the Jewish labor movement and the nurture of other constructive movements and institutions among American Jews. The most cogent champion of labor was *The Jewish Daily Forward,* which grew to be one of the largest and most potent foreign language newspapers in this country. It made a tremendous impact upon the radical circles in Brownsville. Mr. Abraham Shiplacoff was, for a time, as we have noted in a previous chapter, its labor editor. The newspaper taught the immigrant Jewish workers the intrinsic values of trade unionism. It helped to organize unions, it guided, led, and assisted in many of the strikes whose goal was to raise the standards of the worker. It campaigned for social legislation and vigorously opposed and exposed corrupt government.

The phenomenal growth of *The Forward* and of the Jewish labor movement could not have been achieved without the guidance and direction of Abraham Cahan who, except for a few years, served as editor from its founding in 1897 until his death in 1951. Cahan was a typical Russian intellectual, an anarchist for a time, then a Marxist. *The Forward,* in its early years, although not so doctrinaire as the *Abandblatt* and the *Arbeiter Zeitung,* which it replaced, followed the radical ideology of the period. It opposed Zionism and took a negative position on other Jewish issues. In time, especially after World War I, Cahan rediscovered himself as an American and as a Jew, and thereafter manifested a genuine attachment to his people. *The Forward,* in assuming a more positive approach to Jewish life and to Israel, appealed to a wider Jewish public. It met with competition from other papers of the conservative and radical wings—the Orthodox *Tageblatt,* one of the oldest and most influential Jewish dailies, *The Morning Journal,* the Socialist *Warheit,* established by Louis Miller, and the Communist *Freiheit,* but it held its own throughout the years, growing in strength and incisiveness.

In November, 1914, Herman Bernstein, a prominent journalist, together with Dr. Judah L. Magnes and Bernard Semel, established *The Day*—a Yiddish daily purposing to present all phases of Jewish life on a non-partisan basis, and to raise the standard of Jewish journalism. In the venture, they interested three men who are prominently associated with Brownsville—David Shapiro and his partner, Meyer Aronson, who conducted in Brownsville a chandelier business under the name of Shapiro and Aronson, and Morris Weinberg. As a result of a reorganization in the early years, David Shapiro succeeded to the presidency of the daily and became its publisher. Morris Weinberg subsequently bought Shapiro's interest, and has been its publisher to this day. From its inception, *The Day* became very popular, and after it took over the merged *Tageblatt* and *The Morning Journal,* it and *The Forward,* became the principal Yiddish dailies published in New York City.

The Yiddish press—the dailies, the *Tageblatt, The Forward, The Morning Journal, The Day,* and the various weekly and monthly magazines such as the *Amerikaner* and *Die Zukunft*— became an educational medium in the broadest sense of the term. It enriched Yiddish literature by attracting to its ranks some of the outstanding creative literary personalities whose articles and reviews of books and plays enhanced cultural and dramatic productivity.

Although the price of a paper was only one penny, it required considerable effort to introduce and popularize the use of newspapers in Brownsville. The Jew in those days was not interested in news as we understand it today. His reading was confined to novels. Only the wealthy knew what events transpired, and they disseminated their information in the synagogues.

The Isaac Feldman family was instrumental in popularizing the newspapers in the Brownsville section of Brooklyn.³ Isaac Feldman and his family arrived in this country in 1891 and opened a shop on Blake Avenue and Powell Street, where he engaged in making shirts on contract. Frank, the eldest son, finding the work distasteful, chose the job of delivering newspapers. With a bundle of Yiddish papers on his shoulders, he trudged through the streets in all kinds of weather, knocking at doors and pleading with the residents to buy his papers at a penny apiece. Frank's persistence was finally crowned with success—a large number of Brownsville and East New York residents became accustomed to getting their daily papers.

Morris Weinberg, well known as the publisher of *The Day,* was then a resident of this section, and the wholesale distributor for the few hundred Jewish newspapers sent to this part of Brooklyn. His brother, Harry Weinberg, was a newly-arrived immigrant seeking means of livelihood. Aware that Frank Feldman had developed a newspaper route that brought in the munificent sum of some three dollars a week, Morris Weinberg bought the route for his brother for two hundred dollars. When Morris Weinberg retired from the business in 1905, the Weinberg News Company, one of the largest newspaper distribution companies in the city, was turned over to Harry Weinberg. In the beginning, a man could carry papers to the dealers on his back, later, a pushcart was necessary. As the business grew, delivery of papers progressed from a horse and wagon to a fleet of motor trucks.

Of his capital, Frank Feldman used $150 to buy a small English newspaper stand and route at the corner of Fulton Street and Van Siclen Avenue. He spent half the night bringing the papers from New York, and the greater part of the day in personally distributing them among his customers and in canvassing for new customers. With the growth of the business, he took in his brothers as partners. Their energetic distribution of newspapers attracted the attention of the publishers of *The New York World* and *The*

Evening Journal, and thereby won for Frank Feldman and his brothers the distribution agency for the entire twenty-sixth Ward of Brooklyn.

The immigrants of the community were now attending night schools in large numbers to learn English. The Feldman brothers saw a great future for English newspapers in Brownsville and East New York, but they realized that the Jew would not give up his Yiddish newspaper for the English one. They hit upon the idea of making the English papers a necessity in the home, at least for the young folk if not for the elders. They asked the publishers of *The World* and *The Journal* for a number of newspapers to be distributed free each day. These they distributed without any charge for months.

The results were beyond their expectations. The papers were taken not only for the news, but also for the assistance they rendered in mastering the English language. Thus was the foundation laid for the present large newspaper business of the Feldman brothers. They distribute not only daily newspapers, but also magazines and weekly publications, and the territory they control includes not only East New York and Brownsville, but also Queens and a substantial portion of Long Island.

As Brownsville and the surrounding sections grew in population, a need was felt for a local weekly to publicize local activities and to promote the communal needs of this section. Morris Weinberg and David Shapiro became the publishers of *The Brownsville Post—Die Bronzviller Post—*also known as *The Brooklyn-Brownsville Post—*the first, and for a long time the only Yiddish weekly in Brooklyn. Launched in 1910, it enjoyed a circulation of about 14,000 at its peak. When its financial backing fell to a low ebb in the depression of the 1930's, the weekly was discontinued.

Another Yiddish weekly, *The Brooklyn Jewish Progress,* under the management of Victor E. Pomeranz, was also published for a number of years, with its office at 1746 Pitkin Avenue. Pomeranz had previously published, in 1897-1899, a Brooklyn annual known as *Der Anzeiger.* A perusal of the columns and editorials of *The Brooklyn Jewish Progress* during 1912, 1913, and 1917 reveals a liberal approach to the problems of the day. For many years a weekly section was published in *The Morning Journal* entitled "Brownsville, East New York, Eastern Parkway Section," of which Joseph Koplowitz, and later his son Samuel, were manager and editor.

A number of English weeklies were published in the section promoting Brownsville's civic interests, presenting a record of local activities, and featuring historical events and significant personalities. Many of the businessmen, the Pitkin Avenue Merchants Association, the political groups of the section, and other individuals gave financial backing to these undertakings. Most of these weeklies were short-lived, due to financial deficiency, but a few lasted a number of years. One of these periodicals, *The Kings County Chronicle,* is still being circulated in the section. Established in 1937, it has been published since 1940 by Edward Mirabean Herrschaft in his printing office at 175 Shepherd Avenue.

Among the weeklies published in Brownsville and known to the writer are:

1. *The Kings County Observer* (1920-1930) whose editors and publishers included Dr. Isidore Kayfetz, president, and Harry A. Singer, associate manager. For a time Dr. Aaron Roth was editor and publisher, Samuel L. Peckerman, associate editor, and B. Malefski, managing editor.

2. *The Brooklyn Guide* (Sept. 17, 1927), Harry Stadler, president; Harry A. Singer, business manager; Edgar Mels, editor; B. Malefski, managing editor.

3. *The Brooklyn News* (1934-), Harry W. Bobley, publisher; Edward Bobley, editor.

4. *Brooklyn Herald* (1948, 1949), I. Harry Helfgott, editor and publisher; Samuel S. Hyams, Barney Ain, Dr. Irving Sparer, Stewart Rosenon, and Leon Kadansky, contributing editors.

5. *The Community Voice* (May 12, 1948-)

6. *The Brownsville Record* (1945-1948), Paul Backal, publisher and editor.

7. *The Brooklyn Graphic* (1954, 1955).

The Yiddish Theatre

Next in importance to the press, was the Yiddish stage in helping the development of a Jewish mass-culture in America.[4] The
tired, hard-working immigrants flocked on weekends to the Yiddish theatres to seek surcease from their troubles, to enjoy a few
hours of pleasure, and to share spiritual and emotional stimulation
with their co-religionists. The folk-religiosity of Yiddish drama
provided, especially for those who had abandoned Jewish ritual
and no longer attended the synagogue, the religious pageantry of
Jewish life.

After a faltering and shaky start, a period of great expansion
began in the Yiddish theatre. Much that was shown in the theatre
was not artistic; sometimes it was amateurish, and did not serve
the educational or aesthetic needs of the times. But there were also
opportunities to witness the works of talented and even brilliant
playwrights—Jacob Gordin, Solomon Libin, Leon Kobrin,
Sholem Asch, David Pinski, Perez Hirshbein, Shalom Aleichem,
H. Leivick—playwrights whose creative works exalted the Yiddish
theatre. Dramas such as Gordin's *God, Man, and Devil, Mirele
Efros,* Anski's *Dybbuk,* Pinski's *Treasure,* and Shalom Aleichem's
Tevye, became the mighty rocks on which great acting reputations
were forged. Jacob Adler, Bertha Kalich, David Kessler, Kenny
Lipzin, Boris Thomashefsky, Morris Schwartz, Jacob V. Ami,
Samuel Goldberg, Jennie Goldstein, Menasha Skulnick, Mollie
Picon, and others became famous stars who brought the Jewish
theatre to its pinnacle of glory.

Brownsville did not offer the glamour and the at-home
atmosphere of the East Side. During the early years, therefore, it
could not maintain a continuous company through the winter
season. Those interested in a drama or comedy traveled to the East
Side. During the year a number of the theatrical companies came
to Brownsville and presented one or more plays. Sanger's Hall was
often used for these dramatic performances, and also for vaudeville
shows. Louis Goldberg played regularly in Sanger's Hall from 1905

to 1910. As the population increased, this locality supported not only one regular theatre, but also, for a time, two theatres.

In September, 1915, the Liberty Theatre, which had been built by Loew and served as a popular show place, became a Yiddish theatre under the management of Charles W. Groll, a lawyer interested in promoting the Yiddish theatre. Groll married Rose Karp, the Yiddish actress. He first managed the Lenox Theatre in Harlem, and when it closed, he came to Brownsville and managed the Liberty Theatre for eight years. Later, he opened the Prospect Theatre in the Bronx.

The productions in the Liberty Theatre in 1916 included plays by Jacob Gordin, Z. Libin, L. Kobrin, J. Lateiner, M. Richter, I. Solotorefsky. Among the stars were Jacob P. Adler, Boris Thomashefsky, David Kessler, Jacob Cone, S. Weintraub, Rose Karp, Kenny Lipzin, Bessie Thomashefsky, and Sarah Adler. In the following year Jacob B. Ami, who performed in three one-act plays by Perez in the Neighborhood Playhouse in 1915, and who, with Morris Schwartz, established the Yiddish Art Theatre, played in melodramatic repertoire in the Liberty Theatre. He became particularly known for the character of Noteh, the water carrier, which he played in a melodrama written by Kalmanowitz, *The Value of Mother*. In 1921 Bernard and Clara Young starred in this theatre.

When the Jews began to move toward the Eastern Parkway section, the Hopkinson Theatre was opened on Hopkinson Avenue near Pitkin Avenue. It was a large playhouse, with an orchestra and two balconies, and seated nine hundred people.

In 1927 the Rolland, or Parkway Theatre at 1768 Saint Johns Place was erected at a cost of about a million dollars. It was a large and well equipped playhouse. For some thirty years both theatres functioned simultaneously. Then the Hopkinson Theatre was torn down to make room for the parking lot of the East New York Savings Bank, and the Parkway Theatre was taken over for a church.

Oscar Green came to America in 1908 and settled in Boston, where he managed the Grand Opera House until 1922. In that year he came to Brooklyn and became manager of the Hopkinson Theatre until 1928. He returned to the Boston Yiddish Theatre for a year, but came back to the Hopkinson Theatre in 1929, and continued there for a number of years.

In 1932, together with Charles Weinblatt and Guskin, he persuaded Menasha Skulnick to take over the direction of the Hopkinson. Skulnick engaged a company consisting of Herman Yablokov, Bella Meisel, Yetta Zwerling, Frances Weintraub, Seymour Rechtzeit, Isaac Friedman, Bennie Zeidman, Sylvia Fishman—a native of Cleveland, Ohio—and Skulnick's brother-in-law, Isaac Lipinsky.

Collaborating with Israel Rosenberg, who wrote and adapted many plays and lyrics for the Yiddish theatre, Skulnick had a new play written for the opening of the 1932 season in the Hopkinson Theatre. It was a satirical comedy called *Mr. Schlemiel,* with lyrics by Israel Rosenberg and music by Gerechtman. In September, 1933, Skulnick staged a comedy by William Siegel entitled *Menahem Mendel,* adapted by Israel Rosenberg. Skulnick performed in various plays at the Hopkinson, and in other theatres.

While most of the actors began their dramatic careers in Eastern Europe, there were native-born Americans who became proficient in the Yiddish language and made their careers on the Yiddish stage. These included Sylvia Fishman, Freidele Lifshitz, and Philip Finkel.

It was customary to present the main performance on weekends. The other week nights were usually given over to organizational benefits, for which repertoire plays were performed. It was these benefit performances that enabled the theatres to maintain themselves throughout the season. For thousands of Brownsville residents, the Yiddish theatre remained for many years one of the main recreational agencies of the community.

Public Schools and Libraries

IX

The Public Schools

THERE WERE a number of public and private agencies whose purpose was to help the immigrant parents and their native born children to become integrated into American society, and to enable them to adjust to the mounting complexities of a new urban society. Despite their short-comings, no other agency reached a wider segment of the population, or played a more important role in the Americanization of the youth and in the development of a democratic society than the city schools.

Jewish children of school age, with few exceptions, attended the public schools. There was no all-day Jewish school in Brownsville until 1912, when Yeshivah R'Chaim Berlin opened one for boys. Only a small group attended in the early years, no more than two hundred as late as 1918.

An assignment to teach in a Brownsville school was usually a rewarding experience. There was great respect for learning, for the teacher, and for the school. Dr. Julius B. Maller, in his Study of Jewish Neighborhoods in New York City in 1930, found that the Jewish pupils of the schools had a higher average of attendance than the other children, a higher rate of school progress, a higher rating on verbal tests of mental ability, and a smaller incidence of common physical defects except in vision.

Samuel Tenenbaum wrote feelingly of Brownsville's respectful attitude toward the education of its children: [1] "In Brownsville when I knew it, school was a major occupation, not of the children alone but of the whole neighborhood. Every teacher was discussed with the minute detail a jeweler devotes to a watch; the principal of the local public school had the same authority and prestige as the most learned dean of our most respected university. To Brownsville, school represented a glorious future that would rescue it from want, deprivation and ugliness. . . .

"As I recall my childhood, we were all measured in educational potential. Next to an allegation of illegitimacy, nothing more damaging could be said than: 'He has a stuffed head. In school, he's put back or left back.'

"The relative scholastic progress of the children provoked intense jealousy and rivalry among neighbors. On coming home from work, the first question the good Brownsville father asked was, 'What happened in school?' and the child had to bring out the test papers and the marks.

" 'My Milton got all A's.' Milton's mother would look down her nose at Harry's mother, whose son got all B's. 'Don't talk of failure'—then the whole house went into mourning."

To be sure, a considerable number of children were neither interested nor qualified to continue their education, despite their parents' desire. "Workin' and the maturity and independence it implied held in our eyes an immense glamour," William Poster wrote about Brownsville youth in the thirties.[2] "Gathered around a stoop for our nightly philosophical and educational sessions, we spoke passionately of our desires to become plumbers, bricklayers, carpenters, or businessmen. . . . The traditional Jewish passion for higher education, as well as many another 'Jewish trait' simply fell apart under the violent impact of street life . . . and many sons of fairly affluent parents never got past grade school, the lure of punchball, movies, and 'working,' proving stronger than parental authority or desire."

For some sensitive individuals like Alfred Kazin, the well-known author and literary critic, the rigid school discipline in those days and the atmosphere of learning that surrounded it were irksome. "All week long," he states, "I lived for the blessed sound of the dismissal gong at three o'clock on Friday afternoon." [3]

To Matthew Josephson, another famous son of Brownsville, high school appeared as a famous "grind factory." [4]

It is noteworthy that one or two of the local schools acquired a reputation of being "tough" schools with some "tough kids." "Tough" boys were also found in the vocational schools, where their disorderly behavior plagued the school and their teachers. Even though they regarded their classes as a waste of time, the compulsory education law forced them to attend several hours a week. Some were mischievous, even malicious; they knew how to get under the skin of their teachers. Irving Shulman, in his *Amboy Dukes*, painfully describes, albeit in fictional garb, the antics of a typical group of such students. [5]

Truancy was never a serious problem in Brownsville, yet there were times when special efforts were required to enforce the Compulsory Education Law, especially to prevent school dropouts. In 1912 the local school board exhorted the Board of Education to provide at least two more attendance officers. Although District 39 had more than twice the school population and many times the area of the average district, only two attendance officers were assigned to cover the entire territory. Theirs was indeed a difficult task, practically impossible of fulfillment. The number of truants was quite insignificant. Only some twenty cases of Jewish truancy in all of Brownsville, East New York, and Canarsie came before the Attendance Bureau for all of 1930.

In 1898 the systems of New York, Brooklyn, Queens, and Richmond were consolidated with that of Greater New York. Under the direction of Dr. William H. Maxwell, a native of Ireland, a great teacher, administrator, and a visionary ever seeking improvements, the city school system was developed into

one of the most effective in the country.[6] The city was divided
into a number of school districts, each in charge of a local
committee of three or four citizens, whose powers were considerable. Teachers were admonished not to engage in any occupation
that might interfere with their duties. A female teacher who married lost her post. Schools were in session 202 days a year, and text
books and slates were furnished free. In addition to the three R's,
the New York School system included a variety of activities and
specialty subjects—evening classes, vacation schools, music, drawing, cooking, and the like by specialty teachers. There were also
special classes for the handicapped, the blind, the anemic, and
courses of evening lectures, among other activities.

The Brownsville schools were in District 39, and the East New
York schools in District 40. Each was in charge of a local School
Committee, a member of the Board of Education, and a district
superintendent. For many years Mr. Baruch Miller was chairman
of the Brownsville Committee, and Mr. James J. McCabe, district
superintendent. All children were expected to attend the district
or neighborhood school, and since Brownsville was predominately
Jewish, its schools were attended almost entirely by Jewish
students, while most of the teachers were Irish.

The Brownsville schools faced a number of problems. The most
serious problem was to relieve the overcrowded schools and find
room for the new children. A large proportion of the school
population never had the opportunity to get a full day of
schooling. "Nowhere is the congestion crisis in schools more acute
and harder to deal with than in Brownsville," reads a newspaper
interview with District Superintendent McCabe in *The Standard
Union* of April, 1904. "With people moving in constantly, and
with cars beginning to cross the Williamsburg Bridge," he
continued, "the situation is expected to grow worse. We have now
100 part-time classes with approximately 5,000 children in them.
In Brownsville, where the congestion is especially felt, we have
now only four schools. . . ."

Four new schools were opened between 1905 and 1912. On May
31, 1911, more than 30 per cent of the school population in
Brownsville proper was on part time—8,920 children out of a total

registration of 29,000. At the end of the following year, May 31, 1912, the number decreased somewhat to 6,742 out of a total registration of 30,210.

Compared to today's new schools with their many facilities and conveniences, the red or grey brick school houses built in Brownsville in the early days would appear antiquated and inadequate. They would seem anachronistic to the modern parent, but to the immigrant parent they represented progress and a monumental achievement. Contrasted with the European schools, which were forbidden to Jewish children, these schools were palaces. The parents were therefore happy to have the children attend them at least part of the day. The schools were, after all, solidly constructed, spacious, with classrooms that were warm in the cold winters, and they were manned by a staff of professional teachers.

In the 1940's the parents associations initiated an active campaign for new schools. After six years of persistent effort—letters, delegations, bus loads of parents at City Hall budget hearings, and political pressure—the new Junior High School 263 was constructed. A new elementary school, 298, replaced Public School 84.

By and large, the teachers were dedicated and devoted. Those who were nonJewish strove to understand the Jewish children, their immigrant parents, and the homes they came from. Some became an inspiration to their pupils and infused them with high ideals.

Unfortunately, a few teachers made little effort to understand, much less to like Jewish children. Ignorant of the cultural background of their pupils, and uninformed regarding their customs and traditions and the conditions which prevailed in the Jewish home, these teachers looked down on them. Some complained that their Jewish children "lacked culture." In 1912 a formal protest was lodged with the local School Board that during school exercises in the school auditorium, the assistant principal goaded the children by saying, "Sing well, little Sheenies!"

With the entrance of more Jews into the teaching profession, several outstanding Jewish teachers and principals came to the

Brownsville schools. The first Jewish principal was Dr. Oswald Schlockow, who headed the Boys Division of Public School 109 between 1902 and 1917. In 1909 and 1910, among the twenty-five school principals in the area there were three additional Jewish principals, Dr. Saul Badanes, Dr. Leon W. Goldrich, and Dr. Alexander Fischhandler. By this time there were a goodly number of Jewish teachers in the Brownsville schools. In the Boys Division of Public School 84, of which Dr. Badanes was principal, half of the staff of some fifty teachers were Jewish. In the Girls Division of the same school, of which Miss Mary Finly was principal, there were 7 Jewish teachers out of a staff of fifty. In Public School 109, Boys Division, of which Dr. Schlockow was principal, eighteen of the fifty-two teachers were Jewish.

Dr. Oswald Schlockow was an inspiring personality, a great teacher, an eloquent speaker, writer, and social worker. He was principal of Public School 50 in Williamsburg (1918-1927), and in 1927 became District Superintendent of Schools. He was elected president of the Brooklyn Teachers Association in 1924, to which organization he rendered valuable service for many years. He was president of the Hebrew Educational Society between 1920 and 1923, and participated in a rich program of philanthropic endeavors.

One of the most sympathetic and beloved personalities among New York teachers and school principals was Dr. Saul Badanes, for many years principal of Public Schools 84 and 173. In 1935, on the occasion of his seventieth birthday, a volume of appreciation of the Badanes System of Primary Arithmetic was presented to him by a group of educators. The volume was edited by Dr. Paul Radosavlevich, Professor of Experimental Pedagogy at New York University, and by Dr. McQuilkin DeGrange, Professor of Sociology at Dartmouth College.

The school subject which caused the greatest number of pupil-failures occupied Dr. Badanes' interest throughout his life. The method he developed concretized and simplified the teaching of primary number work to little children. He published a series of primers for the first grades, and manuals for the teachers. His work in this field provoked discussion and evoked acclaim among educators. The versatility and profound educational ideas of Dr. Badanes are attested to in his *First Practical Steps in Selecting Gifted Children in a Large City School* (New York, 1927). This problem had absorbed his attention since his early days in 1900. During a half century of activity as an inspiring teacher, philosopher, and thinker, he promulgated his credo: "Do not test, but teach; do not be fooled by the face value of school-room testing, but note what kind of stimuli you offer to your class, and what kind of insight you get in your individual pupil." He died on April 25, 1940.

Among the teachers who taught in Public School 84, when Dr. Badanes was principal were a number who later became local principals—Charles G. Eichel, Samuel Katz, and Maxwell F. Littwin. Another teacher in his school was Eugene A. Culligan, who later became Associate Superintendent of Schools, and then President of Hunter College. "It was my good fortune," wrote Dr. Culligan, "shortly after I began my teaching career, to be assigned to the school of which Dr. Saul Badanes was the inspiring principal."

Principals who served for lesser periods also left their impress on the schools and other positions to which they advanced. Dr. Leon W. Goldrich, principal for a time of Public School 144, became the executive director of the Hebrew Sheltering Guardian Society, and later Director of the Bureau of Child Guidance of the Board of Education.

Dr. Isaac Bildersee was among the many district superintendents who worked in Brownsville. He unleashed a storm of controversy over the issue as to whether or not Hanukkah songs should be sung in the schools along with Christmas carols. His zeal in preserving the doctrine of separation of church and state called for the elimination of both Hanukkah songs and Christmas carols. Among his extracurricular activities was providing country camping for all children. He composed a detailed list of suggestions for setting up country camps.[7] These suggestions, which augmented the Peck Bill, were presented to the State Legislature.

In the early years, comparatively few children attended high schools. Generally only those bent on preparing themselves for a professional career continued their schooling upon graduation from the grammar grades. Many parents were unable to support their grown children; therefore the children were forced to find employment as soon as the law permitted. In a study made of 245,000 employed boys in 1918, it was found that in Greater New York 87.6 per cent between the ages of 16 and 18 years were out of school. Of American-born boys having at least one parent born in Russia, 70.0 per cent under the age of 16 were employed, as against 70.1 per cent for all of Greater New York (3.8 per cent left school under 14 years of age; 22.7 per cent at 14, and 39 per cent at 15 years). The percentage was larger (79.6 per cent) for American-born youth with at least one parent born in Poland (36.8 left at 14 years, and 38.6 per cent at 15 years) [8].

Dr. Lee K. Frankel and Louis 1. Dublin, in their study of the height and weight of 10,043 children between the ages of 14 and 16 years who were granted employment certificates in New York City from July 13, 1914 to April 12, 1915, found that 3,671 or 36.6 per cent were Jews, almost twice as many as might be expected on a population basis. Of this number, 1938 (35.9 per cent) were boys, and 1733 (37.3 per cent) were girls. Their nearest competitors were the Italians, who constituted 18.3 per cent (877 boys and 965 girls).

According to the Bureau of Jewish Research, the continuation schools of the city established for young workers under 17 who could work full time except for a half-day each week to attend classes, had an enrollment in 1926 of 49,917 Jewish students (54 per cent) out of a total enrollment of 92,440 students. Many students who could not afford to continue their education attended evening classes either in public or private schools while holding a job during the day. There were a number of private preparatory schools in the neighborhood in the early years. In many families, one or two of its members attended higher schools of learning, while the rest of the family worked to support them.

High school students attended either Boys High School or one of the high schools that were opened later. It was not until 1924 that East New York finally had a high school—the Thomas Jefferson High School on Dumont and Pennsylvania avenues. Dr.

Elias Lieberman, head of the English Department of Bushwick High School, was appointed its first principal. He has enjoyed a distinguished literary career as editor of *Puck,* literary editor of *The American Hebrew,* editor of numerous anthologies of poetry, and he has several published collections of verse to his credit.

Through his many years as principal of Thomas Jefferson High School, he helped shape the course of the school, which was attended by thousands of boys and girls. When Hebrew was introduced in the New York High Schools, Thomas Jefferson High School was the first to offer the subject. According to Dr. Lieberman, a modern high school student must cultivate a three-fold education—a sound body, good speech, and good manners, "notable for their absence in many quarters."

For those who were unable to attend regular high school there was the continuation school. The original Brooklyn continuation school was founded in 1919, and met on the top floor of Public School 69, at 155 Ryerson Street. Dr. I. David Cohen became head of the school the following year, and numerous annexes were added.

J. Ritchie Stevenson, principal of the East New York Vocational High School for many years, came to East New York in 1922, and began the work that has grown into the East New York Vocational High School. He was particularly interested in boys and girls who, because their abilities were not along the traditional academic lines, often found themselves disadvantaged and rejected.

Most Jewish parents appreciated educational opportunities for their children and endeavored to keep them in school as long as possible, but they were not averse to having their children earn money outside of school hours and during vacations.[8] A considerable number earned part or all of their expenses while attending college or a professional school in New York. Seventy per cent of the 31,000 students enrolled in New York University in 1926 depended wholly or in part upon their own incomes.

In 1928 Dr. Frederick B. Robinson, president of the College of the City of New York attended by a number of Brownsville students, remarked about Jewish students that "so many of them have to earn their living while attending college, some even supporting parents, that they have little time to supplement their curricular activities by taking advantage of and participating in cultural activities such as are found in literary and musical circles. Of course, this condition is not of their making, but it is regrettable nevertheless. And yet we have a fair representation among debating societies, orchestras, and the like."

Since the 1930's a large number of Brownsville and East New York youth have gone into teaching. Jews constitute a large proportion of the teachers in the New York Public Schools, and since there is also a large proportion of Jewish children, the schools are closed on the Jewish New Year and Day of Atonement. Unlike the early days, when the students in the Brownsville schools were mostly Jewish and the teachers non-Jewish, today most of the principals and teachers in Brownsville schools are Jewish.

Many Brownsville and East New York teachers have risen from the ranks to assume positions of principal, assistants to principal, assistant superintendents, examiners, and other positions in the New York City Board of Education and in the City Colleges. They have made a notable contribution to the New York educational staff.

The Brownsville Libraries

No library existed in Brownsville until 1900, when the Hebrew Educational Society moved into its building on Pitkin Avenue and Watkins Street.[9] The Brooklyn Public Library, which had been established earlier, had opened an East Branch at 29 Pennsylvania Avenue in October 1899, but it was some three-quarters of a mile outside the Jewish settlement.

The library and reading room on the second floor of the Hebrew Educational Society building became one of the most popular places in the neighborhood. During the ensuing five years the library acquired a considerable collection of books and employed a staff of librarians at its own expense.

In February, 1905, the Society offered to turn the library over to the Brooklyn Public Library. The library's Book and Administrative Committee reported in March 1905: "Examination of books has shown that the collection is a well chosen one of about 7,000 volumes. The reference works, while not many, are of excellent quality. . . . The committee recommends the acceptance of the generous offer of the Society and the establishment of a branch at Brownsville with the understanding that the present rooms be given to the library rent-free until January 1, 1906. We commend the farsighted liberality and the civic interest of the Hebrew Educational Society which has thus evinced its willingness to dedicate to the public its entire library, which it has created and gradually built up at a considerable outlay." [10]

On May 1, 1905, the Brooklyn Public Library took over, and with the consent of the donors, it received the name of "Brownsville Branch." The four employees of the Hebrew Educational Society Library were examined, and admitted to the proper grades by the Public Library. The new Brownsville Branch contained 7,173 volumes, with a monthly circulation of 3,871.

In 1906 the Building Committee of the Brooklyn Public Library recommended the lease of the library rooms from the Hebrew Educational Society at a rental of $1,000 per year. Under the direction of Leon Solis-Cohen, Assistant Librarian in charge of the branch, the library was reorganized to make its practice conform to the rest of the system. New books were added, and an awakened library consciousness was stimulated in the community. As a result, the yearly circulation doubled in 1906 to 64,627 volumes, of which 22,612 were juvenile fiction. In 1907 the number had reached 124,056 volumes, of which 47,592 were juvenile fiction. Book borrowers increased to 8,033; the total accessions were 10,466. The reading room was continually overcrowded, and the librarians found it difficult to keep up with the needs of juvenile circulation, which sometimes ran over 1,000 a day.

In *The Library Journal* of December, 1908, Mr. Leon Solis-Cohen published an article on library work in the Brooklyn Ghetto, in which he described some of his experiences in the

Brownsville Branch. Here are a few excerpts of the article which describe the insatiable readers of those days:

"To one beginning work in a poor foreign district, many habits of the people may seem objectionable. Such people, nevertheless, make a reading public, which many librarians long for in vain. You are constantly beseeched for more books on sociology and for the best continental literature. Your reading room is full of young people preparing themselves for civil service and college entrance examinations; your reference desk is overtaxed with demands for material for debates. Where there are more youngsters awaiting help than their assistants can serve, you are apt to find some child seeking by himself for material for currents in the latest *Current Literature*. Fully two-thirds of the work in all departments is with children. The little readers are the most insistent, and are very willing to wait a whole afternoon for the return of a book they want. Their reading is an odd mixture of the serious and the childish. Five hundred Yiddish, Russian, and Hebrew volumes have been too few to attract many of the fathers or grandfathers."

Because of the library's inadequate facilities, the Board of Estimates and Apportionment approved on January 25, 1907, a site for a library on the corner of Glenmore Avenue and Watkins Street, the building to be erected under the Carnegie gift. Lord and Hewlett, architects, were assigned to plan the building at a cost not to exceed $50,000. On December 19, 1908, the branch was opened to the public.

The building was taxed to the utmost from its opening day. Solis-Cohen, Miss Lillian Baldwin, and a staff of workers were assigned to this branch. The circulation for the first day was 3,000. In 1909 the Brownsville Branch jumped to first place in circulation among the branches of the Brooklyn Public Library, with a total of 330,338 volumes. Special collections of books in Yiddish, Hebrew, Russian, German, Italian, Polish, French, and Spanish were acquired, and a large number of periodicals subscribed to. In 1911, with Miss Harriet Burgess as branch librarian, the circulation reached 370,311 volumes. In 1940 the Brownsville library possessed 25,000 volumes, 21,000 borrowers, and a staff of one librarian, Alice Tuthill, and eight assistants.

The First Children's Library

The Board of Trustees of the Brooklyn Public Library was quick to recognize the imperative need for another branch library in the section. Its annual report of 1912 pointed out that Brownsville was not only densely populated, but also that its people were avid readers. Accordingly, the City acquired for $15,000 a lot on the corner of Stone and Dumont Avenues, some six blocks from the Brownsville Branch.

Thanks to the foresight, the perspicacity, and the dedication of Miss Clara W. Hunt, Superintendent of Works, who recommended to the Chief Librarian that this be constructed exclusively as a children's library, the new branch became a virtual little Paradise for the youngsters. An experienced children's librarian for many years, Miss Hunt applied herself with admirable devotion to the task of implementing her recommendation. A beautiful two-story building with a mezzanine was completed and opened for the public on September 24, 1914. Mrs. Flora DeGogorza, a graduate of Pratt Institute Library School, and for many years librarian in various Brooklyn Public Libraries, was chosen as branch librarian. It was a glorious achievement! It vindicated the prophetic words Miss Hunt had written on June 22, 1912:

"The Brownsville district deserves the best we can provide. There are more than 27,000 school children within the library radius this year, and the district is growing with mushroom rapidity. Practically all the residents are of foreign birth. If we do not bend our efforts now to giving the children American ideals, we, or those who come after us, will rue it. Every detail should be as perfect as our information, available in the year 1912, can make it, so that the visitor from abroad may see a model children's library indeed. Expense should not be spared in providing the most convenient and artistic furniture and decorations as well as the best book collection. The Brownsville's children's library will be the only one planned and built from the ground up to serve only a juvenile public. . . ."

The great heights the branch attained are reflected in the daily report of Monday, January 4, 1915. The circulation during the four library hours on that day was 2,645 volumes. There was a line of people outside the building extending along the block and around the corner into Christopher Avenue. Inside, another line of people waited to have their books changed.

"Our problems in discipline are not similar to those met in dealing with most children," states the librarian in the Annual Report of 1914. "Books are the center of their interest, and it is around these that our discipline resolves itself. One child is consumed with curiosity to know what book another child is reading. If by chance one child has chosen two or three books for selection, he or she is sure to have them taken away. If a handful of new books in publishers' covers is brought in, the bearer is followed, like a farmer's wife in her henyard, to catch a glimpse of the titles. . . . No other group could be handled with such comparative ease in proportion to their numbers."

Over the years a number of special services were conducted in this library. On April 17, 1915, the Story Hour was begun—a single day's attendance being as large as 270. A number of reading clubs were organized between 1915 and 1936. At first there were only girls clubs. In 1921 Mrs. DeGogorza received a request from a 7A class of boys of a neighboring school who were "attenders of the Brownsville's Children's Branch," requesting her to start a Boys Reading Club. 'We, the undersigned, promise to be quiet and orderly throughout.' "

The letter was signed by thirteen boys, and the reading club they organized continued until 1936. Famous men and women of history, the world of science, and other lands were some of the topics discussed in the programs.

In 1929 the trustees approved Mrs. DeGogorza's project to expand with a department for intermediates or high school youngsters from the 9th grade to age 16. The Young People's Room was placed under the direction of Miss Cecile J. Lynch, and was open between 2:30 and 9 P.M.

In 1930 the Library had a book collection of 18,680 volumes, a registration of 22,064, a circulation of 369,990—the largest in all of its years—and a staff of 14 professional and 7 clerical workers.

When Mrs. DeGogorza retired in 1940 she was succeeded by Miss Anne Jackson as librarian. Since that time the total circulation has decreased for a variety of reasons. There has also been a change in the reading tastes. "These children of newly arrived immigrants were eager readers. Through books a new world was opened to them. They were anxious to possess the treasures which these books contained . . . ," wrote Mrs. DeGogorza. Nevertheless, the beautiful building, covered with ivy, continues to be a vital force in the lives of the many who use it.

The Children's Library on Stone Avenue was a "beyond" to many. It was a "beyond" even in Brownsville to Alfred Kazin, "because they had an awning over the front door; in the long peaceful reading room there were story-book tiles over the fireplace and covered deep wooden benches on each side of it where I read my way, year after year, from every story of King Alfred the Great to *Twenty Thousand Leagues Under the Sea.*" [11]

The Hebrew Educational
Society of Brooklyn

X

Sixty-five Years of Communal Service

THE ORIGIN and development of the Hebrew Educational
Society of Brooklyn (known to many by its initials as the
"H.E.S.") is closely associated with the history and development of the Brownsville Jewish community. Its long and
fruitful career runs almost parallel to that of the community—
some sixty-five out of approximately seventy-five years. The
founding of this institution at the end of the century stirred
intense interest. It was the first Jewish Community Center in
Brooklyn.

The need for such an agency was quite apparent. Immigration
was at its flood tide. Parents and children were learning about
their new America—the parents through the sweatshop, the
pushcart, and the tiny store; the children in the school or on the
street. Like all youth, the children were often in conflict with their
parents. It was to guide and interpret to these newcomers the

world about them, and to help bridge the gap between parents and children, between the secular and religious cultures, between the Old World and New York City and America, that the Hebrew Educational Society was established.

The program of activities was flexible over the years, invoking changes to meet changing needs. The agency came under the influence of different personalities holding disparate views toward life in general, and toward Jewish issues in particular, but some of its original goals and emphases have continued unabated as the focus of its work throughout its almost seven decades of existence. These included the engendering of a warm, neighborly, hospitable and home-like atmosphere one could feel on entering the building; a friendly, vital interest in the individual person, in his family, in his problems and difficulties; constructive work with the small club or group; stressing the roles of music, art, drama, cultural activities, athletics, and homemaking so as to elevate the tone and standards of neighborhood life and to provide media outlets for the creative powers of individuals and groups. "Wherever there is a need we stand ready to serve" has been the Hebrew Educational Society's motto through the years.

The Hebrew Educational Society served as a socializing force, bringing together individuals and groups with different ideas in natural interplay and mutual understanding. It pioneered and experimented in a variety of educational and social projects. It organized the first library and reading room in the neighborhood, a kindergarten, a penny savings bank, farm gardens, a summer vacation school, a country camp, a "golden age" program, a special service for young adults, and other activities, some of which were later taken over by public agencies. For a time it served as the headquarters for a number of the Brooklyn social agencies and movements. It became in a real sense the *Bet Am*, the cultural and recreational center for the entire locality, from which flowed the cultural life within and outside the neighborhood. Fortunately, the complete records of its activities since its inception are intact and available, and we can therefore relate its story in detail.[1]

The Early Development

The Hebrew Educational Society was the first, and for some
time the only Brownsville institution to be established by an
outside community. In the late 1890's, when Brownsville was
being inundated by wave after wave of newcomers, the Baron de
Hirsch Fund became concerned with the new community's needs,
and proceeded to establish the Hebrew Educational Society.[2]

To many who are familiar only with the contemporary role of
American Jewry as the generous benefactor of oppressed Jews the
world over, it may come as a surprise that at the end of the last
century American Jewry was the recipient of the bounty of some
of the wealthy Jewish communities of Europe.

In the eighties and nineties, when the large numbers of Jewish
Eastern European immigrants were coming to this land, many of
the older settlers did not look with favor on this vast migration.[3]
Moreover, the financial drain was too great for them to bear.
Committees were established in all of the large capitals of Europe
to come to the rescue.

The original attitude of hostility toward the newcomers
changed in time. A growing number felt a common tie of kinship
and fraternity with the newcomers; others sensed the historic
import and potential of this mass migration. A group of wealthy
Jews in high places became leaders in the crisis, stimulated and
inspired to positive action by that great philanthropist, Baron
Maurice de Hirsch, who entered the scene at this time. The
number of humanitarian causes to which he contributed was
legion, and he is reported to have exceeded the fabulous sum of
100 million dollars.

Ready to relieve distress anywhere, he realized that the
appalling plight of the vast mass of Russian Jewry called for
immediate and heroic action. To render possible a new existence
for his oppressed brethren, he established in 1891 the Jewish
Colonization Association (J.C.A.) and the Baron de Hirsch Fund.
A group of outstanding American Jewish leaders, headed by Judge

Meyer S. Isaacs as president, was chosen as trustees of the Fund. Abraham Abraham of Brooklyn became one of the trustees. Adolphus S. Solomons was selected as superintendent, a title later changed to "general agent."

The new settlement of Brownsville came to the attention of the Baron de Hirsch Fund in 1897, when a Committee on Homes was appointed to solve the problem of congestion on the East Side. While examining plans of model tenements as a solution of the East Side problem, the committee also investigated the new settlement of Jews in Brownsville and East New York which contained some five hundred Russian-Jewish families engaged in tailoring. This community seemed to offer more favorable conditions than the East Side. Stretches of land were available, and many families owned their own homes. There were also schools and other public facilities in the neighborhood. Dr. Milton Reizenstein, a graduate of Johns Hopkins University, who had written on the subject of housing for low income groups and who later became superintendent of the Hebrew Educational Society, was engaged to aid the committee in its investigations. In 1898 the Fund attempted to combine the model tenement idea with removal to other sections of the city. Land was acquired in Brooklyn and some lots were purchased in the Bronx, but after considerable study the experiment for the construction of model tenements was abandoned, and the property acquired for this purpose in New York and Brooklyn was finally sold.

In the summer of 1898 the Baron de Hirsch Fund, after investigating the social conditions in the Brownsville community, made a modest start by opening a vacation school for a few weeks. The Fund sent a Mr. Joseph Parvin to Brownsville to conduct the vacation school.[4] Seventy children between seven and twelve years of age attended at a total expense of eighty-five dollars.

Joseph Parvin, a Russian intellectural (*Maskil*) who had come to America in the early 1880's, was an interesting personality. Before coming to New York in 1897 he had edited *The Star of Israel,* a semi-monthly Chicago journal devoted to the moral and intellectual progress of American Jews in general and to those from Russia in particular. He was a lover of Zion, a poet, and a social reformer. Some of his writings were published in 1926 in a volume entitled *Bringing in the Sheaves of Zion*.

In the fall of 1898 Mr. Parvin experimented under the auspices of the Baron de Hirsch Fund with an evening class in English to immigrants and with some club work.[4] For its locale, one floor in a small private house on Rockaway Avenue was used from November 15, 1898 to February, 1899. The total expense to the Fund was between $55 and $60 per month. When Adolphus S. Solomons, superintendent of the Fund, visited the little place and observed the disadvantages under which the school was operating, he suggested that the Fund increase the allotment to $70 a month.[5] Larger quarters, which were called the "Baron de Hirsch Hall," were obtained in a small house located at 91 Osborn Street at a monthly rental of $22.50. Here the work continued and expanded in scope. Mr. Adolphus Solomons, who visited the new premises several times, became convinced of the need of the work in Brownsville, and the appropriation was again increased.

Convinced that Brownsville needed an educational institution similar to the Educational Alliance in the Lower East Side, Mr. Solomons [5] enlisted the cooperation of Abraham Abraham, a trustee of the Baron de Hirsch Fund and a leading Brooklyn Jew. Mr. Abraham called on a group of Brooklyn Jews to meet for "the purpose of taking definite action to establish educational schools in Brownsville under the auspices of the Baron de Hirsch Fund."

On the evening of May 24, 1899, the following assembled in the Baron de Hirsch Hall, 91 Osborn Street: Abraham Abraham and Adolphus S. Solomons, trustees of the Fund; Nathaniel H. Levi, Michael Furst, Moses B. Schmidt, Emil Weil, Moses H. Harris, David Michael, E. Newman, Hon. Mitchell May, Rev. Dr. Leon Nelson, Julius Reiner, Edward C. Blum, Dr. Abraham Koplowitz, Maurice Weil, Dr. Max Levy, Dr. Michael A. Cohn, J. B. Grubman, Dr. L. Adlerman, and J. Koplowitz. It was resolved to form a temporary organization. Michael Furst was chosen temporary chairman, and Moses B. Schmidt, secretary. A committee of five was appointed on Plan and Scope, consisting of Simon F. Rothschild, Moses B. Schmidt, Dr. Leon Nelson, Hon. Mitchell May, and Dr. Michael A. Cohn.

On June 8, 1899, a second meeting was held at de Hirsch Hall. Gathered here were orthodox and reform rabbis; American, German, and East European Jews, professionals and businessmen, Democrats, Republicans, Socialists and Anarchists.

On June 21, 1899 the Committee on Plan and Scope submitted its recommendations to the trustees of the Baron de Hirsch Fund. The anxious consideration which motivated the report is expressed in this introductory paragraph.

"Gentlemen:

"Without reflecting upon anyone, the facts are patent that unless drastic measures are adopted and that too, without delay, the present fearful status of affairs in Brownsville will inevitably evolve into a scandal that will reflect not only injuriously upon its 15,000 or more residents, but inflict a lasting blight upon the fair fame of our people throughout the land and especially Greater New York where it is our pride to claim that its position of Jew morally, commercially, and socially, makes him the equal to the best grade of American citizenship."

The report urged the fund to provide a larger and more suitable building than the one then in use, the new building to be suitably furnished and to be under the patronage of the Baron de Hirsch Fund; in which work should be done similar to that of the Educational Alliance in New York, the work to be directed by representatives of the Fund and an Advisory Committee of residents of Brooklyn and Brownsville to be selected thereafter.

The report also recommended the establishment of a kindergarten, library, clubs for literary, musical and social aims, a small gymnasium, scheduled public lectures, readings and social reunions, continuation of the English classes and the Vacation School if the city authorities failed to do so. It also voiced the hope that in time the house be made into a social and literary center for the whole of Brownsville, something that was much needed for there was not a hall, theatre, or other public place of amusement or assembly in the District.

The report set forth details regarding administrative procedures of the proposed organization, and suggested that its name be the Hebrew Educational Alliance of Brooklyn. It then called for an appropriation of $2,750 for furnishing the building and library, and an appropriation of $455 per month for one year to meet running expenses, which included the rental of the building, salaries, and other expenses. In response to this appeal, the trustees of the Fund voted $2,500 for furnishings and $400 per month for maintenance. Thus was the Hebrew Educational Society of Brooklyn established in Brownsville.

Plans for the new organization proceeded rapidly. On November 12, 1899, at the first membership meeting of the Society held in Sanger Hall, the first set of officers and directors were elected. They included Simon F. Rothschild, president; Michael Furst, vice-president; Moses J. Harris, treasurer; and Nathaniel H. Levi, honorary secretary.

As directors, the following were elected: Adolphus S. Solomons, Abraham Abraham, Rabbi Leon M. Nelson, Moses B. Schmidt, Samuel Gabriel, Jacob Brenner, and Frank Pentlarge for a period of three years each; Maurice Weil, Samuel Goodstein, Julius Reiner, Edward C. Blum, Ira Leo Bamberger, Louis L. Firuski, for two years each; and Michael A. Cohen, Mitchell May, D. J. Steinhardt, Silas W. Stein, and Hyman Meyersohn, one year each.

Two of the members of this Board of Directors, Dr. Michael Cohen and Hyman Meyersohn, were residents of Brownsville. Later, other residents—A. J. Grubman, Samuel Palley, Nathan J. Coyne, Michael Fisk, William B. Roth, Samuel A. Telsey, and Dr. A. Koplowitz became directors. Rabbi Leon M. Nelson of Temple Israel not only served on the board, but often chaired the very important educational committee. He served as chairman of the Education Committee until he left Temple Israel in 1903. Dr. Judah L. Magnes succeeded him in 1904, and also came on the board of the Hebrew Educational Society. He filled the vacancy created by the resignation of Adolphus Solomons, who was unanimously elected an honorary member. A fitting set of resolutions and a letter were presented to Mr. Solomons. Rabbi Nathan Krass, who occupied Temple Israel pulpit between 1910 and

1918, likewise served on the board, and conducted a regular forum on Sunday afternoons. Other Rabbis of the community who served on the board over the years were Rabbi Martin Meyer, Simon R. Cohen, Louis Gross, Alexander Lyons, and Israel H. Levinthal.

Next to Mr. Adolphus Solomons, the Hebrew Educational Society owes its growth to the efforts of Mr. Abraham Abraham. Like Mr. Solomons, he was a native New Yorker (born March 9, 1843), but unlike Mr. Solomons who was associated with the English and Sephardic groups, Mr. Abraham came of German-Jewish stock. His father, Judah, was a native of Bavaria, Germany, who came to the United States in 1835. In 1865 he established with Joseph Wechsler the dry goods firm of Wechsler and Abraham in Brooklyn. In 1893 the firm name was changed to Abraham and Straus (A. & S.) and grew into one of America's leading mercantile establishments. Noted for his public spirit, Abraham Abraham gave generous support to movements for the civic, philanthropic, and cultural advancement of the community. He played a leading role in the development of the various Jewish institutions in Brooklyn. He died on June 28, 1911, leaving three daughters; Lillian, wife of Simon F. Rothschild; Florence, wife of Edward Charles Blum; and Edith, wife of Percy Seldon Straus; and a son, Lawrence Abraham.

Not only was Mr. Abraham himself interested in the development of the Hebrew Educational Society, but he also involved both of his sons-in-law, and his daughter Florence. Son-in-law Simon F. Rothschild became the first president of the Society, in which office he served for ten years. Mr. Edward C. Blum served on the Board of Directors, and his wife Florence served as a member and as president of the Ladies Auxiliary for a number of years.

On November 12, 1899, Mr. Abraham Abraham delivered an address at a meeting of the Society in which he expressed his satisfaction at the response to his call for the organization of the society, and his hope that Brooklyn Jewry would give it the support it merits. He then went on to dwell on the task of the society as he saw it, which was the Americanization of the immigrant primarily through learning the English language, the abandonment of the "jargon," and becoming acquainted with American institutions. Subsequent speakers expatiated on the educational, religious, vocational, and recreational projects that were to come under the purview of the society.

A petition was made to the regents of the University of the State of New York for a charter, and on December 21, 1899, the institution was incorporated under the name of "Hebrew Educational Society of Brooklyn." Its object was, as set forth in the charter, "To promote the intellectual and physical advancement of men and women, and to erect suitable buildings containing library, reading, class and lecture rooms and gymnasium." Membership in the society increased during the year to about five hundred, and two collectors were engaged, one for those residing east of Ralph Avenue, and one for those residing west of Ralph Avenue.

Joseph Parvin acted as superintendent until 1900, when Albert Bernard Yudelson was appointed superintendent. He was the first of a group of eight interesting personalities who headed the institution over the years. Dr. Yudelson stayed two years with the Hebrew Educational Society, and then moved to Chicago, where he served as Rabbi of the South Side Hebrew Congregation (1902-1914). He also studied medicine, and became a well known neurologist and Associate Professor of Nervous and Mental Diseases of the Northwestern University Medical School.

Much progress was made at the Hebrew Educational Society during the first years. The new building which was erected on Pitkin and Watkins Street by Dr. Edward Mandel and his partners, Hyman Meyersohn, Krakauer, and Krimsky, was leased by the society at an annual rental of $3,000. Hyman Meyersohn, on whose land the building was constructed, was among those who encouraged Mr. Abraham to interest the Baron de Hirsch Fund in the needs of the Jewish population of Brownsville. The dedication of the new headquarters on May 6, 1900, was a memorable event in Brownsville, and so many sought to attend the evening public reception that police were needed to keep the throng in check.

The people of Brownsville, particularly the youth, welcomed

the Hebrew Educational Society. At last there was to be a center with a library, a social hall, a gymnasium, club and class rooms where boys and girls could meet, form friendships, cultivate their social instincts, expand their spiritual horizons, and bring fulfillment and realization to their hopes for the future.

The Hebrew Educational Society was planned originally to serve as an educational center for the adjustment of the Jewish immigrant to the New World. The objectives, purposes, and activities of the society paralleled those espoused by various institutions in this country, such as Hebrew Institute, or Jewish Educational Alliance. All focused their activities on the education and Americanization of the immigrant.

When negotiations were conducted with Mr. Hill, chief librarian of the Brooklyn Public Library, about handing over the Hebrew Educational Society library to the Public Library, the matter of keeping the library open for circulation on the Sabbath was taken up at the Board meeting. It was decided that the agency would have no objection to having the library open seven days a week provided there should be no circulation of books on the Sabbath until after six o'clock. However, when the Brooklyn Public Library Branch was in the Hebrew Educational Society building, the library was closed on Saturdays.

Among the first paid employees of the society was the librarian, Miss Minnie Shomer, who served until 1903. She was a daughter of the well-known Yiddish writer and dramatist, N. N. Shaike-witch, who used "Shomer" as his pen name. Miss Shomer was for a time also in charge of the clubs. She married Mr. Charles Zunzer, the well known social worker. Mr. Zunzer himself was for a time a volunteer club leader of the Young Boys Educational Club at the Hebrew Educational Society. Miss Shomer was assisted, among others, by Fannie Masliansky and S. Elizabeth Silberstein. When Miss Stewart, who followed Miss Shomer as librarian, resigned, Miss Celia Silbert succeeded her.

The society's earliest activities included classes in English for immigrants, a regents school to prepare students for higher examinations and entry into higher schools of learning, a piano class, manual training classes, a sewing school, dressmaking and millinery classes, lectures in English and Yiddish, concerts, entertainments, socials, and exhibitions of various kinds.

In addition to educational activities, the society conducted a program of activities through a large number of social, literary, and athletic clubs. The Brownsville kindergarten, which Rabbi Godfrey Taubenhaus of Congregation Shaarey Zedek was instru-mental in establishing under the auspices of the Brooklyn section of the National Council of Jewish Women, was taken over by the Women's Auxiliary. On November 5, 1902, the Board of Education rented the Hebrew Educational Society Auditorium for $1,200 a year, to conduct the kindergarten under its auspices. It met in the building until 1908 before moving to the new annex of Public School 84.

Through the generosity of L. Littlefield, a well-fenced plot on Blake Avenue between Osborn Street and Thatford Avenue was secured in 1906 for the purpose of experimenting in vacant-lot farming. After a number of years, the project was taken over by the Betsy Head Playground.

In 1904 a branch of Penny Provident Fund was established, which afforded children an opportunity to save small amounts of money beginning with as little as one penny. Withdrawals were permitted when deposits reached the sum of fifty cents.

While the founders of the Education Committee were con-cerned with the Americanization of the foreigner, they were equally concerned with the religious upbringing of the young. "We believe that it is our duty to keep alive in the children of the community a proper religious spirit and love for Judaism," President Adolph Feldblum stated in his report for the year 1911. In a subsequent report two years later he repeated, "In every branch of our work, the Jewish feature is emphasized. . . ."

Although most of the board members belonged to the reform wing of Judaism, and the reform rabbi of Temple Israel was usually the chairman of the Education Committee, every effort was made not to offend the sensibilities of the orthodox Jews in the community. At a meeting in 1903 the question was raised as to whether or not the society was sectarian. It was stated by the president that the Baron de Hirsch Fund appropriation would cease if this were otherwise.

From the very outset, classes in Hebrew and a Sabbath School were conducted in the building. Prior to 1903 the Beth Abraham School Association, in cooperation with the Hebrew Educational Society, conducted a Hebrew school in the building. According to the articles of agreement drawn up between the society and the Beth Abraham Hebrew School Association in February 1901, the association was responsible for the salaries of the teachers and the supplying of books and stationery. In return, the society was to allow, free of charge, the use of as many classrooms as it could spare. The Hebrew Educational Society was to have a voice in the selection of teachers, in the formation of the curriculum, and in methods of instruction. In 1903 the Hebrew Educational Society took over the school under its own control, and has conducted it now for more than sixty years.

A Sabbath School was opened on October 25, 1902, meeting Saturday mornings from a quarter after ten in the morning until twelve-thirty. It attracted thousands of children over the years. In the 1906 annual report we find that 650 pupils, taught by a staff of 15 volunteer teachers, attended on Saturday mornings, taxing the capacity of the building. Religious services were held for the children at the conclusion of the session. The holiday celebrations and the annual picnic in Prospect Park, sponsored by the Ladies Auxiliary, were outstanding events of the school. High Holy Day services were held during the early years in the auditorium under the auspices of the Brownsville Relief Society and under the direction of N. Getzoff. From time to time well-known Jewish speakers spoke from the Hebrew Educational Society platform. Reverend H. Masliansky, the famous Yiddish preacher, delivered ten lectures in 1901 with an average attendance of 305.

The annual attendance during the first decade varied from 160,000 to 250,000. Practically all of the services were free. The income from fees never exceeded a few hundred dollars a year. The fees for the Hebrew School were five cents a week in 1902. A charge of a few cents was levied for Masliansky's early lectures on Saturday evenings, but they were then offered free. In 1902 the attendance for two of Masliansky's free lectures was 465 against 121 for two of his previous lectures, at which there was an admission charge of five cents.

The annual Hebrew Educational Society budget was between $10,000 and $13,000, of which $4,800 was contributed annually by the Baron de Hirsch Fund. The problem of financing the activities was always present because a large part depended on annual membership which fluctuated from year to year. Membership constituted several classes: life membership, $250; Donor, $50; Patron, $10; Member, $5; Associate Member, $3. A special committee of local residents was appointed on March 16, 1904, to form an Auxiliary Board for the purpose of soliciting local members. On April 2, 1901, the Hebrew Educational Society reported a grand total of 968 members. In 1905 the total number declined to only 605.

The society was assisted in its work by a ladies auxiliary which was organized in the fall of 1900 with a membership of 80, dues three dollars a year. It had a membership of 120 in 1904. Mrs. Ira Leo Bamberger was the first president (1900-1903), with Mrs. Isaac Levy as vice-president, Miss M. Marcus as secretary, and Mrs. Edward C. Blum as treasurer. In 1912, under the presidency of Mrs. Lee Gunst, the activities of the auxiliary were merged with those of the main society.

In her annual report in 1907 Mrs. Edward C. Blum, president, spoke of some of the activities of the auxiliary. It sponsored mothers meetings every fourth Saturday afternoon, at which a lecture was given in Yiddish, followed by a social tea. It also sponsored children's socials on Sunday afternoons, and dressmaking, sewing, and millinery classes. To teach the art of housekeeping, the auxiliary rented and furnished a four-room flat on Pitkin and Stone Avenues, where classes met twice a week in two-hour sessions. Mrs. Otto Kempner, treasurer of the auxiliary, reported $3,398.19 as receipts for the year, and $2,633.56 as disbursements.

The Brooklyn Section, National Council of Jewish Women, which was organized in October, 1896, cooperated with the Hebrew Educational Society over the years in a variety of activities. In its beginnings it received some support for its work from the Baron de Hirsch Fund. To counteract the proselytizing efforts in Brownsville at the beginning of this century, the society organized a Sunday School and kindergarten, maintained social service work, established mothers clubs and a sewing circle.

When the Hebrew Educational Society opened its building, the National Council of Jewish Women housed its classes and clubs in the society's building. Its probation officer and immigrant-aid agent made the society's building their headquarters for their work in this section, and generally cooperated with the society in various other ways during the early years. The presidents of the Brooklyn Council during these years were: Mrs. Godfrey Taubenhaus (1896-1900); Mrs. David Zeman (1900-1901); Mrs. S. Lippman (1901-1902); and Mrs. Otto Kempner (1902-1912).

In September 1902 Hartog Veld became superintendent and served for one year.[6] Dr. Milton Reizenstein, who received his degree of Doctor of Philosophy in 1897 at Johns Hopkins University, assumed the position of superintendent on September, 1903, and served until September, 1910, when he became superintendent of the Hebrew Orphan Asylum of Baltimore. Through his efforts the society had grown into an important institution.

By the end of its first decade, the Hebrew Educational Society was a real educational and social center in Brownsville. A striking aspect of its early history was its active interest in religious education. For a time, in 1918, there was some struggle within the Board of Directors as to what kind of curriculum should be introduced in its religious school. One group within the board felt that it was unnecessary to conduct an intensive program of Hebrew. They requested the Committee on Religious Work to consolidate the Hebrew School and Sabbath School, heretofore conducted as separate entities, into one school, and to prepare a syllabus of instruction which would devote about one-third of the time to the acquisition of a reading knowledge of Hebrew, and two-thirds to the study in the vernacular of the Bible, history, ceremonial, ethics, and the like.

This so deeply offended a number of Board members as to threaten a serious controversy. They held an informal conference at the Unity Club on November 24, 1918, and after a long discussion, decided to request the Committee on Religious Work to seek the guidance of Dr. Samson Benderly. Acting as Consulting Director of the school, and in concert with the committee, a curriculum would be prepared along lines which, while conforming to traditional Hebraism, should also be modern in educational practice and American spirit, outlook, and ideals. An intensive Hebraic school was the ultimate policy which prevailed over the years.

Second Decade of Service

A second period of growth for the Hebrew Educational Society began in 1910 when the late Judge Harry E. Lewis succeeded Nathaniel H. Levi (1909-1910) as president, and Dr. Charles S. Bernheimer succeeded Dr. Milton Reizenstein (1903-1910) as superintendent.

In October, 1909, the Brooklyn Federation of Jewish Charities was incorporated, and on November 11 of that year the Hebrew Educational Society voted to join the federation. The organizational pattern of the federation relieved its constituent societies of soliciting for members and contributions, permitting the trustees and professional staff to concentrate on internal duties and executive work.[7]

Even thus relieved, the budget of the society was too small to meet its needs. For 1911 the total receipts were $10,179.81, to which the Brooklyn Federation contributed $4,800 and the Baron de Hirsch Fund $4,200. The expenditures were $10,610.16. The Ladies Auxiliary of the society received an allotment of $1,600 for that year for their activities, which was subsequently merged with the general allotment to the Society. In 1915 the income was $12,300 and expenditures $12,348. In an address before the Judaens on May 2, 1915, on "Americanizing the Immigrant," Dr. Bernheimer called attention to the herculean task which confronted Brooklyn because of its limited means. "The character of the problem may be illustrated by the situation in Brooklyn, where the largest social and educational agency under Jewish auspices is the Hebrew Educational Society, with an annual budget one-tenth that of the Educational Alliance."

With the steady increase of Brownsville's population and of the society's activities, the need emerged for a larger and better building it could call its own, to replace the old, poorly equipped, and rented structure on Pitkin Avenue and Watkins Street. The federation authorized the Hebrew Educational Society's Board to solicit funds for the erection of a new building. The Brooklyn Federation contributed $12,000, the first contribution made by the federation for a building in this borough.

This sum was augmented by contributions from board members and from friends of the society in Brooklyn and Manhattan. A site was selected at the northwest corner of Hopkinson and Sutter Avenues, where the present building was constructed. Simeon B. Eisendrath was the architect, and Albert E. Kleinert the contractor. Dr. Bernheimer planned practically every detail with the architect. The building included an auditorium, a gymnasium, club and classrooms, music rooms, a roof garden, and other facilities. "It was the best," according to Dr. Bernheimer, "that could be accomplished at the time with the limited funds at the disposal of the organization." The building was dedicated on June 7, 1914.

This major event gave the Hebrew Educational Society a new lease on life. It assumed more the character of a settlement or neighborhood house, preoccupied not only with the programs and projects undertaken within the building, but also with the affairs of the neighborhood and of the community at large. Dr. Bernheimer, one of the eminent social workers in the United States, who died only recently in his ninety-second year, analyzed and evaluated the various phases of social service development in his book, *Half a Century in Community Service,* and in his numerous papers read before professional organizations and printed in sociological publications.[8]

Having done service in non-sectarian settlements prior to his coming to the Hebrew Educational Society, Dr. Bernheimer introduced into his work some aspects of the neighborhood settlement. As has already been pointed out, the Hebrew Educational Society was established from the outside Baron de Hirsch Fund and later supported by the Brooklyn Federation of

Jewish Charities. The nonsectarian settlements were usually founded from the inside by idealists or groups who felt an inner call to ameliorate poor social conditions, and who came to live in working-class neighborhoods in order to share their lives with the lives of those less fortunate.

The Hebrew Educational Society was primarily an educational rather than a social service or social and recreational agency. From its inception it was committed to providing a Jewish religious education for the youth. The clientele were not slum dwellers with a slum psychology; most of them came with a rich traditional culture and with a deep reverence for learning. Dr. Bernheimer recognized these differences, and adjusted his program accordingly. "Brownsville," he stated, "represented a phase of Jewish migration in New York from the Lower East Side to Brooklyn, and took on a somewhat more sophisticated coloring."

Following a basic settlement-house principle of living within the walls of the settlement building on the theory that it enables one to learn to know the community and become an integral part of it, Dr. Bernheimer took up residence in the new Hebrew Educational Society building, and made it his home until he married.

From the days of the Hebrew Educational Society's inception, the arts have entered into its program of settlement work. Under Dr. Bernheimer's direction, the Hebrew Educational Society Music School was organized, and became a significant division of the institution. It has continued over the years, providing individual instruction in every branch of music to hundreds of students for fees within the reach of the neighborhood residents. Scholarships were provided for many who could not meet even the reduced cost. Orchestral instruments were loaned or rented. Theory classes, an orchestra, and a chorus were organized. T. Bath Glasson (1873-1952), a non-Jew, well known as a composer and teacher in various colleges, joined the school in 1910, and served without charge for more than forty years as the executive of the department. He accepted fees only for lessons on his particular instrument. One of his associates was John Lynch, who headed the violin department until his death in November, 1929.

Other manifestations of artistic and aesthetic development were the Brownsville Neighborhood Theatre, under the direction of Maurice Sylbert, and a cultural institute which presented a series of lectures and concerts under the chairmanship of Oscar Bernstein. Exceptionally appealing was a series of Sunday afternoon lectures on topics of general and Jewish cultural interest, which started in the spring of 1915 and continued for several years, by Rabbi Nathan Krass of Temple Israel of Brooklyn, and later Rabbi of Temple Emanu-El in New York. The auditorium was always crowded to capacity, and the doors had to be closed to hundreds eager to hear the lectures and to participate in the ensuing question-and-answer period. It came to be known as the "Brownsville Forum."

Special attention was accorded the club department comprising a large group of junior, intermediate, and senior clubs, the junior, intermediate, and senior congresses, the declamation and debating tournaments, various social affairs, and a mothers club. The roof-garden dances attracted large numbers.

These clubs were led by volunteer club leaders, mostly young men and women who grew up with the Society. They were supervised by professional club workers—a Boys' Worker and a Directress of Social Work. Among those who served during these years were Miss Bertha Brenner, Joseph N. Gilman, David Schneeberg, Louis Spector, and Miss Hillman. The gymnasium came under the direction of Mr. Saul Friedman in September, 1915, and remained under this guidance until 1940, when he retired. Miss Kate Silverstone conducted the girls' classes in the gymnasium. A Hebrew and Sabbath School were regular activities which were continued. Among the teachers were Solomon Goldman, Solomon Grayzel, E. Charles Sidney, Hyman J. Landau, Joseph Allen, Solomon Rivlin, and Joshua Hochstein.

Dr. Bernheimer regarded himself not merely as the head of an institution, but also as a neighborhood and community worker obligated to crystallize opinion and to promote civic progress. With the aid of the Hebrew Educational Society and the Brooklyn Playground Association, he succeeded in persuading the authorities to place the Betsy Head Playground in a more accessible location in Brownsville than was originally contemplated. As a member of the local school board, serving for a time as its secretary, his dynamism and idealism helped to engender a fine spirit of neighborliness. He was for a time president of the Brooklyn Neighborhood Association, and an officer of other communal agencies.

After more than eight years of distinguished service to the Society, Dr. Bernheimer resigned as superintendent on December 30, 1918. The presidents of the Hebrew Educational Society during the period when he was the executive director were Judge Harry E. Lewis (1910, 1911), Adolph Feldblum (1912-1915) and Aron William Levy (1916-1919). Dr. Bernheimer was honored twice by the Hebrew Educational Society in later years. In 1949, when the institution observed its Golden Jubilee, a special luncheon was held in his honor. Some two hundred social workers assembled to salute him on his eightieth birthday. Ten years later, on December 5, 1958, when the Society celebrated its sixtieth anniversary, a luncheon in his honor was tendered on the occasion of his ninetieth birthday, and he was presented a leather-bound volume of letters from distinguished leaders in communal service from every part of the country.

After Dr. Bernheimer's departure, the Hebrew Educational Society was for a short time, from October 1919 to the fall of 1920, under the direction of Herman Brickman, who later became executive director of the Brooklyn Federation of Jewish Charities from 1924 to 1927. Harry Lebau, presently executive director of the Elizabeth Young Men's Hebrew Association, succeeded Mr. Brickman from December 15, 1920 to September, 1922. Dr. Oswald Schlockow was president of the Society from 1919 to 1921.

Four Decades of Service

Another period of growth and change may be said to have coincided with the long term of office held by Rabbi Alter F. Landesman. Under the presidency of Mr. Bernhard Bloch (1922-1924), Dr. Landesman became superintendent in September 1922 and continued until January, 1962, when he retired as director emeritus. He was succeeded by David Kleinstein, who had served as director in the Jewish Centers in Lynn and Buffalo, and as field secretary in New England for the National Jewish Welfare Board.

During the past four decades the perspective, program and objectives of the institution underwent important changes. It bears repetition to point out that the Hebrew Educational Society was originally projected and financed as an educational center, a philanthropic enterprise to help the immigrant family adjust itself to its new American environment. With the decrease in immigration and the subsequent replacement of the immigrant by native-born sons and daughters, the agency took on, for a period of years, more of the character of a settlement house or neighborhood center. The membership was composed mostly of children and adolescents, and the emphasis of the program was on educational, social, and recreational activities.

During the past several decades the Hebrew Educational Society has assumed the functions, scope, and responsibilities of a Jewish community center.[9] In 1921, just prior to Dr. Landesman's arrival at the Hebrew Educational Society, the Jewish Welfare Board, which was organized during World War I to conduct activities on behalf of the men and women in the armed services, merged with the Council of Young Men's Hebrew and Kindred Associations (founded in 1913), and decided to develop Jewish Centers in various parts of the country. The Hebrew Educational Society became a constituent society of the Jewish Welfare Board from the start, and its philosophy and program were greatly affected by the Jewish Center movement.

While the Jewish Community Center shares common elements with other institutions, it is a distinctly American contribution, purposing to enrich Jewish life on a distinctive basis.[10] Since no common philosophy has as yet been elaborated, Jewish Community Centers throughout the land exhibit wide variations of practice, of mood, and even of ultimate objectives. Particularly strong is the division between those who regard the Jewish Community Center as primarily an agency with a discriminating

Jewish purpose, "with which the Jew might identify himself in order to satisfy his specialized Jewish needs," and those who regard it in more general terms as a social work agency. During the past four decades the Hebrew Educational Society has functioned as a Jewish Community Center striving to disseminate and conserve the best of the Jewish heritage and to enhance its importance as a vitalizing force in the life of the Jew. It has not limited its activities to any single age group, but has sought to serve every member of the family, young and the old. The new emphasis was to work *with* people rather than *for* people.

In a booklet entitled, *The Present Role of a Jewish Community Center in a Metropolitan Neighborhood,* Dr. Landesman detailed the activities and objectives of the society, and included the following pronouncement of two basic goals:

"Working With the Neighborhood and Wider Community

"The Hebrew Educational Society is rooted in the Brownsville neighborhood, which has been the setting for its work for the past fifty-seven years. To understand our neighborhood, to develop its potentialities, to help provide or secure needed services has always been its concern. It never viewed itself as an insulated unit, but rather as an integral part of the entire community.

Our Special Tasks as a Jewish Community Center

"In addition to the many needs which the residents of our neighborhood have in common, and which they, with others, seek to satisfy through the various communal agencies, there are special needs which the Jews of our community have. For this they require a special place.

"The Jewish Community Center has been called by some a fourth force in Jewish life, different from and in addition to other religious and ideological forces. In many a metropolitan area like ours, where only a small portion of the Jews are affiliated with any Jewish organization, where few Jewish institutions exist outside a number of small synagogues and schools which restrict their activities either to worship or Jewish educational functions, and where the earlier settlers and established leadership have left for the newer sections, the Jewish Center remains the primary agency around which pulsates whatever general Jewish life there exists in these neighborhoods. It serves as a link to unite all Jews, young and old, regardless of ideological differences. It gives the Jews an opportunity to feel a sense of belonging, and to participate in Jewish communal life.

"The Jewish Community Center offers instruction in Judaism and its values and provides an opportunity for a diversity of Jewish experiences. Since it works with the individual as a whole person through his natural groups and interests, the Center exerts a great influence in the development of an integrated Jewish personality who will find no conflict between his Jewish heritage and the great American environment."

The Hebrew Educational Society's Facilities are Enlarged

In essential harmony with the general principles specified above, many of the regular activities were continued and developed over the years, and many new activities were initiated. Space permits only a brief summary of the diversified activities which were conducted by this agency.

The temporary postwar business recession of 1921 was succeeded by several years of comparative prosperity. It was during this period, in 1926, under the presidency of Isaac Sargent (1925-1926) that the building was enlarged and completely renovated. Also at this time, the Hebrew Educational Society's Honor Society was founded. In 1928, the Brooklyn Hebrew Society of the Deaf was organized in our building. Until 1936 it was sponsored by the Brooklyn Section of the National Council of Jewish Women, and since then exclusively by the Hebrew Educational Society. It has remained the only organization of its kind in Brooklyn, instituting an elaborate program of religious, educational, social, and athletic activities among the Jewish deaf. From 1924 to 1957 the Young Israel Synagogue of Brownsville used the Hebrew Educational Society building as its headquarters for their religious, educational, and social programs. The Sunday evening forums brought eminent speakers to the Hebrew Educational Society's platform.

With the renovation of the building came an upsurge in

activities. The serious economic depression of the early thirties affected the work very seriously. The years 1930 and 1931 were particularly discouraging and trying. The government's measures to create work for the unemployed through the Works Progress Administration, National Youth Administration, and other bureaus, brought a large staff to the society and enabled it to introduce new and needed services. The Works Progress Administration maintained a nursery school for children between two and four years of age. Teachers and clerks were provided for the office, for classes in English for adults, "Home Camp," and other programs. The Works Progress Administration and Recreation Project provided instructors in sculpture, puppetry, woodwork, metalwork, photography, painting, dramatics, music, and other subjects.

In 1931 the Alumni Old-Timers Association was formed under the leadership of Samuel Telsey and Judge Nathan Sweedler, and in 1933 Max Herzfeld, then the president of the society, launched another Women's Association. Mrs. Maurice B. Rich was elected its first president. Over the years the organization has made a valuable contribution to the society's numerous activities.[11]

During the depression period in 1931, the New York Federation of Jewish Philanthropies had to come to Brooklyn's assistance, and in 1937, after two decades of individual and separate existence, both federations combined their campaigns into a single appeal. In 1944 the Brooklyn Federation became an integral part of the New York Federation of Jewish Philanthropies. This marked a great milestone for Jewish Service Agencies in New York and Brooklyn as well as for the Hebrew Educational Society. In 1922 the society's budget was $25,733, toward which the Brooklyn Federation contributed $15,000 and the Baron de Hirsch Fund $1,200. In 1961 the Hebrew Educational Society, including Camp and Fellowship, spent $264,688, toward which the Federation of Jewish Philanthropies of New York contributed $136,285.

The Hebrew Educational Society's Young People's Fellowship

Under the guidance and initiative of the executive director, two important institutions were added to the Hebrew Educational

Society in 1940—its Young People's Fellowship and Camp H.E.S. The fellowship was established in the spring of 1940 through a special grant by the Greater New York Fund. Later, in 1947, the Federation of Jewish Philanthropies assumed the major responsibility for its maintenance. It originated as an experiment in dealing with young adults between eighteen and thirty by providing them with separate facilities, and allowing them more freedom and privacy than was formerly possible in the usual Jewish center surroundings. Its aims were to attract young people who were not identified with any Jewish center, and especially to draw such young people away from the unwholesome atmosphere of cellar clubs. It represented a unique contribution to the Jewish Center Movement, which was experiencing a discernible decrease in young-adult membership. Its work was designed to provide constructive social outlets, richer cultural experiences, and opportunities for the development of leadership. Functioning as an organized unit, its members participated in a program of social, cultural and recreational activities. The major emphasis at Young People Fellowship was not so much program as it was the membership involvement and commitment in the planning and implementation of these activities.[12]

The first quarters for the fellowship were opened on November 12, 1940, at 407 Rockaway Avenue. The response of the young people was immediate and enthusiastic. In 1947 it moved to larger quarters at the Hebrew Free School at 400 Stone Avenue. In 1953-1954, under the presidencies of Seth Marrus (1952-1953), and Mrs. Irving J. Sands (1954-1956), and Clarence J. Shlevin and Mrs. Louis Nathanson as chairmen of the Fellowship Committee, and Richard LaPan as director of activities, a building was acquired at 1212 East New York Avenue. It was purchased by Walter N. Rothschild, then the head of Abraham and Straus, in memory of his father, Simon F. Rothschild. The reconstruction of the building was made possible by funds contributed by the Federation's building fund, members of the board of directors and friends of the Hebrew Educational Society.

Camp H.E.S. Inc.

The need to provide a camping experience for the children of Brownsville had been felt since March 14, 1907, when it was unsuccessfully proposed at a meeting of the board of directors. Not until 1940, at a meeting attended by representatives of the board of directors, the Hebrew Educational Society Women's Association, Mothers Clubs Council, Hebrew Educational Society Honor Society, and friends of the Hebrew Educational Society, was Camp H.E.S., Inc. organized. Dr. David Teplitsky was elected president, Harry Pinesick, vice-president, Mrs. Irving J. Sands, secretary-treasurer, and Milton Mandel, camp director. A small camp site on Lake Tiorati in Harriman State Park was leased from the Palisades Interstate Park Commission, and Camp H.E.S. was opened for the 1941 summer season.

In 1948 the Camp moved to a larger area, taking over the Jewish Child Care Association's Camp Wakitan, a large, attractive site on Lake Stahahe in Harriman State Park. As a result of this change, twice as many campers were accommodated. It was now organized as a co-ed camp where boys and girls from eight to fourteen years of age received a three-weeks vacation under excellent supervision. In 1961 an additional site across the lake was leased to accommodate a group of one hundred boys and girls from fourteen to sixteen years of age. After Camp H.E.S. moved to Lake Stahahe it became an affiliate of the Federation of Jewish Philanthropies of New York in 1949, and received an annual allotment for the care of the free or partially free campers. During the period between 1947 and 1963, Mr. Arthur Meyer served as camp director.

The marked growth of Camp H.E.S. was truly heartwarming. In 1941, the first year of its operation, 186 campers received a two weeks vacation at a total cost of $6,400. During the nine weeks summer season of 1963, 886 campers were accommodated with a budget of $103,101.68, of which $34,292.61 came from the Federation of Jewish Philanthropies, and the balance from campers registration, contributions, and other sources.[13]

In addition to the country camp, the Hebrew Educational Society has shared in the spread of day-camping in recent years. Earlier in this volume it was pointed out that the Hebrew Educational Society itself originated as a vacation school in August, 1898, under the auspices of the Baron de Hirsch Fund. In 1953 The Hebrew Educational Society provided a vacation program for more than 1,500 boys and girls between six and sixteen years of age in two day-camps and in its country camp alluded to above.

Golden Age Club Organized

In the vanguard of a new movement in social work, the Hebrew Educational Society organized in 1946 the Golden Age Club to serve the needs of the aged in the community. From less than 50 people who registered during the first season under the supervision of Walter Zand, and later of Miss Esther Kolatch, the club has grown in membership and daily attendance. In 1951 Miss Lillian Strauss, then the supervisor, reported a total membership of 503—196 men and 307 women ranging in age from 60 to 85. Thirty-eight per cent were married, 35 per cent widows, 19 per cent widowers, 8 per cent divorced or separated, and 1 per cent single. A program was developed for this group that took into consideration the character of the membership, the social patterns developed over many years, and the problems unique to this period in life.

The Golden Age Club remained the Hebrew Educational Society's best "customers." Rain or snow did not keep them from coming daily to the building, which was open to them five days a week from ten o'clock in the morning until ten o'clock in the evening. Under the direction of Mrs. S. Ellenbogen and a number of specialists, a number of special-interest groups were organized to give individual members more attention and to develop new interests.

The largest attendances were attracted to the weekly Sunday night dances to the music of a professional band, the Tuesday evening sings, entertainments, concerts or lectures, the dramatic performances of their own dramatic groups, the Wednesday afternoon tea, and of course, the monthly birthday party and trips to various points of interest.

What attracted so many senior citizens to the Hebrew Educational Society's program was its warm, traditional, Jewish atmosphere. They looked forward to it especially at a Jewish holiday. Some had no other opportunity to observe these special days except through the Hebrew Educational Society's celebrations. The season began with the Succoth celebrations in the society's beautiful Sukkah, and was followed by the Hanukkah and Purim programs. The highlight of the year was the Passover Seder, about which the Golden-Agers began to inquire months in advance.

Much has been done to keep the older members alert and happy in their social relationships, but these people do not forget the needs of others. They are proud of their annual group-gift to the United Jewish Appeal, their successful suppers on behalf of the Federation of Jewish Philanthropies, and their many contributions through their Social Service Club. These make them feel an important, integral part of the larger Jewish Community.

Other Activities

Numerous additional activities were introduced over the years—Friday evening Oneg Sabbath hours, a special Friday afternoon program for local Yeshivah students who found no other time to engage in a recreational program, mothers day-classes in English, a social group for unattached men and women between thirty-five and fifty years of age, an Israeli Group (*Hug Ha-Yisraelim*) to serve the special needs and interests of several hundred families who had emigrated from Israel and moved into the locality for a time. There were also a Sunday day-camp program, a Saturday evening "Teen Canteen," speech improvement classes, tutorial services, and a counseling service made possible through a grant by the Parshelsky Foundation. In 1947 the Jerold E. Rubinton Memorial Playground was constructed on the land adjoining the main building.

Most of the activities which were conducted by the society since its inception were continued and enhanced. During any one year some one hundred different clubs, teams, special interest and hobby groups, fraternal organizations, *landsmanschaften,* mothers clubs, a men's club, family circles, national and civic organizations, group councils and congresses, and various other groups participated under the guidance of trained personnel in a variety of activities designed to meet different individual and group needs and interests.

Since 1922 the following have been associated with the Hebrew Educational Society's group-work program as supervisors, directors of activities, and program directors: Mrs. Herman Brickman (Sybil Hartman), Miss Anna Gelrud (Mrs. H. L. Ginsberg), Florence Sakrais Barth, Fannie Shaber (Mrs. Selig Perlman), Pearl T. Reiss (Scarlet), Henrietta Rosenspan (Singer), Lloyd Rosenblum, Mrs. Morris Dembowitz, David M. Kleinstein, Esther Kolatch, Walter Zand, Richard LaPan, Paul Simon, Harmon Putter, Lillian Strauss, George Weisfuse, Adolph Dembo, and Harold Fontak. T. Bath Glasson, Jan Meyerowitz, and Murray Ditzer have served as directors of the Music School. Conan Feldman and Max Greenberg headed the art department.

The Hebrew Educational Society Gymnasium

During some of the years the gymnasium of the Hebrew Educational Society was the only one available. These were the times when the local public gymnasiums were not open weekends, or only on some evenings. When the Hebrew Educational Society gymnasium was enlarged and newly equipped in 1926, it attracted large numbers who participated in a wholesome and well-rounded athletic program.

For more than fifty years the men's gymnasium has been under the direction of two men who have endeared themselves to thousands who have come under their influence; Mr. Saul Friedman, who directed the gymnasium between 1915 and 1940, and Jules Bender, who has been director since 1940. Mr. Bender was a Hebrew Educational Society boy in his youth, and has distinguished himself as an all-round athlete.

Special Jewish Aspects of the Hebrew Educational Society Program

For many the Hebrew Educational Society was the only, or the major institution of Jewish identification and Jewish education. Here Jews found close associations with other Jews, and a variety of activities and programs which enriched their Jewish knowledge and nourished their Jewish consciousness. Although the society tried to touch the lives of as many as possible, the number was small in comparison to the size of the community and its Jewish population. While the entire program may be said to have enriched the Jewish lives, ideals, and practices of the membership, a certain number of activities were especially conducted for these ends.

The Hebrew School continued to be an integral and important activity of the society. The principals of the school during this period were Jacob Klansky, Simon Greenberg, David Satlow, Aaron Pinta, and David Weitzman. David Cedarbaum, Mordecai Soloff, and Barnett Cohen were among those who headed the Sabbath School. Religious Services, Holiday Celebration, Jewish Book Month, Jewish Music Month, the *Keren Ami,* the annual drives by various groups in the building on behalf of the Federation, United Jewish Appeal, and other *Zedakah* efforts, the adult classes in Yiddish literature, Hebrew, Bible, and the Oneg Sabbath Hours are some of the concrete media through which the Hebrew Educational Society tried to emphasize the Jewish aspects of its program. But more important has been the attitude and spirit which has pervaded the program which was aimed to enrich the Jewish life, ideals, and practices of the membership.

Participation in Communal Activities

The Hebrew Educational Society through the years has always been glad to open its facilities to other agencies, and in turn, has often had occasion to call on others for assistance. The Young Israel Synagogue of Brownsville, a branch of the Marshalia

Hebrew High School, the Brownsville Neighborhood Health and Welfare Council, the Brownsville and East New York Jewish Community Council, the Talmud Torah Council of Brownsville and East New York, the Boy Scouts Council, the *Yiddishe Volks Universitat*, the Jewish Big Brothers and Big Sisters of Brooklyn, the Joint Passover Association, and some of the activities of the Brooklyn Section, National Council of Jewish Women—all were for a number of years housed in the building.

The presidents of the Society since Mr. Bernhard Bloch (1922-1924) were Isaac Sargent (1925-1927), Nathan Sweedler (1928-1930), Herman S. Bachrach (1931-1932), Max Herzfeld (1933-1935), Marshall Snyder (1936-1940), Samuel A. Telsey (1941-1944), Nat Bass (1945-1946), Nathaniel Bloom (1947-1949), Walter R. Hart (1950-1951), Seth Marrus (1952-1953), Mrs. Irving J. Sands (1954-1956), Morris Messing (1957-1959), Clarence Shlevim (1960-1961), David F. Cohen (1962-1965), and Lawrenc Rose (1966-   ).

After sixty-five years of service in the Brownsville community, the Hebrew Educational Society found that due to the changed neighborhood and other factors, its need as a Jewish Center was no longer necessary. It decided to relocate in the contiguous area to its south known as Canarsie, where some of its former members now reside, and where the unique services of the Hebrew Educational Society are needed. Land was purchased on Seaview Avenue and East Ninety-fifth Street where a new center is being erected.

To abandon a neighborhood which one has served for so long a period is not easy. The new nonJewish groups that have moved into the section need social services as much as the older Jewish elements who are now leaving it. The Catholic Diocese of Brooklyn has taken over by purchase both Hebrew Educational Society buildings at Hopkinson Avenue, corner of Sutter Avenue, and also at East New York Avenue and Ralph Avenue, and are using them as religious, recreational, and educational centers for the population presently residing in the neighborhood.

Adaptability has been the keystone of the Hebrew Educational Society's policy since its inception. It plans to continue to serve as a Jewish community center in the new location. Its faith in the continued value of its work comes in some measure from the large number of alumni who have grown up in Brownsville and have since spread over the country. Many of them have made valuable contributions in various fields of endeavor. Many of them have repaid the community manifold for what they have received. What is most encouraging is the deep, affectionate, and positive feeling so many cherish and express concerning the society, the center of their early activities, and which so many like to regard affectionately as the second nostalgic home of their youth.

The Brownsville Hebrew Educational Society has spoken its farewell, but the many friendships will not be closed, and the feasts of companionship and warm human relationships will never be finished.

Young Men's and Women's Hebrew Associations of Brownsville and East New York

XI

A Young Men's Hebrew Association existed in Brownsville for thirteen years, and served the recreational needs of youth above eighteen years of age. It disbanded in 1925 because of failure to procure financial support.

The idea of forming a Young Men's Hebrew Association in Brownsville was conceived in 1911 by a small group of young men to provide healthful recreation for the youth of the community, to promote social welfare, and to encourage an active interest in civic and Jewish affairs. The association was incorporated in 1912. During its formative period the Young Men's Hebrew Association experienced great difficulty procuring proper quarters, with the result that it moved from place to place. It met first in the recreation center of Public School 84. For a time it was located at 27 Amboy Street. Finally it found fairly satisfactory quarters at 461 Rockaway Avenue, where it progressed. In 1917 it joined the Metropolitan League of Young Men's Hebrew Associations, and its members participated in all of the League's activities. Among other accomplishments they won the Metropolitan League Championship in debating.

As the membership increased, and the program of work expanded, the association required larger quarters. It moved into three floors of the Liberty Theatre building at 63 Liberty Avenue. The first floor served for a gymnasium and an auditorium, and the other floors for office, clubs and meeting rooms, and a billiard parlor.

Things were moving smoothly when World War I broke out, and a number of the members were called into the service. The situation of the association became precarious, but the diligent effort of the members who remained and of the girls who had organized a Young Women's Hebrew Association in 1917, saved it from becoming defunct.

When the war was over, and the boys returned, the Young Men's Hebrew Association took on a new lease of life. Many new activities, including classes, lectures, dances, dramatics, and a Junior Young Men's Hebrew Association, and clubs were introduced. New members were enrolled, free religious services were organized for the Holy Days, and a part-time executive was employed.

In the early part of 1921 the Young Men's and Young Women's Hebrew Associations amalgamated into the Young Men's and Young Women's Hebrew Association of Brownsville. It now had a membership of 446 young men above the age of 18, 160 young women above the age of 17, and 50 juniors. The annual budget for 1921 was approximately $5,000. George F. Gottlieb served for 17 months (1921-1922) as the executive director, and endeavored hard to put the association on a firm footing. However, efforts to get funds from the Brooklyn Federation of Jewish Charities and to organize a board of directors from among prominent lay people in the community failed to materialize, whereupon the organization had to disband.

The East New York Young Men's and Young Women's Hebrew Association

It was not until 1938 that a Young Men's and Young Women's Hebrew Association was opened in the populous Jewish sections of East New York and New Lots. Over the years several unsuccessful attempts had been made to organize an association. In the mid-1930's a Committee on Extension Activities of the Metropolitan Section, National Jewish Welfare Board, had undertaken to establish two new "Y's" in neighborhoods needing them most. The committee, headed by Mrs. Edgar Oppenheimer, included Louis Kraft, Executive Director of the J.W.B., and Benjamin Rabinowitz and Meyer Fishman, field secretaries of the Metropolitan Section. The committee was successful in establishing the East Tremont "Y" in the Bronx, and the East New York "Y."

Quarters for the East New York "Y" were obtained on Sheffield and New Lots Avenue. They were inadequate, consisting of a dilapidated loft over a fish store, with some space on the ground floor. The evening of the dedication of this "building" on May 30, 1938, found some 5,000 young boys and girls clamoring at its doors.

To enhance its usefulness, it took over in 1943 the quarters occupied for several years by the Pitkin Jewish Center, housed in a remodeled loft on Sutter Avenue and Junius Street. There it conducted a small day nursery, a games and crafts program, and special summer activities. Dr. Joseph Bass was for a time its president, and Mr. Arthur Lehman, the executive director. Among the executive directors who served the "Y" during the early years were Ben Lambert, Myron Blanchard, and Irving Brodsky. Benjamin Alva Levine was president.

In 1948 the East New York-Brownsville Young Men's and Young Women's Hebrew Association was admitted by the Brooklyn Federation of Jewish Charities as one of its beneficiary societies. Dr. Isaac Rabinowitz, a former director of the B'nai B'rith Hillel Foundation in Brooklyn and now Professor of Hebrew and Biblical Studies at Cornell University, became executive director of the "Y"; and a group of prominent Brooklyn Jewish laymen, among them the brothers Harry and Julius Leventhal, became associated with it. They were profoundly influenced by Dr. Rabinowitz's philosophy of the Jewish Center. It was during the ten-year presidency of Julius Leventhal (1946-1954), that a new building was built. Edward Isaacs, followed as president and was an influential leader. Emanuel Frisch is president at the present time. Commendable support was accorded by Samuel Lemberg, a leader of the Federation. Other members of the Board included Max J. Dym, Reuben Frieman, Paul Paulson, William C. Smerling, Irving Levine, Dr. Arthur Levine, Neil M. Lieblich, Abraham Feit, Dr. Elias Lieberman, Kalman Astow, Jacob Tabb, and others.

The steadily expanding communal service soon achieved community-wide recognition and support, and in 1954 the New York Federation of Jewish Philanthropies granted it a sum of $375,000 toward the construction of a new "Y" building. This sum was to be matched by an equal amount to be raised in a special campaign by its Board of Directors. The goal was reached, and on October 17, 1954 the new, fully equipped building at 2057 Linden Boulevard was dedicated as the East New York Young Men's and Young Women's Hebrew Association. The Board immediately initiated a campaign to raise funds for the construction of a swimming pool, and in 1958 a $130,000 swimming pool was dedicated. In the same year, through the efforts of Edward Isaacs, the "Y" opened a country camp 65 miles from New York City in the Taconic Mountains, in Holmes, New York.

At its twenty-fifth anniversary the "Y", under the direction of Adolph Wasser, executive director, proudly recorded a membership of 5,600—28 full staff members, 110 part-time workers, 120 volunteers, 6 separate camping units, and a comprehensive program of Jewish educational, recreational, and social activities. Its annual budget was $400,000.

The East New York "Y" has pioneered in many directions, and its strong emphasis on the Jewish cultural and spiritual aspects of the program has attracted nationwide attention. In March, 1948 it adopted after lengthy discussion, the following Statement of Principles which has contributed much to the emerging pattern of American Jewish communal life:

Article I—"The aim of the Jewish Community Center is to serve the Jewish people and the total American community through fostering the growth, development and creative self-expression of human personalities on the basis of Jewish conceptions of the meaning, purpose and functioning of individual and social human life. However we may differ as to specific applications of our millennial heritage of human values, as Jews we share a common conviction that Judaism is a way of living human life which can be taught and practiced through and in everyday experience."

Article II—"The program of the Jewish Community Center should consist of a variety of activities for people of all age levels, offering opportunity for creative experience based upon, and permeated by, the spiritual-cultural values of the Jewish way of life."

The Brownsville Boys Club

Sunday, October 13, 1953, marked a milestone in the history of the Brownsville Boys Club when the beautiful $1,250,000 building was opened at Linden Boulevard and Stone Avenue with brief ceremonies by Mr. Abe Stark, its prime mover, and others.

The Brownsville Boys Club had a very humble and interesting beginning. It was organized in March 1940 by a small group of teenagers led by "Doc" Baroff, George Schmaren, Izzy Lesevoy, and Dave Gold, who had been meeting during the winter in an afternoon school recreation center. When boys over 14 were denied the use of the center in order to increase facilities for younger children, some of them embarked on an effort to procure a meeting space. Their success in getting playground space for basketball tournaments at Public School 184 inspired the formation of a club in the Brownsville's Branch Library where regular weekly meetings were held, attended by delegates of the smaller neighborhood clubs. The membership of the club soon skyrocketed from 100 to 700, and a program of sports, social and cultural activities arranged.

The officers and members were exceedingly active. They were particularly stimulated by the ingenious leadership of their president, himself a youth, who sought to have the club governed by the boys themselves, with no adult supervision. They invited guest speakers for the weekly meetings, arranged trips and athletic tournaments, issued a newspaper and distributed theatre passes. They sought and obtained help from the social agencies of the neighborhood, such as the East New York Young Men's and Young Women's Hebrew Associations, the Children's Branch Library, and the Police Athletic League, but they operated without adult leadership from these agencies.

This group became articulate regarding the needs of Brownsville youth for recreational opportunities, and succeeded in arousing a wholesome community consciousness. The club's rapid growth evidenced its sparkling vitality, thereby attracting the attention of various social agencies and leaders.

Mr. Abe Stark became vitally interested in the project, giving it much of his time and effort. He involved a number of public spirited citizens and generous donors to help procure a club house. The Haydn Foundation responded to his appeal with a grant of a quarter of a million dollars. Levitt, the builders, Max Abrams of Esquire Shoe Polish, and others gave substantial gifts. Many fund raising affairs were conducted, including annual hundred-dollars-a-plate dinners. In these fund raising functions, Mrs. Minnie Weingart rendered invaluable assistance. After the first building was constructed, additional wings were added to accommodate additional services.

At present the 3.5 million-dollar club house includes, in addition to a full recreation program, a Golden Age center, a cerebral palsy unit, two child-care centers, an orthodontic clinic, an industrial home for the blind program, and a variety of other programs.

Soon after the building was completed, the operation of the center was given over to the City of New York, to be conducted under the auspices of the Park Department. The Brownsville Boys Club, however, still retains its organization, and assists in a variety of special projects.

Synagogues and Their Rabbis

XII

THE ARRIVAL of the East European immigrants not only spurred the growth of a strong radical trade-union movement, but also stimulated the founding of Orthodox religious institutions and the creation of Conservative Judaism in this country. If the liberal *Daily Forward* was read by many, the Orthodox *Tageblatt* and the *Jewish Morning Journal* were equally to be found in many homes.

Religion was a cogent force in Brownsville, even though a large group of anti-religionists resided in the community. Those who attended a synagogue went to an Orthodox house of worship. Some two hundred places of worship were established from the beginning of the Jewish settlement.[1] Synagogues were a part of practically every Jewish institution: The Home for the Aged, the day nurseries, the various Talmud Torahs, and the Yeshivas. Besides the regularly constituted congregations there were many *"Minianim,"* regular services conducted in the homes of rabbis, Hebrew teachers, or even in rented rooms.

Very few of the synagogue buildings were architecturally

imposing. Most of them were built at a modest cost, with the result that externally and internally they were unimpressive. The small groups that built the synagogues were usually composed of small tradesmen or workers who could not afford lavish sums for buildings.

A majority of the synagogues were organized by *Landsmanschaften,* men originating from the same European town who assembled to fraternize with one another and to engage in common worship. Many such organizations (*hebrot*) were founded here, and became not only the primary social agencies of the neighborhood, but also havens to thousands of the first generation of immigrants who affiliated with them. They provided not only a place of worship and study, but met the immigrant's needs for comradeship, friendship, and fellowship. They were of great assistance in time of distress, offering sick benefits, free loans, cemetery rights, insurance, and a variety of other advantages. Above all, these associations gave the newcomers in a strange land a sense of security, a feeling that behind them was a group ready to be helpful and to respond to a call in time of need.

The annual dues varied. On the average they were from $6 to $12 a year. Since this could hardly cover expenses, extra income was derived from contributions, holiday seats, and special functions. The membership of these congregations was small. *The Eagle Almanac* of 1899 and 1900 reports for the Oheb Shalom Synagogue, the oldest in Brownsville, a membership of 75 in 1899 and 65 in 1900. During 1899 it raised a total of $2,000, of which $1,600 was used for current expenses. It still had an indebtedness of $5,000 on its property, which was valued at $10,000.

Brownsville became known as the "Jerusalem of America." Synagogues did not have to seek a "tenth man" for a *Minyan;* large numbers of Jews attended them for worship and study. Many of the synagogues engaged rabbis, among whom were great Talmudic Scholars who contributed to Jewish learning through their publication of responsa and rabbinic works. They received small salaries and had difficulty eking out a living. Extra income obtained from special services, such as supervising the *Kashruth* of Jewish provisions, helped considerably. Synagogues that were too small to engage a Rabbi usually had a Jewish lay scholar serve as its functionary.

The functions of the Rabbi were many. He was the *Dayan*—(the rabbinical judge), the communal arbiter and counselor. He was in charge of all matters pertaining to marriage and divorce, supervised *Kashruth* (dietary laws); he conducted classes in Talmud, Mishnah and other subjects. Unlike the practice in Europe where the preaching was done usually by the Maggid, the popular religious preacher, in America the Rabbi himself was required to preach frequently, at least once a week.

When the membership of Congregation Oheb Shalom grew in number, they engaged a cantor on an annual basis. Some of the most famous cantors were associated with this congregation. Cantor Friedberg and a choir conducted by Mr. Charry, father of Rabbi Elias Charry, were the first to hold the position. Cantor Grafman followed, then Cantor Kaminsky and his choir, who held the position for seven years, and Cantor Krasnow, who served four years. For two years the synagogue was ministered by the famous Cantor David Roitman and Leove's Choir at a cost of the then huge sum of eighteen thousand dollars a year to the congregation. Leibel Glantz, who later became famous as a cantor in Israel, served for three years. Among the presidents who served this congregation were Simon Rose, William B. Roth, A. Belanofsky, S. Sassulsky, Abraham Valetsky, Sigmund Shapiro, and Gershon Ungar.

The synagogue, through its appeals on the holidays and other occasions, did much to assist various causes and institutions. At one such *Kol Nidre* appeal by Rabbi Finkelstein, the sum of $100,000 was contributed for the *Keren Hayesod*. When Rabbis Kook, Epstein, and Shaprio visited America soliciting assistance for the *Yeshivahs,* the sum of $10,000 was contributed through appeals in the synagogue.

The Oheb Shalom Synagogue continued through the years to play a leading role in the congregational life of the community. It attracted for a time not only the most influential residents, but also a large membership. When Rabbi J. L. Wistenetzky returned to Lithuania, Rabbi Simon J. Finkelstein accepted the position in

1902, and served until his death, April 16, 1947. Rabbi Finkelstein wielded an important influence in the community, and was the author of several legal and homiletical works.[2]

Rabbi Morris B. Tomashov, famous as an authority on Jewish law, served as Rabbi of Congregation Beth Israel of Brownsville on Christopher Avenue, and later on Sackman Street, from 1915 to 1960. He was the founder and co-editor with Rabbi E. Meltzer of *Yagdil Torah,* a monthly journal on Hebrew law. When he came to the United States in 1912, he continued the publication of the journal under the title of *Magdil Torah.* His responsa to questions on Talmud and Jewish jurisprudence were published in a four-volume work, *Avnei Shoham* (Precious Stones). He also was the author of *Tikun Gitin* (1936), a treatise on the Jewish code of divorce. He was active in many organizations. He served as president of the Rabbinical Board of Brownsville and East New York (1935-1960), and was honorary chairman and former vice-president of the Union of Orthodox Rabbis of the United States and Canada.[3]

In 1922 Rabbi Hirsch Dachowitz was selected as the Rabbi of the Congregation Agudath Achim Anshei Libowitz at 248 Watkins Street. He came to the United States in 1922 from Vilna where he was Rabbi between 1907-1922. He was known as an eloquent preacher, Talmud scholar, and was the author of Sermons and Commentaries on the Bible, *Pree Shloimo* (1926), and *Hegyonai Visarapai* (1929). He was a vice-president for a number of years of the Union of Orthodox Rabbis of the United States and Canada, and a member of the Executive Committee of *Vaad Harabonim.*

The forceful, half-blind Rabbi Samuel Elkin preached in the *Etz Hayim*—Tree of Life—Synagogue on Stone and Sutter Avenues. In a moment of ecstasy he sometimes opened the Ark and carried on a dialogue with the Creator about the sad plight in which the Jewish people finds itself. Near Etz Hayim, in the Bobroisk Synagogue on Christopher Street, Rabbi Israel Jacobsen, a follower of the Libowitcher Rabbi, inspired his listeners.[4]

A warm and interesting personality was Rabbi Joshua Heshel Rabinowitz, the Rabbi of Monastritch, whose two grandsons minister at the present to synagogues in adjacent areas. He lived and worshipped in his home on Barrett Street, and won the hearts of hundreds of Hasidim and others who usually celebrated the holidays with him. On Simchas Torah night the block surrounding the house was filled with hundreds of young and old, singing and dancing.

The Young Israel of Brownsville that met for more than thirty years in the Hebrew Educational Society would fill the building to overflowing for its Simchas Torah affairs, Succoth parties, and other events. People would walk for blocks to attend some of the functions arranged in the beautiful Hebrew Educational Society's Succah. The Hapoel HaMizrachi on Hopkinson Avenue was known for its Shmini Azereth gatherings, at which time it would invite as its guests the Rabbis of the community. For many years the Stone Avenue Talmud Torah Synagogue became a center for famous cantors who used to conduct services with their choirs on special Sabbath and Holidays, attracting thousands of worshippers. It was the proving ground for many of the cantors in the country whose reputations were often made or unmade by the keen critics who flocked to hear them.

While a large portion of the Jewish population attended the synagogues on the High Holy Days (Rosh Hashana and Yom Kippur), crowding many buildings and even using rented halls and theatre buildings, a relatively small proportion attended them during the rest of the year.[5] Many were workers or shopkeepers who were occupied on the Sabbath and were not free to attend the synagogue. Since there were very few late Friday night services at that time, many of the Jews of the neighborhood visited the synagogue only on the High Holy Days and on other special occasions, such as Bar Mitzvahs, weddings, and special events.

Today, practically all synagogues alluded to have been razed to make room for housing projects, or have been converted for other uses. Before concluding, let us note some historical data about a few other synagogues.

After the organization of the Oheb Shalom Synagogue, a second congregation, Hebra Torah, was established in 1887, by a small group of learned Jews. In time a number of large synagogues grew out of this organization, bearing the same name of Hebra Torah. This led to some controversy, but subsequently the other congregations assumed different names or merged with other congregations. Thus came about the establishment of the large synagogues, Beth Hamidrash Hagadol on Sackman Street, the Etz Chaim Machzikei Ha-Rav, on Stone Avenue, Hebra Torah Anshei Hesed on Strauss Street, and Hebra Torah Anshei Radeshkowitz on Amboy Street. The *Hebra Torah* Anshei Radeshkowitz constructed a large, beautiful synagogue on Amboy Street near Sutter Avenue where it worshipped until October, 1965. Great Talmudic scholars served as Rabbis of the synagogue; Rabbi Benjamin Fleischer, Rabbi Moshe Rosen, Rabbi Ben Zion Natalewitz, and Rabbi Prybush.

Among the distinguished Rabbis who served in congregations in Brownsville were: Rabbi Moshe Chaim Rabinowitz for forty-two years Rabbi of Congregation Etz Chaim Machzikei Ha-Rav, Rabbi Ben Zion Eisenstadt, author of the biographical dictionary, *Dor Rabbanow We-Saferow*,[6] Rabbis Jacob Levinson and Meyer Pam of Beth Hamidrash Hagodol, Rabbis I. Isaacson and Lipman Levine of Agudath Achim Anshei New Lots, Rabbi Nisim Telushkin for many years head of the Rabbinical Board of Brownsville, Rabbi Solomon Braun, author of halachic works, Rabbi David B. Appelman of Hebra Tehillim Kether Israel, 256 Thatford Avenue, Rabbi Joshua Heshel Gorchicoff of Anshei Zedek, 1760 Park Place, Rabbi D. D. Weitzman of Hebra Torah Anshei Hesed, known as the Strauss Street Synagogue, and Rabbi Isaac Sadin of Alabama Street Synagogue.[7]

While these Hebrot meant much to thousands of the first generation of immigrants, not much was done to make the tradition for which they stood meaningful to their children, the Brownsville born youth. The language of prayer was, of course, Hebrew; in conversation and study it was Yiddish; and only a few had formed schools or junior congregations. The Rabbis were pious and learned men, but they espoused the same conception of their rabbinical functions as they knew them in Europe.

The impression one of the Hebrot made on a Brownsville-born youth is feelingly expressed in Alfred Kazin's *A Walker in the*

City; "Old as the synagogue was, old as it looked and smelled in its every worn and wooden corner, it seemed to me older through its ties to that ancestral world I have never seen. Its very name, Dugschitz, was taken from the little Polish village my mother came from; everyone in the congregation was either a relative or an old neighbor—a landsman. The little wooden synagogue was 'our' place.

"Though there was little in the ritual that was ever explained to me, and even less in the atmosphere of the synagogue that in my heart I really liked, I assumed that my feelings in the matter were of no importance; I belonged there before the Ark, with the men sitting next to an uncle. I felt a loveless intimacy with the place. It was not exclusively a house of 'worship,' not frigid and formal as we knew all churches were. It had been prayed in and walked through and lived in with such easy familiarity." [8]

As the English-speaking American young Jews were growing up, and as their parents were becoming Americanized, the need for some adaptation to the new conditions became apparent. Temple Petach Tikvah on Rochester Avenue, and Temple Sinai on Arlington Avenue became centers of Conservative Judaism in Brownsville, and the Young Israel Synagogue of Brownsville was the answer to a need felt by some of the Orthodox Jewish youth in the community.

The Rise of Temple Petach Tikvah

The organization of Temple Petach Tikvah in 1914, and the erection of its beautiful synagogue on Rochester Avenue and Lincoln Place met a pressing need.[9] It became not only the moving force in the revival of Judaism in the community, but also a model for other synagogues in the country dedicated to the promotion of traditional Judaism. It was all-embracing in its scope, appealing to men, women, young people, and children. Its emphasis was not only on the religious, but also on the educational and social demands of the community.

The service was traditional, and did not jar the sensitivities of those who were brought up on the traditional services in the

Brownsville synagogues. Unlike a Reform Temple, there was no organ. Mixed pews were introduced as well as a mixed choir. The love for cantorial music characteristic of Jews was satisfied by Cantor A. Jassen and his excellent choir. There was the daily *Minyan,* and the *Shamash,* always a man of learning, conducted classes in the Mishnah and other texts.

Above all, the Temple was fortunate in obtaining the services of a young leader, Rabbi Israel Herbert Levinthal, a son of the late distinguished Rabbi Bernard Levinthal of Philadelphia, who served the Brownsville community for more than half a century. The young Levinthal, ordained as Rabbi at the Jewish Theological Seminary of America in 1910, upon graduation served the Bnai Sholom Temple in Brooklyn until he came to Temple Petach Tikvah in 1915. From the beginning of his career Rabbi Levinthal became noted as a great pulpit orator and communal leader. Brownsville needed and made use of his talents.

Preaching on Rabban Simon Ben Gamaliel's interpretation of a Biblical text, "May the beauty of Japheth be found in the tents of Shem," Rabbi Levinthal set forth in lucid and scintillating terms a blueprint of his rabbinical stewardship. He proclaimed: "I shall endeavor to preach and to uphold before you a life which shall represent religion and culture, faith and knowledge, reverence for the old and respect for the new, love for the past and recognition of the present and the future. . . . We must remain true to the spirit and teachings of Israel, but we must also accept in our synagogue the requirements of modern times so as to be better able to make our appeal to the hearts of those who are influenced by the conditions of our day."

Temple Petach Tikvah was located close enough to Brownsville to regard itself as part of the community, and yet it was situated at the edge of a new section that was rapidly developing, and to which the more prosperous were moving. Brownsville had no Conservative nor Reform synagogues. Under the untiring and energetic efforts of William B. Roth, its first president and a group of laymen, most of whom had been associated with the Oheb Shalom Synagogue in Brownsville, and through the inspiring guidance of Rabbi Levinthal, the Temple enjoyed a remarkable growth.

"Within the short time of two months," reads an editorial in the first issue of *The Petach Tikvah News* (Chanukah, 1915), "we have seen an increase of the membership of our Congregation from twenty to one hundred and sixty. Where no organization of its kind existed before, a Sisterhood of a hundred women sprang up to take a healthy interest in the Temple's activities. The rolls of the Junior Congregation show the names of two hundred young men and women. Our Sunday School has an attendance of five hundred children, and our Saturday morning services are attended by five hundred, excluding the children of the school. Moreover, when we hear constant complaints from other denominations that their religious institutions are unsupported, and their churches are empty, it is highly gratifying to know that every seat in the Temple is taken at our Friday night services. In fact, we have been forced to turn away for lack of room many who had come."

The annual meeting held in the Temple on Wednesday evening, January 12, 1916, was a great tribute to the men and women who worked for the erection of the Temple, particularly William B. Roth, who was reelected president. With him were selected A. Belanowsky and Henry Seinfel, vice-presidents; Israel Halperin, treasurer; Victor Schwartz, financial secretary; Henry Greenberg, recording secretary; and a board of trustees consisting of the most influential residents.

The Sisterhood of the Temple was among the first organizations formed by Rabbi Levinthal in 1915. It began with 22 members and increased to 125 after one year. The Rabbi himself, interestingly enough, served as the sisterhood's president during the first year of its existence. Its aim was not merely to help the Temple in the raising of funds, but to give an opportunity to Jewish women to learn about the ideals of the synagogue; to foster synagogue attendance and religious observance in the home, to evince an interest in the religious education of the child; and to become acquainted with current vital problems. At each alternate meeting a speaker of prominence addressed the group. At the end of 1916 the following ladies were selected as officers of the sisterhood; President, Mrs. Mark Feiler; vice-presidents, Mrs. Simon Kugel and Mrs. S. Seiderman.

Petach Tikvah Junior Congregation

A religious and social center for the young people in the neighborhood was a crying need. This was met by Rabbi Levinthal, who organized, on October 19, 1915, a Junior Congregation composed not of children but of young adults. About 150 young men and women formed the nucleus. Its aim was to engage in Jewish study, to attend Friday night services, and to contribute the financial returns from the various affairs for helping the parent-congregation. At the second and fourth Tuesday evening meetings, in addition to the transaction of business, there were literary and musical programs. The congregation's dances, social affairs and other programs attracted such large numbers that at times it had to restrict them to members only. A Men's Club was formed for the adults, and clubs were organized for boys and girls.

Temple Petach Tikvah was among the first synagogues to publish a newspaper, *Petach Tikvah News,* with Paul Reznikoff as its first editor-in-chief. It reached as many as two thousand families every month, and was more than a routine recording of synagogue events. Its editorials, its treatment of current Jewish topics, and the reprint of excerpts from Dr. Levinthal's sermons made it an important educational periodical.

With some five hundred students in its Sunday School, the Temple introduced beautiful and impressive confirmation exercises which were held each Shabuot. It also organized an efficient Hebrew School for boys and girls. For the adults, a weekly Jewish history class was conducted under the personal charge of the Rabbi and Nathan Persky. A library was instituted to give young and old an opportunity to acquaint themselves with English and American-Jewish literature, and Jewish topics of the day. There was hardly an activity in the community in which the Temple was not involved. The congregation took an active part in encouraging the sale of Liberty Bonds, and in canvassing for the Jewish Federation of Charities.

The late Friday night service became a highly esteemed institution in the community. Addresses by Rabbi Levinthal, beautiful music by Cantor Jassen and the choir under the direction of N. Corman, and inspiring worship attracted large crowds to the Temple. People from all parts of Brownsville and adjoining areas walked long distances to attend them, even as they later flocked to hear Dr. Levinthal in the Brooklyn Jewish Center.

After Rabbi Levinthal accepted a call from the newly constructed Brooklyn Jewish Center on Eastern Parkway in 1919, Temple Petach Tikvah continued its various activities under the spiritual guidance of Dr. Raphael H. Melamed (1919-1920), and then for a period of ten years (1920-1929) of Rabbi B. Reuben Weilerstein, both graduates of the Jewish Theological Seminary of America. When Rabbi Weilerstein accepted a pulpit in Atlantic City, Rabbi Jacob A. Dolgenas served from 1930 to 1933, and Rabbi Nathan Rosen from 1933 to 1936. Since 1937 Rabbi Abraham P. Bloch has been Rabbi of the Temple. Cantor Abraham Jassen, after serving from 1915 to 1950, was succeeded by Alvin F. Schraeter, who still maintains that post.

Young Israel of Brownsville, East New York and New Lots

A Young Israel Synagogue of Brownsville and of East New York was organized in 1919. As a rampart of the traditional Jewish way of life, it inspired many to dedicate themselves to the perpetuation of Judaism in America. The local Young Israel Synagogue was part of the Young Israel movement, and modeled itself after the original Young Israel Synagogue of Lower Manhattan, which originated in 1912.[10] It was initiated by, and derived its impetus from the young people themselves, who were eager to ameliorate certain disturbing conditions they observed in Jewish religious life. Beginning modestly with a plan to conduct Friday evening lectures in English, the group called on Dr. Judah L. Magnes, head of the Kehillah, for assistance. It was at his suggestion that the name "Young Israel" was adopted. A constitution was drawn up, with a preamble setting forth the aims of the organization:

1. To arouse and intensify the Jewish consciousness of our young men and women whose Judaism is dormant;
2. To awaken Jewish young men and women to their duties and responsibilities as Jews;
3. To create a feeling of sympathy for the Jewish religion, Jewish life in the past and in the present, and Jewish ideals;
4. To strengthen the bonds of unity among all the divisions of the Jewish people.

The movement began under the leadership of Moses Rosenthal, a Jewish Theological Seminary student who was ordained as Rabbi in 1914. A small group of far-sighted Jewish leaders, headed by Dr. Judah L. Magnes, assisted the group. Professor Israel Friedlander, who was martyred in the service of his people, served zealously as a member of this group.

As some might expect, the strict Orthodox parents of these young people did not all view the new organization with favor. They entertained grave doubts about holding English lectures in the synagogue. The success which greeted these lectures, however, prompted a group of members to form a new organization in 1915 for the purpose of conducting a "Model Synagogue," as they first called it, but soon changed to Young Israel Synagogue. The services were conducted in a room in the Educational Alliance. Such innovations as sermons in English and congregational singing were introduced. There was insistence on proper decorum and the elimination of all commercialism. Not only did the idea take firm hold, but also, in January, 1918, the Young Israel Synagogue, which had remained separate and distinct, merged with the Young Israel under the name of Young Israel Synagogue. Soon after they purchased the old Hebrew Sheltering and Immigrant Aid Society building on East Broadway, where they instituted a rich program of religious, educational and social activities.

Other organizations sprang up in different sections of this city, which duplicated the model established on the East Side. In Brownsville and East New York Solomon Rivlin, a native of Jerusalem and a student at the Jewish Theological Seminary of America, headed a group of young people who founded the Young Israel Synagogue of Brownsville and East New York in 1919. Originally the organization purposed to serve both Brownsville and East New York, but later a separate branch was established in East New York. Other charter members of the local Young Israel were Benjamin Plotkin, now rabbi in Bayonne, New Jersey; Max Zucker, Rabbi at Passaic, New Jersey; Solomon Grayzel, later Rabbi at Camden, New Jersey, and now editor emeritus of the Jewish Publication Society; and Morris Schatz, rabbi in Brooklyn. All were students of the Jewish Theological Seminary at the time. Another charter member was Zvi Hirsch Glickman, ordained in 1922 as Rabbi by the Isaac Elchanan Theological Seminary; he has served as Rabbi in Charlotte, North Carolina and in Washington. These men set a pattern which was followed for a number of years.

In the beginning, the Young Israel held its services and meetings in one of the brownstone houses on Saint Marks Avenue between Saratoga and Howard Avenues, previously occupied by another Jewish organization. A few months later they moved for a short time to the Tiphereth Zion Talmud Torah building at 1887 Prospect Place. Another move brought them to the Stone Avenue Talmud Torah building at 400 Stone Avenue until the end of 1923, when they came to the Hebrew Educational Society at Hopkinson and Sutter Avenues. Here they conducted their program of religious, educational, and social activities for some thirty-three years. Their final move was in 1957 to their own building on Winthrop Street and East Ninety-fourth Street, where they now function under the name of the Young Israel of Brownsville and East Flatbush.

For many years Rabbi Alter F. Landesman, executive director of the Hebrew Educational Society, worked very closely with this group and conducted Friday evening Oneg Sabbath hours and various classes. In later years Young Israel engaged their own rabbi, who served both as their spiritual leader and also conducted the classes. Rabbi Snow became Rabbi in 1939. He was followed by Rabbi Eli Quint, Rabbi. Z. Schussheim, and since 1955, by Rabbi Meyer Lazar.

There were branches of the Young Israel Synagogue in East New York and New Lots. The Young Israel Synagogue of East New York was organized in 1923 and met for a time in rented quarters until it purchased a building on Bradford Street between Sutter and Belmont avenues. In 1957 it merged with the Young Israel Synagogue of New Lots and purchased a building on Sheffield Avenue, at the corner of Hegeman Avenue. Among the active members of the group were Joseph Schechter, Louis Lerner, Al Schreiber, Philip Zuller, and the late Irving Ungar and Harry Hisiger.

The Sephardic Community of New Lots

During the past forty years a large group of Ladino-speaking Sephardic Jews have settled in the New Lots district. They have developed their own distinct community, modeled largely after the pattern of the Levantine countries from which most of them emigrated after World War I. Most of the Sephardim moved into New Lots from the Lower East Side. Like the early East European immigrants, they too sought to escape the crowded tenements for more air and space; hence their exodus to New Lots. More than five thousand of these Jews settled on Malta Street, Williams Avenue, Sheffield Avenue, Alabama Avenue, New Lots Avenue, Hegeman Avenue, and in surrounding streets, mostly in small one- or two-story brick homes with porches and large backyards where they could enjoy the shade of trees and even plant their own vegetable gardens. Several coffee houses and a variety of stores and shops were opened in this new neighborhood.

Three Sephardic Synagogues were also established here: Hesed V'Emet on Malta Street, the Sephardic Center on Williams Avenue, and the Sephardic Congregation of New Lots on Hinsdale Street. To the Hebrew names they gave their congregations, they added the names of the little Balkan or Turkish towns from which they came—Hesed V'Emet de Castoria's Synagogue;

Keter Zion Ankoralese. As a tightly knit group largely isolated from the rest of the Jewish community, the New Lots Sephardim to a large extent reproduced a replica of the Levantine society as they knew it, with its mores and customs, and with its unique social code. The members of the Sephardic community are *sui generis* with their distinctive religious customs and ritual, their individual culinary tastes, and their own jargon, Ladino—an archaic Spanish interspersed with Turkish, Greek, and Latin words.

Most of the males found employment in the garment trades, not unlike the other Jews in the neighborhood, as operators, pressers, and cutters. Some in time advanced to manufacturing and wholesaling. Socially they found an outlet in their clubs and fraternal societies, organized along geographical lines like those of the East European *Landsmanschaften,* and restricted to fellow townsmen of their native country. Since most of the Sephardim are related by blood or by marriage, the community has attained a cohesive character. The coffee house is the rendezvous for the men. Here they assemble for companionship, for discussions on family, clan, and community affairs, for their games, and for some of the elders, the smoking of their water pipes.

Due to the far reaching differences between the Ashkenazic and Sephardic communities their relationship has not been close. Indeed, there is an intimation of antagonism, much more than the suspicions that existed in the early years between the different Jewish immigrant groups from Eastern Europe—the Lithuanian, Romanian, and Galician Jews. The proud Sephardim look down upon the *Yudaks* or *Zug-zuygs,* as they call their Ashkenazic neighbors. Among the Ashkenazic Jews of the community their Sephardic neighbors with their strange names and unique customs are also suspect. An intermarriage occasionally occurs, but it is usually opposed by both sides.

This predilection to live their own lives in a little selfcontained world has persisted not only among the immigrant generation, but even among the second generation. In recent years a noticeable change has overtaken the community. This is to be attributed to the economic, social, and religious changes that have affected the younger generation since World War II. The American Melting Pot has boiled here, too. A notable event took place in 1953 when a group of some two hundred young American-born Sephardim organized a Conservative congregation under the name of Congregation *Tipereth Bachurim*—the United Sephardim of Brooklyn.

With the advent of Rabbi Arnold B. Marans, himself an Ashkenazi, a graduate of the Jewish Theological Seminary, and one who was brought up in the Brownsville community, a program was developed which included not only religious services according to the Sephardic ritual, but also a modern Hebrew school, late Friday evening services, and a social welfare and cultural program intended to bring the Sephardim closer to the general American Jewish community. In recent years many have enjoyed prosperity and have moved to newer neighborhoods, some to suburbia. They have erected a beautiful center in Woodmere, where Rabbi Marans now officiates. The conservative synagogue in New Lots continued to function for a time under the spiritual leadership of Rabbi Abraham Morhaim. Interestingly enough, Rabbi Morhaim is a native-born American Sephardi who was brought up in the New Lots section and was graduated as Rabbi from the Jewish Theological Seminary of America.

The community has witnessed a breakthrough along other fronts. There has been an increasing number of Ashkenazic wives resulting from intermarriage with Ashkenazim, and a great change has taken place among the Sephardic women themselves. Their American-born girls have taken positions in business or the professions, and adopted the American attitude toward woman's place in society. The Sephardim have also taken a leading role in the building of the large and beautiful Sephardic Home for the Aged at 2266 Cropsey Avenue in the Bensonhurst section.

Over the years the community has been led by a number of respected men—Solomon Pardo, Louis Russo, and Bocko Mayo, among others. Like the rest of East New York, the New Lots Sephardic community has lost its residents to East Flatbush, Canarsie, and Long Island.[11]

Brownsville's Contribution to Jewish Survival

XIII

THE PICTURE of Jewish life in this country at the turn of the century appeared very discouraging to many observers. The Judaism which the masses of immigrants brought from Eastern Europe was disintegrating, and was being threatened by the new conditions of American life. Interest in religion was lagging. Radical and secularist movements were proliferating. Zionism touched only a numerically small group, and was considered by many as a philanthropic project. Bright young people were turning to more promising fields of endeavor than those offered in Jewish life. It is no wonder that under such circumstances many feared that Americanization would lead to total assimilation, and despaired regarding the future of Judaism in America.

Amidst such an atmosphere of futility and despair, personalities, institutions, and movements emerged that laid the foundations upon which the vigorous Jewish community of today is built. The Society of the Jewish Renascence (*Tehiyyath Yisrael*), organized in 1918 by Professor Mordecai Kaplan and a group of Jewish leaders, reflected the thinking of those who were gravely concerned about the future of Judaism in America.[1] The society was formed to advance Judaism; it represented an organized effort to introduce into the spiritual life of our people conscious direction in place of aimlessness and drift. It believed that Palestine as a spiritual center would remedy some of the Jewish ills, but it also realized that the vast majority of Jews would remain in the Diaspora, and needed guidance and spiritual readjustment to present day conditions.

This period of growth and change is still close to us, and therefore has not yet been fully evaluated. We shall try to indicate how Brownsville shared in this period of awakening, and how it participated in the activities which operated as factors for the survival and revival of Judaism in the United States. There were many individuals who were animated by the hope that this country would, in course of time, become a great center of Judaism. They were pioneers of the spirit who displayed a burning and passionate devotion to Jewish learning and education, to Hebrew, to Zionism, to the synagogue, and to the spiritual legacy of the Jewish people.

Jewish Education

A momentous event in the development of American Jewish education occurred in 1910, when the New York Jewish Community, through its Kehillah, which was headed by Dr. Judah L. Magnes, decided to organize a community bureau of Jewish education. It set for itself a dual task: (1) to create a sense of community responsibility for Jewish education, and (2) to raise the level of teaching in the Jewish schools.

Dr. Samson Benderly, a native of Safed, was selected to head the Bureau of Jewish Education. He had come to Baltimore at the advice of Dr. Harry Friedenwald, with the intention of completing his course in medicine and returning to practice in his homeland, but he came to realize that his lifework was to be Jewish education in America. Through his indomitable will, stupendous energy, vision, and intellect, he effected a veritable revolution in Jewish education. The ideas Dr. Benderly propounded and the example set by him and the New York Bureau of Jewish Education influenced Jewish education everywhere.[2] Its impact is felt to this day.

Dr. Benderly enlisted the cooperation of a group of kindred spirits who have left an indelible impression on Jewish life—Judah L. Magnes, Israel Friedlander, Henrietta Szold, and Mordecai M. Kaplan. He also activated a group of distinguished laymen on behalf of Jewish education—Louis Marshall, Jacob Schiff, Felix Warburg, Bernard Semel, Samuel Rottenberg, Judge Otto Rosalsky, William Fishman, and others. While Dr. Benderly never elaborated a systematic philosophy, Professor M. Kaplan summarized his effort as seeking to implement Ahad Ha-am's conception of Judaism in the *Galut* (Diaspora) in terms of education.

Dr. Benderly was quick to recognize the indispensability of Jewish education for the survival of Jewish life in America. His activities were based on a positive and sympathetic attitude toward Jewish traditional practices in so far as they represented values in Jewish living, on a strong sense of the unity of the Jewish people, and on a firm belief in the reconstitution of Palestine as the Jewish National home and as a center of spiritual influence throughout the world. Above all, Dr. Benderly recognized the necessity of adjusting and integrating Jewish life with American life. He regarded the public school as a genuine expression of democratic values. It was for this reason that his whole conception of Jewish education in the United States was predicated on the idea of supplementing the public school, not supplanting it.

It was tantamount to an article of faith for Dr. Benderly and the bureau to place special emphasis on the education of girls as well as boys, and also of adolescents. He perceived the essentiality of the Hebrew language and literature as a Jewish survival value. He advocated extracurricular forms of Jewish education, and insisted on the need of a profession of Jewish education.

During the first years of the bureau, great progress was made through the preparation of Hebrew and other textbooks, the publication of a children's magazine, *The Jewish Child,* through the mass activities of the Circle of Jewish Children and the League of Jewish Youth. Music, arts, crafts, dramatics, and dancing were introduced and encouraged. Many other innovations, including a camping program for Jewish education, were instituted in subsequent years. All these innovations did not go unchallenged. "The opposition to the 'Benderly system' was a recurrent experience in his life," wrote Dr. Alexander M. Dushkin, one of his disciples.

As might have been expected, the changes effectuated through the efforts of the bureau could not help but influence the Jewish educational system in Brownsville, where some of the largest Talmud Torahs were located. Moreover, when Dr. Benderly became director of the bureau, his first task was to invite the principals of the leading Talmud Torahs to meet with him for the purpose of working out a uniform program of studies to be pursued in the Talmud Torahs.

The Hebrew Free School

One of the most important Talmud Torahs, which served as an experimental school for many of the ideas introduced by the Bureau of Jewish Education and the Hebrew Principals Association, was the Hebrew Free School of Brownsville, popularly known as the Stone Avenue Talmud Torah. It was one of the largest in the country. For more than a half-century it offered a Jewish education to thousands of children and youth. Its teachers and alumni have included some of the foremost Hebraists and educators of our time. For some forty years this school was under the direction of its principal, Harry Handler, who worked very closely with Dr. Benderly, with the bureau, and with the Hebrew Principals Association, of which he was one of the founders.

From a small society, which originated in 1892 employing two teachers, the Hebrew Free School grew to be one of the largest schools in the community. As its name implies, it was to serve the needy, and the tuition fees even for those who could contribute were low enough—ten cents a week in the early days.

From the 1905 minutes of the Hebrew Teachers Union, which

represented an early attempt to organize the Hebrew teachers of the City, we learn that the teachers of Stone Avenue Talmud Torah were most active in its organization and in improving the lot of the Jewish teachers.[3] At the first meeting of representatives from four schools—the Machzikei Talmud Torah (206 East Broadway), the Stone Avenue Talmud Torah, the Uptown Talmud Torah, and Rabbi Jacob Joseph School—Mr. Getzof of the Stone Avenue Talmud Torah proposed that an *Agudath Hamorim* (Association of Teachers) be organized to protect the rights of teachers. Harry Handler of the same school suggested that it be called the "Hebrew Teachers Union."

The minutes of the union for October 19, 1906, indicate some of the difficulties which confronted the teachers of the Brownsville Hebrew Free School, who were demanding certain changes in their contract with the school, which were subsequently granted. One of the questions which agitated the teachers was a five-day week school in order to relieve them from coming on Saturdays. Customarily, a new contract for one year was entered into at the beginning of each season. Classes were held throughout the year, including the summer months, without any vacation time for the teachers. To appease the teachers, and to afford the board of directors sufficient time to come to an understanding with them, the president of the Hebrew Free School, Isaac Levingson, declared a vacation of one week during the summer of 1906. This became a precedent for a summer vacation in later years. Another demand which provoked controversy was that no more children be registered in a class than there were seats available in the room, and that the maximum number of students be set at forty.

More substantial gains for the Jewish teaching profession were achieved in subsequent years by the present *Agudath Hamorim*—Hebrew Teachers Union—which held its first convention in 1912. Akiva Fleishman, its founder, was concerned not only with improving the lot of the Hebrew Teachers in New York, but also with forming a national organization. The first Congress of Hebrew Teachers in the United States and Canada was held in the Stone Avenue Talmud Torah, and was attended by delegates from all parts of the country.

Among the first acts of the Bureau of Jewish Education under the direction of Dr. Benderly was a survey, in 1911, of the financial status of the Jewish Religious Schools of New York, with full data about 8 of the largest Talmud Torahs. The Stone Avenue Talmud Torah, with an enrollment of 1,100 pupils and a staff of 13 teachers, and the Pennsylvania Avenue Talmud Torah with a register of 600 students and a staff of 6 teachers, were among the 8 largest communal schools in the city. Of the remaining 6, 2 were in Harlem (Rabbi Israel Salanter and Uptown Talmud Torah), 1 in Williamsburg (School of Biblical Instruction, Meserole Street), and 3 in the Lower East Side (Downtown Talmud Torah, Machzikei T. Torah, and Ohel Torah Society, East 6th Street). The total income for the year January 1, 1910 through December 31, 1910 for the Stone Avenue Talmud Torah was $11,340.65, and the expenditures were $11,102.50 or about $10 per capita cost for the year. The salaries of teachers, $7,171.12, accounted for most of the expenditures— about 65 per cent. The total income of the Pennsylvania Avenue Talmud Torah was $6,584.77, and its expenditures $6,837, most of it for teachers salaries—$4,273, or $7.12 per capita cost for the year. Even though the budgets were small, the financing of Jewish education was a problem to which Dr. Benderly and the Bureau gave considerable attention.

The survey revealed that the Stone Avenue Talmud Torah received half of its expenditures—51.9 per cent, or $5,880.77 from tuition fees. Membership dues from 750 individuals, most of whom paid $2.50 a year, accounted for $2,172.16—19.2 per cent. The collection of dues was not easy. Six hundred and sixty-six of the members paid 5¢ weekly; only 63, some of the larger donors, paid annually. The remainder of the income, approximately 29 per cent, came from general donations, entertainments, synagogue seats, rent for local meetings, charity boxes placed in homes, and from appeals made at circumcision ceremonies—*Brith Milah.*

In 1911 the old building on Stone Avenue was razed, and the present building, a substantial four-story-and-basement brick building, was constructed at a cost of about $200,000, a large sum for that time. It contains 19 large classrooms, a synagogue with a seating capacity of 800, and a number of other facilities.

During the early years, Harris Allen, a scholar and Hebraist, was principal of the school. Professor Morris Levine (Moshe Halevi), the well known Hebraist, who later became professor at the Jewish Theological Seminary, followed as principal of the school, and when he left on June 15, 1913, he was succeeded by Harry Handler, one of the school's teachers.[4] Mr. Handler held the position until his retirement in 1952. He was one of the founders and a past president of the Hebrew Principals Association. An original member of the board of license of the Jewish Education Committee, he made many contributions to Jewish Education through significant innovations which he first introduced in his own school, and which later became widespread. He was the first to introduce female teachers in a Talmud Torah, and "knee-pants teachers" in his school, as the young American-born teachers in those early years were called by the older teachers. The first two young teachers in this group, who were graduates of his school and who have since occupied important positions in the New York School System, were Dr. Samuel Streicher of the Board of Examiners, and Barnet Cohen, head of the history department of New Utrecht High School.

Hebrew High School

It was at Mr. Handler's suggestion that Dr. Samson Benderly opened the first Hebrew high-school class in the Stone Avenue Talmumd Torah during 1913-1914. The class consisted of eleven boys who had graduated from the Stone Avenue Talmud Torah, and who, in Mr. Handler's opinion deserved an opportunity to continue their Hebrew education. Among those who belonged to that class were Samuel Streicher, Morris Turetsky, Solomon Heller, Rockmuller, A. Weinstein and his brother, and Benjamin S. Sheinin.

Dr. Benderly asked Mr. Joseph Bragin, who had left the position of principal of the Meserole Street Talmud Torah, to become the principal of this new department of the bureau, and Moshe Halevi (Professor Morris Levine) was the first teacher of the class. Thus came into being the Hebrew High School of the Bureau of Jewish Education. Originally conducted as a boys' school, it became coeducational after 1918, and later it was converted from a free school into a tuition-fee school. For a number of years Dr. David Rudavsky and Rabbi George Ende, both of them former Brownsvillites, headed the Hebrew High School of Greater New York, as this department has been known since 1948. The Hebrew Free School in 1918 consisted of three departments—a boys department, with an enrollment of 1,165 boys, a girls department, with an enrollment of 800, and a high school department. It also served as the center of the Brownsville Branch of the League of Jewish Youth, an organization with a membership of 2,000 adolescents in 1918.

In 1918 a number of Talmud Torahs were admitted into the Brooklyn Federation of Jewish Charities, and the subsidy it granted, combined with the activities subsidized by the Bureau of Jewish Education, enabled these schools to meet better the great demands made upon them. The Stone Avenue Talmud Torah celebrated its affiliation with the Brooklyn Federation on Sunday evening, April 13, 1918, with a large public gathering which was addressed by representatives of the local community and of the Federation. The income for that year was three times that of 1910, $33,470, of which $9,250 came from tuition fees, $8,000 from the Brooklyn Federation of Jewish Charities, $5,928 from synagogue income, and the remainder from other sources.

Tiphereth Israel (Glory of Israel) Hebrew Institute of East New York

For many years the *Tiphereth Israel* Hebrew Institute, known as the Pennsylvania Avenue Talmud Torah, was one of the most vigorous Jewish educational agencies in the city. It was organized in 1905 by a group of East New York Jews who were interested in spreading Hebrew education. Hyman Kaplitzky who became the first president, together with A. L. Cohen, and H. Z. Silver, were the founders who gave impetus to this undertaking. They opened a school in a private house with 18 pupils and 2 teachers. In a few years they enlisted a sufficient number of co-workers to construct a $58,800 school building containing a number of large classrooms, a large Synagogue, and other facilities. The cornerstone was laid on Sunday afternoon, September 11, 1910, and the building was dedicated on June 28, 1914. Some of the most outstanding Jewish residents of the East New York section have been associated with the institution.

In 1917 it had an enrollment of 680 boys and girls, taught by a staff of 12 teachers. In 1920 the enrollment increased to 750 boys and 350 girls. Sessions were held on Sundays from 9 A.M. to 1 P.M., and on weekdays from 4:30 to 8:30 P.M. Besides the elementary Hebrew School, instruction was given in secondary Jewish subjects in the high school department under the auspices of the Bureau of Jewish Education. Affiliated with the school was also a branch of the Circle of Jewish Children of America and League of the Jewish Youth of America. It also had a Hebrew Library. In 1918 it became an affiliate of the Brooklyn Federation of Jewish Charities, and received $3,123 toward its budget of $26,282 of which $7,673.35 came from tuition fees. In 1920 it received $10,083 from Federation toward the budget of $41,338, of which $15,627 came from tuition fees which ranged from 50¢ to $4 a month.

Under the direction of Nahum Aaronson, who was principal of the school for a number of years, and his successors, the Glory of Israel Talmud Torah became known for its intensive Hebrew education. Mr. Aaronson penned many poems to voice his deep feelings whenever some new undertaking was launched by the Bureau of Jewish Education, or by the Teachers Organization, for the good of Jewish education. During the last two decades Dr. Samuel Linick (died November 18, 1965), a leader in Jewish education, was associated with the school both as teacher and as principal.

One of the school's outstanding activities was its Junior Congregation, which included not only the young students, but also many of the older alumni. It was a youth movement that lasted for a half century, exerting a tremendous influence on its members. It conducted a wide variety of educational and social activities, and a number of its alumni are now actively participating in Jewish life in the community.

The Synagogue for Adults, which was an important adjunct of this institution, was served by capable Rabbis over the years, some of them serving also as principals of the school. These include Rabbis Zundel Coblens, M. Finkelstein, Z. Rabinowitz, A. Lehrman, father of Rabbi Irving Lehrman of Miami Beach and Rabbi Moses Lehrman of Detroit, and Solomon Goldman.

Talmud Torah Tiphereth Ha'gro

Until 1961, when it had to discontinue its activities because of changes in the neighborhood, the *Tiphereth Ha'gro* communal weekday school at 405 Howard Avenue offered an intensive Hebrew education to a large number of students. In the 1930's it had an enrollment of as many as 800 pupils, an annual budget of $45,000, and a staff of well known teachers. The *Tiphereth Ha'gro* represents the merger in 1916 of two educational institutions in the neighborhood—the Hagaon Rabbi Elijah Yeshivah (*Ha'gro*) and the *Tiphereth Zion* (Talmud Torah). The latter was established in 1907, and was located at 1887 Prospect Place. Before the merger it had an enrollment of 200 boys and 75 girls. The former was located at 297 Saratoga Avenue, had 150 students, all boys. The merger did not last long, as the Hagaon Rabbi Elijah Yeshivah decided to go alone, and separated. The name of the Talmud Torah remained, however, *Tiphereth Ha'gro*.

Due to a munificent gift of $45,000 from the first president, Louis Rosenman, and a gift of $10,000 from M. Cohen, together with contributions by others, a new building was constructed at Howard Avenue. The first principal was S. Fox. He was followed by the well-known Hebrew writer and poet, Shimon Ginsberg, who was responsible for the introduction of a full Hebraic curriculum in the school. He was succeeded by Rabbi Shemarya Leib Hurwitz, a great preacher, teacher, and gifted writer who had served for many years as principal of the Rabbi Israel Salanter Talmud Torah in Harlem. He was among the first to accord full cooperation to Dr. S. Benderly and the Bureau of Jewish Education in their efforts to improve and to expand Jewish education in this city. After his death, Rabbi Baruch Meir

Rabinowitz, a grandson of the Rabbi of Monastrich, became principal and held the position for twenty years until the school closed.

The school's curriculum provided an intensive Hebrew religious education. The lower classes received daily instruction for an hour and a half; the higher classes were taught three hours a day, and their instruction included the study of Talmud. The school also had a synagogue for adults with a daily *Minyan,* and study groups in Talmud and other subjects, which were attended by a large adult group, and a junior congregation. With the institution were associated many active workers in the community including Jacob Bloom, Joseph Koplowitz, G. Davidson, and M. Donnenfeld, among others.[5]

New Lots Talmud Torah

Another large, active weekday school in East New York was the New Lots Talmud Torah, located at Pennsylvania Avenue and New Lots Avenue. For the past thirty years I. H. Lerner has directed the school which has given a rounded Hebrew religious education to large numbers of students. Rabbi S. Grossbein, its spiritual leader, and lay leaders including Aaron Enteen, have given devoted service. Prior to the construction of the present building, the New Lots Talmud Torah was located at 644 Georgia Avenue. For a time Morris Zeldin, well known Zionist, was principal of the school.

Yeshivah Torah M'Zion

Brownsville proper had another important daily school, the Yeshivah Torah M'Zion, which had a fine building at 628 Stone Avenue, founded in 1912. Four hundred and eighty students were in attendance in 1927. Its presidents included Abraham Solowitz, Zalman Rubenstein, and Ben Werbel, and among its principals was Rabbi Eli Quint. A few years ago it relocated in Canarsie, and is known now as the Seaview Jewish Center Yeshivah Torah M'Zion.

Other Schools

There were additional weekday Hebrew schools in the area. One was *Atereth Tiphereth Israel* Talmud Torah at 479 Ashford Street, popularly known as the Ashford Street Talmud Torah. It was organized in 1913, and for many years was directed by Joseph Baltuch. Another was the Hebrew School of the Hebrew Educational Society to which we have alluded elsewhere. It has given instruction to hundreds of boys and girls through the past sixty-five years.

There were a number of outstanding private weekday schools throughout New York. These were directed by well-known Hebrew educators who were imbued by the spirit of the Hebrew Renaissance, and felt that they could carry out their programs more fully in their own private schools uninhibited by pressures from lay groups. The Beth Sefer Ivri Hathiah at 417 New Jersey Avenue was directed by Zorach Rudavsky, the father of David and Jochanan Rudavsky, prominent educators and Zionists. In 1917 the school had an enrollment of 110 boys and 15 girls, taught by 3 teachers.

Yeshiva Rabbi Chaim Berlin

By the end of the first decade of this century there were only four Jewish parochial schools in all of America. Two of them, the Rabbi Jacob Joseph School and Yeshiva Etz Chaim; were located in the Lower East Side of Manhattan; one in Harlem, the Talmudical Institute of Harlem; and one, Yeshiva Rabbi Chaim Berlin, on 1899 Prospect Place, in Brownsville. Today there are several hundred schools and high schools. Jewish studies were taught in these schools from 9 o'clock in the morning to 3 o'clock in the afternoon, and secular subjects from 3 to 7 o'clock in the evening. The Jewish curriculum, amassing 10,000 hours of instruction during its 7-year period, was patently much more ambitious than the curriculum of the weekday schools, encompassing about 2,600 hours of instruction.

The Yeshiva Rabbi Chaim Berlin originated in 1905 under the name of *Hevrah Tiphereth Bahurim* of Brownsville. It included a Talmud Torah for a few children, and a synagogue, first in a store front on Sutter Avenue, and then on Chester Street. In 1908 a number of Brownsville Jewish leaders established an all-day school which started with 43 children. It soon outgrew its small quarters, and moved to its own building which it purchased at 1899 Prospect Place, assuming the name of Yeshiva Rabbi Chaim Berlin. The school remained in Brownsville until the fall of 1963, when it moved to its new quarters at 899 Winthrop Street in East Flatbush. Among the founders were Abraham J. Lesser, its first president, Abraham Cohen, Barnett Weiner, and Baruch Hershenov.

The curriculum stressed the "subjects of *Chumash, Rashi, Talmud* and *Tosafot,* taught in the spirit of the homeland in good Orthodox tradition. Here the ancient talmudic tradition is continued as of old, but naturally under the influence of modern pedagogic reforms as regards methods." The Bible, the Hebrew language and grammar, and Jewish history were also taught. The enrollment of the school was 200 boys in 1917, 256 in 1925, 435 in 1927, and 500 in 1933.

Under the guidance of well known Rabbis, including its principals, Rabbis Chaim I. Moseson, Moses Shapiro, Eliezer Portnoy, hundreds of boys of Brownsville and surrounding neighborhoods received an intensive rabbinic education, many of the graduates continuing their studies in higher academies of Jewish learning. For some thirty years the principal of the Hebrew Department was Rabbi Moses Samuel Shapiro, a unique personality of integrity and piety, a rabbinic scholar, a Hebrew writer of great literary ability, and a great lover of Zion.[6] The English Department was for many years directed by Isidore K. Zwickel as principal.

The reverence for learning evinced by some of the Brownsville residents was demonstrated when the Yeshiva Rabbi Chaim Berlin found it necessary to move into more spacious quarters. Due to radical changes in the character of the neighborhood, the old synagogue, *Oheb Zedek,* on Howard Avenue, was sold, whereupon the officers succeeded in persuading the membership to contribute a major portion of the money to the Yeshiva. This generous gesture was a heartwarming example of the responsibility Jews felt towards one another.

Yeshiva and Mesivta Torahs Chaim of Greater New York

Under the guidance of Rabbi Isaac Shmidman, dean since 1930 of Yeshiva and Mesivta Torahs Chaim of Greater New York, this school, located at 631 Belmont Avenue in East New York, has graduated hundreds of students well-versed both in rabbinic and secular learning. It was founded in 1926, but four years elapsed before the institution was fully organized. It has been able to provide each year Jewish and English education for 400 students under a well-trained staff. An elementary and high school department are maintained, as well as a number of extracurricular activities. Due to neighborhood changes, the school merged in 1965 with the Yeshiva of South Shore in Woodmere, Long Island.

Chaim Nachman Bialik Day School

In 1946, Dr. Haim Abramowitz as principal, and Dr. Arthur Leivson as president of the board of directors, opened the Chaim Nachman Bialik Day School to afford an intensive Hebraic education. The school met in the building of the Stone Avenue Talmud Torah until 1951, when it affiliated with the Flatbush Jewish Center.

The Yiddish Culture Schools

In addition to the religious schools there were a number of Yiddish cultural schools sponsored by the National Workers Alliance—*Poale Zion*—the Shalom Aleichem *Volks Schulen,* and the Workmen's Circle Schools—*Arbeiter Ring.* The courses common to these schools were Yiddish, Yiddish literature, Jewish history, current events, Yiddish folk songs and dances, and, in

some of these schools, Hebrew. The Jewish festivals were celebrated, although the purely religious holidays were omitted in
some of these schools. The attitude towards Zionism and Israel also
varied with these schools. All had small registrations. Most of them
used rented facilities, and therefore they were found in various
locations. In recent years the Perez *Volks Schule* owned its own
house on Saratoga Avenue near Pitkin Avenue. The schools designated below were extant in the 1920's.

Name of School	*Address*	*Registration*
Hebrew National School	1554 St. Marks Avenue	35 boys
Jewish National Radical School	1701 Pitkin Avenue	25 boys 75 girls
Shalom Aleichem *Volks Schule*	Hopkinson Avenue	100 in 1927
" " " "	172 Riverdale Avenue	
Perez *Volks Schule*	Herzl and Douglas Streets	145
Arbeiter Ring School #3	88 Grafton Street	60
" " " #14	1465 St. Marks Avenue	125
Non-Partisan School	1842 Pitkin Avenue	
Workingmen's School	Labor Lyceum, Sackman Street	

The proportion of children of school-age receiving any kind of
Jewish education in any one year was comparatively small,
approximately 20 per cent of the total school population. Many of
the boys received a brief preparation for their Bar Mitzvah for a
year or less, and many of the girls never attended at all. On the
basis of the surveys made by the Jewish Education Committee of
the Yom Kippur register as compared to the general register, the
Jewish school population of Brownsville proper, exclusive of East
New York and New Lots, was 33,128 in 1923, and 32,358 in 1924.
It was 31,679 on September 28, 1925, out of a general register of
33,638. An actual count of the register of Jewish religious schools
in the neighborhood and their attendance on January 1, 1927,
from the records of the Jewish Education Association, showed a
total of about 4,000 children. Another 500 children attended the
Volksshulen and Workingmen's Circle schools, and it was esti-

mated that possibly 1,000 children, at the most 1,500, studied with private teachers and in private *Hedarim*. This showed a total of 6,000 children, or about 20 per cent, receiving any kind of Jewish education in that year.[7]

There were a few one-day schools in the neighborhood—the Sabbath School of the Hebrew Educational Society, and the Sunday Schools of Temple Petach Tikvah and Temple Sinai. In addition to the elementary education received by the children in these schools, there were a number of Hebrew high-school classes that met in the Stone Avenue Talmud Torah and the Pennsylvania Talmud Torah, and also a branch of the Israel Friedlander classes with a registration of about sixty. If we add a few study groups conducted under the auspices of the Young Israel, Junior Mizrachi, etc., we shall have exhausted the list.

Jewish Educators

Dr. Benderly realized from the very beginning that unless the profession of Jewish Education became indigenous in this country through the enlistment of American-bred young men and women interested in making Jewish education their life work, there was no future for Jewish education here. In this effort he cooperated with Dr. Mordecai M. Kaplan and the Teachers Institute of the Jewish Theological Seminary, who shared these aims and enlarged its program by adding to its faculty distinguished Hebraists and teachers such as Dr. Morris L. Levine, Dr. Zevi Scharfstein, Hillel Bavli, Joshua Ovsay, and Dr. Leo L. Honor. The improved instruction in the Hebrew weekday schools, and the organization of the Hebrew High School by the bureau stimulated a number of students to make Hebrew teaching their profession.

Many of the important leaders in Jewish education received their training at the Teachers Institute. A number have come from Brownsville, where they have received their early Jewish education. These include Dr. Samuel Dinin, registrar and associate professor of Jewish history and Jewish education, Teachers Institute, 1926-1945, Executive Director, Bureau of Jewish Education, Jewish Community Council, Los Angeles, and vice-president and chairman of the faculties of the University of Judaism, Los Angeles; Dr. Moshe Davis, dean of the Teachers Institute and College of Jewish Studies (1945-1951) and now head of the Institute of Contemporary Jewry at the Hebrew University of Jerusalem; Dr. Azriel Eisenberg, Director of World Council of Jewish Education, executive vice-president of the Jewish Education Committee of New York (1949-1966); director of the Bureau of Jewish Education—Cincinnati (1930-40), Cleveland (1940-1945), and Philadelphia (1946-1949).

Dr. Simon Greenberg, vice-chancellor of the Jewish Theological Seminary of America, and professor of Jewish Education, Rabbinical School of the Jewish Theological Seminary of America.

Dr. David Rudavsky, now professor at New York University; former executive director of the Jewish Education Association of Essex County, New Jersey; founder and principal of Florence Marshall Junior Hebrew High School, principal of Hebrew High School of the Bureau of Jewish Education of New York City; Administrator Camp Achvah.

Louis L. Ruffman, associate director, Jewish Education Committee, New York.

Temima Gezari, artist, sculptor, director of art education, Jewish Education Committee, New York (1940-   ).

Rabbi George Ende, principal Hebrew High School, Jewish Education Committee, New York.

Henry R. Goldberg (died 1966) former Educational Director, East Midwood Jewish Center; president, Educator Assembly, Chairman, United Synagogue Commission on Jewish Education.

A number of Jewish educators who have come from Brownsville studied in the Teachers Institute of the Yeshiva University for many years under the direction of Dr. Pinhus Churgin. Many of the graduates of Yeshiva and Mesivta R'Chaim Berlin have also entered the field of Jewish Education, teaching and directing in the various day-schools or Yeshivahs which have been organized in recent years.

One of the foremost leaders in Parochial Jewish education is Dr. Joseph Kaminetsky, a graduate of Yeshivah College and Teachers College, Columbia University, who is director of the Department of Education of *Torah Umesorah,* the National Society for Hebrew day-schools since 1946. Between 1934-1946 he served as educational director of the Jewish Center of New York.

Hebrew in the Public High Schools

With the cooperation of Dr. Stephen S. Wise, Dr. Israel Chipkin, and the leaders of the *Avukah* students organization, Samuel M. Blumenfeld and Abraham H. Cohen, Dr. Samuel Benderly was instrumental in having the public high schools of New York City introduce the study of Hebrew culture and civilization as a regular part of their curriculums. Judah Lapson, one of Dr. Benderly's younger disciples, became the director of the Hebrew Culture Council, through whose efforts this activity has continued over the years.[8]

On May 1, 1930, the Board of Superintendents recommended to the Board of Education of New York City "that Hebrew be included experimentally in the course of study, as an elective subject, in the Thomas Jefferson and Abraham Lincoln High Schools on the opening of the schools in September, 1930."

The Thomas Jefferson High School in East New York, whose principal was Dr. Elias Lieberman, and the Abraham Lincoln High School in Coney Island, whose principal was Dr. George Mason, opened classes in the fall of 1930. Ninety-five students enrolled during the first year. Dr. Samuel Streicher, a graduate of the Stone Avenue Talmud Torah, was the first teacher in Thomas Jefferson High School, and Miss Celia Lewis in the Abraham Lincoln High School. In the Thomas Jefferson High School Hebrew was offered during this experimental period only to students in the upper two years of the commercial course who possessed no previous knowledge of Hebrew.

The progress over the years has been phenomenal. From 95 students in the two high schools in 1930, the number increased to 235 in 1932, and by 1950 to more than 6,500 in thirty-six high schools and colleges.

In 1940 Thomas Jefferson High School, with the largest registration of any school in the City, had 20 classes in Hebrew with a total enrollment of 687 students. The staff consisted of 4 teachers licensed in Hebrew, and 2 other teachers. The New Lots Evening High School, which meets in Thomas Jefferson High School, had an enrollment of 130 students in 3 classes. Junior High School 109 in Brownsville and Junior High School 149 each had 1 class in Hebrew with an enrollment of 46. Two other high schools in Brooklyn attended by Brownsville students, Samuel J. Tilden and Boys High School, also had classes; the former, with 6 classes, had an enrollment of 223 students, and the latter, with 4 classes, had an enrollment of 169.

During this period of growth and progress much was achieved. A staff of trained and licensed teachers was developed, and a syllabus and regents, as well as college entrance credit, secured. The project exercised a profound influence not only on the Jewish, but also on the non-Jewish students. They came to know of the Hebrew Renaissance, and of the role of Hebrew in modern Jewish life. The students of these classes who belonged to the Hebrew Culture Council participated in many extracurricular activities. These included clubs under the supervision of the Hebrew Department, with a varied program including discussions and symposia on cultural subjects, film showings, and learning of Hebrew songs and dances. The students became responsible for the Hebrew assembly program, which they presented before the school assembly once a year. They planned various exhibits of arts and crafts; they produced their own Hebrew publications. For students desiring to supplement their study of Hebrew, courses were offered on Sundays by the Jewish Culture Council. To interest students and parents in Hebrew, the Culture Council produced plays which were presented at rallies and parents meetings. One of the earliest rallies, held at Thomas Jefferson High School, proved so successful that police had to be summoned to handle the overflow audience of students and parents on the sidewalks.

Much of the early success of this project may be attributed to the teachers who brought to the subject of Hebrew not only a record of excellence as instructors, but also a love and devotion for their work. In Thomas Jefferson High School Dr. Samuel Streicher, Mrs. Deborah Pomerantz, Mrs. Florence Friedman,

Abraham Aaroni, Morton Lewittes, and Edward Horowitz, who was the first acting head of a Hebrew department in the city, were among the teachers who over many years rendered dedicated service to the cause.

Zionism in Brownsville

The influence of the Zionist movement was widely felt in Brownsville, affecting wider circles than is indicated by the official enrollment of Zionists in the various groups. Zionism was a strong factor in the communal life despite the large portion of Jewish workers and cosmopolitan Socialists, to whom Zionism and Socialism were mutually exclusive movements. It not only attracted large numbers of adults, but also fired the imagination of young people who had become indifferent to Judaism, offering them a new channel of Jewish expression. It provided a great goal on which Jews could unite.[9]

There was a strong *Hovevei Zion* Society, and also other groups of Zionists in Brownsville as early as 1898. Among the 135 Zionist societies affiliated with the Federation of American Zionists in 1900 was the B'nai Zion Association of Brownsville, which was established in 1897-1898.

With the appearance of Theodore Herzl, the World Zionist Congress in 1897, the establishment of the World Zionist Organization, and the organization of the Federation of American Zionists in 1897, with Professor Richard Gottheil as the first president, and Dr. Stephen S. Wise as the first secretary, Zionism as a movement of hope and redemption began to affect larger numbers of Jews.

Numerous Zionist groups sprouted. In Brownsville, the *Degel Zion, B'nai Zion,* the *Hatikvah,* the Zion Social Club, and other organizations flourished, each sponsoring its literary programs, lectures, and debates. One of the earliest Zionist and literary groups was the *Dorshe Zion*—Seekers of Zion—which met at the Hebrew Educational Society building. On October 31, 1903, a mass meeting held under its auspices attracted an audience of 200 people, and was addressed by the Reverend A. A. Radin, Jacob DeHaas, and A. H. Simon.

The *Degel Zion,* with headquarters on Christopher Street, was another active group in the first decade of the century. The Hebrew-speaking *Dovre Ivrith* group met in the same club rooms. Many young people belonged to one or both of these groups. In 1916 the *Tiphereth Zion* Association of East New York was organized, with a membership of twenty-five. Jacob Dunn was president, and N. Aaronson, secretary. There was also a Brownsville Friends of Zion Club with a membership of twenty-five, and a Zion Club, *Kadimah,* of East New York.

These groups consisted mainly of young people, most of whom were recent arrivals from Eastern Europe, where they had come under the spell of the ideas expounded by Lilienblum, Pinsker, Herzl, Ahad A'ham, and other leaders of the Zionist movement. Since most of the members spoke Yiddish, it became the official language at the meetings. For a number of years the headquarters were in a house at 296 Sackman Street, where lectures, sings, and socials were conducted. During the war years, when many of the famous Zionists lived in this city, lectures were delivered by Ben Gurion, Dr. Ben Zion Mossinsohn, Dr. Shemarya Levin, and other distinguished leaders.

In 1918 the Zionist organization decided that instead of individual clubs, its constituent parts be organized into districts, geographically defined. The Zionist District of Brownsville and East New York was selected to serve as an experiment to prove the feasibility of the plan. The *Degel* and the *Hatikvah* clubs became part of the District. A membership committee headed by Isidore Hassin was formed to serve the entire district, and succeeded in organizing as many as 4,000-5,000 members. As a result, the Brownsville District became one of the largest and most active in the country.

In 1921 the ranks of the American Zionist Organization split into two camps—the Mack-Brandeis Group, in opposition to the *Weizmann-Keren Hayesod* Group. The leading American Zionists, including Judge Julian Mack, Felix Frankfurter, Rabbis Stephen S. Wise and Abba Hillel Silver, Nathan Strauss, Henrietta Szold, and Philip Rosenblum were opposed to *Keren Hayesod* methods proposed by the Europeans to develop the national home under the Balfour Declaration. The issue was fought out at the

Cleveland Convention held in June of that year between the Brandeis group on one side, and the Weizmann group, represented by Louis Lipsky, Abraham Goldberg, Emanuel Newman and Morris Rothenberg, on the other. The administration was overwhelmingly defeated, whereupon the whole Brandeis group resigned from the executive of the American organization. The *Keren Hayesod* was officially established in America, and the task of organizing and popularizing the Zionist fund fell in large measure on the shoulders of Dr. Weizmann and his European delegation, which included Shemarya Levin and Menahem Usishkin.

The Brownsville Zionists sided with Weizmann and Lipsky. According to a very interesting memoir published by Morris Zeldin in the Hebrew Journal *Hadoar,* the Brownsville Zionist District was greatly responsible for the early success of the *Keren Hayesod* in America. The Zionists of Brownsville, East New York, New Lots, and Arlington decided to arrange a reception to Weizmann and members of his delegation at a mass meeting to be preceded by a parade through the streets of Brownsville. Mr. Zeldin was appointed chairman, and together with Isadore Hassin, he went to Manhattan to select a date for the reception. They wanted to make certain that besides Chaim Weizmann, Shemarya Levin, the favorite Yiddish orator admired by many in Brownsville, would attend.

Morris Zeldin recalls how Dr. Weizmann turned to Shemarya Levin and said, "I have heard and read so much about Brownsville, which you call the 'Jerusalem of America.' Tell me, where is Brownsville?"

With a gentle smile on his lips, Levin replied, "Brownsville is Brownsville, and the City of New York is built around her."

A date for the mass meeting was set. The Liberty Theatre was engaged. Admission tickets were printed, and show cards ordered, which were to be placed in stores and other central points. News releases were issued to the newspapers about the route of the parade. Every detail was attended to, except one: the committee failed to consult the *Keren Hayesod* Council, which met and decided that it would be inadvisable to begin the campaign for funds in a neighborhood like Brownsville, which consisted mostly of workers and small businessmen. The rich Brownsvillites had moved to Eastern Parkway, and would have no relations with the Brownsville Zionists.

There was consternation in Brownsville. How could the *Keren Hayesod* Council provoke and disgrace the Brownsville Zionists, who had put so much effort in preparing for the event? Almost all admission tickets were sold. Thousands of Jews, including students of the Talmud Torahs and members of the Young Judaean clubs, had volunteered to participate in the parade. The newspapers had given unusual publicity to the event. Happily, after discussion by the council, Mr. Zeldin was informed that he could proceed with the reception and parade, but no appeal for funds should be made.

A week before the event, a well-known Brownsville builder, Jacob Goell, informed Mr. Zeldin that he felt so strongly about the cause that had brought Weizmann to America that he wished to contribute $2,000 a year for five years to the *Keren Hayesod* in Brownsville, where he had made his wealth. And to the astonishment of Zeldin, he handed him a check for $2,000.

On the day of the parade, tens of thousands of Brownsville Jews participated. The theatre was packed with an audience that only Brownsville could furnish, all in a holiday mood. The matter of a public appeal for funds remained unsettled until the very last few minutes. Zeldin urged Shemarya Levin to make an appeal, or else he would do so himself. After Menahem Ussishkin, the first speaker, explained in detail the purposes of the *Keren Hayesod* and the need for funds to develop the land, Mr. Zeldin introduced Shemarya Levin, who delivered an eloquent address which filled his audience with enthusiasm, and prepared them for the appeal for contributions. When Mr. Zeldin announced Mr. Goell's gift of $10,000 with $2,000 as the first check, the theatre shook with applause and excitement. A flood of gifts followed, totaling $125,000, a truly huge sum for those days. It was a moment of joy and triumph for the Brownsville Zionists. For Weizmann, it was a source of encouragement beyond his expectations. Dr. Shemarya Levin remarked to Weizmann, "In Brownsville was laid the foundation for the *Keren Hayesod*," and to Zeldin he turned to say, "God came to our help."

Weizmann concluded the sensational meeting with an address in which he replied to his critics and outlined his program. It marked a great day for Brownsville, and thereafter the *Keren Hayesod* annual appeal became one of the most important projects of the Brownsville Zionists.

There were other Zionist activities in Brownsville. The Jewish National Fund, with its blue boxes placed in many homes, was a recognized institution. The annual Flag Day and Flower Day were great events for the youth on the Brownsville streets, especially on Pitkin Avenue. The Order B'nai Zion, the Zionist fraternal organization, had a strong group in the Abarbanel Camp.

The annual Purim *Seudah* was another special event, at which time a journal containing material written in a spirit of levity and satire conforming to the holiday mood formed the basis of the program. This was joined later with the annual campaign for the United Jewish Appeal. Another outstanding activity was the *Hebra Shas Zioni* (Study Group in Talmud) which the Zionist District sponsored for a number of years.

Not only individuals, but many organizations were involved in the Zionist spirit and ideals. Some decided to settle in Israel. When the Nahlat Israel Synagogue on Chester Street sold its synagogue because of the change in the population of the neighborhood, it donated the proceeds of $6,000 to the Kfar Habad, the colony established in Israel by the followers of Rabbi Schneierson, the Rabbi of Lubavitch.

The American Jewish Congress

The Brownsville Zionists played a dominant role in the election of delegates for this section to the American Jewish Congress, which was held at the end of World War I.

A large number of East European Jews, apprehensive about recent occurrences abroad, began to agitate through the Yiddish press, the fraternal orders, and numerous other organizations, for the consolidation of all Jewish forces in a new representative organization to be elected on a democratic basis. On November

23, 1914, Dr. Joseph Krinsky, of the Brownsville neighborhood, called a conference in New York City of persons interested in securing full rights for the Jews in belligerent countries after the war. Numerous other conferences were called, and various resolutions adopted.

For several years the question of convening an American Jewish Congress provoked discussion and dissension. It was generally supported by organizations with Zionist sympathies. It was initially opposed by the American Jewish Committee and other organizations, which proposed the calling of a limited conference of delegates from national bodies. The National Workmen's Committee on Jewish Rights, representing various labor organizations, which was established in 1915 to work for the achievement of equal rights for the Jews of all countries, withdrew from the movement after the Russian revolution. It maintained that the need for a congress had ceased with the abolition by the revolution of all restrictions against the Jews of that country.

After protracted discussions and negotiations, the American Jewish Congress finally met in Philadelphia in December, 1918, exclusively for the purpose of defining methods whereby, in cooperation with the Jews of the world, full rights might be secured for the Jews of all lands, and all laws discriminating against them might be abrogated.

Under the direction of the General Board of Elections, of which Professor Isaac Hourwich was chairman, nominations for delegates to the American Jewish Congress were held through conventions in all parts of the country between May 12 and May 14, 1917. The general election, held in all communities on June 10, 1917, proved to be a remarkable demonstration of the popular interest in the congress. Three hundred delegates were chosen by popular vote, one hundred of them in New York City, and one hundred to be selected by the national Jewish organizations.

Brownsville and East New York Jews again demonstrated their strong feelings for the lot of their fellow Jews, and for the cause of an American Jewish Congress. Once again Brownsville justified its epithet, the "Jerusalem of America." It drew the largest vote of any section in the city. This was mainly due to a strenuous six weeks campaign, lasting from four to six hours a night, which was carried on by members of the Zionist District. On Brownsville street corners and in various places of assembly, the issues of the Congress and of the Jewish people the world over were brought to the Brownsville masses.

Brooklyn was divided for election of delegates into two districts. District Seven included Brownsville, East Flatbush, East New York, Borough Park and Bayside, while the rest of Brooklyn, most of whose Jews were to be found in Williamsburg, formed the other district. Brownsville placed two tickets in the field, the Zionist and the Nationalist Socialist. The Jewish Nationalist Socialists, including the Poale Zion and the National Workingman's Circle, conducted a strong campaign on behalf of their ticket, which included Dr. Joseph Krinsky, Dr. J. Globus, M. Moskowitzky, J. Levitzky, H. Glaser, M. Glass, Morris Weinberg, N. Chanowitz, and D. Abrams. Morris Weinberg, who was opposed by many Zionists because of his socialist association, carried on a particularly strenuous campaign, claiming that while he was a Socialist, and supported socialist institutions in Brownsville, he was also known for his support of all religious and worthwhile efforts. In East New York, Morris Binkowitz, Jacob Dunn, Dr. J. Krinsky, and Dr. Morris Robinson appealed for votes.

After a lively campaign, balloting took place on Saturday evening and all day Sunday, June 10. In District 7, 31,000 adults cast their votes. It was the largest number of voters in the whole of New York. The East Side District and the Williamsburg District attracted only half of that number, some 15,000 voters each. When one considers that the large labor element withdrew from the Congress movement, one appreciates all the more the extraordinary size of the local vote.

Thirteen Zionists and two National Socialists (Morris Weinberg and Dr. Joseph Krinsky) were elected. Three of the delegates were Borough Park residents, one of whom, Joseph Barondess, drew the largest number of votes, 19,207. Following is a roster of the delegates and the number of votes cast for them:

Joseph Barondess (Borough Park)	19,207
Dr. Joseph Krinsky	13,040
Gedaliah Bublick (Borough Park)	12,533
C. Zunzer (Borough Park)	12,299
Isaac Allen	11,835
Rabbi Israel H. Levinthal	11,356
Dr. Morris Robinson	10,765
Mrs. Ida Levine	9,187
Morris Weinberg	9,160
Dr. Reuben Finkelstein	8,792
Morris Binkowitz	7,192
Jacob Dunn	7,075
Victor Schwartz	6,488
Abraham Levy	5,920
David Goldberg	5,430

At the Congress held in Philadelphia in December, 1918, Isaac Allen of Brownsville was one of the three secretaries elected.[10]

The Mizrachi

The Mizrachi Organization was called into being to unite all religious elements loyal to Jewish tradition within the ranks of Zionism.[11] "The Land of Israel for the people of Israel in accordance with the Torah of Israel," is its motto. In the early years prior to 1913, a number of Mizrachi groups were part of the Federation of American Zionists. In fact, Jacob DeHaas, secretary of the Federation, aided in the organization of a Mizrachi movement in the United States. With the advent in America in 1913 of Rabbi Meyer Berlin (Meyer Bar Ilon), then the secretary of the World Mizrachi movement, a change occurred. Rabbi Berlin advocated the separation of the Mizrachi from the Federation, but not from the World Zionist movement. In 1916 the Mizrachi designated Rabbi Berlin as its president, succeeding Rabbi D. B. Abramowitz of St. Louis, and its headquarters were established in New York. Substantial results were achieved in enlisting the religious elements of American Jewry. A youth movement took shape in the early 1920's and a Mizrachi women's organization was formed in 1925.

The Orthodox Jews of Brownsville and East New York participated actively in this movement, and provided some of its leadership. In 1917 the Mizrachi established its first significant and highly constructive institution in New York—the Mizrachi Teachers Institute (now the Teachers Institute of the Yeshivah University). It was the first school of higher Jewish learning to use *Ivrit be'ivrit*—Hebrew in all its subjects of instruction. It was located at 86 Orchard Street. Rabbi Jacob Levinson, who came to New York from Chicago, was the first instructor in Talmud, and is reputed to be the first to teach Talmud in Hebrew translation in this country. Rabbi Levinson settled in Brownsville, was for a time Rabbi of Beth Hamidrash Hagodel on Sackman Street, served as president of the Mizrachi Movement, and played a leading role for many years in the Jewish life of Brownsville. Dr. Meyer Waxman, a former resident of Brownsville, became instructor in Bible, history, and history of Jewish literature.

Of the fifteen Mizrachi societies in New York City in 1917, three were in Brownsville and East New York. One was the *Tiphereth Zion Mizrachi* at 417 New Jersey Avenue, organized in 1911, with a membership of forty odd. Albert Schwartz was president, and H. S. Heilig, secretary. There was also the Mizrachi organization of Brownsville, with Isaac Allen as its president.

The third group was the Hebrew League Mizrachi of Brownsville, which met Saturday nights at 1554 St. Marks Avenue. M. Dorfman was president, and Louis Finkelstein was secretary. The youth group of Brownsville, the *Adath Bnei Israel Mizrachi* of Brownsville, was second only to the youth group in Chicago as the most important in the country. Among its founders were Samuel Reifman, Mr. Meyerowitz, and Louis Finkelstein (now Dr. Louis Finkelstein, Chancellor of the Jewish Theological Seminary). Together with *Tiphereth Mizrachi* and *B'noth Jerusalem Mizrachi,* they became the basis for the organization in 1920 of the *Mizrachi Hatzair,* now the *Hapoal Ha-Mizrachi.*

For many years the Brownsville *Ha-Poel Ha-Mizrachi* occupied a house on Hopkinson Avenue, where it carried on a full program of activities, comprising Sabbath religious services, classes in various subjects including Talmud and Bible, clubs for juniors, holiday celebrations, and lectures. They later moved to larger quarters on Herzl Street near Pitkin Avenue, but now have their headquarters on Saratoga Avenue and East 98th Street. Over the years there was also the active East New York Chapter of the *Mizrachi* Women's Organization.

Labor Zionists—Poale Zion

The *Poale Zion,* the National Jewish Socialist Labor Organization, represented a secular radical Jewish labor movement which believed in the possibility of a synthesis of Zionism and Socialism.[12] To its followers, *Poale Zionism* was not only a political movement but also a philosophy of Jewish life. It espoused the establishment of a socialistic commonwealth in Palestine, and advocated the formation of cooperative settlements and workers collectives. Among the leaders of the movement whose thinking profoundly influenced their followers were Ber-Berochow, Dr. Nachman Syrkin, and Hayim Greenberg.

Brownsville had a dynamic *Poale Zionist* organization since its inception. In 1917 the *Poale Zion* of Brownsville met at 1731 Pitkin Avenue. It played a principal role in convoking the first American Jewish Congress and the Brownsville *Poale Zionists,* conducting a vigorous campaign on behalf of their candidates, Dr. Joseph Krinsky and Morris Weinberg as delegates. There was a branch of the Jewish National Workers Alliance (*Varband*) with headquarters at 443 Hopkinson Avenue. The East New York *Poale Zion* met at 539 Schenck Avenue. A National Radical School was conducted at 595 Saratoga Avenue. In recent years the local *Poale Zion* headed, by Abraham Schudroff, have had their headquarters in the Cultural Center at 395 Kingston Avenue.

Although small in numbers, the *Poale Zionists* in America engaged in a wide spectrum of activities. Their interest in the education of the Jewish masses in America prompted them to establish their own system of Jewish education, the secular Jewish folk schools. They published their own organs of opinion, *The*

Yiddish Weekly, Der Kempfer, and the English monthly, *The Jewish Frontier.* They initiated the *Halutz* movement, and were responsible for the organization of the Jewish Legion that fought on the side of the Allied Army in Palestine during World War I. The Palestinian Workers' Fund, started in 1910, led to the organization of the *Histadruth* campaign. They organized the Farband Labor Zionist Order (1900), the Pioneer Women's Organization, and the *Habonim* (Labor Zionist Youth) Organization. They continuously arrayed themselves against the anti-Zionist attitude within the Jewish labor movement and solicited sympathy for the cause from the non-Jewish socialists. The gradual entry of the Jewish trade unions into the sphere of Israel aspirations is to be attributed in a measure to their efforts.

Young Judaea

Brownsville was for many years one of the most active centers of Young Judaea activities. Of the 118 groups of Young Judaea in New York City listed in the Jewish Communal Register of 1917-1918, 28 were in Brownsville and East New York.

Young Judaea as a distinct national organization came into existence in 1909, with Professor Israel Friedlander as its first president, and David Schneeberg as executive secretary. The organization and its program expanded over the years to include hundreds of clubs with a membership of thousands of youths.[13] Through the publications of the Young Judaean Magazine, leaders manuals, guides, handbooks, materials for the observance of the various holidays and on various aspects of Jewish life, history, and Zionism, Young Judaea disseminated among many of the rising generation the Zionist ideals and program, and helped to arouse an intelligent interest in all Jewish affairs, as well as a positive and reverent attitude toward Judaism.

At the Ninth Annual Convention of Young Judaea held in Asbury Park on June 30, 1917, with Dr. David de Sola Pool presiding, Max Cohen reported for the Young Judaea groups of Brownsville. The Brownsville Young Judaeans consisted of ten clubs and maintained a building of their own. The activities included a training class for leaders, a Hebrew and Sabbath School, a Boys' Congregation, sewing and craft circles, dancing, celebrations, and collections for Zionist funds. David Schneeberg, who was a conspicuous factor in the organization of Young Judaea and a dedicated devotee of its work, was familiar with the Brownsville program, since he had served at one time as Boys Worker in the Hebrew Educational Society, and for a time conducted a preparatory school on Pitkin Avenue.

The 1917-1918 Communal Register shows that ten Young Judaea Circles met at 130 Liberty Avneue. Another group of seven clubs met at 373 Saratoga Avenue, and a third group of five clubs at the Hebrew Educational Society building. The Herzelia Club met at Stone Avenue Talmud Torah under the direction of Morris Zeldin, and others met elsewhere.

One of the Young Judaea's most active leaders for a time was Rabbi Simon Greenberg, now vice-chancellor of the Jewish Theological Seminary of America. Beginning as a leader of a Young Judaea Hebrew Club, he later served Young Judaea in various official capacities—as a Supervisor of Brownsville Young Judaea, as City Secretary, as President of New York City Young Judaea, and for several years as a member of the Administration and Executive Committee of National Young Judaea. In 1922, while principal of the Hebrew Educational Society's Hebrew School, he organized more than twenty young Judaean clubs in that institution alone. Among the other leaders of the Young Judaea Clubs in Brownsville were Benjamin H. Block, Sadie Cohem, Sam Streicher, Morris Zeldin, Dr. D. H. Rosenberg, Max Cohen, Dave Tannenbaum, Elias Gartman, Moses Plotkin, David Satlow, Ella Kanefsky.

Hebrew Literary Groups

As a by-product of the rise of Zionism, there followed a resurgence of interest in Hebrew. There was a small but enthusiastic group that believed one of the prerequisites for a regenerated Israel was the cultivation of Hebrew. A new Hebrew literature was being created in Europe, but American Jewry was out of touch with it. To reestablish Hebrew to its former pristine status became the group's chief aim. Hebrew-speaking groups were organized in New York as early as 1880 (*Shoherai Sefat Eber*), but it was not until the beginning of the century that a lively interest became apparent. The prime movers and guiding spirits were a group of young men who had emigrated from Europe, some of whom later entered the Jewish Theological Seminary. Especially active was Morris Levine (Moshe Halevi), who was graduated from the Jewish Theological Seminary in 1909.[14] He became principal of the Stone Avenue Talmud Torah in 1912, and later served as professor of Hebrew Literature and Bible in the Teachers Institute of Jewish Theological Seminary. He immersed himself heart and soul in the Lower East Side Hebrew organization known as *Mefitzei Sefat Eber* (Society for the Dissemination of Hebrew), which was established in July, 1902, and became a Hebrew Forum attracting Hebrew-speaking members from all parts of the city. It exerted a prodigious influence on the spread of the Hebrew movement.

In Brownsville proper, Dr. Meyer Waxman, who is known for his voluminous history of Hebrew literature and for many other scholarly works, together with Dr. L. M. Herbert, who became editor of the Hebrew medical journal (*Ha-Rophe Ha-Ibri*), organized a Hebrew speaking group, *Dobre Ivrith*, which attracted twenty-five members. Rebecca Schildkraut Mehr was corresponding secretary. In 1905 this group was enriched by a zealous worker in the person of Abraham Spicehandler, a young man of eighteen who had arrived from Poland recently and moved into Brownsville. He soon became active in this Hebrew-speaking society and in the Zionist organization of Degel Zion, in whose headquarters on Christopher Street the *Dobre Ivrith* met.

For nearly a half century Mr. Spicehandler, a merchant by occupation, who later moved to the Borough Park section of Brooklyn, devoted his life to the support and dissemination of Hebrew culture in the United States. Every Hebrew cultural enterprise, whether it be the *Histadruth Ivrith*, the Hadoar Publishing Company, the Bitzaron, or the Masad, has been the beneficiary of his time, energy, and even of financial resources.

"His was the voice crying for Hebrew in the wilderness of our times," stated Dr. S. Margoshes.[15]

At the twelfth Zionist Convention of the Federation of American Zionists held in New York in 1908, at which he was a delegate, Spicehandler organized a group urging the Zionist organization to assist Hebrew culture in a positive manner. At succeeding conventions he continued to demand more and more financial assistance for Hebrew publications in the United States.

An effort to organize a Hebrew Federation of all Hebrew speaking groups in this country was made at the annual convention of the Zionists held in Philadelphia on June 16-20, 1905, but the organization did not endure. In the Hebrew weekly *Ha-Lehum* of September 12, 1906, a public request was made to all Hebrew speaking groups in America desiring to federate, to communicate with Dr. Meyer Waxman of the Committee of the *Dovre Ivrith* of Brownsville.[16] While nothing substantive came out of this effort, it pointed up the indefatigable activity of the Brownsville group and the enthusiasm of Dr. Waxman as one of the prime movers of the Hebrew movement in this country. A number of other unsuccessful efforts followed before the *Histadruth Ivrith* was finally organized under Kalman Whiteman's direction in June, 1916. A number of active Hebrew literary groups continued to function in Brownsville—*Ben Jehudah, Zeirai Zion, Ivriah,* and *Barkai* among others. They enlisted the active interest of many of the local Hebraists.[17]

The Contribution
of Brownsville to the
Development of Orthodox,
Conservative, and Reform
Judaism in America

XIV

THE ARRIVAL in 1902 of Dr. Solomon Schechter, reader in Rabbinics at Cambridge University, England, to head the reorganized Jewish Theological Seminary of America was a significant event in American Jewish life. Dr. Schechter believed that the revival of Jewish learning must serve as a basis for a Jewish Renaissance in America.

Under his dynamic leadership from 1902 to 1915, the Jewish Theological Seminary, a small and struggling institution since its founding in 1886, burgeoned into a world center of Jewish learning and became the spiritual fountain head of the new alignment in Judaism—Conservative Judaism.[1] As the acknowledged leader and spokesman of the movement, Dr. Schechter enriched and enhanced its scope and goals, molded its rabbinical leadership, which is represented by the Rabbinical Assembly of America, and integrated its lay constituency into the United Synagogue of

America. Indeed, for a time the seminary was popularly known as "Schechter's Seminary." With his characteristic creative dynamism he assembled a group of renowned Jewish scholars for the seminary faculty; he laid the foundation of the greatest Rabbinic library in the world, to which he brought a great part of the treasured Geniza manuscripts and documents. The seminary exerted an incalculable influence not only in the fields of Jewish learning, but also on Jewish life generally—on Zionism, Jewish education, the organization of the Jewish community, and other movements. It became the center for a group of lay and professional leaders who played an important role in the growth of Judaism in this country. Upon the death of Dr. Schechter, Dr. Cyrus Adler succeeded him as president, and since the death of Dr. Cyrus Adler in 1940, Dr. Louis Finkelstein has headed the great institution.

A number of the Seminary students, as well as lay leaders of the Conservative movement, came from Brownsville and East New York. During the early years, the student body of the seminary was small. Few were ready to enter the rabbinate and become pathfinders. There was, however, a small core of youth who came either from rabbinic homes or from religious families whose imagination was fired by the rise of the Zionist movement, the modern Hebrew Renaissance, and the ideology of such men as Ahad Ha'Am, whose hearts ached for their people as for all mankind. These men were particularly anxious for the perpetuation of the Jewish spiritual heritage in this land and in the world. The program of the newly reorganized seminary, and the great scholars headed by Dr. Solomon Schechter exercised a magnetic attraction which prompted them to seek entrance into that institution.

Among the first students from Brownsville were Louis Finkelstein, Solomon Goldman, and David Aaronson. All became dynamic leaders in Jewish life in America and in the Conservative movement. Dr. Louis Finkelstein is the current chancellor of the Jewish Theological Seminary, a spokesman for Conservative Judaism, and one of the world's foremost scholars and religious leaders.

The late Dr. Solomon Goldman occupied important pulpits in Cleveland and Chicago and served as president of the Zionist organization of America. He was a brilliant orator, writer, and scholar, who enriched Judaism with his many incisive contributions.

Rabbi David Aaronson, for many years the spiritual mentor of the important midwestern community of Minneapolis, was president of the Rabbinical Assembly of America, and has contributed much to the teaching and expansion of the movement.

In 1945 Dr. Solomon Goldman, in paying his tribute as a pupil to a beloved teacher—Professor Louis Ginzberg—described the first impressions of the professor and the seminary made on these three Brownsville youths.[2] "It was as a youth of eighteen that I had the privilege of making the acquaintance of Professor Ginzberg, and the energy of that first impression has never faded from my memory. . . . I came to Professor Ginzberg directly from an institution where the title 'Professor' was for some mysterious reason held to be the equivalent of *Am-Haaretz* and *Apikiros,* ignoramus and heretic, an opinion which had the whole-hearted endorsement of my sainted Uncle Mendle. It was to this uncle, who had been stuffing me for years with the Commentaries on the Torah and Rashi as an antidote to all secular learning, that I first spoke of my interest in the seminary. 'Shlomele,' he pleaded with great anxiety, 'forget it. I hear they have no *Roshe Yeshiva* there, but only professors, *Rahmana Litzlan,* the Merciful One Save Us!'

"His fears only served the more to arouse my curiosity, and in the fall of 1910 I found myself in the presence of Professor Ginzberg.

"The occasion was a wholesome oral examination in Talmud, which students seeking admission to the Junior Department of the Seminary were required to take. Having enjoyed for some time prior the license and anarchy of studying *Varsich,* that is, without any guidance or supervision, I entered the classroom with more than the one sixty-fourth of self esteem which the Talmud allowed the disciples of the wise. I was awakened from my sad and supercilious musings at the sound of my name. 'Mr. Goldman, what tractate have you studied?'

"What in the world did the Professor mean? What possible affinity could there be between this outlandish word and the Gemoro? Professor Ginzberg recognized instantly the limitations of my vocabulary, substituted *Masechet* for 'tractate,' and I blurted out breathlessly, and I fear contemptuously, the name of one Talmudic folio after another, until Professor Ginzberg brought me to a sudden halt with an unceremonious and laconic "Um! You are a *lamdan* (scholar).'

"I agreed with him so confidently and enthusiastically that I could not have suspected a sarcastic note in his voice had it been as loud as an air-raid siren. His first question was simple enough. The second must have been a forerunner of the atomic bomb. I went down ingloriously under its impact, contracting, shrinking. I regained sufficient command of myself to whisper my embarrassment to my friends, Louis Finkelstein and David Aaronson, who were to submit to the ordeal a few moments later very much sobered up. When the examination was at an end, I left the room woefully deflated and strangely enough loving the man who had put me to the blush."

Dr. Louis Finkelstein, speaking more recently of the influence of the Seminary teachers, said: "Through the labors of Schechter, Ginzberg, Marx, Israel Friedlander, Morris D. Levine, Professor Kaplan, we were transported out of the confusion which characterized American Judaism in the early 1900's. On one side was a group of people who maintained that there were no new questions to ask, and consequently no new answers to be found. On the other side was a group who declared that both the questions and answers given in rabbinic Judaism were irrelevant. The task of the founders of the seminary was to teach American Jews that we are not people who accidently happened to exist, but that we are part of a great enterprise, the beginning of which was Mount Sinai. The end of this enterprise cannot be foreseen because it has no end. These giants were able to bring system, organization, and meaning into our world of utter confusion. As a result of their labors we can transmit to our congregants the lessons we have learned here. . . ."

Not only did Dr. Finkelstein, but also the Vice-Chancellor and President of the University of Judaism in Los Angeles—the west coast branch of the Seminary—Dr. Simon Greenberg, also lived in Brownsville. Professor Moshe Davis, Provost of the Seminary, now head of the Institute of Contemporary Jewry at the Hebrew University in Jerusalem, resided in this community and attended the Stone Avenue Talmud Torah as a boy. Other Seminary graduates who lived in Brownsville, and became leaders in American Jewish life are Dr. Meyer Waxman, one of the early graduates (1913), Dr. Solomon Grayzel, eminent Jewish historian, and formerly editor of the Jewish Publication Society of America, and Dr. Ben Zion Bokser, of the Forest Hills Jewish Center.

Following is a more inclusive list:

David Aronson	1919	Harry Jolt	1928
Ben Zion Bokser	1931	Harold Kastle	1948
Elias Charry	1930	Benjamin Kreitman	1942
Morris B. Chapman	1933	Hyman J. Landeau	1920
Samuel Chiel	1952	Philip Listokin	1935
Jacob M. Cohen	1928	Moses Lehrman	1942
Nathan H. Colish	1920	William S. Malev	1925
Moshe Davis	1942	Arnold Marans	1953
Louis Finkelstein	1919	Abraham Morhaim	1958
Max Gelb	1932	Philip Pincus	1935
Milton J. Goldberg	1952	Benjamin Plotkin	1921
Nathan Goldberg	1948	Solomon Rivlin	1921
Israel M. Goldman	1920	Manuel Saltzman	1944
Solomon Goldman	1918	Morris Schatz	1922
Morris S. Goodblatt	1927	Jack Schechter	1957
Solomon Grayzel	1921	Samuel Schwartz	1941
Gerald Green	1953	Ralph Silverstein	1954
Simon Greenberg	1925	Joseph P. Sternstein	1948
Sidney Greenberg	1942	D. Bernard Stolper	1932
Morris A. Gutstein	1932	Meyer Waxman	1913
Edward Horovitz	1927	Aaron J. Weiss	1952
Louis Hammer	1925	Max Zucker	1922
Ario Samuel Hyams	1931		

The Growth of Orthodoxy

The earnest efforts expended by Conservative rabbis on the American scene, and the ferment of the processes of Americanization, influenced considerably the other alignments in Judaism—the Orthodox and Reform camps.

Orthodoxy has become strongly entrenched with an expansive program of activities. Under the leadership of Dr. Bernard Revel, president from 1915 to 1940 of the Rabbi Isaac Elchanan Yeshiva, and his successor Dr. Samuel Belkin, the Yeshiva University has become the bastion of a strong Orthodox movement. English-speaking Rabbis, trained by a distinguished faculty of Jewish scholars, have taken positions throughout the country, where they have introduced decorous synagogue services and have established a network of afternoon and all-day schools for the training of the youth. Other well-equipped Yeshivahs in New York, Chicago, Baltimore, and elsewhere graduate teachers and Rabbis annually. Through their rabbinic and lay bodies, through various publications and comprehensive religious and educational programs, the forces of Orthodoxy are more effectively organized than ever before.

Many Brownsville youths, especially those who received their elementary education in the Yeshivah Rabbi Chaim Berlin, continued to pursue their studies in these higher institutions of learning. On graduation, some entered the rabbinate, others went into the field of Jewish education and kindred vocations, while a large number chose a business career or one of the professions. Among Brownsville and East New York youths who have advanced to highly esteemed rabbinic positions are Rabbi Joseph Hyman Lookstein of Congregation Kehillath Jeshurun of New York, a leading rabbi and educator, professor of homiletics and Jewish sociology at the Yeshivah University, chancellor of the Bar Ilan University in Tel Aviv, Israel, a past president of the Rabbinical Council of America and of the New York Board of Rabbis. Rabbi Herschel Schacter is now chairman of the Presidents' Conference and President of the Religious Zionists of America; Rabbi Paul

Levovitz is president of the Rabbinical Council of America; Rabbi Gilbert Klaperman is president of the New York Board of Rabbis, and was formerly president of the Jewish Book Council; Rabbi Alexander Linchner is now the head of Boystown in Jerusalem; Rabbi Abraham B. Hecht is a former president of the Rabbinical Alliance of America; Rabbi Leon Gewirtz, a graduate of the Chicago Rabbinical College, has served for the past twenty years in Wilmington, Delaware; Rabbi Ephraim Shimoff of Congregation Beth El, Astoria, is president of the Religions Zionists of Greater New York; Rabbi Milton Furst is Assistant to the Dean at Yeshiva University; Rabbi Henry Seigman is executive vice-president of the Synagogue Council of America, and Rabbi Ephraim Sturm is National Director of the National Council of Young Israel.

Among other Brownsville and East New York youth who graduated as Rabbis and occupy pulpits or other positions are:

Morris Appleman	Harold Kanatofsky
Abraham J. Appleman	Mendell Lewittes
Hyman Appleman	Jacob I. Nislick
Aaron B. Dachowitz	Chaim Abraham
Pincus Dachowitz	Pincus
Louis Dunn	Nathan Rosen
Samuel Fink	Paul Rosenfeld
Meyer Edelstein	Joseph Shapiro
Meir Felman	Norman J. Strisower
Aryeh Leib Gottlieb	Leon Weingrowsky
Abraham Halbfinger	Jacob Weitzman
Hyman Heifetz	Abraham Weitzman

Israel Yavne

Rabbi Joseph Kaminetsky, National Director of Torah Umesorah, the National Society for Hebrew Day Schools, is greatly responsible for the rapid development in this country of the all-day schools among the Orthodox Jews in recent years. In these schools the children study religious subjects in the morning and the secular subjects in the afternoon. Many former Brownsvillites are heads of Hebrew Day Schools. These include among others

Rabbi Hirsch Diskind, head of Bais Yaakov of Baltimore; Rabbi Seymour Gewirtz, chief rabbi and head of the Day School, Waterbury, Connecticut; Rabbi Paul Goldberg, Principal of the Yeshiva Academy of Harrisburg, Pa.; Rabbi Joshua Goodman, Principal of Bais Yaakov in Chicago; Rabbi Maurice I. Hecht, Principal of the Lubavitcher Yeshiva in New Haven, Conn.; Rabbi Ephraim Kamin, Principal of the Lower School of HILI in Far Rockaway; Rabbi Nathan Kapner, Hillel Hebrew Academy and Synagogue, Massapequa, Long Island; Rabbi Mannes Mandel, Principal of the Yeshiva of Brooklyn; Rabbi Joseph Nayowitz, Principal of the Yavneh Academy, Paterson, New Jersey; Rabbi Eliezer Portnoy, head of the Yeshiva Rabbi Chaim Berlin; Rabbi Isaac Shmidman of the Yeshiva Toras Chaim in Hewlett, Long Island and his son, Rabbi Morris Shmidman, head of the Hebrew Academy of the Shore Area in Wanamassa, New Jersey; Rabbi David Twersky, head of the Hillel Academy in Perth Amboy, New Jersey; Rabbi Nathan Wadler, Principal of the English Department of the Lubavitcher Yeshivos; Rabbi Morris Besdin, Director, James Striar School of General Studies; and Rabbi London of the Hechel Torah.

Mesivta R. Chaim Berlin

Rabbi Isaac Hutner, who came to America in 1936, influenced a group of layman to found a Mesivta High School and a Beth Midrash for higher learning. The Mesivta R'Chaim Berlin started on a small scale in the building of the Stone Avenue Talmud Torah. In 1940 the Mesivta purchased the building on 350 Stone Avenue, formerly occupied by the Municipal Bank, and refurbished it with dormitories and other facilities. Hundreds of students from the community and other parts of the country and the world came to study here. Many have graduated as Rabbis, occupying positions in various Jewish communities. Others have entered the professions. In 1964 it relocated its quarters in Far Rockaway.

The spirit and atmosphere of the Mesivta reflect the steadfastness and imprint of Rabbi Isaac Hutner's personality. A native of

Warsaw and a descendant of great rabbinic scholars, a grandson of R. Yudel Segal, one of the spiritual leaders of Warsaw, Rabbi Hutner studied in the Yeshivahs of Slobodko, Lithuania, and in the University of Berlin. He lived in Israel for a time, and became closely associated with the late Rabbi Isaac Hakohen Kook and other scholars. Since his arrival in this country he has infused his spirit into the student body of the Yeshivah, seeking to permeate them with his idealism and to inspire them with his unique views and methods which include both the *Mussar* (ethical) and Hassidic trends in Jewish thought. Through such intimate and friendly relationships with his students, he has made an unforgettable impact on their lives.

The Reform Movement

Reform Judaism, too, has been affected by the momentous changes in American Jewish life, and has taken on in recent years a somewhat different complexion than in the beginning of the century. The influx of the more prosperous East-European Jews and of American-born Jews of East-European origin into Reform Temples, the growing number of Rabbis who were drawn from the East-European group, the effects of the World Wars and of Hitler's persecutions of Jews, led to a growing acceptance by the Reform group of Zionism and of some traditional Jewish practices.

In 1922 Rabbi Stephen S. Wise, Reform leader and Zionist, founded in New York City the Jewish Institute of Religion, a liberal rabbinical seminary welcoming men and women of diverse viewpoints. In 1948 the Institute merged with the Hebrew Union College in Cincinnati to form the Hebrew Union College-Jewish Institute of Religion (HUC-JIR). The small group of Zionist Rabbis who were in the Reform movement from the very beginning grew in numbers and in influence. Rabbis Stephen S. Wise, Judah L. Magnes, Abba Hillel Silver, Barnett Brickner, Max Heller, and others were in the vanguard of Jewish life and Zionist activity. They attracted some of the outstanding laymen of the older community such as Louis D. Brandeis, and Julian Mack, among others. Dr. Emanuel Gamoran, an Hebraist and Zionist who was associated with Dr. S. Benderly and the Bureau of Jewish Education, became the Educational Director of the Department of Synagogue and School Extension of the Union of American Hebrew Congregations.

There were no Reform temples in Brownsville, and most of the youth had no idea what Reform Judaism was. But in time, some of the youth, although they came from traditional backgrounds, were greatly attracted by the new Reform leadership. They entered the Hebrew Union College of Cincinnati or the Jewish Institute of Religion in New York. The sons of the two foremost Hebraists and Zionists of Brownsville—Ezra, son of Abraham Spicehandler, and Isaiah, son of Morris Zeldin—were graduated from the Reform Seminary. Dr. Ezra Spicehandler, author and Hebraist, is now professor at the HUC-JIR in Cincinnati. Rabbi Isaiah Zeldin, spiritual leader of the Stephen S. Wise Temple in Beverly Hills, California, was assistant dean from 1948 to 1953 of the Hebrew School of Education and Sacred Music in New York City. From 1953 to 1958 he served as dean of the California School of the HUC-JIR.

Dr. David Seligson is Rabbi of one of the oldest Reform Temples in the country, Central Synagogue of New York. Rabbi Nat Hershfield is serving in Hartford, Connecticut. Dr. Irwin M. Blank is Rabbi of Temple Sinai, Tenafly, N.J. and professor of Jewish Theology, Fordham University. David I. Cedarbaum, assistant-professor of Jewish Education, College of Jewish Studies, Chicago, held the rank of Major in World War II and was the only Jewish Chaplain in the 20th Air Force. He took his post at the headquarters of the 20th Air Force on the Island of Guam on March 7, 1945. Rabbi Mordecai Isaac Soloff has distinguished himself as an educator and author of a series of historical textbooks.

Among other graduates are Rabbis George Ende, Committee on Jewish Education, New York City; Bernard Kligfeld, Temple Emanuel in Long Beach, New York; Lewis Satlow, Temple Emanuel, East Meadow, New York; Robert Miller, Temple Ahavath Sholom, Brooklyn, New York.

Zedakah and Communal Jewish Institutions

XV

Jewish Philanthropy, Social Service, and Mutual Aid Organizations

THE TRADITIONAL VALUE OF *Zedakah*, the human obligation to help the less fortunate, which the immigrant Jews brought with them, was not only retained by the new settlers but also handed down to their children. Though themselves poor and struggling, the Brownsville and East New York residents did not neglect their social responsibilities. Particularly noteworthy is the fact that the East-European Jewish immigrants in Brownsville created a number of important institutions without assistance from the outside.

As needs increased, societies were formed to meet them. Reference has already been made to some of the organizations. The Malbish Arumim societies, Lechem Aniim Society (incorporated in 1908), the Brownsville Relief Hebrew Charity (incorporated in 1904), supplied coal, food, clothes, shoes, payments, and the like.

A *Hachnosoth Orchim* (Public Hostelry) was established for

transients, for those stranded in Brownsville on their way to other cities, or to supply tools to immigrants desiring to make Brownsville their permanent home.

The Hebrew Free Loan Association (Gemiluth Hasadim), was organized in 1901 to assist persons in temporary financial straits, to aid those in need of cash to tide them over a dull business season, or to acquire material or tools, and to help the small businessman establish himself. Similar institutions were established in East New York in 1908.

There were the Sisters of Israel to assist the poor sick with food, medical care and other necessities. The *Linath Hazedek* Society (organized in 1905) was a very important group which aided families who could not afford to call a doctor, although the fee of a home call at that time was only $1. The society rented a small store and kept a day and night vigil so that those in need might have a place where they could appeal for help. When the sick urgently needed nurses or attendants, but could not afford such services, members would volunteer to spend the night attending the sick. In the case of the male volunteers, the service was rendered by them after a hard day's work in the shop. A report was always rendered on the needs of the sick who had been visited, but the patients' names were never mentioned at meetings. Mr. A. Nathan Shafran served as president of the organization for 18 years. In 1929 the society expended more than $5,000 caring for as many as 30 sick persons a day. Some of the ailing were sent to the country for convalescence. To help the sick in a single year, the Society spent $1,407.59 for milk and eggs, $957.75 for chickens, $530.90 for medicines, and $250 for electrical treatments.

The Ladies Free Loan Association of Brownsville (Ladies *Gemilut Hesed*) was founded by 13 women in 1910, with an office at 348 Hopkinson Avenue. It aided without interest charge all who applied for loans. Possessing 1,800 members in 1931-32, the association advanced some $100,000 that year to approximately 1,200 borrowers. Mrs. Rose Finkelstein (one of the founders) was president, Shifre Eisenberg, honorary vice-president, and Mrs. Gussie Davidson, manager. For a number of years Mr. M. Huberman was the association's financial secretary.

In time, as the population increased manifold, the local community was no longer able to cope with the situation alone, and had to seek outside help. When the Brooklyn Federation of Jewish Charities was organized in 1909, it extended affiliation to the United Jewish Aid Societies, the Brooklyn Hebrew Orphan Asylum, the Jewish Hospital of Brooklyn, the Hebrew Educational Society, the Council of Jewish Women, and the Young Men's Hebrew Association of South Brooklyn. These helped to meet the social needs of all Brooklyn, and as might have been expected, Brownsville and East New York were among the principal beneficiaries.

United Jewish Aid Societies of Brooklyn

More adequate and more effective distribution of relief to the needy Jews of Brooklyn was achieved when the United Jewish Aid Societies of Brooklyn were established in 1909 to keep intact families deprived of their bread winners, and to rehabilitate impoverished persons. The society became a constituent of the Brooklyn Federation of Jewish Charities and received increasing annual allotments: $8,000 in 1909, $36,000 in 1914, $100,000 in 1919, and $227,887 in 1927. The funds were still insufficient to meet the growing demands, and proportionately much less than those distributed by the charities of Manhattan, but United Jewish Aid Societies did well under the circumstances.

In 1911 the Aid Societies divided Brooklyn into two districts— Brownsville and East New York in one district, and the rest of the borough in the other.[1] During the year 1911, the Aid Societies in the Brownsville and the East New York District gave relief to applicants among whose families there was a total of 1,420 children. These cases received $5,369.44, while $7,777.70 was spent for 629 cases in the rest of Brooklyn. Of the 398 applicants in the Brownsville and East New York District, 290 were families, 54 widows, 35 deserted women, 2 widowers, 8 single men, and 9 single women. Most of these—296—had come from Russia. Only seven were natives of the United States.

Of the 1,420 children in the families of the applicants, 121 were over 16 years of age, 103 between 14 and 16, 1162 under 14, and 34 were children committed.

The reasons for the relief and the amount given were:			
Sickness	110		$1,682.00
Tuberculosis	90		1,538.67
Lack of work	66		371.80
Insufficient earnings	18		112.12
No male support	71		1,350.35
Old age	5		144.00
Accident	3	all other	170.50
Imprisonment	2		
Other causes	31		
	396		$5,369.44

In 1912 the United Jewish Aid Societies engaged Samuel Rabinovitch, a well-known social worker, as superintendent, a position which he held for more than a quarter century. For that year Mark M. Salomon, president of the society, noted in his annual report that aid was sought by 1,651 applications whose aggregate was 8,830 individuals. Forty per cent, or 667 of the applicants, 133 old and 534 new cases, came from the Brownsville District, and the others, 984, from the rest of the Borough. Not all cases were accepted. Cash relief amounting to $7,763.54 was given to 352 applicants in Brownsville. In 1913, 372 cases, or 36 per cent of the total number came from Brownsville and East New York, and received $10,355 in relief. The nation-wide depression of 1914 and 1915 showed a sharp increase in relief cases due to unemployment. State aid to widows went into effect on January 1, 1916, and eased some of the burden.

Jews sought help whenever possible from their own people, avoiding public charitable institutions. At the National Conference of Jewish Charities held in Richmond, May 4 to 6, 1908,[2] Robert Hebbard, Commissioner of Charities of New York, remarked, "Now I have charge in New York of the public charitable institutions, and fortunately we have in those institutions comparatively few Jews. We do have some; we have got a few consumptives from the East Side, comparatively few from that great Jewish district, Brownsville, where the Jews live out in the country, and that really is a wonderful village to see, as I saw it last Saturday afternoon, stretching for miles-away on the outskirts of the city. We have a few Jews in all institutions, and the question has occurred to me how shall we treat them, especially with regard to the food question. . . ." Incidentally, the commissioner reported that a kosher kitchen was being planned for the new City Hospital on the south side of Blackwell's Island.

In the following decade the case load declined. This was due in part to progressive social legislation (workmen's compensation, pensions to widows) , and in a large degree to the improvement of the general economic conditions and conditions of employment, spread of insurance, decreasing morbidity, a decline in birth rate, the effect of mutual aid societies, modern casework with its emphasis upon rehabilitation as against granting of doles, and the virtual cessation of immigration.

For many years the United Jewish Aid Societies maintained a branch office in Brownsville to serve the Eastern District of Brooklyn. When the Brooklyn and Manhattan Federations merged, a number of affiliated agencies also merged their services. These included the United Jewish Aid Societies. The names of the organizations were changed to designate their new functions more appropriately. Thus the societies met in the late 1930's and early 1940's at 1528 Pitkin Avenue as the East End District of the Jewish Family Welfare Society, and now are part of the Jewish Family Service whose main office is in Manhattan, with two consultation centers in Brooklyn.

Brownsville Builds its Philanthropic Institutions

Some of the largest and most important philanthropic agencies in this section were established by the East-European Jews. They continued to maintain their independent and original organization, not becoming affiliated with the Brooklyn Federation of Jewish Charities, nor with the New York Federation of Jewish Philanthropies when the Brooklyn and Manhattan Federations merged. They have been maintained in accordance with Orthodox

Jewish tradition, one of the main motivations which prompted their original formation. The institutions included the Beth El Hospital (now the Brookdale Hospital Center), the Brooklyn Hebrew Home and Hospital for the Aged,[3] the Pride of Judaea Children's Service, the Women's Hospital, the Jewish Chronic Disease Hospital, two day nurseries, Hebrew Schools, Yeshivahs, and other institutions. Some of the local institutions, such as the East New York Dispensary, the Stone Avenue and the Pennsylvania Avenue Talmud Torahs, were affiliated with Federation for part of their existence. For a number of years the Jewish Board of Guardians and the Jewish Family Service maintained branch offices here. The Brooklyn Hebrew Orphan Asylum, an affiliate of Federation, was for many years located on Ralph Avenue, on the edge of Brownsville. The only affiliates of Federation which were located here throughout their existence were the Hebrew Educational Society of Brooklyn and the East New York Young Men's and Young Women's Hebrew Association.

The East New York Dispensary

The need for a dispensary where poor Brownsville residents might secure medical help and medicine became apparent as early as 1895. A small store was rented at Thatford and Pitkin avenues for the Society for the Aid of the Poor Sick. In the beginning, the few local physicians were apprehensive lest it jeopardize their private practice, but as the population increased they realized that there was enough work for all. The Society bought a small house on Watkins Street, into which the dispensary was moved. In 1909 the house was razed, and on its site a two-story-and-basement building was constructed at a cost of $16,000 and arranged for 12 departments.

The dispensary building was dedicated with fitting ceremony on May 8, 1910. In reviewing the history of the dispensary, Dr. Leon Louria said: "You are to be congratulated that the erection of this building was made possible through funds raised by your own people. No outside philanthropists were appealed to. No more exalting tribute than this can be cited to public spirit and social ethics. That community which properly provides for the health of its citizens is safeguarding and increasing their productive capacity."

The dispensary has rendered invaluable help to the sick of the section. It has served between 20,000 and 30,000 annually in its various clinics, and has issued an equal number of prescriptions. Its staff of between 20 and 30 physicians, and the prominent specialists who have headed the various departments, were drawn from the Brownsville-East New York section. They rendered free and valuable service. The token fees paid by the patients, which varied from 15¢ to 30¢ per visit, and the small additional charges for such special services as X-rays and eye glasses helped to defray part of the expenses. The indigent were accepted free. For a number of years, beginning with November, 1917, the Brooklyn Federation of Jewish Charities granted the Dispensary an annual allotment varying from $2,000 to $3,000. For the year 1917 the total receipts were $8,081, of which $3,536 came from the patients, and $2,916 from Federation.[4]

The Brooklyn Hebrew Home and Hospital For The Aged

The Brooklyn Hebrew Home and Hospital for the Aged, one of the largest voluntary institutions of its kind in the country, was founded in 1907.[5] It provides shelter, maintenance and complete medical, surgical, dental and nursing care for some 1,000 aged men and women. The entire program of the home is maintained in full accord with Orthodox Jewish tradition. Its board of directors, which includes some of the outstanding men and women of the community, and its staff of 600 have constantly aimed at creating an atmosphere in which each individual would find personal comfort, security, self-respect, and companionship. It has an annual outlay of more than $3,000,000.

The Brooklyn Ladies Hebrew Home for the Aged (the original name of the institution) was organized and incorporated in 1907, by a group of philanthropic women of the Williamsburg section in the home of Mrs. Flora Groden on Hart Street. At one of the women's socials she spoke of the plight of destitute old people in the community. She had spent that day in court, and described the case of an old Jew who had been picked up (according to one version on Pitkin Avenue) and charged with vagrancy. He was sent to Welfare Island where he was abused, had his beard pulled by some of the other inmates, and was badly injured when he jumped through a window to escape further torture. She appealed to the women to devote themselves to the assistance of such destitute old people, so that such tragic situations might not recur. Responding to her plea, the women began to canvass among their friends to raise money for a home to shelter the aged. After 3 months the society realized $1,500 from a strawberry festival held at Arion Hall, and soon thereafter the society had 1,000 dues-paying members.

After a few projects, the women accumulated enough money for a building, and on November 9, 1908, they purchased a mansion on Willoughby Avenue. They were not long in discovering the inadequacy of the building for the needs of the community, whereupon the women disposed of it and purchased lots at the corner of Dumont and Howard avenues in Brownsville. A committee consisting of Mr. and Mrs. Samuel N. Berlin and Mr. and Mrs. Bernard Trotsky appeared before the Board of Directors of the Brooklyn Federation of Jewish Charities in November, 1911, and reported that they owned lots free and clear, and contemplated erecting a fireproof home to cost about $55,000, of which approximately $12,000 was then on hand. The Committee solicited Federation's help in their work. Mr. Nathan Jonas, then the president of Federation, appointed a committee of five, with William Meruk as chairman, to meet with the committee from the Home and explore the possibility of affiliation. Subsequently, at a meeting on April 16, 1912, the Federation Committee reported that "the Hebrew Home for the Aged was not prepared to abide by the by-laws of Federation, and therefore was not yet ready to affiliate with us."

Unwilling to relinquish its membership and its fund raising, the Hebrew Home for the Aged carried on its activities independently until 1968, when it affiliated with the New York Federation of Jewish Philanthropies.

A modern three-story building was constructed at the corner of Dumont and Howard avenues, the cornerstone of which was laid on June 23, 1912. With the completion of the building in 1913, the name of the organization was changed to Brooklyn Hebrew Home for the Aged. It opened for admission of inmates in January, 1914, and by the following year the home's population was seventy permanent residents. In 1916 a second four-story building was started on Howard Avenue, and in 1918 the name was changed to Brooklyn Hebrew Home and Hospital for the Aged.

In 1923 the hospital division was officially opened for chronic cases, and as a result the resident population rose that year to 360. The size and scope of the institution were increased by the addition of new buildings in the following years. This enabled the home to institute a more comprehensive medical, surgical and dental program, and to increase the bed capacity to 706 in 1938. Upon the purchase and reconstruction of the spacious 14-story Half Moon Hotel on the Coney Island Boardwalk, the Home transferred all ambulatory residents to it in 1953, and limited the Brownsville buildup to the hospital division.

Among those who served as presidents of the agency were Mrs. M. Groden, Mrs. S. W. Berlin, Mrs. Charles Rosenthal (1916-1926), Mrs. Sarah Werbelovsky (1926-1936), and Mrs. Philip Brenner, who has been serving in this office since 1936, and under whose leadership phenomenal progress has been made. Mention should be made of these active workers and friends: Mrs. J. D. Booth, who was treasurer for fifteen years; Mr. and Mrs. Samuel Coffey, Mrs. Bertha Lurie, Mr. and Mrs. Morris Neinken, Mr. and Mrs. Max B. Marks, Mrs. B. Prensky, Mr. Jacob Krisel, Chairman of the Executive Board, and the Parshelsky brothers, whose munificent gifts made some of the new building possible. For a number of years a very active Young Folks Auxiliary attracted many young people of the community who assisted the home. Among the superintendents who served were Albert Kluger, Dr. Harry W. Rosenthal, Isidor Greenspan, and Mr. Morris Roth. It must be added that the Brooklyn Hebrew Home and Hospital for the Aged is a priceless gem in the crown of Brooklyn philanthropy.

Beth-El Hospital (Brookdale Hospital Center)

The early history of Beth-El Hospital, originally named the Brownsville and East New York Hospital, illustrates how the local community built its own institutions.[6] The need for a public hospital in the heart of this populous community was felt by many for some time. In 1910 a group of public spirited individuals organized the Brownsville Hospital Society for the purpose of raising funds to erect a hospital. The project received the support of every civic and social organization in the community, as well as of every element of the population, of the radical Socialists as well as of the strict Orthodox. The society had 10,000 members by 1917, but several years elapsed before enough money was accumulated to erect the first building. Surprisingly, it did not evoke a response from the wealthy givers, but relied on the nickels and dimes from membership dues and from various affairs conducted on its behalf. For a long time the organization was dubbed "the nickels and dimes hospital."

Sunday afternoon, August 11, 1912, marked a turning point when more than 5,000 men and women paraded through the main Brownsville streets to attend a mass meeting to celebrate the purchase of fifteen lots at $780 a lot on East Ninety-Sixth Street, Rockaway Parkway and Avenue A, on which the hospital was to be erected. Among the speakers were Henry Mehl, president of the society, Rabbi Simon Finkelstein of Oheb Shalom Synagogue, B. Feigenbaum of *The Forward,* Rev. H. Masliansky, Barnett Wolf, the Socialist leader, and others.

In 1914 the society was incorporated as the Brownsville and East New York Hospital, with plans to establish a strictly kosher kitchen. However, it was not until April, 1921, that the first building, a five-story brick structure with a capacity for 90 patients, opened its doors. The long delay occasioned considerable disappointment and complaint. As the community grew, however, and the wealthier residents became interested, there was an upsurge of marked progress. Today the hospital is one of the important medical centers in the city. The facilities have been enlarged by the construction of a number of buildings—a maternity pavilion on Avenue A in 1928, a nurses residence on Rockaway Parkway in 1942, a new 130-bed pavilion, a modern building in 1952, a new clinic pavilion, a residence hall in 1961, and a recently completed 200-bed pavilion at a cost of $3,100,000, increasing the Hospital's capacity to over 450 beds. Most of the funds necessary to erect these structures were derived from contributions by members of the board, the medical staff, and private foundations such as the Brookdale Foundation, grants from the United States Government through the Hill-Burton Act grants, and contributions from the general public.

Along with the increased physical facilities, beneficent progress was achieved in the improvement of the medical services and the introduction of many research projects. Outstanding leaders in the medical profession were named full-time directors of various departments. Among those who have served as president of the Hospital's Medical Staff were many Brownsvillites: Dr. Abraham Koplowitz (1922-1929); Dr. Benjamin Koven (1930-1933); Dr. Maurice Dattlebaum (1934-1935); Dr. Reuben Finkelstein (1936-1937); Dr. Charles E. Panoff (1938-1939); Dr. Jacob Schwartz (1940-1941); Dr. Solomon Hendelman (1942-1943); Dr. H. M. Rabinowitz (1944-1945); Dr. Jacob Halperin (1946-); Dr. Joseph M. Michtom (1947-); Dr. David Kershner (1948-1949); Dr. William Levine (1950-1951); Dr. Benjamin Kogut (1952-1953); Dr. Isadore Feder (1954-1955); Dr. H. I. Teperson (1956-1957); Dr. Abel Kemin (1958-1959); Dr. Harry Bloch (1960-).

The hospital has been served by a group of devoted laymen who have constituted its board and associate board of trustees and by a group of affiliated organizations, women's auxiliaries, and various leagues and foundations. Benne Katz has been serving as president since 1954, and Max DeKaye as superintendent since 1928. In 1932 the name of the Brownsville and East New York Hospital was changed to Beth-El Hospital, and in 1964 to the Brookdale Hospital Center.

The Jewish Chronic Disease Hospital

The Jewish Chronic Disease Hospital, located at East Forty-ninth Street and Rutland Road, is at the edge of Brownsville and serves the entire community. It was established by East-European Jews and their descendants to provide a kosher hospital in Brooklyn for the large number of chronically sick. Since its founding in 1925, it has grown to be the largest voluntary institution of its kind in the country, caring for 810 chronically ill men, women, and children in 1963.

The Home for Incurables, as the institution was originally called, was founded by Max Blumberg and a group of noble-hearted men and women.[7] It obtained a charter from the state in 1926 under the name of Sanitarium for Incurables, and opened the first building it erected at its present location on April 24, 1929, with 52 patients. When its facilities for 250 patients became overcrowded, a second building was added in 1933, with Mr. Joseph Ponemone as chairman of the Building Committee. The name of the institution was changed at this time to the Sanitarium and Hospital for Chronic Diseases, and more recently the present name, Jewish Chronic Disease Hospital, was adopted.

Because chronic diseases are of such long duration—patients at the Jewish Chronic Disease Hospital have been cared for and maintained for periods ranging up to twenty-five years—continuous expansion of facilities was necessary. Additional buildings were opened in 1940, 1950, 1958 and 1960, increasing the capacity to a total of more than eight hundred. In April, 1963, ground was broken for the construction of a new surgical wing.

The Morris and Bessie Masin Pavilion to house the Isaac Albert Research Institute was opened in 1958, and a few years ago the Institute's research work in diabetes, muscular dystrophy, Tay-Sachs disease, and other long chronic conditions was accorded universal recognition. In 1957 the hospital set aside a seventeen-bed ward for the care and study of infants and children afflicted with Tay-Sachs disease—the only ward of its kind in the world.

All measures are implemented to make the lives of the eight hundred patients as pleasant and comfortable as is humanly possible. Among the facilities available at the hospital is a school from elementary through high school under the direction of the Board of Education of the City of New York, a volunteer service, a recreation program, and a social service department. The hospital promotes various study groups, and has a synagogue where services are conducted regularly. Since the hospital is not affiliated with the Federation of Jewish Philanthropies, it conducts its own fundraising projects. In recent years it has been the recipient of generous grants from city, state, and federal agencies, from various foundations, and from others who have helped defray its huge budget. Invaluable cooperation has emanated from the many ladies auxiliaries which have been established in various sections of Brooklyn.

For twenty years Isaac Albert served the Jewish Chronic Disease Hospital as its president. His inspiring leadership and energetic efforts on behalf of the institution were largely responsible for the considerable progress achieved over the years. Mr. Albert was brought up in Brownsville, and spent his early youth in the various clubs and activities of the Hebrew Educational Society. When he grew older he joined the Non-Pareil Club, of which he later became president. Happily, Mr. Albert worked with a devoted board of directors consisting of eminent philanthropists in the community. In 1966 Mr. David S. Rabinowitz assumed the presidency.

Pride of Judaea Children's Service

To care for Jewish orphan children of Brownsville and East New York, a number of local residents organized the Jewish Orphan Asylum of Brownsville and East New York. They collected nickels and dimes and dollars, incorporated their organization in 1916, and established their headquarters at 512 Sutter Avenue near Snediker Avenue. During this early period Joseph Polonsky, a pharmacist, was president, and Aaron Wiener, secretary. They were fortunate in interesting a number of highly respected Jews in their effort. Among them was Max Blumberg, whose service over the years helped to build a number of other institutions in Brooklyn. He became president of the organization in 1920, and continued in this office for two decades.

It was during his term of office that the commodious building known as the Pride of Judaea's Children's Home was constructed on Dumont and Elton Street, at a cost of $300,000. Until recently it cared for about 250 boys and girls. One of Mr. Blumberg's co-workers, the late Jacob H. Cohen, succeeded him as president and headed the institution for twenty-five years. In recent years the institution, under the name of Pride of Judaea Children's Service, has relinquished caring exclusively for orphans and now concentrates on various services to children, particularly those who need psychiatric treatment. Judge Maurice Bernhardt serves as its president at the present time.

Brooklyn Women's Hospital

The large Women's Hospital at 1395 Eastern Parkway is the product of the efforts of the Maternity Aid Society organized in the first decade of the century by a group of Brownsville women. It is the only Brooklyn hospital exclusively for women and children. For twelve years the group collected money, sent doctors to indigent women, and rendered financial aid to the needy who preferred their own doctors. In time these women collected sufficient funds to build a hospital for maternity cases, and in the course of the years, new wings were added. Mrs. Henry Heater was president for about twelve years; Mrs. Samuel Browner, treasurer for ten years; Mrs. Harry Holland, treasurer for six years. Mrs. Jennie Koplowitz, one of the founders, was vice-president and president of the original Maternity Aid Society for many years. Although the organization was founded and directed by women, it was assisted by a number of men, particularly the husbands of the members. Albert M. Leavitt has served as its president in recent years.

Day Nurseries

Several day nurseries have been established in Brownsville and East New York to care for children whose mothers are obliged to work. The Hebrew Ladies Day Nursery was established in 1909, and incorporated in 1910. It maintained until 1961 its very large and well-equipped building at 453 Hopkinson Avenue. It enlisted the support of many Brownsville residents and organizations. Among its presidents were Mrs. Minnie Hershkovitz, Mrs. Lena Fuchs, Mrs. Fannie Edelstein. Its superintendents included Mr. H. Levene and Mr. Edward Todros.

The Ahavath Chesed Day Nursery on 394 Hendrix Street was established in 1917. D. L. Marcus was its first president, and David Emanuel Cohn the first president of the Auxiliary. Lately it has become associated with the Pride of Judaea Children's Service.

For a number of years a day nursery functioned in the Hebrew Educational Society (auspices Works Progress Administration), and another in the Pitkin Center on Sutter Avenue and Junius Street. In recent years, day nurseries supported by public funds have been established in the following housing projects: Brownsville Houses, Howard Houses, Van Dyke Houses.

Moos Hittim—*Passover Assistance*

A project which enjoyed the support of religious, social, fraternal, and political organizations was the annual collection and distribution among needy families of Passover food (*Moos Hittim*).[8] This traditional charity was maintained by the American-born generation with the same earnestness and zeal as by their immigrant parents. It took on special significance during depression periods, when the need was acute. Thus, on Sunday, April 14, 1935, thousands of families of the Brownsville, East New York, and Ocean Hill sections received baskets of Passover food from charity, fraternal, and political organizations. All day, long lines formed outside the headquarters of these organizations, while packages were delivered to families unable to call for the food.

The focus of activity was at Eastern Parkway and Rockaway Avenue, where the three largest organizations were occupied all day long in distributing food. The Nonpareil Social and Athletic Club distributed food to 800 families. It had raised $10,000 for this purpose on the previous Saturday night at its all-star show in the 106th Infantry Armory. One-fourth of these proceeds was expended for food, and the remainder was allocated to charity institutions in the neighborhood. The Huron Club at 1700 Eastern Parkway aided 2,000 families. The Jefferson Democratic Club delivered packages in cars from a store at Rockaway Avenue to over 1,200 families. The Frank Radest Democratic Association cooperated with the *Lechem Aniim* Society, which distributed food all year round to take care of its cases. The Sutter Club, the Sunrise Democratic Club, the Brownsville Democratic Club, and the Pitkin Democratic Club all made deliveries on the following day, each averaging 300 packages. In addition to these organizations, various synagogues—including the Young Israel Synagogue, which made this project an important part of its program—and numerous local charity groups were likewise engaged in the work, either delivering packages or distributing cash.

The Joint Passover Association of New York subsidized by the Federation of Jewish Philanthropies, has taken over some of the work. It opened three offices in Brooklyn, one in the Hebrew Educational Society to serve all of East Brooklyn. It investigates all cases between Purim and Passover, and depending on the family's size, mails a check with which the family may purchase its holiday needs. In order to avoid duplication, it clears all cases with other organizations engaged in *Moos Hittim* distribution.

Mutual Aid Societies

Hundreds of mutual aid societies, *Hebrot,* known under different names, flourished in New York. Most of these organizations were *Landsmanschaften*—societies whose members hailed from the same European towns. Some were fraternal orders. Others combined the functions of synagogues with their mutual-aid activities. All helped their members in emergencies arising from

death, sickness, or other occasions of distress. They offered some
security in crises in which the members might otherwise be com-
pelled to depend on charity.

Most of these societies met in the Lower East Side. According to
the Jewish Communal Register of New York City, there were
1,000 Mutual Aid Societies in 1917-1918, with an aggregate
membership of over 100,000. In 1938 the Yiddish Writers Group
of the Federal Writers Project reported some 3,000 *Landsmanschaften* in New York with 500,000 members. In one
hall in the Lower East Side, the Central Plaza Annex, they found
250 such organizations meeting regularly. The business and protocol of practically all these groups were conducted in Yiddish.

The benefits these societies offered varied, but practically all of
them came to adopt the same pattern of operation—acquiring a
common cemetery, burying the dead, and visiting bereaved families. Besides meeting these primary needs, many established houses
of worship. Some included welfare privileges such as "sick benefits," allowance for tombstone and *Shiva gelt,* aid to indigent
members, and small loans without interest or security.

Each society engaged a doctor who charged reduced rates for
visits to members. The souvenir journal of the Kartuz-Berezer
Social and Benevolent Association issued on the occasion of its
fortieth anniversary banquet in Park Manor on December 21,
1935, reveals an arrangement with a doctor for their Manhattan
members, with a second doctor for their Bronx members, and with
Dr. Hyman W. Karp of 1645 Prospect Place for their Brooklyn
members. Their organization boasted two hundred members, a
Ladies Auxiliary, and a Young Men's Benovolent Association.
Like many other *Landsmanschaften* they contributed to a number
of philanthropies. They were particularly helpful to their hometown in Russia, where they built a synagogue, a fence around the
cemetery, contributed to the Passover Fund (*Moos Hittim*) and to
the charitable society (*Lechem Aniim*) of Bereze. They contributed toward the construction of a hospital which was never
completed.

In this, as in many similar journals, we find nostalgic expressions in poetry and prose of these immigrants for their native towns. They reminisce about days gone by, very much in the manner of the popular Yiddish song, *Mein Shtetele Belz.*

Since the end of World War II, the number and influence of these mutual-aid societies has declined. The American-born youth could generate no interest in these *Landsmanschaften* associated with towns from which their parents hailed, but which were altogether unknown to them. Family circles and fraternal organizations were substituted to fill the new need. The Pan Judaea Lodge, Order B'nai B'rith, The Conqueror and Maimonides Lodges, Knights of Pythias, the Brookboro Club, the Non-Pareil and the Huron Clubs, are among the new organizations which have attracted the American-born generation.

Jewish Fraternal Organizations

The Jewish fraternal organizations played a leading role in Jewish communal life.[9] By 1917 there were as many as twenty-eight Jewish fraternal orders in this country, with a total of about a half million, or 500,000 members. With the exception of B'nai B'rith, which abandoned insurance and kindred benefits in 1900, all the orders provided benefits which included sick and life insurance (usually $500), a burial fund, and in some cases, also accident and disability insurance. In addition to the material benefits, the members found their lodges a source of camaraderie, a valuable training school where they became conversant with parliamentary procedure, and a forum where they could hear and participate in discussions of crucial problems affecting the Jewish people.

The leaders of these orders generally took a leading part in the convocation of the American Jewish Congress and in the upbuilding of Israel as a National Jewish Homeland. They contributed generously to worthy causes, some establishing and maintaining their own philanthropic institutions. Due to changes with respect to insurance features, and to the fact that many American-born Jews of the second and third generations formed their own lodges and joined non-sectarian fraternal orders, most of the smaller orders have ceased to exist. Even the larger orders have lost their former influence.

Many Brownsville and East New York residents were active in the various fraternal organizations. In 1917, twenty-five lodges belonged to the Independent Order Brith Abraham with a membership of some 5,000. One of the oldest and largest lodges of this order is the Young Friends Lodge (Number 147), founded at the end of the century with 23 members. It had in 1917 as many as 2,300 members. Captain Isaac Frank was its president, and B. S. Glassberg its secretary. One of its most active members was William Rader, one of the pioneers of Brownsville. He served 18 terms as president of the Lodge, was Deputy Grand Master of the Order, Chairman of Endowment, and Grand Treasurer. His son, George also had been active in this order. One of the other lodges, the Joseph Levy Lodge 113, had 1,300 members at this time. In recent years the Fraternal Center of Brooklyn, 693 Ralph Avenue, housed a number of societies and fraternal groups.

The Brownsville and East New York Jewish Community Council

The Brownsville-East New York Jewish Community Council, founded in 1944 through the efforts of the Men's League of Brooklyn, was for a number of years one of the most effective affiliates of the Brooklyn Jewish Community Council.

Its aims and purposes were primarily to unite all Jewry of Brownsville and East New York in one representative council that should have authority to speak in its name whenever occasion warranted it; to cooperate with the national organizations, through the Brooklyn Jewish Community Council, on all matters affecting the welfare of the Jewish people; to promote and foster formal Jewish education for children as well as adult Jewish education; to establish cooperation among the local organizations for the benefit of all; and to cooperate with all organizations engaged in combating all forces of racial or religious discrimination, and to help safeguard and defend the civil, political, economic, and religious rights of the Jewish people whenever such rights were challenged or threatened.

At the monthly meetings, which were held in the Hebrew Educational Society of Brooklyn, and at the annual conventions and other gatherings, the Community Council was able to bring together the leaders of the Jewish community of Brownsville and East New York.

One of the most active committees was the Education Council composed of all the principals and presidents of the Hebrew schools in the area. It worked in cooperation with the Jewish Education Committee and the Brooklyn Jewish Community Council to improve Jewish education, to help raise funds to finance Jewish education, to encourage larger registration in the schools, and greater interest on the part of parents in the Jewish education of their children.

The Jewish Community Council sponsored lectures and forums, concerts of Jewish music, and arranged for the observance of special events of Jewish significance on a community-wide basis. The Council was strongest during the decade of 1944-1954. When the community underwent changes and the Brooklyn Jewish Community Council was unable to give it special professional leadership, it lost much of its effectiveness, and a few years ago it ceased to function as a neighborhood Council.

Adath Israel of Brownsville

For many years the Adath Israel of Brownsville was an active communal organization which commanded the cooperation of prominent residents of the community.[10] Its headquarters served as a central address for various coordinating and communal efforts. It housed the local Zionist District, the Jewish National Fund, the United Jewish Appeal, and various other activities. Organized April 1, 1914, primarily to provide burial grounds and orthodox funerals for its members, it served also as a communal agency concerned with local, national, and international Jewish institutions, especially with the development of Israel.

The two houses purchased by the organization at 1846-1848

Pitkin Avenue served not only as its own offices, but also as quarters of the Zionist District and of some of the activities it conducted, such as a court of arbitration. After it sold the Pitkin Avenue property, the Adath Israel moved to 485 Hopkinson Avenue. In 1936 it had about 2,000 members who paid annual dues of $3.25. Each member was also responsible for an initiation fee of $50, which could be carried as a mortgage against his cemetery plot, payable to his heirs at the time of the funeral. It owns burial plots in Montefiore, Beth David, and Mount Lebanon cemeteries.

The annual meetings, which are attended by large numbers, have been high points in the communal calendar. At these meetings announcement is made of the organization's annual contributions, amounting to several thousand dollars, to local organizations such as hospitals, homes for the aged, the Chronic Disease Hospital, Talmud Torahs, and various Zionist funds.

World War I

XVI

LIKE ALL other American communities, Brownsville shared in the distress that engulfed our country during the war period. Once the United States entered the war, all classes became a united citizenry that rallied to the support of its land and government. But such unanimity did not prevail prior to that time. The overwhelming majority of the Socialist Party had been strongly opposed to the war, and in accordance with the non-interventionist-pacifist platform adopted at St. Louis, they were committed to agitate against it.[1] The Yiddish Socialist daily, *The Forward*, followed the pattern of other Socialist newspapers and also opposed the war. In October, 1917, it was denied the use of the mails.

There was widespread opposition to the war, especially to the conscription law, among the immigrant sections in New York including Brownsville. The Central Powers, Germany and Austria, were fighting against Czarism, and Jews had sufficient reason to welcome its destruction. Once the United States entered the war, however, there was a marked reversal of attitude. *The*

Forward editorially conceded that "it is no longer a capitalistic war. Neither is it imperialistic or nationalistic. It is a war for humanity."

The Forward's rival, *The Warheit* (Truth), was much quicker to favor support of the Allied Powers. The war divided the Socialist Party into two groups, one group adhering to the St. Louis platform which denounced the war, conscription, and every phase of activity on its behalf; the other remaining loyal to our country's actions. In the fall of 1917 the Socialist Morris Hillquit, who was denounced as a traitor for his position on the war, rolled up 144,135 votes, or 28 per cent of the ballots cast for the office of Mayor of New York. John F. Hylan was elected mayor.

The Socialists drew a big vote in Brownsville in those years. The political campaigns were spirited.

There were a few who found themselves in difficulties because of their intransigent, negative positions on the war. They included those who opposed conscription and chose prison rather than participate in the war. A reading of the columns of the Brownsville Yiddish weekly, *The Brooklyn Jewish Progress,* for this period, reveals the popular excitement and the deep emotional upheaval that stirred some of the people. The weekly's June 5, 1917, issue reported that H. L., a school teacher, was sentenced to a year in prison for refusing to register. On June 22, its editorial urged the freeing of H. L., whom it characterized as a martyr, and it pointed up the alleged illegality of the conscription act. On June 8, it reported a meeting at Independent Hall attended by several thousand people for the purpose of repealing the conscription act.

The overwhelming majority, however, backed the war effort with all their heart and with all their might. They resented and condemned the attitude of those who were opposed to the war effort. They insisted that this was no time to espouse unpatriotic ideas.

Many Brownsville young people joined the armed forces and some distinguished themselves. Benjamin Kaufman, who attended Public School 149, Erasmus Hall High School, and Syracuse University, won the rank as Sergeant of Company K, 308th Infantry. On October 4, 1918, he fought in Argonne. Nine governments heaped awards upon him, and his own country gave him the Congressional Medal of Honor. Harry Margolin won the First Congressional War Medal. A goodly number made the supreme sacrifice on the foreign battlefields.[2]

The spirit which permeated the vast numbers of the community is perhaps best illustrated by the activities of the young members of the Non-Pareil Club, presently one of the best known in Brownsville. "It was the World War that made the Non-Pareil Club just as it has made nations, millionaires, and no doubt paupers," asserts its history.[3] The club was a kind of unofficial recruiting station. Young men joined the club, enlisted, donned uniforms, and went to war. Noah Seedman, in an "impassioned address" urged more volunteering, and was himself commissioned an army field clerk to General Pershing's headquarters.

"I was the first one to sail to France," he recalled later in an interview for *The New York Post,* "and it was Ike Albert's little Ford that took me from the clubhouse direct to the pier."

Men in the service were not required to pay dues. The home contingent bought Liberty Bonds and helped in the bond campaigns. They escorted the volunteers to Camp Upton, and the father of Al Mesler, a member, took rye bread from his bakery as a gift to the boys in camp. Packages were sent overseas. There was a secretary to handle correspondence with members in the service. When the body of Al Witover, killed in action, was shipped home, the club members carried the coffin on their shoulders all the way to Mount Judah Cemetery, in lieu of having it carried on the caisson provided for the military funeral.

When the war was over, the friendships cultivated during those years continued. It was a kind of comradeship that can be cemented only among men who have faced danger and death together. One of the club members, Herman Jaffe, related how Hyman Rapps saved his life at Saint Mihiel. In the engagement begun on General Pershing's birthday, Jaffe was injured in the recoil of a big gun fired by the 59th Coast Artillery, and needed immediate attention. Disregarding his own safety, Rapps took the captain's car, placed Jaffe in it, and drove him through the battlefield to a first aid station.

The World War affected everyone, those on the homefront as

well as those on the fighting line. To meet the prodigious cost of the war, the government floated four Liberty Loans, and a Victory Loan after the Armistice. Campaigns of publicity, heretofore undreamed of in their intensity, publicized the bonds, and many in the community bought them in denominations as small as $50, or even in the form of "Thrift Stamps." Prices skyrocketed; the cost of living pyramided. To conserve food and essential materials, "gasless Sundays" and "meatless meals" were introduced. Various organizations did all they could to keep in touch with the boys away from home. On September 7, 1917, a farewell dinner for the soldiers about to leave for camp was held in the Hopkinson Manor. Rabbi Israel H. Levinthal's address on that occasion received considerable notice at that time.

Several hundred Brownsville and East New York boys were associated with the 77th Division, which originally contained about 12,000 Brooklyn men.[4] The story of the 77th Division is one of the great sagas of the war. It was given the name "The Lost Battalion" after it had been cut off in the Argonne Forest where it fought heroically for six days without food and reinforcements until rescued. The 77th went to Camp Upton on September 10, 1917, and just one year later was "digging in" on the Aisne in France. In the ensuing months of the savage war a number of men from Brownsville and East New York lost their lives, and a larger number was wounded.

Eventually Germany was forced to surrender, and a weary world saw the end of war. On November 11, 1918, the Armistice was signed, and millions began to dry their tears. On January 8, 1918, President Wilson promulgated his Fourteen Points, which many hoped would end war for all time. The boys returned home. Gradually the scars of the war commenced to wear off, and people returned to their normal routines.

A grateful community, including the war veterans who remembered their comrades in arms, paid tribute to those who had fought for their country. Two monuments were erected, one in Brownsville and one in East New York, to commemorate the men who died during the War. A large limestone monument with an approach of broad steps flanked by walls was erected in Zion

Memorial Park, located at East New York and Pitkin avenues, Legion and Grafton streets, on the land which was originally presented to the city in 1896 by P. L. Vanderveer. The central wall of the monument depicts a winged female figure with sword and shield, in bas-relief. The sculptor was Charles Carey Rumsey. It was presented by the Citizens Memorial Committee, of which Alexander Drescher was chairman, and by the following organizations: Soldiers and Sailors Committees of the American Legion, Veterans of Foreign Wars, and Jewish Veterans of the Wars of the Republic. It was unveiled on November 1, 1925. The bronze tablet at the base reads:

TO COMMEMORATE THESE WHO AT THE CALL OF THEIR COUNTRY
LEFT ALL THAT
WAS DEAR
ENDURED HARDSHIP, FACED DANGER AND FINALLY PASSED OUT OF
SIGHT OF MEN BY THE PATH OF DUTY
AND SACRIFICE GIVING UP
THEIR LIVES THAT OTHERS MAY LIVE IN FREEDOM.
LET THOSE WHO COME AFTER SEE TO IT THAT THEIR NAMES
BE NOT FORGOTTEN
BY THE
CITIZENS MEMORIAL COMMITTEE
AND SOLDIERS AND SAILORS MEMORIAL COMMITTEES
OF THE AMERICAN LEGION,
VETERANS OF FOREIGN WARS AND JEWISH VETERANS OF THE
WARS OF THE REPUBLIC
COMPRISING LOCAL BOARDS 82 TO 88

Two bronze tablets, one on each side of the figure include the Roll of Honor, commemorating 86 men, most of them Jewish, as will be noticed from the list on page 292.

A bronze statue called the "Dawn of Glory" and representing a soldier's dream, by Pietro Montana, stands on a granite base mounted on a set of granite steps in Highland Park, Jamaica Avenue, facing Cleveland Street. It was dedicated as a memorial to the boys from the East New York-Cypress Hill Section who entered the service of the United States Army and Navy during the War. It was unveiled in July, 1925. In the granite base are carved the words:

IN HONOR

OF THOSE

WHO FOUGHT FOR

OUR COUNTRY

1917-1918

1917 ROLL OF HONOR 1918

Abramson, Harry	Goldstein, Philip	Rigrod, Daniel
Ashe, Isidore	Goodman, Jacob	Robinson, Joseph
Bass, Morris	Graham, James B.	Rochlin, David
Bergrin, Jacob	Gustamolsky, Moses	Rosenberg, Sidney
Berlin, Isaac	Heitman, Conrad	Rosenthal, Joseph
Boisa, Benche	Kaplan, Samuel C.	Rykus, William
Borker, Jacob	Keller, Harry	Sultman, Benjamin
Britman, Harry	Krinsky, Louis	Schmeling, Fred S.
Brooks, Zelig	Krupnick, Morris	Schreck, Jack
Chester, Benjamin	Kunofsky, Isidore	Shafran, Samuel J.
Cohen, Herman	Krichevsky, Joseph	Shapiro, Abraham
Cohen, Charles C.	Levine, Frank	Siegel, Harry
Cohen, Max	Levine, Jacob	Siegel, Henry
Cohen, Ralph	Levy, George	Siegel, Jack
Cohen, Simon	Levy, John	Smith, Charles
Dattlebaum, Harry	Levy, Leo	Solomon, Nathan
Dietter, Otto	McIver, Raymond A.	Solovei, Samuel
Doctor, David L.	Mackler, Isidore L.	Spinazola, Nicholas
Dropkins, Isidore	Mintz, Edward	Sullivan, Frank X.
Feldberg, Harry	Mirgenthaler, Charles P.	Swirzky, Joseph
Finkelstein, Samuel	Moskowitz, David	Thomsen, Gustave W.
Fitzpatrick, James	Muscowitz, Michael	Walthauer, George M.
Ford, Christopher	Packer, Samuel	Wanswer, James D.
Forman, Harry	Paskoff, David	Werther, Aaron
Friedman, Abraham	Priskinsky, Joseph	Weyuker, George
Friedman, Israel Joseph	Rabinowitz, Harry	Witover, Louis
Friedman, Robert P.	Rapaport, Philip	Zimmerman, Morris
Friedman, William	Reisen, Benjamin J.	Zuckerman, Samuel

The bronze tablet on the back lists 108 names. Among the Jewish names on this list are:

Bergman, S.	Grossman, S.	Schneider, B.
Besman, H. B.	Halpern, J.	Sielsky, L.
Cowen, J. M.	Meshover, G.	Simon, A.
Edelstein, E.	Mintz, H.	Stolzenberg, A. L.
Glasser, F.	Novoselsky, S.	Wachtel, M.
Goldstein, P.	Saltzman, B.	Wiener, H.
	Samuels, S.	

A bronze tablet on a low, slanting, granite base in Salem Fields Cemetery, Norwood and Jamaica avenues, was erected by the Veterans Corps in memory of soldiers of Hebrew Faith who had served in the World War, 1917-1918. At the other edge of Brownsville, in Saratoga Park, Saratoga and Howard avenues, Halsey and Main streets, the residents of Districts 31-32 erected a memorial in 1921. It is a bronze figure of an angel in relief, against a granite upright by James S. J. Novelli. 106 names are listed, of whom a number are Jewish. The bronze tablet reads:

E PLURIBUS UNUM. IN MEMORY OF THE HEROIC DEAD BY RESIDENTS OF DISTRICTS 31-32 OF THE CITY OF NEW YORK, 1921.

Brownsville—East New York Politics

XVII

BROWNSVILLE and East New York took their politics seriously. Election campaigns lasted for weeks and even months. The discussions and debates held on nearly every street corner, in the various halls, and in other places of assembly, were spirited. All means of propaganda known at the time were utilized. Election results were awaited eagerly. People would stay up until all hours on election night to learn the fate of their candidates and issues.

While the political history is generally the history of Democratic and Republican machines, the voting habits of the Brownsvillites could not be taken for granted. Issues and personalities meant much, and the citizens of Brownsville were inclined to vote for new people and for new parties. The parties or candidates who stood for liberalism, or who espoused liberal causes were fervently courted. Consequently, the Socialist Party was able to elect their candidates here for a number of years.

The most exciting and noisiest campaign was conducted by the Municipal Ownership League in 1905, when William R. Hearst was candidate for mayor. For many weeks before election day there were parades and fireworks. Thousands of workers marched under Hearst banners, shouting in rhythmic unison, "Hearst, Hearst, Hearst!"

Tons of circulars explaining the principles of municipal ownership covered the streets and sidewalks. Mass meetings were held every day at Metropolitan Sanger Hall, on Pitkin Avenue and Watkins Street. The platform of the Municipal Ownership League was similar in many respects to that of the Socialist Party. George B. McClellan, a scholar and charming gentleman, was the Democratic Party candidate, and Algernon Lee the Socialist candidate. When the returns were in, McClellan was the winner over Hearst by a plurality of only 3,500 votes. The publisher demanded a recount, alleging that the election had been fraudulent, and accused Tammany of stuffing the ballot boxes. In Brownsville Hearst received more votes than the combined vote for the Democratic and Republican candidates. Judge Alex Rosenthal won his election as judge of the Municipal Court on the Independence ticket, and Joseph Falk was elected alderman.

In 1912 Oscar S. Strauss, a former ambassador to Turkey and well known as a Jewish leader, ran for Governor of the State of New York on the Bull Moose Party ticket. When he came to Brownsville during his campaign, over 10,000 people tried to get in the Metropolitan Sanger Hall to hear him. In the election held on November 5, 1912, Mr. Strauss polled a large vote in Brownsville, far ahead of all the other candidates, while in East New York William Sulzer, the successful candidate, exceeded his opponent's vote.

In 1915 the Equal Suffrage Amendment: "Shall the proposed amendment to section one of article two of constitution, conferring equal suffrage upon women be approved?" was disapproved in the State. It also lost in Brownsville and East New York, but proportionately more were in favor of it, especially in Brownsville. In the 23rd Assembly District (Brownsville) 7,130 voted for it, and 7,692 voted against it. In the 22nd Assembly District (East New York) the vote stood 8,423 in favor, and 11,597 opposed. In 1917 the suffrage amendment was adopted in the State by a vote of 353,566 for, and 249,803 against. Of course, Brownsville and East New York favored it at this time.

Earlier, the 22nd and 23rd Assembly Districts gave an overwhelming vote for John Purroy Mitchell as mayor. East New York was also active in the election campaign of Grover Cleveland when he ran for President. As Mayor of Buffalo and Governor of New York, Mr. Cleveland had made an admirable record as a reformer. The election was very close; it hung upon the vote of New York State, which he carried by only 1,149 plurality in a total vote of nearly 1,200,000. He was elected.

Over the years many reformers and liberal issues succeeded with the voters. But this attitude was short lived. Political life in Brownsville, much more than in East New York, was affected by the liberal voting pattern of its residents. Many of the voters belonged to the Jewish labor movement and to the needle-trade unions originally organized by Jewish Socialists. This accounts for the influence the socialist orientation exerted among the Jewish working class. The unions were concerned not only with the struggle to improve working conditions, but also with the search for a just and righteous order. In the union halls the current fundamental social, political, and economic issues were discussed, and the workers were urged to exercise their ballot in the election campaigns in order to help bring about social improvement. This was in accordance with the trend of the times. Social experiment was the order of the day, and demands for social and economic reforms characterized the general American social scene.

The essentials of liberal, humanitarian, and radical values appealed especially to the Jewish voters because they were indigenously more receptive to liberalism. They were ready to innovate and experiment. As a result, a liberal position on the issues of the day had to be taken not only by the Socialist Party or other leftist parties, but also by the opposing parties and leaders as well. Candidates for office in Brownsville had to be popular speakers, able to debate the issues of the day on the street corners and in the halls. The voter had to be convinced ideologically. An appeal to party or group loyalty was not enough. That is why liberals like Franklin D. Roosevelt, Herbert Lehman, Robert Wagner, Sr., Governor Alfred E. Smith, Fiorello LaGuardia, and

Henry Wallace proved so popular with the voters here. It is for the same reason that Emanuel Celler, because of his liberal record, has been able to represent this district in Congress for some forty years.

At the beginning of the century, Brownsville proper was of minor importance as far as politics was concerned. Ocean Hill, and other sections of East New York where the Irish predominated, had taken over the control from the old Dutch families of New Lots for some time. A number of the colorful political figures and key leaders of the city, of both Republican and Democratic Parties, as well as of other parties, lived in the district.

As Brownsville grew in population, the Irish political leaders, who dominated the Democratic Party and held on tenaciously to their posts, came to recognize the importance of the new population. They began to work and share in the patronage with the Jewish, Italian, and other ethnic groups.

In 1906 a very important reapportionment of the 23rd Assembly District took place, and Brownsville became part of this district. Patrick F. Lynch became the first Democratic leader of the district, holding the post until 1911. It was Pat Lynch who took notice of Hyman Schorenstein and welcomed him into the Democratic organization. Hyman Schorenstein regarded Pat Lynch as his political mentor, and under his tutelage began to understand the new world of politics which was then opening to him. Known as "Hymie" to his many friends, he became one of the most colorful political figures, and one of New York State's best known Democrats. His lack of a formal education did not prevent him from rising to an important position in the councils of the Democratic Party. He became a close friend of the great political figures of the time—President Franklin D. Roosevelt, Governor Alfred E. Smith, Mayor James J. Walker, James A. Farley, and United States Senator Herbert H. Lehman. All of these officials stopped at Mr. Schorenstein's home on Bristol Street when they were campaigning in Brooklyn. It was Mr. Schorenstein who led the now famous revolt at the Democratic State Convention in 1932 that resulted in making their Lieutenant Governor Lehman the party's choice for Governor.

Mr. Schorenstein entered the political world at an early age and became a district captain before he reached the age of twenty-one. Upon the death of Mr. Lynch in 1911, James J. Monahan became the leader of the district, and then James M. Power. Mr. Schorenstein was one of the most active workers, and when Mr. Powers resigned as leader in 1917, he was chosen as his successor. He worked hard to become acceptable to all factions. As soon as he took over the reins, he immediately began to put the 23rd Assembly District back into the Democratic column.

He began by entering into a fusion agreement in 1921, when he succeeded in electing Captain Isaac Frank, the first Jewish police captain in Brownsville, to the Board of Aldermen, and Joseph Ricca, representing the Italian community, to the assembly. This feat he repeated in 1923.

Although the district became overwhelmingly Jewish, Mr. Schorenstein continued to work with the original Irish leadership. As his co-leader he selected Agnes Riley, wife of one of the old-time contenders for the crown of leadership, and for secretary he chose John Lynch, son of his old leader, Patrick Lynch. He surrounded himself with a group of young Jews of the neighborhood who became a tower of strength to him and to the organization. They included Aaron L. Jacoby, Walter R. Hart, Emanuel Celler, Michael Kern, Harry A. Singer, Albert Martin Cohen, Perry Parmer, Samuel Seiderman, and Sam Perlman. After a political battle within the local party, Dr. Maxwell Ross succeeded in winning the leadership of the 23rd Assembly District in 1937.

Another important figure in political life was Hyman Raphael (Rayfiel), a most interesting and beloved personality. From a beautiful tribute written in his memory by Katherine Dangerfield, a reporter for *The Brooklyn Eagle,* we gather some facts about his life. He was born in Austria, January, 1866, and came as a penniless immigrant at the age of fifteen to this country. An Irish contractor, one Patrick Mooney of New Brunswick, Canada, gave him his first job as a hod carrier. Under that job his health broke down, and he took a job in a silk mill in Hoboken, New Jersey, and later became a conductor on the Second Avenue trolley line in New York.

At the age of 30, and father of a family of 8 children, Mr.

Rayfiel began to study law. While studying for the bar he took the Civil Service examination for Court Interpreter, passing first on the list with marks of more than 98 in German, and 96.70 in Hebrew and English.

Magistrate John F. Hylan named him Chief Clerk of the newly-opened New Jersey Avenue Police Court in 1907. Meanwhile, his political star had risen. He was appointed City Magistrate and later Justice of the Special Sessions. Well-read in general literature and in Hebrew learning, he became known in those pioneering days for his kindliness, generosity, and his keen interest in a variety of activities and institutions. His son, Federal Judge Leo F. Rayfiel, has continued in the legal footsteps of his father, and has been serving for many years as District Judge of the United States Court, Eastern District of New York.

Until World War I, the political vote was about equally divided between Republicans and Democrats, although the Socialist vote began to rise about 1910. Among the Jewish residents of Brownsville who were elected to office during this period were: Office of Alderman—Alexander Drescher, 1910-1911, and 1916-1917; Isadore (Izzy) Rosenbloom, 1913, office of State Assemblyman—Isaac Sargent, 1908-1909, Louis Goldstein, 1910, and Nathan Finkelstein, 1915.

The Socialists in the Assembly and Board of Aldermen

World War I brought about a change in the voting pattern of the district. The war brought a critical period of troubled soul-searching for many people, including those in the Jewish labor movement. There was a widespread sentiment of opposition to the war among some of the sections in New York, among which was Brownsville. This expressed itself in the heavy vote which Brownsville gave in those years to the anti-war Socialist Party. The political campaigns were spirited, and the street-corner meetings were anything but orderly discussion sessions, often turning into hissing, and sometimes riotous affairs.

In the November 1915 election, Abraham I. Shiplacoff, prominent Brownsville Socialist and labor leader, was elected to the

State Assembly by a substantial vote, and as a lone Socialist in the entire New York State Assembly, made a good record. Out of a total of 17,202 votes cast in the Brownsville district, 7,057 votes went to Shiplacoff, the Socialist, and 5,279 for Marshall Snyder, the Democratic candidate, while Harris, the Republican candidate received 4,926 votes. Shiplacoff was reelected the following year by a great and increased plurality. In 1917 Barnett Wolff was elected Alderman on the Socialist ticket, receiving 9,602 votes defeating Alexander Drescher who only polled 5,157 votes on both the Democratic and Republican tickets. Mr. Shiplacoff followed Mr. Wolff as alderman, serving in 1919-1920. He received 12,238 votes. Socialism was at its peak.

The great Socialist wave not only swept the Brownsville candidates into office, but was also equally successful in other sections. When the four-year-old war came to an end on November 11, 1918, the Socialist Party, while weaker, was still in business, although there was a general hostility to it by large segments of the public.

The anti-Socialist sentiment was very strong at this time. It was intensified by the attitude of Mitchell Palmer, who succeeded Gregory as Attorney General, by the position taken by the American Legion, by Congress, and by many others. In New York State the Legislature appointed a committee to investigate the scope, tendencies, and ramifications of seditious activities on the part of a large number of persons within the State of New York, and to report the result of the investigation to the State Legislature. The body took its name from its chairman, Senator Clayton R. Lusk, of Cortland, New York. It became known as the "Lusk Committee." The associate counsel of the committee was Archibald Ewing Stevenson. The committee came into existence upon motion of the Union League Club of New York City, and became generally known as a "witch-hunting" committee.

On November 4, 1919, five members of the Socialist Party were elected to the New York State Assembly, representing assembly districts in Brownsville, Bronx, and New York. For Charles Solomon of Brownsville, it was his second term. It was also the second term for Louis Waldman (8th Assembly District, New

York), and for Samuel Orr (4th Assembly District, New York) it was the third term; and for Samuel A. DeWitt (3rd Assembly District, Bronx) the first term.

As they were to assume their seats in the assembly, Speaker Sweet called the Socialist assemblymen before the bar of the House and accused them of having been elected on a "platform absolutely inimical to the best interest of the State of New York and the United States." Upon motion of the majority leader, the five were suspended until their cases could be heard by a Committee of Assembly.

The action created a profound sensation throughout the country. For years the Socialist Party had been recognized in every State of the Union. Its right to vote and to be represented had been unquestioned, and Socialists elected to office had served without hindrance. The New York and Brooklyn newspapers criticized the action. The districts which these men represented sent delegations representing all political parties to Albany to state their indignation. Mass meetings were held protesting this arbitrary proceeding in Albany. Charles Evans Hughes sent a letter to Speaker Sweet, rebuking his stand.

On January 13, the Bar Association, after a long and bitter debate, adopted a resolution by a vote of 174 to 117 opposing the exclusion by the assembly from its membership of any man because of his affiliation with the Socialist Party, not because of any personal unfitness. Among its reasons it stated that "any attempt by a majority to exclude from the Legislature those who have been duly elected to its membership merely because of their affiliation with a political party, when seeking by constitutional and legal methods to bring about any change in our Constitution and laws, and if successful, must destroy the right of minorities and the very foundations of representative government."

It further resolved that the president of the association appoint a special committee who should appear before the assembly or its Judiciary Committee and take such action as might, in their judgment, be necessary to safeguard and protect the principles of representative government which were involved in the proceedings then pending. John G. Milburn, president, then appointed

Charles Evans Hughes, Morgan J. O'Brien, Joseph M. Proskauer, Louis Marshall, and Ogden L. Mills as members of this committee.

Despite tremendous opposition by various segments of public opinion, the assembly went on with its proceedings to expel the Socialist members. The suspension took place on January 7, 1920; the trial began on January 20, and ended on March 11. It took Chairman Martin three weeks to frame the report which was handed up on March 30. The vote of the committee was by no means unanimous—7 to 6. Action on the report took place on March 31 after a debate of twenty-two hours, in which more than a third of the assembly participated. Charles Solomon of Brownsville and August Claessens were declared expelled by a vote of 116 against 28; Louis Waldman by a vote of 115 to 28; and Samuel A. DeWitt and Samuel Orr by a vote of 104 to 40.[1]

The anti-radical hysteria somewhat subsided in the following years. Socialists again began to be accorded their civil rights. By that time, however, the Socialist Party had lost its former strength. Charles Solomon was finally able to hold his seat in the State Assembly when he was elected for the third time in 1920.

Charles Solomon (1889-December 8, 1963) was born in the Lower East Side, and later moved to Brownsville. Throughout his career he was an uncompromising fighter for social justice in all its forms. He served as alderman in 1917 and 1918. He began his practice of law in 1923, He was an unsuccessful Socialist candidate for Lieutenant Governor in 1922, for State Comptroller in 1925 and 1929, for State Senator in 1930, and for United States Senator in 1932. He ran unsuccessfully for Mayor of New York in 1933, and for Governor in 1934.

In his political thinking in later life he turned first to the American Labor Party, and later, denouncing the Communists, who had infiltrated the party's left wing, to the Liberal Party. In 1936 Mayor Fiorello LaGuardia appointed him to the Magistrate's Court. He was reappointed in 1950, and served until the end of 1959, when he retired because of the statutory age limitations. His career on the bench was often marked by unorthodox and often unexpected rulings.

August Claessens and William Morris Feigenbaum have given us an account of the activities of the Socialist assemblymen in Albany.[2] According to Mr. Claessens, the Socialists introduced, in the decade between 1912 and 1922, about a hundred bills, "many measures that were considered fantastic, visionary, and revolutionary that were enacted into law some twelve years later as the New Deal measures in Congress and in many state legislatures." Mr. Shiplacoff was Socialist floor leader in the Legislature, and his disputes with Democrats and Republicans were many and spirited.

Among some of the measures which the Socialists introduced were a series of municipal-ownership bills, labor and social legislation bills—including one calling for an eight-hour day, one asking that all wages be paid in cash instead of by check, and others asking for the abolition of private employment agencies, the raising of age limit for the employment of children, and bills to provide for a system of old-age pensions and for a social-insurance system that would offer protection and assistance in all cases of sickness, old age, unemployment, death, and accident not covered by compensation. There was also a bill introduced by these Socialists providing for the establishment of day nurseries. There was a bill to abolish the death penalty in New York State, a bill to increase State scholarships so that more poor youths might be able to attend college, a bill to stamp out ticket speculators, a bill calling for the election of members of the Board of Education of New York City, and other measures, many of which are now on our statute books.

Evans Clark and Charles Solomons have published a pamphlet describing the activities of the Socialists in the Board of Aldermen.[3] It, too, provides us with interesting reading and indicates that the road to progress is slow, that it has taken some fifty years for some of the measures proposed by them to be finally adopted—under different party labels of course.

In the nineteen-twenties the Socialist Party split into left and right wings. By 1922 the Communists were strong enough to establish their own daily, *The Freiheit,* in opposition to *The Forward.* By 1929 the Socialist Party was a shadow of its former self. When the amazing innovations of the New Deal came into being during Roosevelt's first term, the needle-trade unions, exhausted from fighting the Communists, gave wholehearted support to the New Deal. They broke with the Socialist Party leadership, who insisted on abiding by their old dogmas.

As some of the New Dealers began to dream of a third party modeled on the British pattern, many of the trade unionists in New York City worked hard on behalf of the American Labor Party. It was set up in 1936 as a branch of labor's Non-Partisan League (LNPL) whose purpose was to reelect Franklin D. Roosevelt. When the Communists infiltrated and finally captured the American Labor Party, the Liberal Party was organized.

Socialism as a political party lost its former influence, and almost disappeared. The Jewish unionists, the Socialist press, the fraternal bodies, and the Socialist Party had determined to free themselves from its binding dogma. Threatened by Communism and its doctrines, they became more concerned with the practical present than with a Utopian future. Socialists by conviction and long association, who exhorted over the years the masses of trade unionists to vote only the Socialist ticket, severed their connections with the Socialist Party, and sought to realize their socialist aspirations elsewhere.

The Republicans and Democrats of Brownsville, faced by the strong opposition given them by the Socialist Party, used every means to regain their powers. The entire election district had to be re-gerrymandered in 1920, and a fusion of the Democratic and Republican Parties effected to insure the Socialists' defeat. When Mr. Schorenstein became Democratic leader in 1921, he set it as his main objective to put the 23rd Assembly District back into the Democratic column. At first he had to enter into a fusion agreement, but by 1927 he succeeded in getting his candidate, Walter R. Hart, elected alderman without fusion. Walter R. Hart, a member of the Board of Aldermen (1925-1937), of the City Council (1929-1949), and State Supreme Court Justice (1949-1964), has been one of the most active Democrats in Brownsville.

In the State Senate, Jacob J. Schwartzwald and the present incumbent, William Rosenblatt, have represented the district for many years. For a decade the East New York District was represented by Jacob H. Livingston (1926-1935), a lawyer, and active in various philanthropic activities of the community. He was then elected State Supreme Court Justice in the November election of 1935. Daniel Gutman, now Dean of New York Law School, was elected in 1938 to the State Senate, and later as judge of the Municipal Court. He also served as counsel to Governor Harriman. He took an active part in numerous religious, philanthropic, and social service activities. Herbert I. Sorin, now a judge, also represented the district in the State Senate. Simon J. Liebowitz is the present incumbent of the 10th Senatorial District. Ben Werbel served in the State Assembly.

In the United States Congress Brownsville, which is part of the 10th Congressional District, has been fortunate in being represented since the Sixty-eighth Congress (March 4, 1923) by Congressman Emanuel Celler, distinguished legislator and humanitarian.

Many others have served or are at the present time in the city, state, and federal government. Mr. Abe Stark has distinguished himself in city government. He was swept into office as President of the City Council of New York in 1953, reelected in 1957, and then elected as Borough President of Brooklyn in November, 1961, and reelected in 1965. Judge Nathan R. Sobel, raised in Brownsville, served as counsel to the minority leader of the New York Legislature from 1928 to 1935; counsel to the speaker of the New York Assembly in 1935; counsel to the Governor of New York, 1937-1942, and has served as Judge of the County and Supreme Courts since 1943. Judge Samuel Simon Leibowitz, one of the ablest criminal lawyers in America, became Judge of Kings County Court in 1941. Emanuel Greenberg (b. 1892, d. October 5, 1962) was appointed in 1936 by Governor Herbert H. Lehman as Judge of the State Court of Claims, and re-appointed in 1940.

Nathan Sweedler (b. May 11, 1885, d. August 26, 1960), who lived in his youth with his family in Brownsville, was elected to the Municipal Court in 1929 and served until 1940. He was founder in 1927 of the former Good Will Court in Brooklyn, a free, non-sectarian tribunal for the amicable settlement of disputes.

Among others who are at the present time serving on the judicial bench are Judge Arthur Dunaif, an old Brownsvillite whose family has been active in a variety of philanthropic activities. Before appointment as magistrate, and later to Special Sessions Court, Judge Dunaif served as Deputy Market Commissioner. Judge Maurice Matzkin served as Deputy Hospital Commissioner, prior to his appointment as judge. Judge Irving P. Kartell, and Judge George Rader are holding judicial positions. Councilman Morris J. Stein also spent his youth in this community.

A number of Brownsville and East New York residents have risen to various important positions in public life. Jacob L. Holtzman (b. March 10, 1886, d. July 11, 1963) was a member of the State Board of Regents from 1949-1958, and an active leader in the Republican Party. During his term as regent, he was particularly active in a plan to provide special educational television programs for school children and adults. He was chairman for the Board of Regents of a special committee on television for education. Although his program, on which he worked for several years, did not eventuate, his labors were largely responsible for the daytime educational television programs that began on Channel 11, and are now shown on Channel 13. In 1953 the New York Newspaper Guild awarded him the Page-One Award for his efforts on behalf of educational television.

In November, 1965, Aaron E. Koota was reelected as District Attorney of Kings County. Prior to that he served as chief of the Rackets Bureau, and became known as "Racket Buster Extraordinary." He spent much of his youth in Brownsville. Many have served in the District Attorney's office. Michael Kern, a former president of the Kings County Criminal Bar Association and now Judge of the Civil Court, served as assistant District Attorney for fourteen years, and was active in the Democratic Party. Others include Abraham Brodsky, David Epstein, Louis Ernest, Abraham Greenberg, Abraham Horwitz. Marshall Snyder (1887-1966) was a member of the New York State Assembly in 1918, assistant District Attorney (1921-1922), and for forty years was Counsel of the Greater New York Savings Bank. Samuel Gitlin was assistant Attorney General.

Aaron L. Jacoby, well-known as the Superintendent of the

Brooklyn Hebrew Orphan Asylum, and active in the political and philanthropic life of the community, was a member of the New York State Public Service Commission, and is presently a member of the Parole Commission of the City of New York. Colonel David (Mickey) Marcus was Commissioner of Corrections.

Albert M. Leavitt, Democratic leader for fourteen years of the 15th Assembly District, and director of numerous social agencies, is Chief Clerk of the Kings County Surrogate's Court. Solomon E. Senior, who was raised in Brownsville, is chairman of the Workingmen's Compensation Board. Many have served as secretaries to the Judges in this county, including Beattie Markowitz, A. Frederick Meyerson, and William H. Kurland, the present Republican Leader of this District. The late Nathan Math, who was very active in East New York, was Tax Commissioner. Abraham L. Doris, was Deputy Controller. Jack Kranis was Councilman. Judge Arthur Hirsch, a Deputy State Tax Commissioner has held various positions including that of Judge of the Civil Court. Louis H. Pink was former State Superintendent of Insurance and head of Associated Hospital Service; Milton Mullen served as Chief Housing Coordinator for the City of New York.

Politics is a slice of life. The various political clubs which have existed in Brownsville and East New York under different names and in different locales, have played an important role, functioning not only at election times, but throughout the year. A party organization is strongest where the needs of voters are most compelling. Some of these clubs have been led by life-long politicians who have learned through long experience that the successful politician must like people and be willing to serve them. Politics requires indefatigable energy. Despite the tough requirements, however, it has had enough appeal to recruit a number of interesting personalities that have captured public attention. Some have been accused of seeking and of holding political positions for their own personal gain and power. But there have been those who have held on to these positions because they saw in them a means to promote the American democratic way of life, which expresses itself through popular elections. And elections are won or lost in the precinct.

Between the World Wars

XVIII

THE POSTWAR DECADE of the 1920's saw many changes in American life. Despite a slight depression in 1920, there was an economic upsurge, and the period was one of relative economic security. The "business of America is business," said President Coolidge, and freed from the anxieties of war, the Americans dedicated themselves to making and spending money. Wealth now began to appear in places heretofore unknown, which resulted in such enhanced optimism that people began to talk about an era "with a chicken in every pot, and two cars in every garage." Many new inventions appeared on the market, including the radio, and "talking" movies. It was a busy period for the stockbrokers and the salesmen.

War prosperity also reached Brownsville, and as a result, many of the older settlers and their children were able to abandon their old tenements and purchase new homes being constructed in large numbers in the Eastern Parkway and adjoining sections. Row upon row of two-family homes were constructed on Union, President, Crown, Carroll, and other streets in these sections.

The beautiful and newly-constructed Brooklyn Jewish Center, as well as Temple Petach Tikvah, now attracted large numbers of those who had recently moved into the area. In Brownsville proper, in New Lots, and in East New York new synagogues were constructed, or old ones remodeled. The local institutions like the Home for the Aged, the day nurseries, the Hebrew Educational Society, the Beth El Hospital also enjoyed prosperity, and renovated their physical facilities or built additions. There was greater generosity on the part of the community. Foreign relief, local charitable agencies, and the Zionist causes, which had received great impetus since the Balfour Declaration in 1917, benefited greatly from increased benefactions.

A marked change in the country's political character also occurred. Weary of Wilsonian democracy and idealism, and disillusioned about the war and its aftermath, the three Republican presidents, Harding, Coolidge, and Hoover were swept into office between 1920 and 1932. Isolationism, laissez-faire, intolerance with non-conformity, and hostility to foreigners and radical ideas characterized the political life of this period. Legislatures were "purged" of Socialists, and aliens suspected of radicalism were deported. Immigration was restricted by federal laws.

This restrictive political climate found particular repercussions in Brownsville, which had a large radical group. It dealt a severe blow to the Socialist Party, which had been very strong in Brownsville during the war years and had elected its candidates to office. Charles Solomon, to whom we have already alluded, was expelled from the New York State Legislature with his socialist comrades, and the campaign was on to save Brownsville's political soul. A coalition of Democrats and Republicans drove the Socialists from power. The "Ypsels," a strong group of young Socialists, dwindled to a handful, as did the party itself. Thenceforth the community became solidly Democratic.

The Depression Decade

The period of prosperity in the late 1920's came to an abrupt and dreary end in October, 1929. For more than a decade—from the great crash on Wall Street, in which millions of investors lost their savings, and which pulled down the whole economy, until World War II—America experienced one of the most devastating financial depressions in its history. Millions of Americans were to bear deep scars of this economic catastrophe for the rest of their lives.[1]

Arthur Granit wrote about Brownsville in his novel, *The Time of the Peaches*, "Situated so that one could see the spires of Manhattan on a clear day, and close enough so that one could get there by subway, the district served as a supply center for the garment industry of New York. With the depression, Brownsville was assailed on all sides. The men began to lose their jobs and appear wheeling baby carriages. Soon they began to shop for their wives and argue with the peddlers. And as times grew worse, the long, fascinating noses of our Jews got closer to the ground and began to sniff through the very walls to see what was transpiring on the other side."

The failure of the Bank of the United States on Thursday, December 11, 1930, added to the afflictions.[2] During the period there were 1,345 bank suspensions, but the Bank of the United States was the largest bank to suspend payments. When this mammoth institution closed its doors, it had more than 400,000 depositors with some $160,000,000 in deposits. Much of the garment industry transacted its business through the bank, and so did many of the shopkeepers and businessmen in Brownsville and other Jewish sections of New York. The bank's thrift deposits held the small savings of many poor people as well as the deposits of a number of charitable institutions. Many prominent Jews of the community were associated with the bank, either as shareholders or as directors.

The Bank of the United States was incorporated in 1913 by Joseph S. Marcus, and through mergers with other banks it increased its capital and scope of activities. On May 13, 1929, it merged with the Municipal Bank and Trust Company, which was started in Brownsville, and had its main office on Stone and Pitkin Avenues. At the time of the merger the Municipal Bank had 20 branches, 16 of them in Brooklyn.

Strenuous efforts were made by State Superintendent of Banking, Joseph A. Broderick, Governor Franklin Delano Roosevelt, Lieutenant Governor Herbert H. Lehman, and a number of leading bankers to solve the bank's problems by merger, but they were unsuccessful. According to Broderick, "an evil fate seemed to hang over the Bank of the United States no matter what efforts were made in its behalf." On the eve of its closing he warned the Clearing House bankers that "the Bank of the United States had thousands of borrowers, that it financed small merchants, especially Jewish merchants, and that its closing might and probably would result in widespread bankruptcy among those it served."

Mr. Broderick asked for $30,000,000 in subscriptions from member banks of the New York Clearing House to put the Bank of the United States on its feet. The bankers refused. "Then I warned them they were making the most colossal mistake in the banking history of New York. I told them I considered the bank solvent, as a going concern, and that I was at a loss to understand the attitude of askance which the Clearing-House banks had adopted toward the real estate holdings of the Bank of the United States. I told them I thought it was because none of the other banks had ever been interested in this field, and therefore knew nothing about it."

On December 11, when runs had begun on several of the bank's branches, Broderick ordered it closed. Depositors had withdrawn $20,000,000 within four days. The failure of the bank, the subsequent investigation and trials, the trial and conviction of two executive officials of the bank, the trial and acquittal of the bank's general counsel, and the trial and acquittal of the State Superintendent of Banking on charges of neglect of duty, filled the columns of the daily papers for some time. The depositors' claims against the bank after the state took it over amounted to $137,000,000. Of this amount, 45 per cent, or $67,000,000, was repaid by 1932, and under a plan of reorganization depositors were assured of receiving almost full payment. While much of the assets of the bank was invested in real estate, which required time to liquidate and was one of the main causes for the bank's difficulties, depositors were able to recover the major portion—89 per cent—of their deposits.

Many were the hardships and privations which were suffered

during this interval. On June 16, 1932, the Hebrew Ladies Day Nursery of Brownsville requested that its $6,500 savings account receive preference in the liquidation, since the money was urgently needed to care for the children attending the nursery.

As the depression continued, more and even more were out of work. By 1932 there were over 12,000,000 unemployed in the country, 750,000 of them in New York City. The situation called for aggressive government action. President Hoover clung to the belief that relief was a local responsibility, with the result that during the first and worst years of the depression public relief was improvised by the cities. In 1932 family allowances in New York City fell to $2.39 a week, and only half of the families who could qualify were getting it.

Private institutions were helpless in the face of mounting needs. Many who had formerly supported them had only paper assets and could not continue their former bounties. The Brooklyn Federation of Jewish Charities had to reduce its allotments to its constituent societies because it could not collect on the pledges made in its last campaign. Even the more affluent New York Federation of Jewish Philanthropies failed for the first time in fourteen years to raise its necessary quota, and in May, 1931, adopted the largest deficit budget in its history.

The long and severe depression affected both old and young. It depressed their minds and spirits, and robbed many of them of their self-respect. It fell with particular severity on the young people. Instead of being presented with hope of a bright future, they were to behold long lines of unemployed men and women waiting outside the relief station on Pitkin Avenue and elsewhere. The popular song of the period was "Brother, Can You Spare a Dime?" and the apple and the apple vendor became a symbol of the times. Some people lost hope of ever finding a job, and thought of themselves as a lost generation. Civil Service and teaching jobs became highly prized, but the examinations were made stiffer and stiffer. There were many who found it hard to get a permanent teacher's license, and had to spend years teaching as substitutes. Some young people had to postpone marriage, and some young people who were getting married were moving in with the wife's family. The young writer, artist, or musician found it particularly hard.

The depression was at its lowest ebb when Franklin Delano Roosevelt was elected President of the United States in 1932. He used the first hundred days of his administration to rescue the country by introducing sweeping emergency measures. A string of new symbols and an entire alphabet of new agencies came into being. There was relief for the unemployed, federal insurance against bank failure, protection for labor unions, and an attempt made to restore a balance between industry and agriculture. Above all, an effort was made to restore self-confidence and hope, the stuff on which economic rescue and well being depends. One of President Roosevelt's major government agencies was the National Recovery Act (N.R.A.)

The N. R. A. and the Schechter Poultry Case

The New Deal, with its National Recovery Act (N.R.A.), offered all unions a brilliant organizational opportunity. The Amalgamated Clothing Workers, which had 177,000 members in 1920, received per capita payments for only 7,000 in 1932. The Ladies Garment Workers with 105,400 in 1920 fell to 40,000 in 1932, many of whom paid no dues. After the passage of the National Recovery Act the International Garment Workers Union increased its membership within a year to almost a quarter-million, or about 250,000, and many other unions also enjoyed appreciable growth and substantial improvement in work conditions.

On an appeal made by Brownsville wholesale poultry dealers, the Schechter Brothers, the United States Supreme Court in a unanimous decision on May 27, 1935, declared the National Recovery Act compulsory code system to be unconstitutional.[3] It was one of the most damaging blows delivered to the New Deal. Joseph Schechter, with his three younger brothers, Martin, Alex, and Aaron, operated the two largest slaughterhouse markets in Brooklyn, one of them in the Brownsville section. The petitioners ordinarly purchased their live poultry from commission men at the West Washington Market in New York City, or at the railroad terminals serving the city, but occasionally they purchased from commission men in Philadelphia. After the poultry was trucked to their slaughterhouse markets, it was sold, usually within twenty-four hours, to retail poultry dealers and butchers. Poultry so purchased was immediately slaughtered, prior to delivery, by *Schochtim* employed by the petitioners.

The Schechter corporations were indicted on eighteen counts for violating the Code of Fair Competition for the Live Poultry Industry of the Metropolitan Area in and about the City of New York, "approved by President Roosevelt in an executive order dated April 13, 1934." In addition, they were found guilty of conspiring to violate the Recovery Act and the code. Two of the counts charged violation of the maximum hour and minimum wage provision of the code. Section 1, Article 12, prohibited paying an employee less than fifty cents per hour, and Section 1, Article 3, prohibited permitting a slaughterhouse employee to work more than forty-eight hours in a week. Ten counts charged violation of the minute code regulations such as requiring "straight killing," that is, "the practice requiring persons purchasing poultry for resale to accept the run of any half coop, coop, or coops, as purchased by slaughterhouse operators, except for culls."

The remaining six counts charged that an unfit chicken had been sold to a butcher, that poultry had been sold without inspection or approval as required by New York City ordinances, that false, or no reports had been made concerning daily range of prices and volumes of sales for certain periods, and finally, that sales had been made to butchers or dealers who had not been licensed by New York City. On all of the nineteen points the Schechters were convicted in the Federal District Court for the Eastern District.

An appeal was taken to the Circuit Court of Appeals for the Second District, where the decision of the lower court was sustained on seventeen counts, but was reversed on two counts charging violations of maximum hour and minimum wage provisions. The Court held that the regulation of hours and wages was not within the power of Congress. Both the Schechters and the Government appealed from the court decision to the Supreme

Court. The cases were argued before the Court on May 2 and 3, 1935, with great legal strength on both sides.

On May 27, 1935, the final decision was read by Chief Justice Hughes. A separate opinion concurring in the Hughes decision was read by Justice Cardozo, who spoke also for Justice Stone. In its decision the Court brushed aside the emergency justification by stating that "extraordinary conditions do not create or enlarge constitutional power." It regarded the code-making authority thus conferred as an unconstitutional delegation of legislative power. "Such a delegation of legislative power is unknown to our law and is utterly inconsistent with the constitutional prerogatives and duties of Congress."

No one was more disappointed and irritated by the decision than President Roosevelt. In a press conference on Friday, May 31, 1935, he stated that the Supreme Court decision "takes the nation back to the horse and buggy stage of 1789, when the interstate commerce clause was put into the Constitution."

The consequences of the decision on the appeal of the Browns-ville chicken dealers were stunning. The compulsory action of the 778 codes and supplements which had been put into effect was suspended. Donald Richberg, N.R.A. Administrator, issued a statement that the decision of the court had made codes of fair competition unenforceable as a matter of law, and appealed to employers to continue voluntary adherence until some new structure could be set up. On June 1, President Roosevelt approved dismissal of 411 court suits which had been instituted by the Government against N.R.A. Code violators. On September 5, 1935, the Blue Eagle was abolished as a symbol of the National Recovery Act and on December 21, 1935, the President issued an order terminating the life of the National Recovery Act within the next ten days.

The Spread of Communist Influence

The economic depression furnished fertile ground for the spread of Communist influence and infiltration. The climate was almost ideal for Communist propaganda to gloat that the capitalist world was in violent dissolution. The Party claimed a meteoric rise in its roster of followers and "glittering admirers." New terms were coined to describe the new ferment, and phrases like "united front," "transmission belts," "fellow travelers," "boring from within," "party line," and the like, filtered into our national vocabulary.

Except for the Fur Workers Union, which came under Communist domination under Ben Gold's aggressive leadership, the needle-trade unions, with which many Brownsville residents were affiliated, repulsed, the Communist effort to gain control of the unions. The anti-Communist socialist *Forward* held its ground against the Communist *Freiheit,* which was established to combat it. In the 1930's, however, the Communists attracted a new element, the American intellectuals. They mobilized within their ranks thousands of American youth, youth leaders, social workers, writers, Hollywood stars, and liberals. Alfred Kazin portrays, in his *Starting Out in the Thirties,* not only his development as a young Brownsville intellectual, but also the entire era of "great causes," and the literary-radical milieu of that period.[4]

In the 1930's a large number of those who were intellectually alert were "Reds," or at least on the periphery of their dogma. A considerable number were either unable or unwilling to distinguish between the Communist slogans and their promises. They envisaged themselves as being concerned with a new and better society. Many of the Jewish youth who were brought up in Socialist homes fell in line, aroused by an aura of social conscience and sentimental Utopia. Some became "militants" who could not understand why the older and more experienced Socialists would not unite in a "United Front" with the Communists. In 1932 they consolidated under Norman Thomas and the Milwaukee Group under Mayor Daniel Haan to defeat the Socialist Morris Hillquit. Soon thereafter the Socialist Party lost its influence.

After 1935 the Communists rode to new influence on the United Front, attracting many respectable and important figures. Although numerically small, the Communist Party became the magnet to draw a group of sympathizers and liberals. In February, 1931, a party organizer boasted that it had in the New York District alone "100 different mass organizations," some national and some local. Some of these Communist-led societies had followers in Brownsville.

The Communists rendered some effective service during the height of the depression. They organized "Unemployed Councils" to call hunger marches demanding relief and unemployment insurance. They did social work among city unemployed, investigating cases of neglect and organizing neighbors to resist evictions for non-payment of rent. The Brownsville Unemployed Council, with its office at 646 Stone Avenue, called for a convention on July 9, 1933, stating in its Yiddish and English brochure, "Hundreds of families are being thrown out of their homes in Brownsville because of the no-rent policy of city relief agencies. The Home Relief Bureau is helping the Roosevelt Government to recruit young men into Civilian Conservation Corps at $1 a day to prepare them for war at home and abroad, to drive down wages, and cut relief allowances to their families. The police are being used to beat up and arrest starving workers who resist evictions and demand relief.

"In order to build up a powerful organization of workers on every block and in the neighborhood, the Brownsville Unemployed Council is calling a Convention, Sunday, July 9th, 10 A.M., 105 Thatford Avenue, of workers representing organized and unorganized houses and blocks and all organizations that are anxious to help win these demands:

1. Stopping of evictions of all unemployed families.
2. Payment of rent by the Home Relief Bureau.
3. Increased relief to meet rising cost of living.
4. Full relief to single workers.
5. No stationing of police at the Home Relief Bureau."

The famous march on Washington and other street demonstrations had many Brownsvillites among their participants. These demonstrations sought to arouse the people to the consciousness that government can serve society. Although the radicals obtained a stranglehold on many sections of the nation and infiltrated various circles, strong opposition to the Communist Party was engendered in Brownsville. The debates on the street corners and in the halls were heated. The American Labor Party took to the streets at least six weeks in advance of election, and to the side streets as well. Speakers like Vito Marcantonio attracted thousands, and streets had to be closed off. But as one of the active workers has stated, thousands came to hear the minority party's speakers, but when it came to voting, they voted for the majority party, the Democratic Party.

While America was preoccupied with the depression and domestic problems, the apostles of fascism, nazism, and militarism were wooing the peoples of Spain, Italy, Japan, and Germany. On the Sunday President Roosevelt proclaimed the bank holiday, the National Socialist Party of Adolf Hitler was voted into power. The Loyalist cause directed against the dictator Franco in Spain appealed to liberals throughout the world, and became a symbol of democracy's struggle for survival. Many American youths volunteered for the Abraham Lincoln Brigade and the Loyalist armies in Spain, risking their lives for the democratic ideals they cherished.

This writer received a letter from one of the Hebrew Educational Society's club members written in Spain on November 17, 1937, in which he said:

"In the nine months I have been in Spain I have had the opportunity to see that the same forces that are persecuting the Jews in Germany and Poland are slaughtering helpless men and children here in Spain. I can say definitely, for I have seen fascist airplanes shot down, and upon examining the wreckage of many of them, they all proved to be of either German or Italian make. You have heard how the Abraham Lincoln Brigade, which is composed of Americans like myself who believe in Democracy and that the defeat of fascism in Spain is the defeat of fascism throughout the world, successfully captured the towns of Quinto and Belchite near Saragossa where the civilian population wept with joy on being released from the torture and horrors of fascism. When we left the town of Quinto we donated to the civilian population enough money to provide each child with a new outfit.

"I and my fellow Americans and the people of Spain appeal to you to join the campaign to aid Spain together with the American Committee to aid Spanish Democracy and the American Medical Bureau to aid Spanish Democracy, which is also providing the orphan children of Spain with homes throughout the world."

In the meantime Hitler and nazism were gathering strength, preparing for World War II. The Jews throughout the world were filled with anxiety, and sought ways to assist their harassed brethren. Few realized, however, what overwhelming tragedy awaited the great mass of European Jews.

World War II

XIX

LESS THAN twenty-five years after World War I the second and more devastating World War II erupted. Free men everywhere were cognizant of issues at stake. It was a war against tyranny under various names—fascism, nazism and Japanese militarism. The German Nazis, in their lust for world mastery, revealed during the long and bitter struggle which lasted three years and nine months, hitherto unsuspected depths of human savagery and bestiality, particularly when they feasted upon the torture and extermination of practically most of European Jewry.

It was not until the latter part of 1942 that America could begin to place her total strength into the contest, but in the succeeding years, until the terrible ending came with the atomic explosion over Hiroshima and Nagasaki, the war was fought in Europe, in the Pacific, in China, Burma, and India, on land and on the seven seas. Soldiers, sailors, and marines, infantry, riflemen and fliers, paratroopers, Seabees and army engineers, Americans of every color, and every creed and class, did the fighting and dying.

Brooklyn had some of the largest training centers, and supplied the largest number of Army and Navy fighting men that ever rallied to the colors for any single comparable community— 326,000 men, 7,000 of whom made the supreme sacrifice.[1] The men of Brownsville and East New York shared in this struggle, this time perhaps with a greater interest in the outcome, because the enemy was a Nazi.

Brooklyn was the headquarters of the largest port of embarkation in the world, from which sailed half of the armies overseas, and a third of their supplies. During World War II the Brooklyn Navy Yard grew to be the largest in the world, employing nearly 75,000 at the peak of its activity. Brooklyn industry contributed to the making of everything that brought America final victory, everything from combat helmets to atomic bombs.

A number of these factories were located in East New York. Thus the United States Cabinet Bed Company on Milford, Atlantic, and Montauk avenues employed some 250 men and 75 women in the manufacture of ordnance parts such as ammunition and artillery supplies, and was commended by the New York Ordnance District for its performance. The Ideal Clamp Manufacturing Company, 435 Liberty Avenue, employed some 250 persons in manufacturing special clamps for armed forces, and won its "E" award on the basis of "outstanding performance" in all types of manufacture.

The war years affected every family—the boys who were drafted or volunteered, and those who remained at home. When the stars began to twinkle in the windows, denoting children in service, and flags bearing the names of servicemen began to appear in the halls of nearly every organization, those left behind (particularly the mothers) could not rest. There were some like Mrs. Skolnick, who had as many as eight sons in the service. Mrs. Rosenberg had lost two sons in the war. These women, and many like them, left their homes to work for victory. Numerous victory clubs sprang up. CDVO (Civilian Defense Volunteer Organizations) hummed with activity. The clubs sold War Bonds, ran knitting circles, wrote letters to soldiers, gathered scrap metal, helped with block observances honoring fallen soldiers, and cooperated with the National Red Cross and the Air Raid Wardens. In cooperation with government agencies, canteens were set up for soldiers home on furlough. The *Landsmanschaften* and fraternal organizations raised large sums for Russian War Relief.

Brownsville responded nobly in the campaigns for the sale of War Bonds. The Loew's Pitkin Theatre, under the direction of Mr. Al Weiss and the chairmanship of Abe Stark, rallied mass support. In the first seven bond sales, it came first, and in the eighth it came second. All in all, $15,000,000 worth of bonds were sold in Brownsville. Mrs. F. D. Roosevelt attended the eighth bond rally and purchased a bond.

The opening of a second front in Europe was long opposed before it was undertaken. It meant that American boys would have to fight and die on the soil of Europe. On the other hand, there were those who believed that only a western front could drain away enough of the Hitler army to bring victory. The feelings of a large representation of Brownsville came to expression in one of the most colorful and largest rallies held during this period at the Parkway Theatre on Eastern Parkway and St. Johns Place. Thousands of people jammed the theatre to hear the famous Russian-Jewish dramatists and poets, Michaels and Pfeffer, speak. They also read their poetry. They were on a visit to America to represent Russia, who was then our ally. It is sad to contemplate in retrospect their death under the Stalin regime. What ingratitude! The meeting at the Parkway Theatre was overwhelming.

The Second Front was finally opened, and the day was referred to as D-Day. Brownsville was so excited about the event that it planned a parade. It was the only section in Brooklyn which held a parade on D-Day. The parade was sponsored by CDVO, and included among its other sponsors, political parties, parent associations, victory clubs, and churches.

The war finally ended in 1945. As some of the boys began to return, home-coming parties and celebrations were held everywhere. Those who had made the supreme sacrifice were not forgotten. Some of the War Veteran Posts, such as the Harold S. Helfgott Post No. 130, J.W.V., were named after fallen comrades. Plaques and tablets were placed in the various institutions to perpetuate their memory.

Undesirable Elements

XX

Juvenile Delinquency and Crime

THERE WERE general obedience and respect for law and order in the community. In decency and respectability Brownsville could match any other neighborhood in New York or elsewhere. This is not to make the claim, however, that the community was free from juvenile delinquency and from criminal offenders. Considering that it was one of the most densely populated sections of the city, containing many poor who were struggling with their day-to-day problems, the juvenile delinquency statistics were not inordinately large. One of the reasons was that Jewish philanthropic agencies were concerned with preventive measures to keep the number of delinquents to a minimum.

The Brooklyn Federation of Jewish Charities supported the Brooklyn Jewish Big Brother and Big Sister Committee which had its offices for a number of years in the Hebrew Educational Society building. The Brooklyn Big Brothers and Big Sisters Association,

Incorporated, affiliated in 1925 with the Brooklyn Jewish Social Service Bureau, which had offices at 285 Schermerhorn Street. In September, 1933, it became known as the Brooklyn District Office of the Jewish Board of Guardians. It maintained a district office in the Brownsville area at Stone and Pitkin Avenue until 1951, when it transferred its services to the Borough Hall office.

Dr. Julius B. Maller of Columbia University studied the records of Jewish boys and girls who were brought before the Children's Courts of New York City during the 24 years from 1909 to 1933.[1] Of the 249,594 children arraigned in Manhattan, Bronx and Brooklyn, 19.5 per cent, or 48,668 came from Jewish homes. The rate among Jews was about 1/3 the rate that prevailed among non-Jews, and was less than 1/2 what would be expected from the proportion of Jewish children to the total child population. The rate of arraignment of Jewish girls was even lower, less than 1/4 the rate among non-Jewish girls. The causes of the delinquencies, as well as the manner of the disposition, indicated that a Jewish case brought before the court generally represented a less serious problem than that of a non-Jewish case.

Despite the increase in the percentage of Jews in the city, there was a consistent decline in the proportion of Jewish arraignments, which dropped from 30 per cent in 1909 to 19 per cent in 1930. Most of the Jewish delinquents were native Americans of foreign born parents, the majority of whom had emigrated from Russia and Poland.

Dr. Sophia M. Robison's study, *Can Delinquency Be Measured?* published in 1936 by the Welfare Council of New York, contains pertinent information about juvenile delinquency in Brownsville and East New York.[2] Her first germane observation was that it is difficult to define delinquency. It should be interpreted as more than a legal term usually applied only to individuals who come before the Children's Court. It should include "recorded conduct proscribed by the Children's Court Code, whether apprehended by the law or not." Thus, in studying the delinquent behavior of children between seven and fifteen years of age, she selected not only the cases that came before the Court, but also cases of delinquency which came to the attention of private social agencies which deal with children who display anti-social as well as anti-legal behavior. She found that court figures alone are not only inadequate, but are actually misleading as an indication of even the approximate extent of juvenile delinquent behavior in New York City. The legal definition is inept and therefore unsatisfactory, both as a distinguishing description of delinquency and as a tool for statistical measurements, because the label "delinquency" includes such miscellaneous categories as peddling and begging, disorderly conduct, malicious mischief, and ungovernable behavior. A considerable number of the cases she studied were referred to court for minor offenses of which 70 per cent were dismissed.

Bearing in mind all the difficulties and reservations which Dr. Robison has pointed out in interpreting the delinquency statistics, let us examine the data gathered by her concerning the extent of juvenile delinquency in various sections (Health Areas) in Brownsville and East New York.

Brownsville, East New York, New Lots and Canarsie, comprising more than 30 per cent of the Brooklyn Jewish population estimated to be 794,913 in 1930, accounted for about the same proportion of all delinquency cases (360 out of a total of 1,085 Jewish cases for all of Brooklyn) that came before the Children's Court (856 cases, of whom 627, or 73 per cent were dismissed), or were serviced by some corrective or preventive social agency.

The number of cases was not uniform in all the Health Areas, although each area had approximately the same total population of some 25,000. A few Health Areas, 57 and 59 in Brownsville, and 61 in East New York, had an appreciable number of Jewish delinquents. With a population of 71,862, or 21 per cent of the total population, these areas accounted for 184, or 40 per cent of all cases of juvenile delinquents that came before the Court. Eighty-four, or 45 per cent of the cases were dismissed. Health Area 56, with a population of 24,860, and lying in the heart of Brownsville, between Hopkinson Avenue and East 96th Street, East New York Avenue and Blake Avenue, accounted for 33 cases in all, of whom 27 were Jews, 5 Catholics, 1 Greek Catholic. Seven of the Jews were under the care of a Jewish social agency. Nineteen cases in all appeared in the Children's Court, of whom 10 were dismissed, 7 placed on probation, 2 remanded or committed, 1 referred to the Crime Prevention Bureau, and 5 sent to probationary schools. The offenses which brought them to the attention of the authorities were; ungovernable behavior, 12; desertion of home, 6; peddling without a license, 4; stealing, 3; burglary, 3; disorderly conduct, 2; truancy, 1; violation of railroad law; unclassified, 1.

Health Area 58.20, lying directly south of Health Area 56, between Hopkinson Avenue and East 96th Street, and Blake and Hegeman Avenues, with a population of 24,105, accounted in all for 25 cases, all of whom were Jews. Except for the 4 who were known to social agencies, 21 appeared in Children's Court, of whom 13 were dismissed upon arraignment, and 8 were placed on probation. The offense which led most of them into trouble was peddling without a license, for which 11 were brought into court. Seven were accused of stealing; 2 of disorderly conduct; 3 of ungovernable behavior, and 1 of desertion of home. Health Area 58.10, with a population of 25,558, had even less cases—14 in all, 13 of whom were Jews. Ten appeared in Children's Court, and 7 of the cases were dismissed on arraignment, 2 placed on probation, and 1 remanded or committed.

The area with the largest number of cases was Health Area 59, with a population of 25,710 and lying between Sutter Avenue and Livonia, Hopkinson, and Van Sinderen avenues. It was a mixed neighborhood. Of the 5,909 families 4,688, or 79.3 per cent were Jewish. Of the total number of 94 cases (89 boys, 5 girls), 72, or 76.6 per cent were Jews; 8 Catholics, 2 Greek Orthodox, and 12 Protestants. Seventy-three of the total number of 94 cases appeared in Children's Court, of which 40 were dismissed upon arraignment, 23 placed on probation, 2 committed after having been on probation, and 8 remanded or committed. The offenses which brought them into trouble were stealing, 20; disorderly conduct, 16; ungovernable behavior, 19; peddling, 9; burglary, 8; desertion of home, 4; truancy, 2; violation of railroad law, 2.

In East New York, the Health Area which accounted for the largest number of cases was Health Area 61, with a population of 27,290 and lying between Alabama Avenue and Schenck Avenue, Liberty Avenue and Dumont Avenue. It accounted in all for 60 cases, of whom 33 were Jews, 21 Catholics, and 6 Protestant. Only 46 of the total number of cases appeared in Children's Court, of whom 23 were dismissed, 20 placed on probation, one committed after having been on probation, and 3 remanded or committed. The offenses included burglary, 10; stealing, 10; peddling, 9; ungovernable behavior, 9; disorderly conduct, 8; desertion of home, 3; truancy, 2.

Juvenile delinquency among Jews declined in the following years. Dr. Sophia M. Robison, in her study of delinquency among Jewish children in New York City, based on records of the Jewish Board of Guardians, found that in 1952 only 226 Jewish families were involved, or about 3 per cent of the 5,762 juvenile offenders.[3] This figure assumes even greater importance when we realize that the Jewish population under 15 years of age was estimated by the HIP study to have been 27.2 per cent.

As compared to 1930 figures we find a striking difference. In 1952, all of Brooklyn had only 106 Jewish children referred to court as against 856 in 1930. While the number of Jewish delinquents declined, the behavior of those that were brought to court was no different than that of the nonJewish delinquent. Only 35.4 per cent of the cases were dismissed in 1952, as against 67.1 per cent two decades earlier. The offenses which brought these cases to court were wrongful appropriation of property—burglary, robbery, stealing, auto stealing (43 per cent); injury to persons (10 per cent); sex offenses (8 per cent); ungovernable behavior (20 per cent); habitual truancy (16 cases in all of Brooklyn). There were no cases for peddling or begging without a license, which was one of the leading offenses which brought Brooklyn Jewish children to Court in 1930.

Since only 226 children were brought to Court in the course of a whole year for all of New York City, of whom 106 appeared in all of Brooklyn, health area rates are necessarily very insignificant. In almost 2/3 of all the health areas in New York City there was not a single Jewish child referred to court, and even in those health areas where a few children did get into difficulty, the number was small, and showed no appreciable cluster of Jewish delinquents. There were only 11 Health Areas in all of New York that had 5 or more Jewish cases in Court. Only 2 health areas in East New York (New Lots) had any cases, Health Area 62 with 1 case, and Health Area 63 with 2 cases. Health Area 61, which in 1930 had an appreciable number of cases, did not have a single case in 1952. As for Brownsville proper, it accounted for 37 of the 106 Brooklyn cases, and 4 of its health areas, 56, 58.10, 58.20, and 60, had between 6 and 8 cases, many fewer than in 1930. Health Area 58.20 had 21 cases in 1930, 7 in 1952. Health Area 58.10, which lies more in the East Flatbush section than in Brownsville proper, had in the course of the year 8 Jewish children in the court, the largest number of Jewish children for any one health area in 1952. It had only 10 cases in 1930. Due to a shift in population, Health Area 57 had only 1 case, and Health Area 59, which had the largest number in 1930, accounted for only 4 cases in 1952.

JUVENILE DELINQUENTS
BROWNSVILLE AND EAST NEW YORK

1930 and 1952

	Brownsville			East New York	
Health Area	No. 1930 (Children's Court & Field Agencies)	No. 1952 (Children's Court Only)	Health Area	No. 1930 (Children's Court & Field Agencies)	No. 1952 (Children's Court Only)
51	40	2	61	33	0
52	10	2	62	9	1
56	27	6	63	23	2
57	42	1	64.10	—	0
58.10	13	8	64.20	17	0
58.20	25	7	75.10	—	0
59	72	4	75.20	10	0
60	39	7			
Total	268	37		92	3

	1930		*1952*	
	N. Y.	Brooklyn		
Total No. all of Children's Court	1396	856	Total No. All N. Y. — 226	
Social Agencies	921	229	" " " Brooklyn — 106	
Total cases	2317	1085		

The "Combination," or "Murder, Inc."

All large cities have been plagued by gangsterism at times. Herbert Asbury in his *Gangs of New York,* published in 1928, chronicles the more spectacular exploits of many of the gangsters who terrorized New York during the last century. The dubious honors of these gangs were not confined to any one racial or national group. Brownsville, East New York, the Ocean Hill Section, New Lots, and other neighborhoods of Brooklyn were not spared. They too became for a time infested by gangs similar to other sections of New York. In the early part of 1940, Brooklyn's District Attorney, William O'Dwyer and his assistant, Burton Turkus, startled the nation by their exposure of a crime syndicate called the "Combination" that had been operating major rackets for a number of years across the country.[4] Their inquiry revealed the national scope of the Combination's connections. Wherever the locale, whether it was Manhattan, Cleveland, Chicago, Philadelphia, Detroit, New Orleans, Miami, Boston, or Los Angeles, the underworld of each of these communities and other communities was "in," each mob cooperating, while at the same time operating its own rackets.

The avalanche of publicity of the crime revelations fell upon Brownsville. This was due to the fact that one of the syndicate, Abe (Kid Twist) Reles, who turned State's witness, originated, with some of his "troopers," from the East New York section. None of them lived in Brownsville proper, but one of their main hangouts was in a candy store located at Saratoga and Livonia avenues.

Some of the Brownsville residents were quite stirred up over what they regarded as the "undeserved bad name" the disclosures of the murder ring were giving their community. Most of Brownsville, physically and spiritually, lived far removed from the small criminal group; many were even unaware of its existence. Regardless from where these professional hoodlums came, they were a cruel reality. How they got that way, how they prospered in this wicked business, and how they were eliminated, do belong to the history of the total community.

It is sad to report that in the twenties and thirties a number of the underworld leaders in a few of the large American cities were Jews. This was a shocking and new phenomenon in Jewish life. The Jewish gangster was without ancestry, a product not of Jewish but of American urban life.[5] The immigrant Jew was a law-abiding citizen; the Jewish gangster was the son of the immigrant, rarely if ever the immigrant himself.

Among the factors that contributed to the rise of the Jewish mobster was the need for self-defense. Many in the East Side and elsewhere originally formed small gangs either to defend old Jews and pushcart peddlers who were attacked by hoodlums, or to defend themselves from attacks. Some of the leaders of these "defense" groups later became professional gangsters, prominent in the underworld.

Before the era of bootlegging, the Jewish hoodlums relied on the wars between labor and management. The "strong arm" terrorist racket tactics were common practice in the early unionization of the Jewish trades, especially the garment industry. Harry W. Neuberger, a former deputy commissioner of police of New York, wrote in 1915: "It is no exaggeration to say that at least 75 per cent of our gunmen and gangmen are directly or indirectly supported throughout the year by legitimate business. Associations of employees as well as those of employers have constant use for them. . . ."[6]

District Attorney O'Dwyer and Mr. Turkus, through their investigation, exposed a new pattern in crime. After the repeal of the prohibition law, the large city underworld lords realized that the time for free-hand killing and costly competition was over. Crime, like business had passed the era of rugged individualism, and should ape big industries. Thus, a "Crime Trust," called the "Combination" was formed, and patterned after American big business. It set up its own rules and its own "judicial system." The racketeers in each zone were governed by an "inner circle" of overlords whose decisions were law. These were the "big shots" who directed the various enterprises, arranged murders, and acquired heavy bank accounts. Below them were the vice-presidents.

The term "Murder, Inc.," originated by Harry Feeny of *The New York World Telegram*, has remained. It was a bit journalistic, for murder was not the Combination's business; the rackets were. It did no murders for outsiders, and no killings for a fee. The Crime Trust, according to Reles, never intended to commit murder out of passion, excitement, jealousy, personal revenge, or any of the usual motives which prompt private, unorganized murders. It killed impersonally, and solely for business considerations.

The Combination exercised control over a wide ramification of trade and industry; gambling, prostitution, narcotics, policy games, bootlegging, slot machines, and the loan shark racket. It dominated certain trade union locals and had a financial stake in various night clubs and cabarets. It operated certain legitimate enterprises, and "muscled in" on others by exacting tribute from businessmen by threats or use of violence. Racketeering was costing the United States, according to a New York State Crime Commission report of 1931, between twelve and eighteen billion dollars annually. The East New York, Brownsville and Ocean Hill branch played a specialist's role in these rackets. They became the "Enforcement Squad," the "Extermination Department" for the syndicate.

When Reles turned State's witness, he gave details to the District Attorney of more than fifty murders committed by his group in New York City, Brooklyn, New Jersey, Sullivan County, and elsewhere. He himself had a hand in some dozen killings. Except for three innocent victims, all the murdered were "insiders," mobsters themselves who were eliminated for various reasons, mostly out of fear that they knew too much and might endanger the Combination. According to their code, loyalty to the group transcended friendship, even blood ties. Therefore, the murder of friends and pals, was no occasion for outrage. Over a ten-year period, some two dozen men were found stabbed, strangled, hacked to bits, or cremated, and left in the gutter, the vacant lots, or in stolen automobiles in Brownsville, East New York, Ocean Hill, and elsewhere.

Frightening as this record is, the situation across the country was no better. According to Turkus, there was a list in 1940 of some 200 murders, all unsolved, and during the previous 10 year period upward of 1,000 murders were committed from coast to coast.

The Reles-Maoine Combination began as a small local gang, rising to prominence by mergers, trade agreements, and by wiping out its rivals. As for Abe Reles, he was a notorious hoodlum and a leader of thugs in the Brownsville-East New York section for some seventeen years.

Leo Katcher and Malcolm Logan, in a series of articles in *The New York Post* (April 8-10, 1940) , described the growth of the gang. After Reles and his friends Herschel (Harry) Strauss and Motel (Bugsy) Goldstein graduated from "pinching" fruit from pushcarts to stealing bundles from trucks and extorting dollar and five-dollar bills from small storekeepers, they were ready for bigger "conquests." In the neighboring Ocean Hill section there was a gang of Italian mobsters led by Harry (Happy) and Louis Maione. The Maiones had found the Italians in their neighborhood as vulnerable to blackmail as were the Brownsville merchants. Occasionally the Reles gang would invade that section and stage fights with the Italian gang, but later they decided their feud was unprofitable and formed a loose alliance, each mob respecting the other's territory. Both gangs were, however, negligible factors in Brooklyn's underworld. In the 1920's the substantial Brownsville gangs were led by the four Amberg brothers—Hymie, Oscar, Joey, and Louis—and the three Shapiro brothers—Irving, Meyer, and Willie.

While limiting their reign to their own domains in Brownsville and East New York, these seven had seized control of a number of profitable rackets. The Prohibition era, which lasted for some thirteen years from the time it began on January 17, 1920, offered an especially profitable field for their talents. They coerced an established local brewery into taking them in as silent partners, and their thugs acted as salesmen. With fists, brass knuckles, and blackjacks, they "convinced" the East New York and Brownsville speakeasy owners that their brand of beer was the best. With the speakeasies came the slot machines and other rackets. In 1935 the Amberg brothers dared to defy the gang dominated by Louis (Lepke) Buchalter. Their murdered bodies were found in garages and blazing autos. Abe Reles and his partners were arrested each time, but released for lack of evidence.

Most young people find a niche in the moral world, and many achieve distinction. It is a fact, nevertheless, that individuals who have to struggle from poor and low social strata have traditionally been more prone to delinquency. To boys who live under such conditions, few prospects are as exciting and inviting as truancy, gang warfare, vandalism, and theft. There must be other preconditions of delinquency which modern students have been trying to discover in order to eliminate it. The boy who becomes a member of a crime syndicate must have some special qualities. "You have got to have criminal tendencies in you," insisted Reles. When a reporter of *The Forward* visited some of the homes of these hoodlums, most of the folks had the same story to tell. "All the children are doing well, are married, earning an honest living. Only he! That one! He was different! He got into trouble in school! He got into bad company! We tried this, we tried that, but it did not help!"

A variety of characters and individuals became associated with the syndicate. By the end of 1939 there existed in this country an organized underworld, a government within a government, whose tentacles reached everywhere. It was not until a decade later that the Kefauver Senate Committee dramatized much of the danger, and made the vast public conscious of it. In New York and Brooklyn there flourished, as elsewhere, a crime mob that was exacting tribute from large and small businesses.

District Attorney William O'Dwyer promised, before taking office in January, to hunt down the Brooklyn racketeers and gangsters with a staff of non-political aides who could be trusted to get results. He said, "If everybody stays on his toes, the professional racketeer, gunman, hoodlum, I mean the fellow who stands out on the street corner like a light house, could not remain in Brooklyn one minute."

That was no empty promise. Together with his assistant, Burton Turkus, and other aides, he soon linked various crimes with powerful underground czars like Lepke Buchalter and Luciano. He also spread his web into other counties including Sullivan, the Bronx, and into other states including Illinois, California, New Jersey, and Pennsylvania. Samuel J. Foley, then the Bronx District Attorney, spoke of it as "the most important clean-up of underworld characters that I have know in fifteen years as a law officer."

"It is a good thing O'Dwyer was elected District Attorney of Kings County," said William Dickelman of Sullivan County. "We've been the dumping ground for the last ten years, and until now we've been up against a stone wall." Thomas E. Dewey was conducting his investigations in Manhattan. Mayor LaGuardia and his Police Commissioner, Valentine, were determined to drive these cutthroats out of their sinister machinations.

Abject terror seized these mobsters. The most powerful of them, Lepke Buchalter, who controlled the clothing industry in Metropolitan New York and was regarded as the "worst industrial racketeer in America," became panicky. He went "kill-crazy" trying to destroy every possible witness against him. It has been reported that during his infamous career he ordered the murders of as many as seventy victims. To save their skins many of the mobsters were ready to talk, and when apprehended they lost their bravado. It was at this time that Reles, who was feared by so many and had hurt so many, turned State's witness.

The die was cast. In May, 1940, the case began against Harry (Happy) Maione and Frank (The Dasher) Abbandando for slaying George Rudnick, who was stabbed 34 times with an ice pick in the Ocean Hill section on March 24, 1937. On May 23, 1940, a jury found both Maione and Abbandando guilty of first degree murder, but with appeals and legal moves, they managed to hold out until February 19, 1942.

On June 12, 1941, "Pittsburgh Phil" and his pal Bugsey went to their doom. Lepke (Louis) Buchalter and "Mende" Weiss,

Buchalter's operations manager of Manhattan, paid with their lives for murdering Jacob Rosen, a partner in a New York and New Jersey clothing company, who refused to pay tribute to the Lepke mob.

Additional convictions followed, and at last Brownsville was no longer on the front pages. The new generation did not become involved in such problems. They lived under different social and economic conditions, and could find more useful and rewarding outlets in American life. As Professor William M. McCord has pointed out, racketeers flourish to cater to desires Americans periodically declare illegal: drink, sex, gambling, or security from economic competition. Bootlegging went out when drinking returned to the domain of legitimate business. Labor unions have won recognition and acceptance, making mobs of strike breakers no longer a lucrative business. To be sure, the problems of crime, of labor racketeering, of underworld penetration of business and of various other walks of life, still remain an important aspect of American life. This has been brought out boldly in recent disclosures (September and October, 1963) before a Senate Investigations Subcommittee. These revelations have nothing to do with our Brownsville story. They only remind us that there was a period in our history when Brownsville, too, felt deeply the evils of syndicated crime.

The sordid story has been told in some detail to indicate how widespread the evil was. The syndicate did not reside in any one block or neighborhood or even city. It was an affliction of the entire American community. If the mobsters victimized many, they too were, in a sense, the victims of an era that spawned such criminals. Brownsville was part of the community and should bear its portion of guilt. In all fairness, however, it should be remembered that Brownsville proper contributed perhaps the least to this group.

The Glory of the Community

XXI

ALL KINDS of people were to be found in Brownsville. It had its saints and its sinners, its rich and its poor, its learned and its ignorant. In the course of our account of the development of the community, we had occasion to point out some of the faults and frailties, the weaknesses and failings, the shadows that at times marred the image of Brownsville. But Brownsville also produced distinguished sons who brought glory to the community. Some attained national and international fame. To the glory of the community should also be added the vast host of humble, kindly, common people, even the lonely and the poor, who did not attain fame, but who daily vindicated the loftiest ideals of constructive citizenship. Their lives were a blessing and a sure foundation for a wholesome community. The glory that was Brownsville's rests upon its collective efforts to develop a community of promise. From a straggling, struggling, real estate development it blossomed, unassisted from the outside, by the efforts of poor but zealous East European immigrants into a veritable beehive of hundreds of thousands of earnest, busy, productive workers.

These people built houses of worship, institutions of learning, and charitable and social associations. They shared a sense of close kinship with Jews throughout the world, and responded generously to every call for assistance. They reacted instantly and feelingly to every outrage, upheaval, or injustice here or abroad. They were motivated by a liberalism which expressed itself in a dedication to humanitarianism, to their spiritual heritage, and to the democratic ideal that human dignity and human equality are the inalienable prerogative of every individual.

Brownsville was fortunate in that great personalities came to live here: Rabbinic scholars, Jewish educators, labor leaders, writers, Zionist leaders, professionals and laymen, *feine balabatim* whose profound influence on the community won for it the cognomen, the "Jerusalem of America."

Since Brownsville and East New York were only sections of a big city, it was not unexpected that many young people left the neighborhood when they were ready to enter upon a career. They remained here only during their early and formative years, and sought to achieve their reputations and fame elsewhere. We have no definitive criterion, therefore, of telling how many were fortunate in rising on the ladder of success. We are aware only of those who publicly acknowledged their Brownsville origin, and to whom our attention has been called.

To discuss at length the many distinguished personalities who have come from Brownsville would lead us far afield. Their biographies and accomplishments are chronicled in various organs. We shall, therefore, limit ourselves merely to a listing and a brief mention of some leading men in a variety of fields of endeavor.

Dr. Isidor Isaac Rabi

Modern man's interest in the sciences and his passage from the Machine Age into the Space Age, have profoundly affected every aspect of our society and culture. One of the world's great scientific minds, whose interest is not only his own specialty of physics, but the meaning and place of science and the scientific tradition in our general culture, is Dr. Isidor Isaac Rabi.[1] His distinguished career indicates a brilliant scholar: winner of the Nobel Prize in physics in 1944; Higgins Professor of Physics, and now University Professor at Columbia University; winner of the 1964 Priestly Memorial Award. He has occupied a large number of important positions in both academic and public capacities. Under President Eisenhower he was chairman of the President's Science Advisory Committee, and also one of the prime movers of the International Atoms for Peace Conference in Geneva in 1955. He has taken a lively interest in the scientific development of Israel, particularly in the Haifa Technion.

Dr. Rabi was born on July 29, 1898, at Rymanow in the old Austria-Hungary Empire. His parents brought him to New York a year later. For a time his father, David, worked in a Lower East Side sweatshop, and then moved to Brownsville, where he ran a small grocery store.

It was the neighborhood public library that influenced young Rabi. "I was a kid who read a lot," he recalled recently. When he was eleven years old he had read straight through the children's shelves and turned to the science shelf, beginning with a book about the Copernican theory, and continued through the shelf.

General David Sarnoff

While all his childhood memories go back to the East Side, General David Sarnoff, who is world-famous for his contributions to the development of communications and broadcasting, and who has headed the Radio Corporation of America and the National Broadcasting Company, also lived in Brownsville during his youth.

Dr. Louis Finkelstein

Dr. Finkelstein was born in Cincinnati, Ohio in 1895, and came to live in Brownsville in 1902 when his father, Rabbi Simon I. Finkelstein, became Rabbi of the Oheb Shalom Congregation in Brownsville.[2] Dr. Finkelstein was educated in the local schools, participated in various local Jewish activities such as the Hapoal

Ha-Mizrachi, attended City College and Columbia University
(Ph.D. 1918), and received his ordination as Rabbi from the Jewish Theological Seminary of America in 1919.

Many religious leaders and thinkers of our time have sought to
face the challenge of modern life by adopting their basic theological concepts to the changing social and environmental needs. The
essence of the present world-struggle appears to them to be not
material, but spiritual and ethical. How to develop a pattern of
life in which man, rather than technology, will be central to the
purpose of society, is the chief problem which concerns them. One
of the distinguished religious leaders in the modern world is Dr.
Louis Finkelstein; Rabbi, scholar, author, chancellor of the Jewish
Theological Seminary of America, and leading spokesman of Conservative Judaism in the world.

Under his leadership the Seminary has expanded into a great
university of Judaism with a dozen schools and institutes in New
York, Los Angeles, and Jerusalem. Under the pioneering steps
initiated by Dr. Finkelstein, it embarked on a number of inter-
group activities purposing to apply the lessons of disparate
religious heritages to the common moral and ethical problems
that face contemporary society. These include the Institute for
Religious and Social Studies; the Conference on Science, Philosophy, and Religion; the Institute of Ethics, and the Herbert H.
Lehman Institute of Talmud Ethics.

Besides Dr. Finkelstein, a large number of Jewish religious
leaders and educators spent their youth in Brownsville. We have
alluded to many of them in this volume. These include such outstanding personalities as the late Dr. Solomon Goldman, Dr. Simon
Greenberg, presently Vice-Chancellor of the Jewish Theological
Seminary, Dr. Moshe Davis of the Hebrew University, Dr. Solomon
Grayzel, former Editor of the Jewish Publication Society, Professor
Meyer Waxman, Dr. Ben Zion Bokser, Rabbi Joseph H. Look-
stein, Rabbi Herschel Schachter, Chairman of the President Con-
ference, Rabbi Irving Lehrman of Temple Emanuel, Miami Beach,
Rabbi David Seligson of the Central Synagogue, New York, Dr.
Azriel Eisenberg, Dr. Joseph Kaminetsky, and Dr. Samuel Dinin.

Colonel David Marcus

Men of East New York and Brownsville have participated in the wars of our country, and many have given their lives for the preservation of American ideals. One of Brownsville's famous sons, whose life story has become a semi-legend since World War II, is Colonel David Marcus.[3] He lies buried in the West Point Cemetery among the more than three thousand graves. He is the only West Pointer who died fighting under a foreign flag, and his gravestone bears the simple legend: "Colonel David Marcus—A Soldier for all Humanity." The contribution of "Mickey" Marcus to Israel's amazing war of Independence in 1948 has assured him, in the words of David Ben-Gurion then Prime Minister of Israel, "an undying place of honor in our history."

Ted Berkman, in his biography of David Marcus entitled, *Cast a Giant Shadow,* which has also been made into a screen play, portrays in great detail the unique character and interesting personality of this great American Jew.[4] David Daniel was born on Washington's birthday, 1902, at 103 Hester Street, in the East Side, where his father eked out a living at a vegetable pushcart stand. Before David was six the family moved to East New York, and when he was eight, the father became ill suddenly and died. The family then moved to an apartment at 354 Powell Street in Brownsville. David attended Public School 109, Boys High School, the Hebrew Educational Society gym, and the West Point Military Academy. When he resigned his army commission in 1926, he studied law, and was appointed Temporary Magistrate in 1936 by Mayor LaGuardia. In 1940 he became Commissioner of Corrections. When World War II broke out, David went back into uniform, won a number of decorations, and compiled an astonishing record as an expert in military government.

When he returned from World War II, he responded to the call by an emissary of the *Hagana* to help Israel in its war for Independence against the armies of seven Arab governments. When the very life of Israel was at stake, he became a commander of troops in the fight to relieve the siege of Jerusalem. He was accidentally killed by an Israeli sentry, who mistook him for an

Arab prowler. In Brownsville, Junior High School 263 on Sutter Avenue and Chester Street is named after Colonel David Marcus, memorializing one of its famous sons.

Honorable Abe Stark

Abe Stark has distinguished himself in city government. As the votes were coming in on the television screen on November 2, 1964, indicating Mr. Stark running far ahead of his Democratic ticket, the television commentator commented that this should not come as a surprise for "Abe Stark is as well known in Brooklyn as the Brooklyn Bridge." He was swept into office as President of the City Council in 1953, reelected in 1957, and then elected Borough President of Brooklyn in November, 1961, and reelected in 1965. In 1953, as later in 1964, he ran ahead of his Democratic ticket, and received more votes than the combined total of his two major opponents.

Mr. Stark's popularity is due to his many years of activity with youth, in philanthropy, in medical education, in Israel, in practically every project dedicated to the amelioration of human suffering, and in people generally. Mr. Stark was born on the East Side on September 28, 1894, and came to Brownsville with his parents in 1910. Early in his life he began to work, and by dint of his zeal, his integrity, and his business acumen succeeded in becoming a prominent clothier on Pitkin Avenue, serving as President of the Pitkin Avenue Merchants Association, and involving himself in many constructive communal endeavors. His elite men's clothing store came to have the reputation of a political and social welfare office to which hundreds, regardless of political party, race, or color, came with requests for help. It was at this time that he became enthusiastically involved in the Brownsville Boys Club, which he headed. It was chiefly through his devoted efforts that buildings for the club were erected on Linden Boulevard, at a cost of three-and-a-half million dollars.

He was the leader of a twelve-year fight to make possible a medical education for deserving students. As a result of his campaign, more than 1,000 physicians are now practicing medicine who might never have had the opportunity to take the State Board Examinations. He waged a similar fight for recognition of the Chicago Medical School.

ENTERTAINERS AND FILM STARS

A number of entertainers, film stars, playwrights, radio commentators, producers, and others associated with the entertainment world were either born in Brownsville, or have resided here during part of their lives. They include Danny Kaye, George Gershwin, Gabriel Heater, Steve Lawrence, Samuel Levenson, Joey Adams, Phil Silvers, Henny Youngman, Jerry Lewis, Sandy Baron, Joe Papp, Al Lewis, Sol Hurok, Ted Ashley, and Martin Weldon.

Danny Kaye

Famous as a son of East New York is Danny Kaye, known throughout the world as a great entertainer, raconteur, actor, and comedian. David Daniel Kaye was born on January 25, 1913. His parents, Jacob and Clara Kominski, lived on Bradford Street, and sent this youngest of their three sons to Public School 149. There he first took part in a school minstrel show, playing the part of an enormous watermelon slice. Upon graduation from elementary school, he attended Thomas Jefferson High School for a time.

Danny's mother died when he was thirteen. Danny took a job for a brief period as an errand boy for a dentist, Dr. Samuel Fine, who lived across the street, and whose petite daughter Sylvia later became Danny's wife. As a song writer, author and producer, she was of great help in his career.

While Danny was clowning in a candy store on Sutter Avenue, an old vaudeville star named Bert Lee dropped in to buy a packet of cigarettes. Lee watched Danny's antics and suggested that he might pick up a few jobs in the summer resorts. The rest is a saga of success that elevated Danny to the very peak of the entertainment profession. Soon he found himself working on a circuit which supplied entertainment for summer hotels in the Catskill Mountains. He received his big theatrical opportunity when he appeared with Gertrude Lawrence in Moss Hart's *Lady in the Dark*. His solo spot was a song called "Tschaikovsky," written by Ira Gershwin. After years of persevering struggle, Danny triumphed in various media of entertainment—stage, screen, cabaret, radio, and television, winning for himself the appreciation and admiration of kings and commoners at home and abroad, and a permanent place in show business's gallery of the great.[4]

George Gershwin's Birthplace

On Thursday morning, September 26, 1963, a bronze plaque was unveiled marking the two-story house at 242 Snediker Avenue, East New York, where George Gershwin, the famous composer of such works as *Rhapsody in Blue, Concerto in F,* and *Porgy and Bess,* was born on September 26, 1898.[5] He died on July 11, 1937. The plaque was presented by the American Society of Composers, Authors, and Publishers, of which Mr. Gershwin was a member.

George Gershwin lived in East New York for only a few years before the family returned to Manhattan. The house between Sutter and Belmont avenues was surrounded by trees when the Gershwins lived there. Ira, the older brother and well known lyricist, recalled in an interview with John S. Wilson, published in *The New York Times* (September 23, 1963), eating grapes from a vine that grew in the fenced yard surrounding the house. He played in an open field on the Sutter Avenue side. The house had a front room, a dining room, a kitchen, and possibly a maid's room on the ground floor. Upstairs there were three or four bedrooms, one of which was rented for $3 a week. The rent for this spacious house was $14 a month, and George's father was then earning $35 a week as a skilled designer of uppers for women's shoes, an income that enabled Mrs. Gershwin to employ a maid.

The appearance of the house has changed since those days. In 1914 it was bought by Harry Bilowitz, who turned it into a two-family house. Six years ago it was sold to Pedro and Maria Vargas, who now live there.

George Gershwin, at his premature death at the age of thirty-eight, "had not only changed the pattern of popular music in America, but had also quickened the pulse of music throughout the western world. He had given music a new racy speed, and for the first time in history, an American accent."

Other Entertainers and Radio Commentators

In *Earl Wilson's New York* we read about Phil Silvers who showed Wilson some of the Brooklyn neighborhoods.[6]

"You should see Brooklyn—with a Brooklynite, if you can arrange it. Better yet, with a Brooklynite who's gone from there and missed it," states Wilson.

"I remember riding past Tapscott Street in Brownsville; there were two elevated lines overhead. 'This is the high-class part of Brownsville,' he said."

"Jerry Lewis," Phil said, "was born right here—right here—but brought up in Newark. We realized at an early age," he said laughing, "that Jerry didn't belong in Brooklyn."

Sol Hurok

"Sol Hurok Presents" has become a byword in the cultural life of the country.[7] The most noted musicians, dancers, and dramatic companies have appeared under the management of this famous impressario. Sol Hurok was born in Pogar, Russia on April 9, 1890, and came to the United States in 1905. His start as manager of music artists could be dated from about 1911, while he lived in Brownsville and booked concerts for labor groups. He was for a number of years manager of the Brownsville Labor Lyceum and active in the Socialist Movement. In his *Memoirs* he devotes a section to "Bohemia in Brownsville."

> *"Brownsville in those days was a steaming microcosm of culture in the heart of Brooklyn, alive with intellectual striving and artistic hungers. It was no garden spot to the eye, but it was a lush garden for the mind. In South America, Cuba, Mexico, in the capitals of Europe, I have met musicians,*

*artists, and writers who first budded in Brownsville. . . .
Mark Warnow, the successful band leader, has since re-
minded me of violin concerts he played for me at the Sunday
School of the Labor Lyceum at 219 Sackman Street.*

*"There was never any lack of audience for speakers, for
concerts, and I was kept busy supplying the artists and organizing the events. Elsewhere in New York in those days
music was not big business. But music thrived in Brownsville. So, having tried my managerial wings on our local
talent, and what smaller artists the Wolfson Musical Bureau
could furnish—my first contact in the business—I began to
have bigger ideas."*

In 1911 Hurok arranged to have Zimbalist play at the Brownsville's New Palm Garden for the benefit of the Socialist Party. The
concert was a sensational success. Brownsville was enriched by a
great musical event, and the Socialist Party by a tidy sum for its
treasury.

For a Russian immigrant who arrived in Philadelphia in 1905,
peddling needles and hardware in his youth, Hurok has come a
long way. On November 17, 1965, Mayor Robert Wagner of New
York presented him with the City's scroll of honor for being the
"outstanding impressario of the Twentieth Century."

Joe Papp, Park Impressario

More than 2,000,000 people in New York have seen Shakespeare
productions free during the last decade due to the efforts of Joe
Papp, producer and founder of the Shakespeare Festival Summer
Theatre.[8]

Joseph Papirofsky was born in 1921 in the Williamsburg section,
where he attended Public School 141 and Junior High School 147.
When Papp was fourteen, his family moved to Brownsville. "I
remember I used to go out to . . . coal for the stove, and I got
chased by railroad detectives. They were horrible.

"My father was a trunkmaker," he says, "so you see why we
didn't make out.

"He still lives in Brownsville and goes to the same synagogue except now all the windows are smashed and they barely have enough for a *minyan*—a prayer quorum."

Papp lived "a very generally hard kind of existence." When the war broke out, he joined the Navy, where he served on a baby flattop in both the Atlantic and the Pacific. After the war he studied acting in California, worked for the Columbia Broadcasting Company. And so on to Shakespeare.

In writing recently (July 12, 1964) about Papp's Mobile Theatre with its fifty-eight performances of Shakespeare at thirty-nine different locations in New York City, Howard Taubman characterized Papp as a "man with a mission" who "cultivates a public with a Mobile Dream." Papp's great contribution has been to bring classic plays and players to audiences that have seldom, if ever, encountered the living theatre.

Other Artists

One of the first radio commentators was Gabriel Heater, whose family were among the first settlers in Brownsville. He married the daughter of Dr. M. Hermalin, a well known Yiddish writer and resident of Brownsville.

Martin Weldon (d. 1966) was director of news and public affairs for radio station WCBS. Prior to that position, he was vice-president and news director of WNEW radio and its parent company, Metromedia, Inc. Under his direction, Metromedia won a Peabody Award and other honors. In his youth, like Gabriel Heater many years before him, he participated in a number of the amateur dramatic performances which were presented at the Hebrew Education Society.

Himan "H.L." Brown, well known movie and television producer, also grew up in Brownsville.[9]

Danny Kaye and many other famous celebrities in the television and entertainment field have been clients of Ted Ashley, a son of Brownsville, now in his early forties. He is one of the leading agents wielding a tremendous influence in the entertainment industry.[10] From an office boy he catapulted in nine years to the presidency of his agency, the Ashley Famous Agency, one of the giants in the business.

Members of a well-known Brownsville family, Miss Fannie E. Holtzmann, together with her brother, the late David M. Holtzmann in the law firm of Holtzmann and Holtzmann, specialized in theatre and literary law. Their clients have included Gertrude Lawrence, Noel Coward, Fred Astaire, Ina Claire, Anton Dolin, Alicia Markowa, to cite a few. Mr. Holtzmann was founder and treasurer of the Shaw Society of America, and had been a friend and occasional counsel of George Bernard Shaw.

In the Field of Medicine

Among the most respected professions, especially among Jews, is the practice of medicine. Traditionally the physician was not only among the most cultured of the community, but he usually played a leading role in its welfare. From the very beginning of the establishment of Brownsville, doctors participated actively in the life of the community. Gerald Green, whose father was a doctor in Brownsville for forty years, has depicted in great detail in his novel, *The Last Angry Man* the life of a Brownsville doctor. For forty years the doctor lived in the neighborhood, treated all people as equals, invested them with dignity that all too often was not appreciated, grew angry at all injustice, carried on his profession as a general practitioner, believed in medical ethics, and lived up to his beliefs.

One of the first physicians to settle in Brownsville was Dr. Michael Cohn, a well-known leader in the anarchist movement, but at the same time concerned with the various philanthropic efforts of the community.

Dr. Simon Frucht, a heart specialist, took an active part in the founding and maintaining of a branch of the Thomas Davidson Society in Brownsville.

A very unusual personality was Dr. Morris Robinson (1880-1962), who practiced medicine here for a half century and was beloved by the community as a Jewish scholar and a great lover of man.[11] After studying in the various Yeshivahs of Lithuania, and receiving ordination as Rabbi, he immigrated to America in 1901. He continued to study rabbinics as one of the first six students of the Yeshivah R'Isaac Elchanan on Henry Street. He decided, however, to take up medicine as a career, and to eke out a living he taught in the Stone Avenue Talmud Torah and elsewhere. When he was graduated from Long Island Medical College in 1912, he opened an office in Brownsville, where he practiced until his death in 1962. All classes of people came to his office, to consult him not only on medical questions, but also on personal problems and Jewish law. He was a great lover of Jewish books and of Zion. He worked on behalf of the American Jewish Congress, the Hagana in Israel, led groups in Talmud, lectured on various rabbinic subjects, and published articles in Hebrew, Yiddish, and English.

Many other physicians, including Doctors J. Krimsky, H. D. Rosenberg, M. Canick, David Applebaum, and Jacob Pearlstein were active in the Zionist and other Jewish causes.

Many of the sons of the early settlers became prominent as physicians, some practicing in Brooklyn, others elsewhere. Abraham Jacob Rongy, who came to the United States from Russia with his parents in 1893, lived here for a time. Distinguished as an obstetrician and gynecologist, and author of a number of works in the medical field, he served as vice-president of the American Jewish Congress 1925-1926, and was chairman of the National Council of the Zionist Organization of America.

Dr. Abraham Koplowitz also became an obstetrician and gynecologist, and served as president of the Kings County Medical Society. Other Brownsville natives who served as presidents of the Kings County Medical Society and the Brooklyn Academy of Medicine include William Linder (1932), Dr. Morris J. Dattlebaum (1941), Leo Schwartz (1944) and Dr. David Kershner (1958-1959), consulting surgeon at Beth El Hospital and formerly director of surgical services at the Jewish Chronic Disease Hospital.

Dr. Israel S. Wechsler (May 26, 1886—December, 1962), one of the most famous neurologists of his time, professor, and author, president of the International Congress of Neurologists, and president of American Friends of the Hebrew University, came to Brownsville with his parents when they arrived in this country from Rumania in 1902.[12] They later moved to the East Side of Manhattan.

Another important neurologist and psychiatrist who belonged to an old Jewish family in Brownsville was Dr. Irving J. Sands (March 27, 1891—October 21, 1958). He served on the faculty of the College of Physicians and Surgeons of Columbia University as Associate Clinical Professor of Neurology from 1919 until his retirement in 1956, and also rose to the office of president of the New York Neurological Society.

Dr. Lena Levine (1904-1965) was a highly esteemed psychiatrist, gynecologist, author, lecturer, and marriage counselor. She was a pioneer in the Planned Parenthood Movement, and served as associate director of the Margaret Sanger Research Bureau of New York. She taught in the New York School for Social Research, was the author or co-author of several books and numerous articles on marriage and sex problems.

Among other psychiatrists and neurologists who came from Brownsville are Doctors Harold E. Berson, Abraham Rabiner, Milton Malev, Peter Glauber, and Eli Gerchick.

The number of physicians who came from Brownsville was legion. Among other names called to our attention are Doctors Morris Ant, Benjamin Ashe, Hyman Berkman, Edward and Herman Bronstein, Mortimer Burdman, J. L. Bernstein, Meier Brodman, Jacob Beilly, Meyer Berger, Bernard Blinn, Matthew Brunner, Joseph Cohen, Lester Cohen, L. Canick, Samuel Cohen, William S. Collens, Jay M. Cornell, George B. Doroff, David Farber, Leo Faske, Bob Feldman, Reuben Finkelstein, Hyman Feinerman, Aaron Feinstein, Albert J. Globus, Milton Goldfein, Morris Geshwind, Milton Gitlin, Harold G. Grayzel, Herman Greenbaum, Bernard Greenberg, Martin H. Greenfield, Nathan Ratnoff, Benjamin Koven, Morris Koven, Hyman W. Karp, E. M. Katz, Hyman Krakauer, William Levine, Jay Lambert, Isaac Lorberblatt, William Mandelbaum, Jack Meltzer, Abraham I. Pickar, Henry and Max Pilzer, Henry Plotkin, Harris M. Rabinowitz, Louis Radin, Morris Rivkin, George Richmond, N. Reibstein, Ed Saltzman, Abraham M. Sands, Sol L. Shandalow, A. V. Shapiro, Bernard Seidenberg, Meyer Sklar, Monroe Schneider, W. Starr, H. I. Teperson, Bernard Tillis, Herbert Volk, Herbert Wolfson, Benjamin Purow, and Charles Windwer.

A number of the Brownsville boys went into the profession of dentistry, including Doctors Henry Adelson, Nathan J. Coyne, Simon Shapiro, Myron Wisoff, Carl Bier, Nathan Borkow, Abraham Eisen, H. Feinerman, Benjamin Perlow, M. Nelkin, Howard Hoffman, A. and G. Lieberman, and L. Weinman.

In 1912 the Kings County Dental Society was organized as a result of a merger of the Brooklyn Odontological Society of Brownsville and the Eastern District Dental Society. Over the years the society had chapters in Brownsville and in East New York. In 1917, the society sponsored the first school clinic at Public School 109 and donated a monthly contribution towards its maintenance. Dr. Simon Shapiro, who was among the founders of the Kings County Dental Society, was its second president.

The Legal Profession

In our review of the political life in the community we had occasion to refer to the large number of Brownsville and East New York men who have held public office. Some, like Abe Stark, Brooklyn Borough President, State Supreme Justice Samuel S. Liebowitz, Judge Henry Epstein, Abraham Shiplacoff, Socialist Leader, Jacob L. Holtzmann, member of the State Board of Regents, Aaron Koota, District Attorney of Kings County, Federal Judge Leo Rayfiel, Moses M. Weinstein, Majority Leader of New York State Assembly, Judge Gustave Rosenberg, formerly Chairman of the Board of Higher Education, and Henry E. Schultz, honorary chairman of the Anti Defamation League and a member of the Board of Higher Education, City of New York, have attained more than local fame.

Among the large number who have entered the legal profession, (many of whom have held various positions of responsibility) are Isaac Allen, Judge Joseph Allen of Baltimore, Nat

Azarow, Isadore Beerman, Oscar Bernstein, Sol Block, Louis M.
Brass, Abraham H. Brodsky, Herman E. Cooper, Benjamin Dia-
mond, Bess Dick, Arthur, Charles, and John Dunaif, Jerome
Edelman, Jay Emanuel, H. Broadman Epstein, Alexander Falk,
Abraham Feit, Charles H. Fier, Herman and Maurice Finkel-
stein, Julius P. Fischler, Harold L. Fisher, Martha Gibbell, Ben-
jamin Geduldig, Milton J. Goell, Nathan L. Goldstein, Samuel
Greenberg, Harry and Samuel Halperin, Milton Hertz, Fannie,
David, and Jacob L. Holtzmann, Samuel S. Hyams, Charles Jo-
seph, Alexander Kopp, George Kossoy, William Kramer, Philip
Krimko, Simon H. Kugel, Morgan Lane, Jacob Livingston, Irving
Ostrow, Harry Pinesick, Bernard and Louis H. Pink, Benton and
George S. Rader, Jerome Reiss, Albert A. Sarafan, Oscar Schach-
ter, David Schatzow, George and James Schenker, Benjamin
Schor, Noah Seedman, Howard Shankin, Isaac Siegmeister, Mar-
shall Snyder, Harry P. Solomon, Herman Soloway, Bernard R.
Stave, Martin Stone, Isaac Strahl, Charles Stuback, Samuel A.
Telsey, George Tonkonogy, Louis and David Wallach, S. Bertha
Warters, Frank Wasserman, Morris Willner, Gerson C. Young,
and Paul Zuber.

Among those who have been associated with Federal Government Agencies are: Murray Stein, water pollution enforcement director of the Department of Health, Education and
Welfare; [13] Herman Wolkinson in the Federal Judiciary Department and Joseph L. Weiner, formerly director of Civilian Supply
War Production Board, and special counsel and director of public
utilities division, Securities and Exchange Commission.

Social Welfare

Some of Brownsville's youth entered the social service profession. Dr. Philip R. Goldstein, whose family settled early in
Brownsville, recently retired after forty years of association with
the National Jewish Welfare Board. He published an autobiography entitled *Centers in My Life.* From it we learn that Moses A.
Leavitt (August 6, 1894—June 21, 1963) , was one of the members
of the Strivers Club, which met at the Hebrew Educational Society

at the beginning of the century. Dr. Goldstein was for a time the leader of the society. Leavitt became one of America's most distinguished social workers, and one of the most creative public servants of American Jewry. He entered social work with the United Hebrew Charities in 1923, and in 1929 joined the Joint Distribution Committee (J.D.C.), becoming its executive vice-chairman in 1947. During the most turbulent period in recent Jewish history, when the Nazis oppressed and exterminated millions of our people, Mr. Leavitt gave dedicated and indefatigable leadership in the vast rescue and migration programs. As administrative head of the J.D.C. he supervised the expenditure of more than $550,-000,000 to the Jews of Europe, North Africa, the Near East, and Israel. He served on numerous government and private organizations concerned with social welfare.

The late William Posner, assistant director of Jewish Community Services of Long Island, one of the outstanding social workers in this country, and whose scholarly papers had a profound influence on Jewish social work, also spent his youth in this community, and was associated with the Young Israel of Brownsville.

Among others who have made their careers in social service and group work are Dr. Solomon Green, associate professor of group work in the Yeshivah School of Social Work, and Leonard Blocksberg, professor of group work at Boston University. Hyman H. Bookbinder, formerly assistant director of Office of Economic Opportunity is now director of the Washington office of the American Jewish Congress. Julius Nierow, father of Peter Nero, well-known pianist, is associated with the New York City Youth Board. Dr. Morris Goldman is a specialist in public health. Max C. Gettinger is Executive Director of the Atlanta Jewish Social Service Federation. A number have served as executive directors of Jewish Community Centers and Young Men's Hebrew Associations; Harry Lebau in Jersey City, Herman Jacobs in New York and Detroit, Dr. A. Auerbach in Pittsburgh, Leo Okin in Seattle, and his brother Jerry in Patterson, New Jersey. Carl Lampner is now at Har Zion Temple in Philadelphia and Al Mintz is Executive Director of the Brockton Young Men's Hebrew

Association. Joseph Cohen was former Executive Director of United Synagogue Youth. Among others are Reuben Bennett, former Executive Director of the Brownsville Boys Club and now in California, Brothman of the Newark "Y," and Sol Kutner, Assistant Director of the Wilmington Jewish Community Center. Irving Brickman, Stanley Foodim, Irving Ladin, and Eli S. Levy, graduates of schools of social work, are serving Jewish Social Service Agencies. George Wolk is Regional Director of B'nai B'rith, Pittsburgh.

The Teaching Profession

Many Brownsville youth have entered the teaching profession, especially since the 1930's. They are to be found in large numbers among the teachers in New York and in the suburban elementary schools, high schools, and local colleges as teachers, assistant principals, principals, and professors. Many are to be found on the faculties of various universities in the country. Among the first of the Brownsville boys to establish a distinguished career in the Board of Education of New York City was Dr. Samuel Streicher. He attended the Stone Avenue Talmud Torah, and was one of the first students to attend the Hebrew High School established by the Bureau of Jewish Education. He entered the school system and rose to the office of principal of Seward Park High School; and on February 23, 1944, was elected by the Board of Education as a member of the Board of Examiners. J. Greene is also a member of the Board of Examiners. Dr. Jacob Bernstein, principal of the East Midwood High School, Joseph Shapiro, principal Samuel J. Tilden High School and Carl Cherkis, principal, Canarsie High School, also came from this neighborhood. Likewise, Gustave G. Rosenberg, for many years chairman of the Board of Higher Education; Jacob Jackowitz, school-editor of *The Evening Mail, The Sun, The New York Globe,* and *The World Telegram* School Page; Charles Cogen, formerly chairman of social studies at Bay Ridge High School, and now president of the American Federation of Teachers; Miss Ida Klaus, director of personnel of the Board of Education, Jacob Landers, assistant superintendent of schools in New York, in charge of coordinating the board's integration activities, and formerly coordinator of the Higher Education Horizons Program, a project to increase the educational and cultural opportunities of students from low income and minority areas, lived here in their youth. Jacob Zack is another assistant superintendent. Dr. David D. Denker, President of New York Medical College, Flower and Fifth Avenue Hospitals, was brought up in Brownsville. A former newspaperman turned social scientist, he was associated with Rutgers University 1952-1967 as assistant to the president and professor of social science. He helped develop a medical school in that university.

Among other professors in universities and colleges we may mention Meyer Schapiro, Professor of the arts at Columbia University, Milton J. Rosen, Professor of chemistry at Brooklyn College, and Solomon Simonson, head of the Department of Logic and Mass Media at Yeshivah University. Dr. Maxwell Karshan was Professor of biological chemistry, College of Physicians and Surgeons, Columbia University. Dr. Aaron J. Teller is Dean of the School of Engineering and Science at Cooper Union; Dr. Abraham Tanenbaum is Professor of Education at Columbia University; Dr. Wallace Schoenberg is Dean of Admissions, York College. Dr. Selma (Ginsberg) Wasserman is Professor of Education and Dr. Harvey Gerber is Professor of Mathematics in Simon Fraser University in Vancouver. Dr. Louis Landweber is Professor at the University of Indiana. Dr. Maurice Korman is Chairman of the Division of Psychiatry of Texas South Western Medical School. Dr. Louis Weinberg is Professor of Electrical Engineering at City University, New York. Dr. Samuel Konefsky is Professor of social sciences in Brooklyn College. Dr. B. Eisenstadt is associated with the history department of Brooklyn College, and Donald Kagan with that of Cornell University. Harold Nirnberg is Dean of Long Island University.

Businessmen and Philanthropists

A list of those who had their start in Brownsville and have succeeded in the business world would fill many pages. It should be noted that many of them became equally distinguished as philanthropists who have devoted much of their time and effort for worthy causes.

Let us briefly mention a few of these leaders. In 1906 Samuel Rubel was a coal and ice peddler in Brownsville, and later became the owner of the Rubel Ice Company and the Ebling Brewery. The Lazrus family, who control the Benrus Watch Company, were brought up in Brownsville and East New York. Benjamin Lazrus (b. 1894), founder and retired president of the Benrus Watch Company, is well-known as a philanthropist. He served in 1948 as campaign chairman of the Federation of Jewish Philanthropies of New York. He is vice-president of Temple Emanuel of New York, and has been active in many religious, philanthropic and educational endeavors. His brother, Oscar, has been a tower of strength in the Union of American Hebrew Congregations.

Frank Cohen, a graduate of Public School 149 of East New York, became an important industrialist. He was president of the American Steel Corporation of Cuba, and the American Caramel Company, and Chairman of the Board of Empire Ordnance Corporation, and affiliated groups. He took an active interest in Jewish education, was connected with the Bureau of Jewish Education, and served as vice-president (1915-1920) of the American Association for Jewish Education. His wife, Ethel Silberman Cohen, has continued through the ESCO Foundation to further Jewish Cultural interests in this country and in Israel.

David Shapiro, of the Shapiro and Aronson Lighting Fixtures Company, became publisher of *The Day*, which was later taken over by Morris Weinberg, another Brownsville builder. In January, 1964, Mr. Weinberg observed his eighty-eighth birthday and his sixty-third wedding anniversary. On February 28 of the same year he noted his fiftieth anniversary with *The Day Jewish Morning Journal*, the Yiddish daily. President Lyndon Johnson, as well as many leaders in all walks of life, took cognizance of this triple celebration. For Morris Weinberg, the Yiddish language and Yiddish literature are integral parts of the whole framework of Jewish life, and he has devoted a lifetime to their advancement.

Jacob H. Cohen, who died on July 6, 1964, at the age of ninety-two, was founder and president of the Forest Box and Lumber Company, Long Island City, from 1905 until his death. Born in Odessa, Russia, he came to the United States in 1900. Over the years Mr. Cohen contributed to a large number of Jewish religious, educational, charitable, health, and other organizations. He was an honorary vice-president of the Jewish Education Committee of New York; honorary president of the Pride of Judaea Children's Services, of which he was president for twenty-five years; honorary president of Temple Sinai on Arlington Avenue, of which he was president for twelve years, and of the Herzeliah Hebrew Teachers Institute of New York.

On July 1, 1964, Vincent Tracy interviewed Irving Goldman, who related how he was raised in poverty in Brownsville, and how through the assistance of J. J. Shubert, who loaned him $5,000, he started what has since grown into the largest scenic supply house. Mr. Goldman also became interested in other enterprises, including the construction of the International Plaza in the World's Fair.

Moses Ginsberg was a great builder. Samuel Rothenberg took an active interest in the construction of the Brooklyn Jewish Center, of which he was president, and in Jewish education. He had his factory in Brownsville. Isaac Albert, who was associated with his brothers in I. Albert Company Chandeliers, was not only a successful businessman, but also, for twenty years, headed that great institution, the Hospital for Jewish Chronic Diseases.

Dr. Moses Spatt, dentist, real estate dealer, president of the Brooklyn Jewish Hospital, and for many years president of the Brooklyn Jewish Center, spent his youth in Brownsville, where his parents were among the earliest settlers.

Samuel Sennett (1901-1964), was president of the Howard Stores Corporation, a men's clothing chain, from 1947 to 1957. He began as a clerk with the company at the age of eighteen and worked his way up. In 1960 he became president of Royal Palm Clothes, and was earlier a vice-president of the Hat Corporation of America. He was a former chairman of the executive board of the Brooklyn Hebrew Home and Hospital for the Aged, and participated in numerous philanthropies.

One of the first families to settle in Brownsville was the Telsey family. Their son, Samuel A. Telsey (1881-1960) was among the first Brownsville boys to be graduated from Columbia College (1903) and from Columbia Law School (1905). He organized the Brownsville Savings Bank, and was its president until it merged with the East New York Savings Bank. He was also president of the American Title and Guarantee Company, and Board Chairman of the Marshall Mortgage Corporation. In 1933 he became a vice-president of the Hebrew Immigrant Aid Society (H.I.A.S.), and in 1947 became its president. During the 1930's and 1940's, when the Hebrew Immigrant Aid Society was a vital factor in the escape of many Jews from Nazi persecution, Mr. Telsey was a leader in the organization and in the direction of its European headquarters in Paris. Since his early childhood, he and his sisters were associated with the Hebrew Educational Society, of which he was for a time the president. He also served as a director of the Brooklyn Jewish Center and the Beth El Hospital.

William B. Roth was associated with the State Bank. Dr. Samuel Silverman was president of the Food Dealers Bank. Jacob Leichtman is the founder and president of one of the large banks in the city, the Bank of North America. Harry Strongin has headed the Consolidated Mutual Insurance Company, and Nat Bass, a member of the Board of the Bank of North America and president of American Press Board, has held a number of communal positions.

The Brandts and the Frisches have owned many motion picture houses in the city. Emanuel Frisch, of the Randforce Amusement Corporation, has participated in a wide variety of philanthropic activities, and is now president of the East New York Young Men's Hebrew Association. Max Abrams was associated with the Esquire Shoe Polish Company; David Teitelbaum with the United States Stationery Company, and the Holland family with the Holland Farms and other milk concerns, and the Simon Holland and Son Steel Construction. M. Rubin is president of the Levy Bakeries.

Other Professions

Many Brownsville and East New York youth achieved in other professions. Shelley Winters and Dorothy Tree became known as actresses. Manfred Schwartz has his paintings on exhibit in major private and public collections. Keila achieved a reputation as a sculptor. Temima Gazari has distinguished herself in teaching Jewish art, and for the exhibition of her works. Simon Friedman has pursued a career as a commercial artist, and Theodore Soontup as an architect.

Jacob Robinson and Harry Wiles are known for their inventions. Morton Hamermesh is a nuclear scientist in the Argonne Laboratory in Chicago. Admiral Arthur R. Gralla is with the Joint Chiefs of Staff.

Selma Kaye, singer, performed with a number of opera companies. Murray Garber, Chaskell Ritter, D. Mann, and the late Schicoffs, both father and son, served as cantors. Max Weinstein, Henrietta Miller Berliner, Samuel Charry, Pearl Greenwald, Edward Novick, R. Nazer, are among many who have taught music in the New York public school system. Toscha Seidel, Kalman Fleisig, Ben Richman, cellist, Sidney Saltzman, clarinetist, have performed with symphony orchestras.

Eli Lazarus and Rosenblum are inspectors in the New York Police Department. Benjamin Lorber is widely known in the field of international insurance, and served for many years as an executive of International Universal Pictures, Music Corporation of America, Decca Records, as their Director of Insurance. Many have become accountants. Jacob Sobelsohn, founder of the Sobelsohn School of Accounting, has won the respect of an entire generation of those entering and practicing in the accounting profession. Sol Weiner was president of the Northwestern Chapter of the Pennsylvania Institute of Certified Public Accountants. Seymour Scheer, formerly with the New York State Banking Department, is executive vice-president of Bank Leuhmi.

George Brazilier, T. Delacorts, head of Dell Pub. Co., and David Winston entered the publishing field

SPORTS

The native-born youth of Brownsville took a keen interest in all forms of sport, both as participants and spectators. Some distinguished themselves, and entered professional ranks.[14]

Sid Gordon and Baseball

While the baseball fever has always run high in this community, there have been few players to reach the majors and become stars. One of the famous American athletes of our time, Sid Gordon (born August 13, 1918), did not begin to play baseball until he became a student at Samuel Tilden High School. He lived on East Ninety-fifth Street in the East Flatbush Section adjoining Brownsville. He took part in games in the Parade Grounds in Brooklyn and in the Betsy Head Park.

His rise in baseball came after a long and hard struggle. Between 1942-1949 he played with the New York Giants (1941-1943, 1946-1949). He became so popular with New York fans that in 1948 his hometown admirers gave him a "Day" at Ebbets Field. He played with Boston (1950-1952), with the Milwaukee Braves in 1953, and with Pittsburgh in 1954-1955. Gordon achieved many honors during his career. He hit 202 home runs, and was one of the few men in the history of the game to hit 2 home runs in one inning.[15]

Al McCoy (Al Rudolph) —World Middleweight Boxing Champion (1914-1917)

For a time Coney Island was the fistic capital of the world. Later a number of neighborhood fight clubs entered this field. A number of boxers and prize fighters lived in this area. An Irish name was associated with a fighting nature, therefore some Jews took advantage of it. Al McCoy was a pseudonym for Al Rudolph (born October 23, 1894).[16] He launched his professional ring career in 1908 and became a popular club fighter in Brownsville, where his father operated a kosher butcher store. He was the first southpaw to win a world championship. He wore his crown from 1914 until November 14, 1917, when he was stopped by Mike O'Dowd in Brooklyn in six rounds. He retired on July, 1919, after being knocked out in three rounds by O'Dowd in a title return bout in St. Paul, Minnesota.

David Marcus, an inter-collegiate welterweight champion in
1923, began to box as a lightweight at the United States Military
Academy in 1920, when the sport was introduced at West Point.
He fought as a professional under the name of Danny Mars, and
taught boxing in Hawaii in the United States Army. Sam Mosberg,
another Brownsvillite, was gold-medal winner in the lightweight
boxing class at the 1920 Antwerp Olympics.

The Eastern Parkway Arena was a popular spot for boxing and
prize fight fans. Among those who participated were Ruby Goldstein, Dan Rosenberg, Joe Blick, the Silvers Brothers, Al Davis,
and Lew Feldman.

Basketball Stars

Brownsville and East New York delivered a host of basketball
stars into colleges and professional ranks. Ben Gould, the sports
writer, a Brownsvillite himself, in writing on the development of
basketball as a sport in Brooklyn, points out that "these sharp-
shooters did not develop overnight." [17] A systematic program in
public schools, high schools, and community centers, produced
these stars. The gymnasium of the Hebrew Educational Society
was the training ground for many of the local players. The roster
of the Society's players includes such names as George Newblatt,
Jules Bender, Max Posnack, Allie Schuckman, Moe Goldman,
Boris Nahamkin, "Red" Holtzman, now coach of the New York
Knickerbockers, Norman Drucker, George Slott, Jack Krugman,
Al Zuckoff, Aaron Salzman, Harry Feingold, Sid Katz, Venty
Leibowitz, Sam Schoenfeld, Rip Kaplinsky, Irving Torgoff, and
Ben Puro, among others.

In community center competitions, Public School 84 won top
borough honors (1910-1914). Public School 150 also became a
consistent winner. In 1926 Brooklyn enjoyed an unprecedented
record of successes when Barney Ain, coach of Community
Centers, piloted five straight winners in Junior and Senior play of
the League of Neighborhood School Centers to give Brooklyn top
rating. The best all-around teams of this or later periods came from
Brownsville: the Oaklands of Community Center 66; the Dux

Club of Community Center 184; and the Wallace Club of Community Center 183.

When some of these boys entered Thomas Jefferson High, Bushwick High, or Alexander Hamilton High, they contributed their strength to its teams. Thomas Jefferson had great coaches in John McNulty, Mac Hodesblatt, Sam Schoenfeld. John McNulty had an unusual team in Mac Posnack, Charley Rabinowitz, Gus Glotzer, Phil Marenberg, Jo Zausner, Allie Schuckman, and Slim Steinhouse. They turned in spectacular performances in gaining the city's final round in the first Public School Athletic League season, only to lose to Manhattan's Clinton High Five, led by George Gregory.

The Saint John's Wonder Five of 1927-1928, 1929, and 1930 was one of the greatest college teams, winning sixty-four out of sixty-eight games. In 1932 the same group won the championship of the American Professional League, where they played under the name of the Brooklyn Jewels. Two of them, Mac Posnack and Allie Schuckman came from Brownsville, played in the Hebrew Educational Society, and graduated from Thomas Jefferson High School. The other members of the team were Mac Kinsbrunner, Rip Gerson, and Matty Razonia. Their amazing playing toppled the stiffest opponents with incredible ease. Thousands now turned out to see the games, and the Saint John's gym proved too small; even the larger hundred and sixth Regiment Armory proved inadequate. At the suggestion of Ned Irish, the Madison Square Garden officials were convinced that the teams were ready to play in that arena, and on December 29, 1934, the Saint Johns played there against Westminster College. In the following years George Slott, Rip Kaplinsky and Hy Gotkin, graduates of Thomas Jefferson and known as "the Gold Dust Twins," played for the Saint John's team.

A most spectacular player was Harry Boykoff, one of the tallest men in basketball in his time, six-feet, nine and a half inches. Under the training of Coach Mac Hodesblatt of Thomas Jefferson High School, and Joe Lapchick of Saint John's, Harry became one of the ablest of the college stars.[18] He was selected twice for the Annual All Star Game in Chicago, in 1943 and in 1946. After one of Harry Boykoff's best nights (February 3, 1943), when the Redmen of Saint John's defeated Saint Joseph's, the *New York Times* reporter wrote, "In all the nine and a fraction years that college basketball has been played in Madison Square Garden, there never was a more spectacular performance than the one Harry Boykoff gave last night."

Another great day in Boykoff's spectacular career came in January, 1947, in Madison Square Garden when Saint John's overwhelmed Saint Francis by 71-52, with Harry Boykoff scoring 54 points. It was the "greatest one man basketball act ever presented on the Madison Square Garden floor," wrote a *Times* man. With Boykoff in that year of great college basketball was little Hy Gotkin, also a graduate of Thomas Jefferson High School.

The best team of the 1935-1936 season was the Long Island University Blackbirds, under the masterful coaching of Clair Bee. In 1939 and 1941, Long Island University won the national crown in winning forty-two out of forty-three games. A number of these players came from the Brownsville area: Jules Bender, Leo G. Merson, Irving Turgoff, and Bromberg. Jules Bender was the highest scorer in New York City, and Merson was third. When Captain Bender achieved a forty-three game victory string, Clair Bee said of him, "He was undoubtedly one of the all time greats in 'one-on-one.'"

Jules Bender (born 1919) is instructor of physical education at Boys High School. He is an all-around athlete, and has been director of the Hebrew Educational Society Physical Education Department for the past twenty-five years, where he had an opportunity to train many a basketball and handball player, and referee many close games.

Many Brownsville and East New York boys played for the tremendously successful City College Club whose famous coach, Nat Holman, developed teams over the years. In 1931 the team became famous by winning seventeen out of eighteen games. Among the Brownsville boys who played with the City College team in 1931-1934 was Moe Goldman. The team he captained in 1934 won fourteen games and lost only one. Other outstanding players who came from this area were Sam Winograd, Louis Wishnewitz, Jerry Domischeck, and Norman Drucker.

New York University also claimed a number of robust players from the Brownsville area: George Newblatt (1928-1930), Sid Tanenbaum (1947), Boris Nahamkin (1952-1954), and Milton Gross. George Newblatt, one of the boys who played in the Hebrew Educational Society, won All-American as Captain of New York University in 1930.

Boris Nahamkin, who, like his father, played in the Hebrew Educational Society gym, was a member of the New York University team in 1952-1954. He led the New York University's career scoring with a record of 1,076 points.

Sidney Harold Tanenbaum (born October 8, 1925), captained the New York University team in 1947, and was, according to Wilbur Woods, sports editor of *The New York Sun* (1947), "the finest all around basketball performer ever to don Violet livery." He was selected on the All Met first team in each of his four varsity seasons. Twice he was named winner of the Hagerty Award as the outstanding player in the Metropolitan New York Area. He received the 1947 Bar Kochba Award as America's outstanding Jewish athlete.

Brownsville and East New York also turned out many competent referees who were called to officiate at many crucial games: Nat Krinsky, James Moskowitz, Artie Musicant, Sammy Schoenfeld, Jules Bender, Lou Eisenstein, Norman Drucker, and Mickey Fisher.

Handball

With handball growing into a popular sport, the Hebrew Educational Society and the Brownsville Boys Club have become the hub of the one-wall handball play in the Metropolitan area. Mac Orenstein, Harry Goldstein, Morris Shapiro, Irving Kerzner, and Kenny Davidoff are among the most skilled players of the game. For the past several years the Hebrew Educational Society gym was the annual locale for the AAU Championships in one-wall handplay. Vic Hershkowitz, perhaps the greatest player in the history of handball, usually carried off the trophies. Steve Sandler won it in 1961, and Ken Davidoff in 1963.

WRITERS AND THEIR IMAGE OF BROWNSVILLE

Many of the Brownsville youth became writers, and distinguished themselves in all fields of literary endeavor. Among the oldest is Gabriel Heater (born September 17, 1890), editor, author, and for many years a well known radio news commentator. Miss Gertrude Tonconogy, author of "Three Cornered Moon," came from Brownsville. Her father was a highly respected lawyer. Dr. Harry Schwartz, on *The New York Times* editorial staff as a specialist on Communist Russia and China, spent his youth in this community. Norman Podhoretz, the editor of *Commentary* magazine, lived with his parents in Brownsville. In his life story, *Making It,* he tells us how he reached a high position in Manhattan's literary-intellectual establishment. Milton J. Goell, author of a number of books of poetry; Leonard Speigelgass, the playwright, a son and grandson of the first Jewish settlers of Brownsville; Murray Schizgall, the playwright; Al Capp, famous for the comic strip "Lil' Abner"; Barry Hyams, dramatic critic; Elias Ginsberg (Gilner), Charles Reznikoff, author, poet, and editor; Milt Gross, sports writer; Robert Lewis Shayon, H. Turkin, David G. Plotkin (Kin), are among others who spent their youth here.

At the turn of the century, John Paley, Yiddish writer and editor of the Jewish *Daily News* and the Jewish *Gazetten,* resided here. David M. Hermalin (born May 12, 1865, Vaslin, Rumania), Yiddish novelist and playwright, also lived in Brownsville. Jacob Katzenelson, Hebrew writer, lived here for a time.

The distinguished biographer and critic, Matthew Josephson, spent his youth in this community.[19] He is the son of the late Julius Josephson, a local banker, and a well loved personality. Matthew made Paris his "second country" and became an intimate of the original group of surrealists, authors and painters. He is known for his excellent biographies: *Zola and His Time, Jean Jacques Rousseau,* and *Victor Hugo.*

"The image of the writer turned public man," he wrote, "appealed to me powerfully in Zola, as it did also in the figures of Rousseau and Hugo of whom I wrote later."

The film play of *Zola*, by Heinz Herald, produced by Warner Brothers, was one of the best film plays of the year. With the publication of *Robber Barons* in 1934, and the *Great American Capitalists* (1861-1901), Josephson changed his focus from literary to economic history. His many writings include prose, poetry, and a number of translations from French into English.

Another famous son is Alfred Kazin, the distinguished literary critic. His works, *The Contemporaries,* a collection of a number of his critical essays, and his earlier work on American literature, entitled, *On Native Grounds, an Interpretation of Modern American Prose Literature,* are regarded among the most incisive works of literary criticism written in this century.

In 1951 Alfred Kazin published *A Walker in the City* in which he recaptures the Brownsville of his boyhood years and describes the section as he knew it in the late twenties and in the early days of the depression. He writes about his friends, school, neighbors, the life in the streets, and his family life, which centered in his mother's kitchen where dresses were made, friends were received, and Sabbath Eve (Friday evening) was observed with its special dishes, discussions, and games. Aside from its nostalgic flavor, the book is couched in an appealing lyrical prose.

Kazin does not feel completely separated from his birthplace. "Every time I go back to Brownsville it is as if I had never been away," he begins the book. "From the moment I step off the train at Rockaway Avenue an instant rage comes over me, mixed with dread and some unexpected tenderness."

"Rage, dread and tenderness, their mixed odor gives this book its wistful charm," wrote critic Lewis Gannett,[20] "but I doubt that he is yet quite clear what he owes to or what he regrets in the Brownsville where he grew up. Perhaps he is intentionally vague and elusive, flashing from one mood to another, to emphasize the complex quality of uprootedness in the lives of many young Americans, including himself."

A number of writers raised in Brownsville during the twenties and the period of the depression have tried to set down their impressions of the place. A few have done distinguished work which was well received both by the critics and the public. All share an intense and vivid sense of the place and depict passionately remembered childhoods, but few are deeply tinged by a love and a deep understanding of the locality. Their works appear as if they had been written by persons who had never struck roots here, and had revolted against the environment in which they were nurtured.

The image of Brownsville some of these writers create is usually unfavorable. They portray with photographic reality the drabness of the town, the scene of untold misery and deprivation where Murder, Inc. ran riot, without suggesting a spark of inner life to transcend it. They generally fail to suggest the other side of Brownsville, the warm mutual helpfulness of decent people, and the organized struggle for betterment that are part of the story of the neighborhood.

In this latter group is David Dortort's *Burial of the Fruit*.[21] Its central character is "Honey" Halpern, who was deprived of a father early in life and thrown upon the streets while his mother worked to support him. Thrust into a jungle atmosphere where survival is for the toughest, he grew up a sadistic, depraved killer who becomes a trigger man in a Murder, Inc.

Irving Shulman's *Amboy Dukes* depicts the experiences of one of a number of gang groups which infested the neighborhood.[22] Isidore Rosen's *Will of Iron* is a character study of a Jewish matriarch living with her family in Brownsville's slum during the depression years.[23] While the picture of Jewish family life is interesting, and in spots is told with taste, the people in it seem to have no other idea than to make a little more money and to live prosperously. John Connors, reviewing the novel in *The Saturday Review of Literature* states, "The dreamers who peopled Zangwill's stories are singularly absent."

The Hebrew novel by Haim Abramowitz entitled *By Bread Alone* (*Al Halehem Levado*) is not much different. The title derives from the Biblical dictum, "Man does not live by bread alone," and its characters are hedonists concerned with the problem of bread, how to live better. Morris Bernstein, the ne'er-do-well father, hardly ekes out a living in his small fruit store. His wife, Rose, a former beauty with a shadowy past, is concerned to have her daughter, who is continually dressing herself, marry well. The son Irving, a student whom the parents are anxious that he become a dentist or lawyer, is busy with his studies and Communism. Thus, the life of a Jewish family in Brownsville, pointing up the differences between the two generations, comes alive in this novel.

Leon Kobrin, the Yiddish novelist and playwright who has depicted the crowded tenement life in the early twentieth century New York, takes Brownsville as the locale for a number of his stories and treats it understandingly. *Ore der Bord* is a novel which describes the rise and fall of a poor and pious Jew during the real-estate boom in Brownsville in 1903, and throws light on the psyche of the Jewish immigrant.[24]

Benjamin Rosenblatt, who recently died at the age of eighty-five, a former teacher in the Eron Preparatory Schools, has also depicted life in Brownsville in many of his stories. Also written feelingly about various aspects of life in Brownsville is a volume of Yiddish poetry by David Seltzer, entitled *Bronzviler Gegang* (Brownsville Song).[25]

A number of articles published in *Commentary* by writers born here are concerned with Brownsville. Among them is Samuel Tenenbaum's very interesting "Brownsville's Age of Learning" in which he sets down his memories of Brownsville.[26] William Poster in *Commentary*, and Felix Morrow in *The Menorah Journal* also have described the town as they saw it.

A commanding work of fiction about Jewish immigrant life is *Call It Sleep*, by Henry Roth.[27] When it appeared in 1934 it was hailed as the most talented novel written by an American-Jewish writer. It was recently reissued in paperback. The events in *Call It Sleep* cover a period of two years and are funneled through the mind of a sensitive boy, David Schearl, who is six years old at the start of the book. The novel, a mixture of story, realism, and ecstatic phantasmagoria, depicts with great detail the world of Brownsville and the Lower East Side in the 1930's.

In *The Time of the Peaches*, Arthur Granit, a writer and teacher who was brought up in Brownsville, has also produced a surging novel about the world of poor Jews living in Brownsville

during the depression years.²⁸ He depicts realistically the community imprisoned in its poverty, isolation, and hysteria, but he
tells it with a tender yet humorous touch. To quote one of the
perceptive reviewers of this book, Theodore Solatorof, "He makes
a kind of poetry out of Jewish poverty, without falsifying his
subject, the pathology."

In Kazin's *A Walker in the City*, the ghetto is made to open out
in all directions, so that the walker may escape from the confine-
ments of his Jewish culture into the world beyond Brownsville.
Granit limits the action to the one block in which his whole gallery of characters lives. The block is not Pitkin Avenue with its
big businesses, but one of the drab and ugly streets. "We had a
railroad a block away, an elevated paralleling that, and then one
going right through our street over our heads. As we conversed,
suddenly the plates on the kitchen table would begin to
dance. . . ."

The characters who inhabit this block, shut in and agitated by
their own individual troubles and obsessions, are viewed through
the eyes of a group of children who live in this block—Bibi, who
becomes a gangster and is killed in a fight; Richles, who becomes a
noted physicist; Robby, who opens a business; and Usher, who
becomes a dentist. Reminding us somewhat of Shalom Aleichem's
heroes, Granit's characters, too, often act foolishly and meanly, but
their intentions are good. They are little people who are struggling with their day-to-day problems, and often manifest great
human qualities. There are wildly funny incidents, but there is
pathos, too, a haunting sense of loneliness and despair.

A dramatic and challenging story about Brownsville is Gerald
Green's novel, *The Last Angry Man*.²⁹ Columbia Pictures made a
successful picture of it; *The Reader's Digest* published it in digest
form, and the Book of the Month Club included it among its
books.

Gerald Green (born 1913), the son of a Brownsville doctor,
attended the local schools and the Columbia School of Journalism,
and later held a position with the International News Service, and
became the producer of National Broadcasting Company's, "Wide,
Wide, World." He has since written a number of books on a
variety of subjects, the latest being *To Brooklyn With Love*.

The Last Angry Man is largely autobiographical. It recreates scenes of the author's boyhood in Brownsville. The shifting population of Negroes, Jews, Poles, the gang fights, the filthy, swarming, noisy streets, that mound of poverty, failure, degradation—it is all in the novel.

In an interview with Siegfried Mandel for *The Saturday Review of Literature* (February 2, 1957) Green said, "A slum area such as Brooklyn's Brownsville where I was born, is a savage place shadowed by tragedy and humor. I don't hold with sentimental views popularized by writers like Shalom Asch that the poor are citadels of virtue. You can blame environment only so far, whether it is Brownsville or Hollywood, in its effect on people. Some people invite ruin because they don't assume responsibility for their acts; possibly they get away with too much."

Epilogue

The Passing of A Jewish Community

UP TO 1940 Brownsville was an exciting neighborhood, busily preoccupied with building institutions, and alive with the sense of aiming toward a more meaningful life and a happier society. Since the end of World War II it has begun to decline. As the second and third generations of youth grew up and graduated from schools and colleges into the affluent postwar American society, they sought to establish themselves in other environments. The growing prosperity and the change in the ethnic complexion of the area prompted a wholesale exodus, beginning about 1960, of the remaining Jews, with the result that the Brownsville Jewish community has practically disappeared.

It would be hard to imagine a sharper contrast between Brownsville as it was fifty or even a few years ago, and as it is today. It is scarcely identifiable except in a geographic sense. Much of old Brownsville has been razed to make room for a number of public housing projects. The new housing units, as well as the remaining old tenements are now occupied by Negroes and Puerto Ricans, New York's newest immigrants. It is now part of the vast Negro and Puerto Rican "ghetto" which, interspersed with small pockets of white residents, stretches from Williamsburg on the East River southeast to East New York. The exodus of Jews from East New York and New Lots has not been so complete. There still remains a considerable Jewish community in these sections.

The changes brought with them a number of problems and imposed hardships on many. They became particularly trying for the elderly and the large number of small shopkeepers who had spent most of their lives in Brownsville. They felt rooted in the life of the neighborhood. There was the vexing question of what disposition to make of the many synagogues and public institutions, the symbolic reminders of the continuity of the Jewish community. Rabbi Abraham P. Bloch of Temple Petach Tikvah recently described the plight of some of the institutions that have been the pride and delight of Brownsville.[1] A number of them were leveled to make room for new public projects, but many others have been transformed into varied kinds of establishments. Of a dozen congregations, only two have established new synagogues in border-line communities within walking distance. The others lacked a minimal quorum of active members to warrant relocation. In some cases no effort was made to erase the religious symbols and insignia before surrendering ownership.

There was the problem of disposing of the assets of these institutions. Without an overall communal body authorized to submit and enforce suggestions in such situations, each group was left to its own devices in arriving at a decision. It should be stated to the credit of some of these organizations that they generously contributed of their funds to worthy institutions in other Jewish communities and in Israel. The interiors of some of these synagogues were replicas of old-world synagogues which have long since vanished. The replicas in America, as Dr. Abraham P. Bloch comments, are about to share the same lamentable fate.

Next to the Lower East Side, there was no other district in the country so well-known to the East European Jewish immigrants as Brownsville. For some three-quarters of a century it was a first home for vast numbers of immigrants and their American born children, or perhaps a way-station in their pilgrimage toward success in other communities. Moving from one section to another was not uncommon, and even became part of a pattern of life. It was regarded as a hallmark of success.

In the preceding pages we took the reader through the streets, the shops, the market place, the work, the schools, the libraries, the theatres, the various educational, charitable, welfare, and recreational institutions. In a sense we took them into the hearts of the people. We detailed the *Shulen,* or synagogues, the *Landsman-schaften,* or countrymen organizations that were situated in the area. We discussed the various social, political, radical and reform movements which periodically stirred and agitated the community.

As we look back in retrospect and reflect on some of the aspects of the Brownsville experience, we find that it was a period of both material growth and cultural change. The material gains were particularly striking. Starting with little or nothing, and living under the most trying conditions, large numbers succeeded in extricating themselves from the fetters of poverty and establishing at least a modicum of economic security. From a dirt road, Pitkin Avenue evolved into a metropolitan thoroughfare. From a village, Brownsville grew to a great town with thriving suburbs in East New York, New Lots, East Flatbush, and Eastern Parkway.

So far as the inner lives of the people were concerned, there was also noticeable development and change. Brownsville was a mass-experiment in Americanization, which continued uninterruptedly for a number of decades. The process did not come easily, nor was it without its formidable obstacles. For years the community was a target for censure and even ridicule. It was misunderstood by some of its own native sons, and derogated as inferior. At times the pressure was perilously close enough to induce disillusionment and despair.

It is the glory of the pioneers of the early days that they did not lose hope. Sustained by an invincible faith, they were determined to find a way in the new land. With all their failings and short-comings, their tribulations and anxieties, they emerged victorious from their long struggle. There was a love and warmth of home and family. The neighborhood was more than a collection of disjointed, separate homes. It was a community where one could find comradeship, mutual understanding, and affection for one's fellow beings. There was noticeable consciousness of solidification with the Jewish people here and everywhere.

For those who felt stifled by the Brownsville atmosphere, there was every encouragement by the school, the library, the synagogue, the public forum, and the various social and educational agencies, to help them make their way into the larger city and the culture it would offer. For Matthew Josephson, the writer, Brooklyn was a "good place to get away from"; accordingly, he went to Paris to live for a time. Alfred Kazin, the literary critic, yearned from his earliest youth to make his way "at least into the great world that was anything, just out of Brownsville." Doubtless many others looked forward hopefully to the time when they would find a place in the larger community, and in time many did.

One of the assets that enabled many to adapt to the new American way of life was their ability to draw inner strength from the spiritual heritage they had brought with them. Though many came originally from townlets or villages, they were not necessarily villagers. Reinforced by a profound respect for knowledge and learning, they were quick to take advantage of the cultural opportunities available to them. Following the leadership of a small group of immigrant intellectuals there emerged here, as in the East Side and in other Jewish immigrant sections, the intellectualized worker. Irving Howe has described him as a human type that is rare in this country. He may have lacked a formal conventional education, but he struggled "throughout his life to pick up scraps of knowledge in the faith that knowledge was virtually a mode of redemption. Earnest, self-taught, independent of mind, he remained eager for self-definition and an awareness of the forces that had shaped his life." [2] He was particularly concerned that his children should receive the education denied him.

Although Brownsville was an isolated corner, a provincial world removed from the cross currents of the metropolitan city, and despite the freedom of the Jews to transplant their culture here, only a small proportion were able to transmit to their American offspring a full appreciation of their rich Jewish cultural heritage. As for the movements, goals, and values which motivated Jewish life in Eastern Europe at the end of the century, only a few found a fruitful soil here. The *Yiddishkeit* that was created here had a unique American stamp.

The Brownsville Jewish community has now disappeared. For all its limitations, it was a noble school of experience. Some rich spiritual reservoirs must have existed here to sustain the vast population. How else are we to explain the glorious saga of the East European Jewish migration to America which we are witnessing at the present time? The East European Jewish immigrants, particularly their children, are coming into their own. The respect and hunger for learning which were characteristic of East-European Jewish life did not disappear here. It survived, even if mostly in secular form. The children and grandchildren of the immigrants who filled the schools and colleges are now beginning to distinguish themselves in the political, academic, literary, artistic, and social life of this land. They have gone beyond Brownsville. A paraphrase of what Zalman Joffeh said of the passing of the East Side applies equally to the passing of Browns- ville: [3] "We may have lost Brownsville, but we have gained the world—at least New York."

For legions of Jews who have spent some time of their lives here, Brownsville is still a fresh and vibrant memory. For others it is a palpitating, heroic story of intrepid East-European Jewish immigrants and their children during the past three-quarters of a century. Its heart is no longer here, but its heartbeat will continue to pulsate through the years.

Bibliography

BIBLIOGRAPHICAL NOTE:

The material for this book has been collected from a wide variety of sources over a period of many years. Reference to these sources is made in the notes that follow, and through the body of the book.

SOURCES

1. *Newspapers and Periodicals*

The English, Yiddish, and Hebrew newspapers, periodicals and magazines served as one of the main sources.

The now defunct *Brooklyn Daily Eagle* covered almost the entire period. The Old Timers Column of *The Eagle* offered particularly interesting and valuable information. *The Eagle* also published a variety of works during its existence which contain pertinent information. Among these should be mentioned the Consolidation Number, January 2, 1898; *Brooklyn and Long Island in the war;* a record of deeds and casualty lists, 1918; *The Eagle and Brooklyn;* the record of the progress of *Brooklyn Daily Eagle,* together with the history of the City of Brooklyn, Ed. Henry W. B. Howard, assisted by Arthur N. Jervis, two volumes 1893; "Historic and Beautiful Brooklyn," six pamphlets, including one on New Lots, 1946; *Pictorial History of Brooklyn,* October 26, 1916. The volumes of the *Brooklyn Daily Eagle Almanac* (1886-1929)

376

also contain useful data. The other Brooklyn dailies; *The Standard Union,* *The Brooklyn Daily Times, The Brooklyn Times Union,* also contain information relating to our subject. *The New York Times,* especially its obituary columns, and its columns on "Man in the News;" *The New York Sun,* *The New York Herald, The New York Tribune, The Evening Post, The* *World Telegram,* especially its Brooklyn section, *The Daily News,* especially its Brooklyn section and Old Timers columns, and *The Journal American* were examined in connection with certain events. Fortunately, many of the items relating to the community are found among the clippings which are catalogued and collected in some 150 scrapbooks on file in the Library of the Long Island Historical Society. A. J. Virginia, Scrapbook of articles, clippings, etc. dealing with Jews, especially those of New York and Brooklyn (Boston, 1910) in the Jewish Division, New York Public Library, contains some items relating to our story.

The Yiddish press, including *The Yiddishe Gazetten,* which had a special column in the early years known as the Bronzviller Pinkos, *The Forward,* *The Morgen Journal,* and *The Day* were especially helpful. They not only carried news, but included many articles, editorials, and other material pertaining to the community. *The Jewish Morning Journal,* Sunday section for society news of Brownsville, etc., edited for more than a decade by Jacob Koplowitz, was found most valuable since it carried short historical sketches of the various synagogues, institutions, and personalities of the community. The Hebrew periodical, *Hadoar,* has also carried from time to time interesting items and articles about Brownsville, and some of its personalities.

Many local weeklies were published over the period such as *The Kings* *County Chronicle, The Brooklyn News, The Brooklyn Guide, The Chat,* and others, bearing various names, and also the Yiddish weeklies, *The Brownsville* *Post* and *Brooklyn Jewish Progress.* Except for a few issues, these periodicals are not available. The writer has collected clippings from these publications over a period of years which he found valuable in compiling the story of the community.

Besides *The American Hebrew,* which covers the period, there were several Anglo-Jewish weeklies published in Brooklyn which contain some pertinent material—*The Brooklyn Jewish Chronicle; The Brooklyn Jewish Voice; The* *Brooklyn Examiner* (title varies—*Jewish Examiner, Examiner* (1929-1955), edited by Louis D. Gross, and later united with *American Hebrew* to form *The American Examiner.*

2. Government Documents

Many government documents are available in the Historical Division of Kings County Clerk. Particularly valuable were the State Census and Federal Census Reports. The writer has carefully examined the state census documents for 1845, 1855, 1865, 1875, 1892, 1905, 1925, and the Federal Census reports beginning with that of 1820. The History Division of the Kings

County Clerk's office also contains the old town records of Flatbush and some for New Lots, the Supervisors and Council Minutes, Land Conveyances, maps, and other material of historic value. The Municipal Library in the New York City Hall also contains much material.

3. *Minutes, Records, Reports, Journals, and Other Articles of Organizations.*

The archives of the Hebrew Educational Society, which include the minutes of the Society since its founding, addresses by Abraham Abraham, Adolphus Solomons, Simon F. Rothschild, Mayor Gaynor, annual reports, brochures, journals, programs, anniversary publications, publications by the various clubs and organizations that met in that agency over the years, some of the correspondence of Dr. Charles S. Bernheimer, who also served as secretary of the local school board, and other valuable material were available to the writer, and were closely examined by him. The annual reports of the Brooklyn Federation of Jewish Charities and affiliated societies from 1910 until it was merged with the Federation of Jewish Philanthropies in 1943; the reports of the Brooklyn Jewish Community Council; the *Temple Petach Tikvah News,* of which the first three volumes were made available to the writer by Rabbi Israel H. Levinthal, are a few items in this category that deserve special attention.

4. *Personal Interviews with Leaders and Old Timers of the Community.*

The service of the writer for forty years as the executive director of the Hebrew Educational Society has brought him in contact with most of the personalities, events, and institutions recorded in the book.

5. *Autobiographies and Personal Memoirs.*

Charles Reznikoff: *Family Chronicle:* Early History of a seamstress, by Sarah Reznikoff. Early History of a sewing machine operator by Nathan Reznikoff. *Needle Trade* by Charles Reznikoff, New York, 1963.

By the Waters of Manhattan, New York, 1929.

Morris R. Cohen, *A Dreamer's Journey,* Boston, 1949.

Charles S. Bernheimer, *Half a Century in Community Service,* New York, 1948.

Emma Goldman, *Living My Life,* New York, 1931.

Margaret Sanger, *An Autobiography,* New York, 1938; *My Fight for Birth Control,* New York, 1931.

Impressario, a Memoir by Sol Hurok in collaboration with Ruth Goode, New York, 1946.

A. Frumkin, *In the Spring of Jewish Socialism; Memoirs of a Journalist* (Yiddish), New York, 1940. It includes a chapter on the life of Dr. Michael Cohn.

American Spiritual Autobiographies, Ed. Louis Finkelstein, New York, 1948. It includes a chapter on the Life of Rabbi Simon Finkelstein.

Alfred Kazin, *A Walker in the City*, New York, 1941; *Starting Out in the Thirties*, Boston, 1965.

Matthew Josephson, *Life Among the Surrealists, a Memoir*, 1962.

Norman Podhoretz, *Making It*, New York, 1967.

Samuel Tannenbaum, *Brownsville's Age of Learning, Commentary*, August, 1949.

William Poster, *It was a Dark Night, Commentary*, May, 1950.

Danny Kaye, "The Happiest Man," (A Tribute to His Father), *Readers Digest*, March, 1963, pp. 94.

Emanuel Celler, *You Never Leave Brooklyn, an Autobiography*, New York, 1953.

PRINTED MATERIAL

General History of Brooklyn and Brownsville—East New York

Charles Warren Hamilton, *Handbook of the Town of New Lots*, 1874.

Henry R. Stiles, *History of Kings County*, two volumes 1884.

Henry Isham Hazelton, *The Boroughs of Brooklyn and Queens. Counties of Nassau and Suffolk, Long Island, New York 1609-1924*, seven volumes, New York, 1925.

Peter Ross, *History of Long Island*, 2 volumes, New York, 1902.

Eugene Armbruster, *The Eastern District of Brooklyn*, Brooklyn, 1942.

Harold Coffin Syrett, *The City of Brooklyn*, 1865-1898, Columbia University Press, 1944.

Ralph Foster Weld, *Brooklyn is America*, Columbia University Press, 1950.

Program and Official Directory of *Who's Who in East New York*, 1936.

Good Old East New York; Commemorating the 75th Anniversary of the East New York Savings Bank, compiled by Alfred Osterland, 1943.

Frederick Heidenreich, *Old Days and Old Ways in East New York*, 1948.

Alter F. Landesman, *The Early History of Brownsville, Journal of Long Island History*, IV, No. 1, pp. 18-27.

Rae Glauber, *All Neighborhoods Change*, A Survey of Brownsville, Brooklyn, 1963.

Margaret Freeman, *The Brownsville's Children's Branch of the Brooklyn Public Library*, 1940.

Florence Adamson, *Brownsville, A Study of the Recreational Facilities*-The New York School of Social Work, 1943, published by the Brooklyn Council for Social Planning.

Milton J. Goell, *Brownsville Must Have Public Housing*, 1940.

Walter Laidlow, *Population of the City of New York*, 1890-1930.

The History of the Jewish Community of Brownsville

Samuel P. Abelow, *History of Brooklyn Jewry*, Brooklyn, 1937.

Leon Wexelstein, *Building Up Greater Brooklyn*, with sketches of men instrumental in Brooklyn's amazing development, Brooklyn, 1925.

Jacob Wax: *A History of Brownsville,* a series of articles published in *Kings County Chronicle,* 1927-1928. In collaboration with B. Botwinick, a series of articles in Yiddish were published in *The Forward* (January 2-February 12, 1930). These articles cover phases of life in early Brownsville.

Max Halpert, *The Jews of Brownsville,* 1880-1925. Demographic, Economic, Socio-cultural study. Doctor's Degree Dissertation, Bernard Revel Graduate School, Yeshivah University, New York, 1958.

Leonard Plotnick, *The Sephardim of New Lots, Commentary,* January, 1958.

Felix Meyerowitz, "Golden Jubilee," *Menorah Journal,* June, 1928.

Burton B. Turkus and Sid Feder, *Murder, Inc.* The Story of the Syndicate. Farrar, Straus and Young, 1951.

Jewish Communal Register, 1917-1918.

The Jewish Landsmanschaften of New York, New York, 1938.

M. C. Horowitz and L. J. Kaplan, *The Jewish Population of New York Area,* 1900-1957, Federation of Philanthropies of New York, 1959.

Background Studies of Jews in America

Louis Finkelstein, Ed. *The Jews:* Their History, Culture and Religion (New York, 1960).

Mark Wischnitzer, *To Dwell in Safety:* The Story of the Jewish Migration Since 1800 (Philadelphia, 1948).

C. Bezalel Sherman: *The Jew Within American Society*—A Study in Ethnic Individuality, Detroit, 1960, 1965.

Moses Rischin, *The Promised City,* New York Jews 1870-1914, Harvard University Press, 1962.

Lloyd Gartner, *The Jewish Immigrant in England 1870-1914,* Detroit, 1960.

Hertz Burgin, *Geschichte fun der idisher arbeiter bewegung* in America, New York, 1912.

The Early Jewish Labor Movement in the United States, translated and revised by Aaron Antonovsky (New York, 1961) based on *Di Geshikhte fun der Yiddisher Arbeterbevegung in di Farynikte Shtaten,* Ed. by E. Tcherikoven, two volumes (New York, 1943-1945).

Melech Epstein, *Jewish Labor in United States 1882-1914,* New York, 1950.

Oscar I. Janowsky, Ed. *The American Jew, A Reappraisal.* In addition to an analysis of the inner life of the American Jew by 19 outstanding contributors it contains brief and valuable bibliographical notes on various aspects of Jewish life in America.

Nathan Glazer and Daniel Patrick Moynihan, *Beyond the Melting Pot,* Cambridge, Mass. 1963.

Nathan Glazer, *American Judaism,* Chicago, 1957.

The Lower East Side: Portal to American Life (1870-1924). Ed. by Allen Schoener, 1966, The Jewish Museum, New York, 1966.

Notes

INTRODUCTION

1. Henry Roth, *Call It Sleep* (New York, 1935), p. 12.
2. Samuel Joseph, *Jewish Immigration to the United States from 1881 to 1910* (New York, 1914). *The Early Jewish Labor Movement in the United States*, translated and revised by Aaron Antonovsky (New York, 1961), pp. 51–74.
3. *New York Herald*, Jan. 17, 1909.
4. Moses Richin, *The Promised City* (Cambridge, Mass., 1962), pp. 61–68; Charles S. Bernheimer, Ed. *The Russian Jew in the United States*, p. 104; C. Bezalel Sherman, *The Jew Within American Society* (Detroit, 1965).
5. William Poster, *'Twas a Dark Night in Brownsville, Commentary*, May 1950, p. 460.
6. Ray Ginger, *Age of Excess—The United States from 1877 to 1914* (New York, 1965), pp. 19, 152–153, 289.
7. *Impressario*, a Memoir by Sol Hurok (New York, 1946).
8. Samuel Tannenbaum, *Brownsville's Age of Learning, Commentary*, Aug. 1949, pp. 174, 176.
9. C. Bezalel Sherman, *The Jew Within American Society*, pp. 164–167.
10. *The Early Jewish Labor Movement*, trans. and revised by A. Antonovsky, p. 142.
11. William Poster, art. cit. *Commentary*, May, 1950, p. 466.
12. Jane Jacobs, *The Death and Life of Great American Cities* (New York, 1961).

THE FIRST JEWS IN EAST NEW YORK

1. For the early history of New Lots and its Villages, Henry R. Stiles, Ed., *History of Kings County* (Brooklyn, 1884–I, *History of the Town of New Lots* by Charles Warren Hamilton, I, pp. 306–326) ; Peter Ross, *A History of Long Island*, 2 vols.; vol. I, pp. 514 ff. Eugene Armbruster, *The Eastern District of Brooklyn* (Brooklyn, 1942) ; *Historic and Beautiful Brooklyn, New Lots*, published by *The Brooklyn Eagle* (1946) : Program and Official Directory of *Who's Who* in East New York (1936) ; Frederick J. Heidenreich, *Old Days and Old Ways in East New York* (1948) ; Alter F. Landesman, *The Early History of Brownsville, Journal of Long Island History*, IV, 1, pp. 18–27.

2. Levy's full name was Asser Levy Van Swellem, which indicates that the family came originally from Schwelm, Westphalia. For his life and activities see David de Sola Pool; *Portraits Etched in Stone*, early Jewish settlers, 1682–1831 (New York, 1952), pp. 198–201; Leon Huhner, Asser Levy, "A Noted Jewish Burgher of New Amsterdam," Publications of American Jewish Historical Society, No. 8 (1900) pp. 9–23; Charles P. Daly, *The Settlement of the Jews in North America*, Ed. with notes by Max J. Kohler (New York, 1893), p. 22, note 19; Isaac Markens, *The Hebrews in America* (New York, 1888), p. 9.

3. Teunis G. Bergen, Register in Alphabetical order of the Early Settlers of Kings County, Long Island, New York (New York, 1881), pp. 138, 167.

4. Court and Road Records 1668–1776, vol. 2, p. 70 (Historical Division, Kings County Clerk's office).

5. Ibid. No. 109, p. 79. There is also a reference to a case dated 1668 against Dirck Jane Hoagland, see Flatbush Town Records, Liber D, Court Minutes, vol. II, 1670 to 1682, p. 85 (No. 214) old page 222; T. G. Bergen, op. cit. pp. 138, 145–147.

6. Flatbush Town Records, Miscellaneous Vol. II, 1658 to 1799, paper No. 6899. For another case dated April 8, 1667 in which Auke Jans is involved see Flatbush Town Records, Liber D, Court Minutes, Vol. I, 1664–1670 (April 8, 1667).

7. Flatbush Town Records, Liber D, Court Minutes, Vol. II, pp. 87; 113 (No. 228) ; 365 (No. 341).

8. Flatbush Town Records Liber C. Deeds 1666–1686, p. 275. (IN Re: Negro Slave and Indian Slave.) The original document together with a translation has since been published in full by Dr. Abraham G. Duker under the title "The Sale of a Negro Slave in Brooklyn in 1683," in *Essays in American Jewish History*, Am. J. Archives (Cincinnati, 1958), pp. 63–68.

9. New York State Census, 1855, 1865, 1875 (Historical Division, Kings County Clerk's office). References to the family and their business are found in Warren C. Hamilton, *Handbook of New Lots*, 1874–5; Henry R. Stiles, *History of the County of Kings and City of Brooklyn from 1683 to 1884;* Obituaries in *New York Staats Zeitung*, Nov. 15, 1909, and *Brooklyn Daily*

Eagle, Nov. 18, 1909; "Who's Who in East New York" (pamphlet); *Brooklyn Eagle*, April 24, 1913. The copies of early newspapers quoted are in the Long Island Historical Society Library.

10. *City of Brooklyn* published by the *Brooklyn Eagle* (Brooklyn, 1886), p. 277.

11. *Brooklyn Eagle*, Oct. 4, 1931; "Who's Who in East New York" (pamphlet).

12. New York State Census, 1865; Stiles, pp. 308, 317, et passim.

13. Obituary, *New York Times*, Aug. 22, 1922.

14. *Weekly Recorder*, Aug. 6, 1906.

15. *Three Years in America* (1859–1862), trans. by Charles Reznikoff with Introduction by Oscar Handlin, Jewish Publication Society, 1956.

16. Samuel P. Abelow, *History of Brooklyn Jewry*, pp. 295–296; "Who's Who in American Jewry" (New York, 1938–9), p. 275.

17. "Who's Who in American Jewry" (New York, 1926), p. 310.

18. *New York Tribune*, Dec. 16, 23, 24, 25, 1875; Feb. 14, March 11, 20, May 10, 1876. *New York Staats Zeitung*, Dec. 16, 1875. Abraham Caan, *Bleter fun mein Leben* (New York, 1926–1931), Vol. 2, p. 81. Moses Rischin, *The Promised City* (Cambridge, Mass., 1962) p. 89; *Good Old East New York* compiled by Alfred Osterland (Brooklyn, 1943); "Thrilling Mysteries of the Rubenstein Murder Never Before Brought to Light!" (a pamphlet issued in 1876 by Samuel Stern). In this 15 page pamphlet Stern informs us that he was voluntarily assisting the District Attorney to defeat any effort to prove an alibi. He reprints a letter from the father of Sarah Alexander from Vilna *Guberna* (Province), dated Feb. 10, 1876. The object of the publication was to raise the sum of $50 to be appropriated for the erection of a tombstone over the murdered woman's body. There is a copy of the pamphlet in the Jewish Division of the New York Public Library.

19. Brooklyn Daily Eagle Almanacs, 1887–1900; American Jewish Year Book (1900–1901), p. 329; Savenir Programs and Annual Journals issued by Temple Sinai.

20. Cf. Rudolph Glanz, Jews in Relation to Cultural Milieu of Germans in America Up to 1880 (New York, 1947); Eric E. Hirshler, Jews from Germany in United States (New York, 1955).

JEWS MOVE TO BROWNSVILLE

1. Kings County Register's Office Conveyances, Lib. 1681, p. 391 (July 17, 1886).

2. Ibid. July 7, 1887, p. 324.

3. In a series of articles on various phases of the Early History of Brownsville which were published in *The Forward* in 1930 by B. Botwinick on the basis of material supplied to him by Mr. Jacob Wax one of the first settlers who had written much in various periodicals about Brownsville, the honor of being the first settler is given to Jacob Cohen. Many of the writings on early Brownsville have followed this source.

4. L. 1741 p. 333 (June 1, 1887) ; L. 1800, p. 412 (April 9, 1888).

5. L. 1740, p. 177, May 26, 1887. On Nov. 2, 1887 Mrs. Anna Kaplan, the wife of Elias, acquired a house from Mr. John Power, one of the main builders of the time.

6. Elias Kaplan, by Jacob Wax in *Kings County Observer*, 1930 (Aaron Roth, Editor, S. L. Peckerman, Associate Editor). The series of articles in *The Forward* of that year also includes an article on the life of Elias Kaplan. The writer wants to acknowledge his thanks to Dr. Louis Kaplan, son of Elias Kaplan, who in a personal interview shared his knowledge of his family with him.

7. Among those involved in property transactions during 1888 were Morris Lazarus (Feb. 8) ; Simon Levy (April 3) ; David Levy (April 18) ; Moses Lowenthal (April 26) ; Solomon and Dora Wolff (May 1) ; Max Mittenthal (May 3) ; Max Gittelsohn (June 8) ; Morris Levy (June 20) ; Jacob and Abraham Goldstein (July 1) ; Samuel Balsam (July 3) ; David Blumberg (July 18) ; Abraham Cohen (Oct. 16) ; Max Israel (Nov. 26) ; Henry and Eva Schreiber (Nov. 27) ; Morris Aronsen (Nov. 27). For the year 1889 there are property conveyances recorded in the names of Hilel and Becky Waxburg (March 5) ; Zigmund Rosenfeld (April 16) ; David Axelrod (April 29) ; Arnie and Israel Solomon (May 3) ; Aaron Cohen (May 14) ; Solomon Blatheis (June 15) ; Anne and Thomas Rosenbloom (June 17) ; Louis Ratner (June 24) ; Al Pasternack (June 26) ; Simon Schnapir (July 1) ; Morris Ribstein (July 8) ; Jacob Bleustein (July 18 and 31) ; David Simon (July 31) ; Solomon Morris (Aug. 10) ; Morris Lubliner (Aug. 24) ; Joseph Morris (Sept. 4); Abraham Natelson (Sept. 6); Bernard Kaminowitz (Sept. 9); Barnett Shapiro (Sept. 4) ; Arne Goodman (Sept. 4) ; Anna Axelrod (Oct. 3); Bernard Hershkowitz (Nov. 11).

8. *The Early Jewish Labor Movement in the United States,* translated and revised by Aaron Antonovsky (New York, 1961), pp. 153–155; Jacob Riis, *Children of the Poor,* New York, 1892, pp. 44–47. Samuel Joseph, *History of the Baron de Hirsch Fund* (New York, 1935), pp. 26–27.

9. *Vital Statistics of New York and Brooklyn* by John S. Billings, Washington, 1894.

10. Dr. Leon Horowitz, *The Jews of Galicia,* Menorah 1899, vol. 27, pp. 357 ff. *The Early Jewish Labor Movement in the United States,* transl. and revised by Aaron Antonovsky from the original Yiddish Ed. by Elias Tcherikover (New York, 1961); Samuel Joseph, *Jewish Immigration to the United States from 1881 to 1910* (New York, 1914); Lloyd Gartner, *The Jewish Immigrant in England 1870–1914* (Detroit, 1960); Moses Rischin, *The Promised City* (Cambridge, Mass., 1962).

LIFE IN THE EARLY JEWISH SETTLEMENT OF BROWNSVILLE

1. Quoted by Samuel Joseph, *History of the Baron de Hirsch Fund* (1935), p. 44.

2. Charles Reznikoff, *By the Waters of Manhattan* (New York, 1929); with Nathan Reznikoff his father (1871–1942), *Early History of a Sewing Machine Operator* (New York, 1936); *Family Chronicle; Early History of a Seamstress,* by Sarah Reznikoff. *Early History of a Sewing Machine Operator* by Nathan Reznikoff (New York, 1963).

3. *The Early Jewish Labor Movement in the United States.* Transl. by Aaron Antonovsky, p. 166; *United States Industrial Commission, Reports,* Vol. XV. *Immigration and Education, House Doc. No. 184. 57th Congress.* First Series (Washington, 1901), p. 346; Bureau of the Census, *Twelfth Census of the United States 1900,* Vol. IX, *"Manufactures" part 3. "Selected Industries"* (Washington, 1906), p. 296.

4. The contemporary account mentioned in these pages refers to an article in *The Sun* (July 2, 1899) which described the Brooklyn Ghetto. A copy of this article has been supplied to the writer by Mr. Samuel Hollander.

5. C. Bezalel Sherman, *The Jew Within American Society—Study in Ethnic Individuality* (Detroit, 1965); Lloyd Gartner, *Jewish Immigrant in England,* (Detroit, 1960), pp. 84–93.

6. Prof. Morris Raphael Cohen and his family lived at that time in Brownsville. He describes their experiences during the depression in his autobiography, *A Dreamer's Journey,* p. 80.

7. Interview with Sidney Blatt printed in *Brooklyn Guide,* 1928. M. R. Cohen describes his early school experiences on pp. 78–80 of *A Dreamer's Journey.* Jacob Wax, "Joseph Lack, First Rabbi to Minister to Brownsville," *The Brooklyn Guide,* Jan 28, 1928. Cf. John Higham: *Social Discrimination Against Jews in America,* 1830–1930 A.J.H.S. XLVII. I, p. 1–33; Samuel Abelow, *History of Brooklyn Jewry,* p. 12–13; New York Tribune, June 29, 1899, p. 11; William M. Feigenbaum, *The Jewish Daily Forward,* April 24, 1927. To be sure there was to be found also a wholesome relationship among many who resided here. Henry Hock in Old Timers Page, *Brooklyn Eagle,* March 19, 1949, records his early wholesome experiences when his family, together with the one colored family in the neighborhood by the name of Willet, and the Grallas, a well known Jewish family, lived in the same house on Thatford Avenue.

8. How "Dickey" the dog that belonged to Abraham Horn, one of the first expressmen of Brownsville, saved the day in 1889 is told in an account of *Tashlih* in Brownsville by J. Koplowitz, Brownsville Column, *Morning Journal,* Sept. 12, 1937. See article on Brownsville by Botwinick based on materials supplied by J. Wax, *Forward* (Jan. 1930).

9. *The Sun,* 1899, art. cit.

10. M. R. Cohen, *A Dreamer's Journey,* pp. 80–81.

11. Harry L. Klinger, *World Telegram,* Oct. 8, 1955; Tourney Holmes, *A Sports History of Brooklyn, Brooklyn Eagle,* July 3, 1949; Old Timers Column of *Eagle,* Jack Spiegel, *Eagle,* April 21, 1951; George L. Fallon, *Eagle,* Sept. 18, 1949; Robert Ryder, *Eagle,* Feb. 27, 1944; John Masterson, *Eagle,* July 9, 1944; Wm. D. Breen, *Eagle,* May 28, 1944.

12. *Yiddishe Gazetten,* May, 1894.

13. *The Sun,* 1899, art. cit.

14. *The Brooklyn Eagle,* Dec. 24, 1893.

15. *A Dreamer's Journey,* p. 81.

16. The story of the beginnings of the Oheb Shalom Synagogue has been told by Jacob Wax in the *Brooklyn Guide,* 1928, and in the series of *The Forward* articles on Brownsville by Botwinick, (Jan.–Feb. 12, 1930) from material supplied by Mr. Wax. Jacob Koplowitz has written about it in his Brownsville section in the *Morgen Journal. The Synagogue* published a 40th Anniversary Journal in which some of the history is told.

17. *The Sun,* 1899, art. cit.

BROWNSVILLE'S GROWTH TO THE LARGEST JEWISH COMMUNITY IN NEW YORK

1. For sketches of the life of the builders in Brownsville, East New York, and Eastern Parkway sections see Leon Wexelstein, *Building Up Greater Brooklyn* (Brooklyn, 1925).

2. A special issue of the local weekly—*Brooklyn-Guide-Kings County Observer* was dedicated to Mr. Roth, on June 11, 1930 in which a detailed biography of his life was printed. Mr. Jacob Wax also published in the Jewish Day at that time an article, "The Builder of Brownsville."

3. The information was given the writer by Mr. Alfred Shillito.

4. The Executive Committee of the Brownsville Board of Trade included the following prominent businessmen and leaders in 1912. Mayor Aronson, Abraham Belanowsky, Julius Cassileth, Max Dwork, Jacob M. Elias, Charles Fleischer, Meyer Forsichbaum, Moses Ginsberg, Jacob Goell, Dr. Mark Gordon, James Jarcho, Julius Josephson, Abraham Kaplan, Nathan Kovensky, Israel Lack, Solomon Leibowitz, Isaac Levingson, Harry Lindenbaum, Osias Maller, Isaac Marshall, Simon Nager, Jr., Hyman Rayfiel, Harry Reisler, Marcy Rosenblum, William B. Roth, Samuel Sassulsky, Moses W. Saxe, Victor Schwartz, Samuel Seiderman, Isaac Siegmeister, Arthur H. Selinger, John A. Shepherd, Samuel A. Telsey, George Tonkonogy, Jacob Wax.

5. The Board of Directors of the Pitkin Avenue Merchants Association included in 1941 the following: Howard Launsbach, pres., Samuel Stofsky, and Clinton O. Chichester, vice-pres., Irving S. Mandel, treas., Alfred L. Kranz, sec., Henry M. Feldschuh, attorney, Philip Klewansky, chairman of the Board, and Thomas Atkins, Joseph Boxer, Jack Fisher, Adolph Frey, Irving Glick, Henry J. Iles, Samuel N. Koplowitz, William Metz, Benjamin Molitz, William Metz, Joseph Rosenberg, Abraham Stark, Sam Weinstein, Alexander Weiss, Samuel Zweig, Louis Askwyth, Louis Friedman, Reuben Block, Louis J. Cohan, Philip Stadler, Abraham Gratenstein, Solomon Kochman, Sidney Kaufman.

6. The first officers of the Brownsville Neighborhood Council were: Alter F. Landesman, president, Arthur Blyn and Mrs. Bessie J. Portnoy, vice-presi-

dents; Max Weiner, treas. and Miss Alice M. Tuthill, secretary. The Committee Chairmen were: Broadman Epstein, Arbitration; Milton Goell, Housing, Dr. Maxwell Ross, Legislative, Mrs. Murray Hoffstetter, Nominating; Charles W. Chambers, Public Relations; Samuel Koplowitz, Public Safety; Nathaniel Worman, Recreation, and Mrs. Esther Ziv, Social Service.

Among the active participants over the years were District Superintendents Charles E. O'Neill, Isaac Bildersee and Thomas Nevins; the ministers, Rev. W. B. M. Scott, Rev. Boise S. Dent and Father George Ford; Thomas J. Atkins, Paul Backal, E. Blackwell, Sam Bass, Minnie Cohen, Irene Eisenberg, Sarah Fox, Rae Glauber, Blanche Gitlitz, S. Gorelick, Jack Gordon, Ann Jackson, William Kurland, Albert Leavitt, Dr. Emanuel Lichtman, Ethel Jaffe, Mollie Slutsky, Sally W. Seltzer, Clara Tabb, Gertrude Robbins, Terry Rosenbaum, Dr. Sidney Wasserstrom, Dr. Teits Mildred Wickson.

7. Florence Adamson, *Brownsville (A Study of the Recreational Facilities of the Brownsville Section)* Brooklyn Council for Social Planning, Brooklyn 1943; Alexander Dushkin, *Jewish Population of New York City, Jewish Communal Register of New York City 1917–1918*, pp. 75–89; Max Halpert, *The Jews of Brownsville* (Doctoral Dissertation), New York 1958; Bureau of Jewish Social Research, *Jewish Communal Survey of Greater New York*, New York 1928; C. Morris Horowitz and Lawrence J. Kaplan, *Jewish Population of the New York Area 1900–1957*. New York, 1957; *Survey of Jewish Population in New York City* by Dr. Julius B. Maller, auspices Union of American Hebrew Congregations, New York 1933; Julius B. Maller, *A Study of Jewish Neighborhoods in New York City, Jewish Social Service Quarterly, X, No. 4,* pp. 271 ff.

8. *Population of the City of New York 1890–1930*, compiled and edited by Walter Laidlaw (Cities Census Committee, 1932), pp. 294–295.

9. *Health Center Districts, New York City.* Statistical Reference Data 1929–1933 (Committee on Neighborhood Health Development, Dept. of Health, City of New York, 1935), p. 63. The average rate for the five year period (1929–1935) was 7.52 per 1000 population. For causes of Death for District, see ibid., pp. 69–75.

RADICAL AND SOCIAL REFORM MOVEMENTS

1. August Claessens, *Didn't We Have Fun!* Stories out of a long and merry life (New York 1953) .

2. Gregory Weinstein, *The Ardent Eighties* (New York, 1928) ; Moses Rischin, *The Promised City*, especially chs. 7 and 8 *(Voices of Enlightenment and The Great Awakening)* , pp. 115–168.

3. Maurice G. Hindus: "The Jew as a Radical." *The Menorah Journal*, Aug. 1927 (XIII, No. 4) , pp. 367–379.

4. Morris R. Cohen, *A Dreamer's Journey*, p. 98.

5. Ibid, pp. 98–99.

6. Morris Hillquit, *History of Socialism in the United States* (New York,

1906) ; Herz Burgin, *Die Geschichte fun der Yiddisher Arbeiter-Bewegung,* pp. 309–353; Y. S. Herz, *The Jewish Socialist Movement in America,* New York, 1954.

7. Leon Kobrin, *Meine Fufzig Yohr in Amerika* (Buenos Aires, 1955).

8. For a description of a Yom Kippur Party in Brownsville see Jonathan Finn—*In Memoriam, The Reconstructionist,* June 10, 1966, pp. 23–24.

9. A Frumkin, *In the Spring of Jewish Socialism, Memoirs of a Journalist* (Yiddish) New York, 1940—issued by Frumkin Jubilee Committee, pp. 203–280; *Jewish Daily Forward,* July 12, 1939.

10. Emma Goldman, *Living My Life,* p. 8.

11. B. Botwinick, *The Forward,* Feb. 3, 1930.

12. Algeron Lee, *Universal Jewish Encyclopedia,* vol. 9, p. 510: *The Jewish Daily Forward,* Feb. 8-10, 1934.

13. Herz Burgin, *Die Geschichte fun der Yiddisher Arbeiter-Bewegung,* pp. 359–360; 678–690;

14. See L. Gartner, *The Jewish Immigrant in England,* pp. 127 ff.

MARGARET SANGER OPENS FIRST BIRTH CONTROL CLINIC

1. The material of this section is based mainly on *Margaret Sanger, An Autobiography* (New York 1938), and *My Fight for Birth Control* (New York, 1931).

THE WORKERS, THEIR TRADE UNIONS AND THE JEWISH LABOR MOVEMENT

1. The following works have been found valuable in the preparation of this section:

Herz Burgin, *Die Geschichte fun der Yiddisher Arbeiter-Bewegung* (New York, 1915) ; *The Early Jewish Labor Movement in the United States.* Translated and Revised by Aaron Antonovsky from the original Yiddish, Edited by Elias Tcherikover, (Yivo Institute for Jewish Research, New York, 1961) ; Melech Epstein; *Jewish Labor in the United States 1882–1914,* 2 vols., published by Trade Union Sponsoring Committee (New York, 1950) ; Ben B. Seligman: *Needle, Thread and Thimble.* The story of Jewish Labor in the United States, *Jewish Frontier,* Sept. 1953, pp. 38–60; *Gewerkschaften*—Issued by the United States Hebrew Trades on Occasion of its 50th Anniversary as a Trade Union. Ed. by H. Lang and Morris C. Feinstone. Bernard Weinstein, *Di Yidische Yunyons in Amerika* (New York, 1929), Fertzig Yohr in *der Yiddisher Arbeiter Bewegung* (New York, 1924); Bezalel Sherman: *The Jew Within American Society, especially* pp. 161–172; Moses Rischin, *The Promised City,* section 9—*Labor's Dilemma,* pp. 171–194.

2. Jacob Wax, "Organization of the First Union in Brownsville" (one of a series of articles on History of Brownsville, *Kings County Observer; The Forward,* Jan. 1930.

3. Abraham Rosenberg, *Die Cloakmachers un Zeyere Unions* (New York, 1920), p. 81.

4. Abraham Rosenberg, *Erinnerungen vun a Cloakmacher,* Herz Burgin, *Geschichte vun der Yiddisher Arbeiter, Bewegung,* (New York, 1915), pp. 765–768; Dr. B. Hoffman, *Fufzig Yahr, Cloak Operators Union,* pp. 65–72; Melech Epstein, *Jewish Labor in the United States,* I, p. 226; Rischin, *The Promised City,* pp. 192–193.

5. *The Brooklyn Eagle,* June 3, 1895.

6. Herz Burgin, op. cit. pp. 871–872, 877.

7. Ibid, p. 756; Jewish Communal Register of New York, 1917–1918, p. 709.

8. Ibid., p. 806–807; *Jewish Communal Register,* p. 705.

9. For a listing of these locals see *The Jewish Communal Register of New York City, 1917–1918,* Labor Organizations, pp. 700–712.

10. Melech Epstein, op. cit. p. 372.

11. H. Burgin, op. cit. pp. 430–442, 468–469.

12. Dr. B. Hoffman (Zivyen), *Fufzig Yahr Cloakmacher* Union 1886–1936, pp. 127–134; I.L.G.W.U. Convention Report, June 3, 1900.

13. H. Burgin, op. cit. pp. 597–601.

14. Ibid. pp. 718–720.

15. Ibid. pp. 579–580; L. Levine, *Women's Garment Workers,* (New York, 1924) 144 f.; G. Boone, *The Women's Trade Union's League* (New York, 1942) ; *Forward,* Dec. 7, 10, 14, 16, 21, 1909, Feb. 15, 1910; C. S. Bernheimer, *The Shirt-Waist Strike,* (New York, 1910) ; Theresa Malkiel, *The Diary of a Shirtwaist Striker,* (New York, 1910) ; Richin, *The Promised City,* pp. 247–250.

16. H. Burgin, op. cit. pp. 706–710; B. Hoffman, op. cit. pp. 173–218; Richin, *The Promised City,* pp. 250–252; *Forward,* June 12, 30, July 2, 6, 9, Aug. 8, 28, 1910; *Yiddishes Tageblatt,* July 8, 1910; Meyer London, *The Cloakmaker's Strike,* New York, 1910.

17. H. Burgin, op. cit. pp. 716–718, 808 f.; Matthew Josephson, Sidney Hillman, New York, 1952.

18. B. B. Seligman, *Jewish Frontier,* Sept. 1953, p. 38.

19. A. S. Sachs, *Di Geschikte fun Arbeiter Ring,* 1892–1925 (New York, 1925) 2 parts.

20. Ibid. Vol II, pp. 504–523; "The School Almanac—The Modern Yiddish Schools throughout the World," published by Central Committee of Workmen's Circle Schools, Philadelphia, 1935, contains a number of articles describing the program and development of these schools: Dr. Chaim Zhitlovsky, pp. 5–14; A. Golomb, pp. 15–26; F. Geliebter, pp. 27–65; H. Bezprozvanip, pp. 67–90; Z. Yefroikin, pp. 91–101; N. Chait, 113–118, and others.

YIDDISH CULTURAL ACTIVITIES
THE YIDDISH AND ENGLISH PRESS

1. C. Bezalel Sherman, *The Jew Within American Society,* pp. 166–168.

2. Mordecai Soltes, *The Yiddish Press, an Americanizing Agency,* New York,

1925; Samuel Margoshes, The Jewish Press of New York City. Jewish Communal Register, 1917, pp. 596–663; Richin, *The Promised City,* pp. 115–130; The Foreign Language Press in New York (W.P.A. 1941); J. C. Rich, *Sixty Years of the Jewish Daily Forward,* Forward Assoc., Ronald Sanders, *The Jewish Daily Forward, Midstream,* Dec. 1962, pp. 79–94.

3. Jacob Wax—"The Feldman Family which Introduced Newspapers to Brownsville and East New York," (article in *Kings County Observer,* July, 1930).

4. *Lexicon of the Yiddish Theatre* compiled and edited by Zalman Zylbercweig, vol. 1, 1931; vol. 2, 1934; vol. 3, 1959; vol. 4, 1963, vol. 5, 1967. David S. Lifson, *The Yiddish Theater in America,* New York 1965; David Pinski, "The Yiddish Theatre," *Jewish Communal Register* (1917–1918), pp. 572–578; *The Forward,* March 18, 1927.

PUBLIC SCHOOLS AND LIBRARIES

1. Samuel Tenenbaum, "Brownsville's Age of Learning," Commentary, Aug. 1949, p. 174.

2. William Poster, " 'Twas a Dark Night in Brownsville," *The Commentary,* May, 1950, p. 465.

3. Alfred Kazin, *A Walker in the City,* pp. 17–21.

4. Matthew Josephson, *Life Among the Surrealists*—A Memoir, p. 23.

5. Irving Shulman, *The Amboy Dukes* (New York, 1947).

6. Samuel P. Abelow, Dr. William H. Maxwell, Brooklyn, 1934; First Annual Report of Superintendent of Schools, 1899.

7. Rae Glauber, *All Neighborhoods Change,* pp. 94–99.

8. Walter William Pettit, *Self-supporting Students in Certain New York City High Schools* (N.Y. 1920).

9. The material in this section is based mainly on Margaret F. Freeman's unpublished study (available in the main building of the Brooklyn Public Library), *The Brownsville Children's Branch of the Brooklyn Public Library —Its Origin and Development.* (Brooklyn, 1940).

10. Ibid. p. 16; Minutes, Board of Trustees, Brooklyn Public Library, March 21, 1905.

11. Alfred Kazin, *A Walker in the City,* p. 91.

THE HEBREW EDUCATIONAL SOCIETY OF BROOKLYN

1. The archives of the Society include the minutes from the time of organization to the present, annual reports, special issues and publications of individual groups, correspondence, newspaper and magazine clippings, programs, photographs, and various other items. Much of the material in this section is also based on the personal knowledge of the writer who was executive director of the Society for the larger part of its existence.

2. Samuel Joseph: *History of the Baron de Hirsch Fund,* 1935, passim, and pp. 266–270.

3. J. A. Mandel, "The Attitude of the American Jewish Community to East European Immigration," *Am. J. Archives* (June 1950) ; Richin, *The Promised City*, pp. 97–98.

4. At the end of 1899, Mr. Joseph Parvin presented to Rev. Leon M. Nelson of the newly organized Hebrew Educational Society a detailed report of his activities in Brownsville under the auspices of the Baron de Hirsch Fund. It is in the archives of the Society; Joseph Koplowitz, "Early History of the H.E.S.," *Morning Journal*, Feb. 17, 1935.

5. The H.E.S. was one of the many efforts of Mr. Adolphus Solomons, a leading Jew of his time. For his life see: Publications of the Am. J. Hist. Soc. No. 20 (1911), 166–170; *Jewish Encyclopedia* XI, 459; *Universal J. Encyc.* 9, 643.

6. For the life of Hertog Veld (1856–1924) see: *The Jewish Center*, March 1924 (II, No. 2) pp. 33, 50.

7. Samuel P. Abelow, *History of Brooklyn Jewry*, pp. 263–279; Harry P. Lurie, *A Heritage Affirmed* (The Jewish Federation Movement in America, Philadelphia, 1961), pp. 78–83, 115, 415 et passim.; Annual Reports, Brooklyn Federation of Jewish Charities; Charles S. Bernheimer, "The Federation as a Social Agency," Jewish Charities, Aug. 1917.

8. Charles S. Bernheimer, *Half a Century in Community Service*, New York, 1948, pp. 19–39; 45–46, 65, 135–138, "Americanizing the Immigrant" (address before Judaeans, May 2, 1915) in American Hebrew, June 18, 1915; Boys Clubs (Baker & Taylor Company, New York, 1914) ; "A Social Settlement for Jewish Immigrants," *American Hebrew*, July 16, 1909; "New Plans of the Hebrew Educational Society of Brooklyn," Jewish Charities, Dec. 1910; "Settlements and the Underworld" Jewish Charities, Aug. 1911; "Settlements and Other Agencies," *Jewish Charities*, June 1913; "Need of Y.M.H.A. in Brownsville," *American Hebrew*, November 5, 1915; "The Social Settlement," *The Jewish Center*, Feb. 1922.

9. Alter F. Landesman, *Forty Years of Service in a Congested Metropolitan Neighborhood*, (Hebrew Educational Society, 1939) ; *The Present Role of a Jewish Community Center in a Metropolitan Neighborhood* (Hebrew Ed. Soc. 1957) ; Philip Goodman and Alter F. Landesman, "Jewish Cultural Activities in the Jewish Community Center," pp. 119–148, in *Aspects of the Jewish Community Center* (New York, 1954) ; Alter F. Landesman, "Jewish Activities in Community Centers." Jewish Center, vol. 3, No. 3, (Sept. 1925), pp. 48–51; Policies Affecting Our Work with Intermediate Age Groups, Jewish Center (vol. 8, No. 2, June 1930), pp. 18–32.

10. Benjamin Rabinowitz, *The Young Men's Hebrew Associations 1854–1913*, (New York, 1948) ; *Aspects of the Jewish Community Center*, Louis Kraft, Editor (New York, 1954) ; Oscar Janowsky, *The Jewish Welfare Board Survey* (New York, 1948) ; Louis Kraft, A Century of the Jewish Community Center Movement, (New York, 1953) ; Graenum Berger, *The Jewish Community Center* (New York, 1966).

11. The presidents of the Women's Association following Mrs. Rich were: Mesdames Samuel Salzman (1935–1937); Irving J. Sands (1938–1940); Nat Bass (1941–1942); Stuart Steinbrink (1943–1944); David Merksamer (1945–1946); Michael Kern (1947–1948); Morris Abrams (1949–1950); Sol Rubinton (1951–1952); Louis H. Baretz (1953–1954); Louis Nathanson (1955–1956); David Farber (1957–1958); Isidor Stern (1959–1961); Max Grolnick (1961–1962); Everett Kirsten (1963–1966); Lawrence Rose (1967–).

12. The directors of activities of the Fellowships included Milton Mandel, Bernard Segal, David Suher, and Richard LaPan (1949–1962). The chairmen of the Fellowship Committee included William B. Rothenberg, Seth Marrus, Mark R. Keshen, Nathaniel Bloom, Sol Rubinton, Albert M. Cohen, Clarence J. Shlevin, Arnold Heller, and Mrs. Louis Nathanson.

13. The presidents of Camp H.E.S. included Dr. David Teplitsky (1941–1943); Everett Kirsten (1944–1945); Seth Marrus (1946–1950); Clarence Shlevin (1951–1954); Sol Rubinton (1955–1956); Nathaniel Bloom (1957–1961); Mrs. Irving J. Sands (19621963); Isidore Mones (1964–1966); Morris Abrams (1967–). The Camp Directors who succeeded Mr. Milton Mandel included David Kleinstein, Richard LaPan, Rabbi Meyer Greenberg, Arthur Meyer (1947–1962), George Weisfuse (1964–1965); Harold Fontak (1966–1967).

SYNAGOGUES IN BROWNSVILLE

1. A brief history of a number of synagogues in Brownsville was printed by Mr. Joseph Koplowitz from time to time in his Sunday Column in *The Jewish Morning Journal*. The Jewish Communal Register of New York City 1917–1918, pp. 251–285 includes a listing of synagogues in Brownsville and East New York for that year. *Brooklyn Communities-Population Characteristics and Neighborhood Social Resources,* vol. 1, published by the Community Council of Greater New York (1959) lists 83 synagogues for Brownsville and 41 for East New York. Samuel P. Abelow, *History of Brooklyn Jewry,* pp. 52–54, 70–71.

2. *American Spiritual Autobiographies,* Ed. Louis Finkelstein (New York, 1948), pp. 243–260, 269–270; Samuel P. Abelow, op. cit. pp. 158–159.

3. *New York Times* (obituary—Jan. 7, 1960).

4. Nisim Gordon, *Day-Morgen Journal,* Oct. 24, 1963.

5. Alter F. Landesman, *A Survey of Brownsville,* 1927. An estimate based on actual attendance on 2 Sabbaths (Sept. 17 and 24, 1927) in a large number of synagogues indicated that no more than 10 per cent of the total population above 10 years of age attended synagogues on the Sabbaths.

6. For biography of Rabbi M. C. Rabinowitz, see Abelow, op. cit. pp. 70–71. For biographical note about Rabbi Ben Zion Eisenstadt, see *Jewish Encyclopedia* V, p. 83.

7. Among other Rabbis of the community were Samuel J. Beckerman, Jacob Canick, Abraham Chinitz, B. L. Diane, L. Edelman, Mandel Freidin,

Z. Finkel, Simon Gelshevsky, A. Goodblatt, K. Kamelhar, J. Laks, M. Lax, Alex Levine, Herman Mantel, M. Moinester, Mordecai Nissenbaum, Jacob E. Rabin, Shaya Rotter, Eliezer Schwartz, Harris Semer.

8. Alfred Kazin, *A Walker in the City,* pp. 42–44.

9. I am indebted to Rabbi Israel H. Levinthal who has made available to me bound copies of the first three years issues of Temple Petach Tikvah, and for some of the facts related here. Rabbi Abraham P. Block has filled in on the more recent history. The presidents of the Temple have been: William B. Roth (1915–1932); Samuel S. Seiderman (1932–1937); Max Storch (1938-), Louis Halperin (1938 acting), Harry S. Krinski (1939–1948), Bernard Isacowitz (1949–1961), and Louis E. Schwartz (1962-).

10. Hyman Goldstein: "History of the Young Israel Movement" (in collaboration with Messrs. Max Oxenhandler, Harry G. Fromberg and Louis L. Cohen). *The Jewish Forum,* Dec. 1926. The presidents that have served the Young Israel Synagogue of Brownsville since its inception include: Solomon Rivlin, Benjamin Plotkin; William Raphael, Charles Rubinstein, Ephraim Bennis, David Weinstein, Herman Wolkinson, Charles Liss, Joseph Weiner, Louis Fisch, Joshua Simonson, Arthur Lookstein, Hy Koppel, Hy Levine, Morton London, Morris Burstein, Leibe Gewirtz, Moses Fuchs, Hy Gewirtz, Abraham Halbfinger, Bernard Herschberg, Bernard Seltzer, Joseph Gellis, Irving Greenstein and Isaac L. Zwebner.

11. Leonard Plotnik, "The Sephardim of New Lots," *Commentary,* Jan. 1958, pp. 28–35. The writer is indebted for some of the facts to Rabbi Abraham Morhaim.

BROWNSVILLE'S CONTRIBUTIONS TO JEWISH SURVIVAL

1. M. Kaplan: "The Society of the Jewish Renascence," *The Maccabean,* Nov. 1920.

2. *The Jewish Education Magazine,* Summer Issue 1949 (Vol. 20, No. 3) was dedicated to the memory of Samson Benderly. In it Dr. Isaac B. Berkson, Dr. Alexander M. Dushkin, Prof. Mordecai M. Kaplan, Dr. Judah L. Magnes, Israel Chipkin, David Rudovsky, Emanuel Gameron and others wrote about the life, personality, and influence of Dr. Benderly. Nathan H. Winter, Jewish Education in a Pluralistic Society: Samson Benderly and Jewish Education in the United States, New York 1966, Isaac B. Berkson, *Education and the Jewish Renascence,* Jewish Ed. Summer Issue 1963 (Vol. 33, No. 4, pp. 198–208), "Jewish Education Achievements and Needs in *The American Jew,* in *A Composite Portrait,* Ed. by Oscar Janovsky.

3. The Minutes of the Hebrew Teachers Union are now in the Yivo. I am grateful to Mr. Lipschitz for making them available to me. For the history of the *Agudath Melamde Israel* (1891) and *Agudath Moreh Israel* (1901), see Daniel Persky, *Fifty Years of Teaching Hebrew in America* (in Hebrew) in *Hadoar,* Tebeth 27, 5711 (Jan. 5, 1951).

4. Many of the facts related in this section were related to the writer by the late Harry Handler. The Stone Avenue Talmud Torah is one of the very few institutions in Brownsville that still functions at the present time. The M. Machtay family and M. Slavin have been active workers in recent years.

5. The late Jacob Bloom well known as an author and *Mohel* furnished the facts for the early history of the Talmud Torah.

6. For life of Rabbi M. S. Shapiro see Isaac Rivkind, *Hadoar*, Nov. 23, 1962; N. Goldberg, *Hadoar*, Jan. 25, 1963; Simon Zak, *Hadoar*, Oct. 18, 1962.

7. Alter F. Landesman, *A Neighborhood Survey of Brownsville*, 1927.

8. Judah Lapson: "A Decade of Hebrew in the High Schools of New York City, *Jewish Education*, April 1941, (Vol. 13, No. 1), pp. 34–45; The "Hebrew Culture Council and Two Decades of Hebrew in Public High Schools of New York City," *Jewish Education*, Summer 1950 (Vol. 21, No. 3), pp. 17–19, 59.

9. The writer is indebted for much of the information about Zionist activities in Brownsville to Mr. Morris Zeldin.

10. Bernard Richards, Jewish Communal Register, 1917–1918, pp. 1385–96: *American Jewish Year Book*, 1917–1918; Harry Schneiderman, article on American Jewish Congress, *Universal Jewish Encyclopedia*, I, 247–252; *Yiddishe Tageblatt: Jewish Morning Journal*, and *Jewish Forward*, June 13, 24, 1917.

11. Mizrachi Jubilee Publication of Mizrachi Organization of America (1911–1936), Ed. by Dr. P. Churgin and Leon Gelman, New York, Feb. 1936; Samuel Rosenblatt, *The Mizrachi Movement* (New York, 1940); Teachers Institute of Yeshivah College, Twenty-Fifth Anniversary (Journal), New York 1944; Hyman R. Grinstein, "Orthodox Judaism and Early Zionism in America," in *Early History of Zionism in America*, Am. J. Hist. Soc. and Theodore Herzl Foundation (N.Y. 1958), pp. 219–227.

12. C. Bezalel Sherman, "The Beginnings of Labor Zionism in the United States" in *Early History of Zionism*, Am. J. H. Society Publications, 1958, pp. 275–288, L. Spyzman and Baruch Zuckerman, *History of the Labor Zionist Movement in North America* (Yiddish), New York, 1955 (2 Vols.); *History of J. Labor Movement* (Yiddish) Yiwo (New York 1943–1945), p. 113.

13. Norman Schanin: *Forty Years of Young Judaea*, Jewish Ed. (Summer) 1950 (Vol. 21, No. 3), pp. 37 ff. *Young Judaea Magazine*, passim.

14. Moshe Halevi, *Kitvei Moshe Halevi*, New York 1931 (5691), pp. 253, 263.

15. Dr. S. Margoshes, *The Day* and *Jewish Journal*, June 11, 1963; Okiva Ben-Ezra, Abraham Ha-Ivri, *Hadoar*, Feb. 23, 1968 (24 Shevat, 5728), pp. 275–276.

16. Daniel Perski, *Hadoar*, Jan. 8, 1946 (16 Shevat, 5706), p. 263.

17. There was a large group of Hebraists in the community. They included among others, J. Ovsay, Okiva Ben-Ezra, Meyer Kogan, Morris Zeldin, Johanan Rudavsky, Nahum Aaronson, Benjamin Hirsch, Jehudah Kraushar, Harry Handler, Dr. M. Canick, Dr. Rubin, Mr. Papush, M. Uberman, Saul Sapir, T. Appelbaum, Chesne Tarshis, Mr. Commoner, A. Schachnai, Dr. M.

Robinson, David Sherman, Dr. and Mrs. Samuel Linick, David Shur. According to Okiva Ben-Ezra (*Hadoar,* Feb. 23, 1968) the home of Rebecca and Zevi Mehr was the first Hebrew speaking home in Brownsville.

THE CONTRIBUTION OF BROWNSVILLE TO THE DEVELOPMENT OF ORTHODOX CONSERVATIVE AND REFORM JUDAISM IN AMERICA

1. For the history of the rise of the Conservative Movement, *see* Moshe Davis, *The Emergence of Conservative Judaism* (Philadelphia, 1963), Norman Bentwich, Solomon Schechter, (Philadelphia, 1938).
2. *The Portrait of a Teacher* by Solomon Goldman. Louis Ginzberg, Jubilee Volume, American Academy for Jewish Research, 1945, pp. 1–5.

JEWISH PHILANTHROPY, SOCIAL SERVICE, AND MUTUAL AID SOCIETIES

1. Annual Reports of Brooklyn Fed. of Jewish Charities, 1912, 1913.
2. Nat. Conference of Jewish Charities, Proceedings, 1908.
3. In Dec. 1967 the Brooklyn Home and Hospital for the Aged has announced its affiliation with the New York Federation of Jewish Philanthropies.
4. *The Brooklyn Eagle,* Nov. 19, 1909, May 9, 1910; Sam Kaplowitz, East New York Dispensary, *Morning Journal,* Oct. 25, 1942; Annual Reports, Brooklyn Federation of Jewish Charities, from 1918 on.
5. Samuel P. Abelow, *History of Brooklyn Jewry,* pp. 232–238; Current reports and data supplied by the hospital.
6. Samuel P. Abelow, op. cit. pp. 222–227; Tina Levitan, *Islands of Compassion, A History of Jewish Hospitals of New York, 1964;* Current Reports and Data supplied by the hospital.
7. Samuel P. Abelow, op. cit. pp. 227–230; Current Reports and Data supplied by the hospital.
8. *Brooklyn Eagle,* April 15, 1935; Annual Reports, Joint Passover Association.
9. "Jewish Fraternal Organizations" by Leo Wolfson, *Jewish Communal Register* (1917–1918), pp. 859–862, Listing of Mutual Aid Agencies, pp. 865–978; Alfred S. Kohanski, Fraternal Orders, *Universal Jewish Encyclopedia,* Vol. 4, pp. 419–422; Reports in Sunday Section, *Jewish Morning Journal,* 1933–1942.
10. Samuel P. Abelow, *History of Brooklyn Jewry,* pp. 255–256 Jacob Goell was president of the Adath Israel for 20 years until 1935, and Jacob Wax was honorary secretary for many years. Besides these two officers, the founders included Isaac Allen who framed the Charter, Moses Bernstein, Moses Ginsberg, Herman Moscowitz, Jacob Meiman, Joseph Koplowitz, George Tonkonogy, Harris Reisler and Gershon Ungar. In recent years Morris A. Zeldin and Ben Werbel held the office of president. Among others who were active in the organization may be mentioned Morris Becker, Harry Cooper, Ike Frankel, Julius Grabel, H. Luwish, M. Machtay, Jacob Rothstein, Jacob Solovei, Morris Sapir, L. Shepeloff, I. Shleefstein, Hon. Jacob S. Strahl, Max Wolinsky and Samuel Zacharin.

WORLD WAR I

1. Morris Hillquit, *American Socialists and the War* (Milwaukee, 1917).
2. J. George Feldman and Louis A. Falk, *Jews in American Wars*, N. Y. 1942, pp. 57–59.
3. *The New York Post*, April 27, 1940.
4. *Brooklyn and Long Island in the War*. A Record of Deeds and Casualty Lists (Brooklyn Eagle Library No. 207), March 1919. A number of articles in this volume were prepared by Charles G. Milham. For Roster of Brooklyn Men, 77th Division, see pp. 47–58; For Roll of Honor, 106 Inf. and list of wounded, see, pp. 19 ff. For Pershing's Report, see p. 85. *Historical Markers and Monuments in Brooklyn*, pub. by Long Island Historical Society, 1952 (compiled by Edna Huntington).

BROWNSVILLE—EAST NEW YORK POLITICS

1. Louis Waldman with Introduction by Seymour Stedman: Albany: *The Crisis in Government—The History of the Suspension, Trial and Expulsion from the New York State Legislature in 1920 of the Five Socialist Assemblymen by Their Political Opponents* (New York, 1920); State of New York Legislative Document No. 35, Proceedings of the Judiciary Committee of the Assembly in the Matter of the investigation by the Assembly of the State of New York as to the qualifications of Louis Waldman, August Claessens, Samuel A. Dewitt, Samuel Orr and Charles Solomon to retain their seats in said body (Albany, 1920, 3 vols); New York State—*Seditious Activities*—Joint Legislative Committee. *Revolutionary Radicalism*, 4 vols. Clayton R. Lusk, Ch. Report written and compiled under supervision of Committee by Archibald E. Stevenson.
2. August Claessens and William Morris Feigenbaum, *The Socialists in the New York Assembly, New York 1918* (Rand School of Social Science).
3. Rae Glauber, *All Neighborhoods Change*, pp. 16 ff. Evans Clark and Charles Solomon, with Foreword by Algeron Lee, The Socialists in the New York Board of Aldermen (Rand School of Social Science).

THE DEPRESSION DECADE

1. For a general account of the period see Caroline Bird, *The Invisible Scar* (New York, 1966); Irving Bernstein, *The Lean Years* (New York, 1960); Broadus Mitchell, *Depression Decade, From New Era through New Deal*, Vol. IX. *The Economic History of the United States* (1947); *Boondoggle that Helped 38 Million People*, by Sherwin D. Smith, *The New York Times*, May 2, 1965.
2. The story of the failure of the Bank of the United States was set forth in the columns of *The New York Times* as well as in the other newspapers of the period. *The New York Times*, Dec. 12, 1930; "The Story of the Bank," by

R. L. Duffus, *New York Times*, June 5, 1932; R. Werner, *Little Napoleons and Dummy Directors* (New York, 1933); Nathan S. Jonas, *Through the Years.*

3. Eriksson, Erik Mckinley, *The Supreme Court and the New Deal; a study of* recent constitutional interpretation, Los Angeles, 1941; Invalidity of NRA codes—Opinion of Supreme Court of U.S., together with the concurring opinions of Justices Cardozo and Stone in the case of A.L.A. Schechter Poultry Corp. and others v. the U.S. of America, etc. Washington, U.S. Gov't. Printing Office, 1935. 74 Congress 1st session Senate Document No. 65; A.L.A. Schechter Poultry Corporation, Schechter Live Poultry Market, Joseph Schechter, Martin Schechter, Alex Schechter and Aaron Schechter, petitioners v. U.S. of America, New York 1935 (In Supreme Court of U.S. Oct. term 1934 Nos. 854–864).

4. Alfred Kazin, *Starting out in the Thirties* (Boston, 1962); Nathan Glazer, *The Social Basis of American Communism,* (New York 1961); Eugene Lyons, *The Red Decade* (Indianapolis, 1941); Irving Howe and Lewis Coser, *The American Communist Party* (New York, 1962).

WORLD WAR II

1. Kaufman, *American Jews in World War II,* 2 vols. (Dial Press, 1947). See story about Sgt. Irving Strobing, a Signal Corps man of 605 Barbey Street who was on radio duty in May 1942 when General Wainwright was forced to surrender his last remaining men to the Japanese. Concerning Sgt. Meyer Levin, see p. 23; for Brooklyn's share in the war, *see Brooklyn Eagle,* "Brooklyn and Long Island in the War."

JUVENILE DELINQUENCY AND CRIME

1. Julius B. Maller, "The Maladjusted Jewish Child," Jewish Social Service Quarterly, Vol. 9 (1933), pp. 285–295.

2. Sophia Moses Robison, *Can Delinquency Be Measured?* (New York, 1936), see Appendix C. Table 61, pp. 246 ff; Table 67, pp. 260–263.

3. Sophia M. Robison, Report to Jewish Board of Guardians of New York City on Delinquency among Jewish Children in 1952. I am grateful to Dr. Robison for the specific information on the Brownsville area. See her study of "Delinquency among Jewish Children in New York City," pp. 535–541 in *The Jews, Social Patterns of an American Group,* Ed. by Marshall Sklare, (Glencoe, Ill., 1957).

4. Burton B. Turkus and Sid Feder, *Murder, Inc., The Story of "The Syndicate"* (Farrar, Straus and Young, New York 1951); Joseph Freeman; "How Murder, Inc. Trains Killers," *American Mercury,* Oct. 1940; "Murder Monopoly," *Nation,* May 25, 1940, p. 645. Meyer Berger, *Murder, Inc.* "Justice Overtakes the Largest and Most Cruel Gang of Killers in United States History." *Life,* Sept. 30, 1940, p. 86; Gang Pattern, *New York Times,* Aug. 4, 1940. "The History of a Gang;" "A Tough Kid" by Leo Katcher and Malcolm

Logan, *New York Post,* April 8, 9, 15, 1940; *Forward,* March 23, 1940; *World Telegram,* March 18, 1943; *The New York Sun,* April 4, 1940.
5. Joel Slonim, "The Jewish Gangster," *The Reflex,* July 1928, pp. 36–41.
6. Harry W. Newburger, "The Gangster and the Politician," *American Hebrew,* Jan. 1, 1915; "The Gangster in Business," ibid. Jan. 8, 1915; Editorial, ibid. entitled "The Gangsters of New York," Melech Epstein, pages from "My Stormy Life," *Am. J. Archives,* Nov. 1962.

THE GLORY OF THE COMMUNITY

1. Tina Levitan, "The Laureates, Jewish Winners of Nobel Prize," New York, 1960; *New York Times,* Nov. 11, 1957 and Oct. 28, 1964.
2. *Universal Jewish Encyclopedia,* 4, pp. 306–307; *Register,* The Jewish Theological Seminary of America, 1964–1966.
3. Ted Berkman, *Cast a Giant Shadow*—The Story of Micky Marcus, who Died to Save Jerusalem, (New York, 1962) ; "This was Micky Marcus," by Lowell M. Limpus, *Saturday Evening Post* Dec. 4, 1948: *Micky Marcus* by Judith Halperin and Phyllis Kreinik (New York, 1949) .
4. Kurt Singer, *The Danny Kaye Saga* (London, 1957) ; *The Life Story of Danny Kaye* by Dick Richards of the *Sunday Pictorial* with an Introduction by Sid Fields (London, 1949) .
5. *New York Times,* Sept. 27, 1963; Louis Untermeyer, *Makers of the Modern World,* (Simon and Schuster, New York) pp. 712–716.
6. "Earl Wilson's New York," *New York Post,* July 28, 1964.
7. *Impressario,* A Memoir by S. Hurok in Collaboration with Ruth Goode, 1946; "S. Hurok, Immigrant Who Spreads Culture," *New York World Telegram,* Nov. 17, 1965, p. 31.
8. "Close Up: Park Impressario," by Paul Weiss, *The New York Post,* May 15, 1964, p. 39; Cindy Hughes, "Papp Glances Backward," *World Telegram,* Brooklyn Section, April 27, 1964; *New York Times,* July 11, 1964.
9. "Himan Brown," Federation Campaign Report, Feb. 19, 1965 (Federation Family Portrait) .
10. *Saturday Evening Post,* Oct. 24, 1964.
11. *Akiva Ben Ezra, Hadoar,* July 26, 1963, p. 643.
12. Interview by Simon Boker with Dr. David Wechsler, brother of Israel S. Wechsler printed in *Day Morning Journal,* Dec. 12, 1962.
13. "Murray Stein, Water Pollution Foe," *New York Times,* Aug. 4, 1964, p. 14.
14. Bernard Postal, Jesse Silver and Roy Silver, *Encyclopedia of Jews in Sports,* (New York, 1965) ; Herbert U. Ribalow, *The Jew in American Sports* (New York) .
15. Frank Waldman, *Famous American Athletes of Today* (New York, 1951) pp. 105–126.
16. B. Postal, etc. *Encyclopedia of Jews in Sports,* op. cit.
17. Ben Gould, *The Brooklyn Eagle,* Aug. 21, 1949.
18. Harold U. Ribalow, *The Jew in American Sports,* pp. 238–249.

19. Matthew Josephson, *Life Among the Surrealists, A Memoir* (New York, 1962).

20. *New York Herald Tribune*, Oct. 29, 1951.

21. David Dortort, *Burial of the Fruit* (New York, 1946). Reviews by Schiffman in *Brooklyn Eagle*, Feb. 2, 1947, p. 36 and Jane Morin, *The Community Voice*, May 19, 1948, p. 8.

22. Irving Shulman, *The Amboy Dukes* (New York, 1940).

23. Isidore Rosen, *Will of Iron* (New York, 1952). Review by John Cournos, *Saturday Review of Literature,* 33:34 No. 4 (1950).

24. Leon Kobrin, *Ore die Bord* (1918), republished in Warsaw 1929, then rewritten and published in *Goldenem Shtrom* (Warsaw, 1936).

25. *Bronzviler Gesang* by David Seltzer (New York, 1937).

26. *The Commentary*, Aug. 1949.

27. *Call It Sleep*, by Henry Roth, with an afterword by Walter Allen, (New York, Avon Books). For reviews see Leslie A. Fiedler, "The Jew in the American Novel," (*New York Times*, 1959); Irving Howe, A Review, *New York Times Book Review*, Oct. 25, 1964.

28. Arthur Granit, *The Time of the Peaches*, (New York, 1959); Reviews— Theodore Solataroff, "The Brownsville Syndrome," A Review, *The Commentary*, 1960, pp. 538–541; Dr. S. Margoshes, *The Time of the Peaches*, *The Day*, Jewish Journal, June 25, 1960, p. 6; Moses Duchovney, Jews in Brownsville described in New Novel, *Day—Jewish Journal*, Dec. 20, 1959, p. 4.

29. Gerald Green, *The Last Angry Man* (New York, 1956). Reviews by James Kelly, *Saturday Review*, Feb. 2, 1957.

Acknowledgement

I am grateful to Seymour Janovsky of the Thomas Jefferson High School Alumni Association; to Dr. Joseph Kaminetsky, and to Dr. David Farber for their information about some of the personalities mentioned in this section.

A. F. L.

EPILOGUE

1. Abraham P. Block, "Synagogues for Sale," *Jewish Spectator*, April 1966, pp. 20–22.

2. Irving Howe, *The Lower East Side:* Symbol and Fact, in the Lower East Side: *Portal to American Life* (1870–1924)—the Jewish Museum, New York 1966, p. 14.

3. Zalman Joffeh, "The Passing of the East Side," *The Menorah Treasury*, Philadelphia 1964, pp. 628 ff.

Index

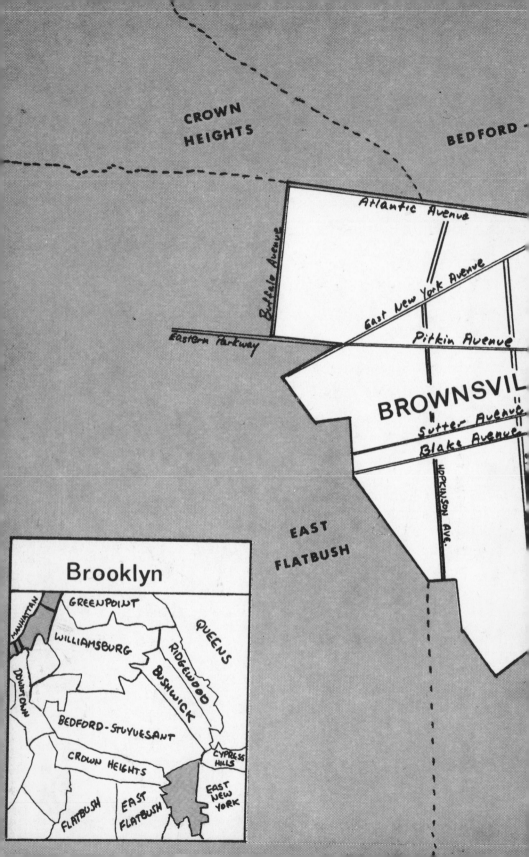